Lecture Notes in Artificial Intelligence   **12758**

Subseries of Lecture Notes in Computer Science

Series Editors

Randy Goebel
  University of Alberta, Edmonton, Canada
Yuzuru Tanaka
  Hokkaido University, Sapporo, Japan
Wolfgang Wahlster
  DFKI and Saarland University, Saarbrücken, Germany

Founding Editor

Jörg Siekmann
  DFKI and Saarland University, Saarbrücken, Germany

More information about this subseries at http://www.springer.com/series/1244

Naoaki Okazaki · Katsutoshi Yada ·
Ken Satoh · Koji Mineshima (Eds.)

New Frontiers in Artificial Intelligence

JSAI-isAI 2020 Workshops
JURISIN, LENLS 2020 Workshops
Virtual Event, November 15–17, 2020
Revised Selected Papers

 Springer

Editors
Naoaki Okazaki
Tokyo Institute of Technology
Tokyo, Japan

Katsutoshi Yada
Kansai University
Osaka, Japan

Ken Satoh
National Institute of Informatics
Tokyo, Japan

Koji Mineshima
Keio University
Tokyo, Japan

ISSN 0302-9743   ISSN 1611-3349   (electronic)
Lecture Notes in Artificial Intelligence
ISBN 978-3-030-79941-0   ISBN 978-3-030-79942-7   (eBook)
https://doi.org/10.1007/978-3-030-79942-7

LNCS Sublibrary: SL7 – Artificial Intelligence

This Springer imprint is published by the registered company Springer Nature Switzerland AG
The registered company address is: Gewerbestrasse 11, 6330 Cham, Switzerland

Preface

The twelfth JSAI International Symposium on Artificial Intelligence (JSAI-isAI 2020) was held during November 15–17, 2020. JSAI-isAI has hosted a number of international workshops annually since 2009, providing a unique and intimate forum where AI researchers gather and share their knowledge in a focused discipline. It has been supported by Japanese Society for Artificial Intelligence (JSAI), the premier academic society of artificial intelligence in Japan (established in 1986).

Initially, JSAI-isAI 2020 was planned to be held at the Campus Innovation Center of the Tokyo Institute of Technology, Japan. However, we decided to go entirely virtual in response to the global health crisis caused by COVID-19. Even with this difficult situation, JSAI-isAI 2020 hosted four workshops (JURISIN 2020, LENLS17, SCIDOCA2020, and Kansei-AI 2020) and had 5 invited talks and 57 oral presentations for 198 registered participants from 19 countries.

The fourteenth International Workshop on Juris-Informatics (JURISIN 2020) was organized to discuss legal issues from the perspective of information science. Compared with conventional AI and law, this workshop covers a wide range of topics, including any theories and technologies which are not directly related with juris-informatics but have a potential to contribute to this domain.

The Logic and Engineering of Natural Language Semantics 17 (LENLS17) workshop focused on the formal and theoretical aspects of natural language. It is an annual international workshop recognized internationally in the formal syntax-semantics-pragmatics community. It brings together researchers working on formal theories of natural language syntax, semantics and pragmatics, (formal) philosophy, artificial intelligence, and computational linguistics for discussion and interdisciplinary communication.

The fourth International Workshop on SCIentific DOCument Analysis (SCIDOCA 2020) gathered researchers and experts who are aiming at scientific document analysis. Recent proliferation of scientific papers and technical documents has become an obstacle to efficient information acquisition of new information in various fields. It is almost impossible for individual researchers to check and read all related documents. This workshop hosted technical paper presentations and system demonstrations that cover all aspects of scientific document analysis.

Kansei-AI 2020 was the second international workshop on Artificial Affective (Kansei) Intelligence. The scope of this workshop was science and engineering research related to value judgements made through the five senses, such as image processing, tactile engineering, acoustics, machine learning, sensitivity engineering, and natural language processing.

This volume, *New Frontiers in Artificial Intelligence: JSAI-isAI 2020 Workshops*, is the post-proceedings of JSAI-isAI 2020. From the 50 papers submitted to the workshops of LENLS17 and JURISIN 2020, 19 papers were carefully selected and revised, following the comments of the workshop Program Committees. The acceptance rate was about 38%. This has resulted in an excellent selection of papers that are representative of some of the topics of AI research both in Japan and worldwide.

It is our great pleasure to be able to share some highlights of these fascinating workshops in this volume. We hope this book will introduce readers to the state-of-the-art research outcomes of JSAI-isAI 2020, and motivate them to organize and/or participate in JSAI-isAI events in the future.

May 2021

Naoaki Okazaki
Katsutoshi Yada
Ken Satoh
Koji Mineshima

Organization

JURISIN 2020

Workshop Chairs

Ken Satoh — National Institute of Informatics and Sokendai, Japan
Nguyen Le Minh — Japan Advanced Institute of Science and Technology, Japan
Yasuhiro Ogawa — Nagoya University, Japan

Steering Committee

Yoshinobu Kano — Shizuoka University, Japan
Takehiko Kasahara — Toin Yokohama University, Japan
Nguyen Le Minh — Japan Advanced Institute of Science and Technology, Japan
Makoto Nakamura — Niigata Institute of Technology, Japan
Yoshiaki Nishigai — Chiba University, Japan
Katsumi Nitta — National Institute of Informatics, Japan
Yasuhiro Ogawa — Nagoya University, Japan
Seiichiro Sakurai — Meiji Gakuin University, Japan
Ken Satoh — National Institute of Informatics and Sokendai, Japan
Satoshi Tojo — Japan Advanced Institute of Science and Technology, Japan
Katsuhiko Toyama — Nagoya University, Japan
Masaharu Yoshioka — Hokkaido University, Japan

Advisory Committee

Trevor Bench-Capon — University of Liverpool, UK
Henry Prakken — University of Utrecht and University of Groningen, Netherlands
John Zeleznikow — Victoria University, Australia
Robert Kowalski — Imperial College London, UK
Kevin Ashley — University of Pittsburgh, USA

Program Committee

Thomas Ågotnes — University of Bergen, Norway
Michał Araszkiewicz — Jagiellonian University, Poland
Ryuta Arisaka — National Institute of Informatics, Japan

Marina De Vos	University of Bath, UK
Juergen Dix	Clausthal University of Technology, Germany
Randy Goebel	University of Alberta, Canada
Guido Governatori	CSIRO, Australia
Nguyen Le Minh	Japan Advanced Institute of Science and Technology, Japan
Tokuyasu Kakuta	Chuo University, Japan
Yoshinobu Kano	Shizuoka University, Japan
Takehiko Kasahara	Toin Yokohama University, Japan
Mi-Young Kim	University of Alberta, Canada
Sabrina Kirrane	Vienna University of Economics and Business, Austria
Makoto Nakamura	Niigata Institute of Technology, Japan
Yoshiaki Nishigai	Nihon University, Japan
Tomoumi Nishimura	Osaka University, Japan
Katumi Nitta	Tokyo Institute of Technology, Japan
Yasuhiro Ogawa	Nagoya University, Japan
Monica Palmirani	University of Bologna, Italy
Ginevra Peruginelli	ITTIG-CNR, Italy
Juliano Rabelo	University of Alberta, Canada
Seiichiro Sakurai	Meiji Gakuin University, Japan
Ken Satoh	National Institute of Informatics and Sokendai, Japan
Akira Shimazu	JAIST, Japan
Kazuko Takahashi	Kwansei Gakuin University, Japan
Satoshi Tojo	Japan Advanced Institute of Science and Technology, Japan
Katsuhiko Toyama	Nagoya University, Japan
Serena Villata	CNRS, France
Yueh-Hsuan Weng	Tohoku University, Japan
Masaharu Yoshioka	Hokkaido University, Japan

LENLS 17

Workshop Chair

| Koji Mineshima | Keio University, Japan |

Workshop Co-chairs

| Elin McCready | Aoyama Gakuin University, Japan |
| Daisuke Bekki | Ochanomizu University, Japan |

Program Committee

| Alastair Butler | Hirosaki University, Japan |
| Richard Dietz | University of Tokyo, Japan |

Naoya Fujikawa	University of Tokyo, Japan
Yurie Hara	Hokkaido University, Japan
Magdalena Kaufmann	University of Connecticut, USA
Kristina Liefke	Ruhr University Bochum, Germany
Yoshiki Mori	University of Tokyo, Japan
David Y. Oshima	Nagoya University, Japan
Katsuhiko Sano	Hokkaido University, Japan
Osamu Sawada	Kobe University, Japan
Wataru Uegaki	University of Edinburgh, UK
Katsuhiko Yabushita	Naruto University of Education, Japan
Tomoyuki Yamada	Hokkaido University, Japan
Shunsuke Yatabe	Kyoto University, Japan
Kei Yoshimoto	Tohoku University, Japan

Sponsored By

The Japan Society for Artificial Intelligence (JSAI)

The Japanese Society for Artificial Intelligence

Contents

LENLS

Logic and Engineering of Natural Language Semantics (LENLS) 17

Koji Mineshima

Keio University, Tokyo, Japan
minesima@abelard.flet.keio.ac.jp

1 The Workshop

LENLS is an annual international workshop on formal syntax, semantics, and pragmatics of natural language and related fields, including computational linguistics, philosophy of language, and mathematical logic. This is the seventeenth time it has been held since its inception in 2005. As with other JSAI-isAI2020 workshops, this was the first time that LENLS was held online. It was held over two days on November 15 and 16, 2020. There were two one-hour invited talks and seventeen 30-minute presentations based on submissions. In spite of the uncertain situation of the first online conference, we received as many paper submissions as usual.

The invited speakers were Yohei Oseki (University of Tokyo) and Patrick Elliott (MIT). Yohei Oseki reported under the title "Building machines that parse like people" on his research on linking theoretical linguistics with natural language processing, with a focus on syntax and morphology. Patrick Elliott proposed a new framework for dynamic semantics under the title "Classical negation in a dynamic alternative semantics", which attracted a lot of attention.

Research presentations based on the submitted papers can be divided into three groups. First, in the area of semantics and pragmatics, a wide variety of topics were discussed, including degree and comparative expressions, factive predicates, conditionals and interrogative sentences in Japanese, honorifics and politeness. There were also presentations on topics such as type-theoretic analysis of negation and event semantics, coercion and selectional restrictions, and discourse modeling using epistemic inquisitive semantics. Second, in the field of mathematical logic and its applications, there were presentations on typicality in default reasoning and analysis of resemblance in measurement theory. Third, topics closer to computational linguistics included natural language inference with automated theorem proving, semantic parsing and knowledge acquisition, and semantic similarity judgment.

One of the distinctive features of LENLS is that researchers from different fields discuss the common themes of language, computation, and logic from an interdisciplinary perspective while taking into account each other's goals and methods. Initially, we had to make a difficult decision on whether to hold the workshop or not, but when it was over, it turned out to be a very fruitful workshop as usual for developing the interdisciplinary study of natural language.

2 Acknowledgements

I would like to express my sincere gratitude to the program committee of LENLS and to Dr. Naoaki Okazaki, JSAI-isAI2020 Chair, and Dr. Katsutoshi Yada, Vice-Chair, for their efforts in organizing the workshop online.

A Semantics for "Typically" in First-Order Default Reasoning

Gergei Bana[1(✉)] and Mitsuhiro Okada[2]

[1] University of Missouri at Columbia, Columbia, MO, USA
bana@math.upenn.edu
[2] Keio University, Tokyo, Japan
mitsu@abelard.flet.keio.ac.jp

Abstract. We present a new semantics for first-order conditional logic, which is a generalization of that of Friedman, Halpern and Koller [7]. We utilize Fitting's embedding of first-order classical logic in first-order S4 to define our semantics. We explain our semantics by showing how it works on the connective expressing "typically implies". We argue that it has a number of good properties, in particular, it is more adjustable to special situations than that of [7]. For example, we can make sense of nested conditional implications even when a conditional implication does not necessarily hold on the entire set of possible worlds, but where-ever it is satisfied, the conclusion is typically satisfied.

1 Introduction

In this work we consider first-order semantics for logics of conditionals in the sense of Adams [1]. Following Friedman, Halpern and Koller [7], we explain our semantics through applying it to "typically implies" (typically as an adverb), though the method works in general for conditional implication. We denote conditional implication by $\phi \mapsto \psi$, and in our specific case one reads it as "ϕ typically implies ψ". We denote classical implication by $\rightarrow$. The main characteristics of $\mapsto$, as well known, is that it is non-monotonic; $\phi \mapsto \psi$ does not imply $\phi \wedge \chi \mapsto \psi$. While birds typically fly, penguin birds do not typically fly, in fact typically do not fly. There are various such non-monotonic systems running under the names of default reasoning, defeasibe logic, conditional logic, and so on. Here we focus on conditional logic (or logics of conditionals), and our starting point is the line of research from Adams [1] through Burgess [5] to Kraus et al. [10] and Friedman et al. [7] on conditional implication and its use in default reasoning. This line of research uses a possible world semantics framework (a source of which is David Lewis's use of possible world semantics), with a hierarchical structure. These hierarchical structures can be adopted to express levels

G. Bana—Part of the work was done while G. Bana was at the University of Luxembourg supported by FNR under the PolLux project VoteVerif (POLLUX-IV/1/2016). M. Okada was supported by JSPS-AYAME, KAKENKI 17H02265, 17H02263, 19KK0006, and 21H00467.

N. Okazaki et al. (Eds.): JSAI-isAI 2020 Workshops, LNAI 12758, pp. 3–20, 2021.
https://doi.org/10.1007/978-3-030-79942-7_1

of typicality and atypicality. Most of them are for propositional formulas only, but [7] presents a first-order approach. Halpern recently applied their method to computer security studies [9].

Here we present yet another improved semantics for conditional implication in a first-order setting that has a number of appealing features and explain it through formalizing "typically implies" with it. Our starting point for the spirit of semantics is Friedman, Halpern and Koller [7], which we are going to generalize. We agree with their detailed criticism of other semantics in the literature, for example, related to the "lottery paradox". The lottery paradox [11] has the form $\forall x(\mathsf{T} \mapsto \neg\mathtt{Winner}(x)) \wedge (\mathsf{T} \mapsto \exists x\mathtt{Winner}(x))$ meaning that "everyone typically loses, and typically someone wins", and it fails to be satisfiable in most other semantics for conditional logic. But we also phrase some criticism of [7] itself. One of our criticisms is the following: In [7], given a set W of possible worlds, satisfaction of predicates such as "is bird", "can fly" etc. is defined on each $w \in W$, but then the interpretation of "typically implies" is defined on the whole W. Finally "typically implies" is defined to be satisfied on each possible world w if and only if it is satisfied on W. As a result, it is either satisfied on every w or fails on every w. Consequently, if ("x is an animal" $\mapsto$ "x can fly") fails on W, the statement ("x is a bird"→("x is an animal" $\mapsto$ "x can fly")) also fails unless "x is a bird" is not satisfied on any w, even if ("x is a bird" $\mapsto$ "x can fly") holds. That is a bit strange given that when "x is a bird", "x is an animal" does not add further restriction in standard interpretations of "is a bird" and "is an animal". In our semantics ("x is a bird"→("x is an animal" $\mapsto$ "x can fly")) can be satisfied when "x is a bird" holds on some w. Similarly, we can make sense of the sentence ("x has a headache in the morning" $\mapsto$ "x takes painkiller in the morning") $\mapsto$ "x feels well at noon" even if ("x has a headache in the morning" $\mapsto$ "x takes painkiller in the morning") itself is not satisfied on the whole of W, only on a part, and on that part the conclusion is typically true. We can do this, because we consider satisfaction not on the whole W, but on subsets of W instead, and simulate satisfaction on $w \in W$ by a trick using Fitting's embedding of classical logic in S4 [6], which is a way of formalizing forcing (a variant of the forcing model construction, which was originally introduced in set theory by Paul Cohen). This approach is motivated by our earlier the work in [2–4], where we used Fitting's embedding to describe satisfaction apart from "negligible" sets in the context of measure theory (originally in the context of computer security). We also underline the relevance of our semantics by pointing out its connection to the semantics of Burgess [5] for the propositional setting. We arrive at a semantics similar to that of Burgess by resolving another issue with the semantics of Friedman et al., namely, that for any formula ϕ, the set of possible worlds where ϕ is satisfied, must behave well, such as be measurable.

Our framework to define the semantics is similar to that of [7], in that we start from some set W of possible worlds that has a hierarchy of atypical subsets. For example, birds typically fly but penguins are atypical, while penguins are typically healthy while sick penguins are atypical. More technically, for each subset S of W (or, more generally, each well behaving set such as σ algebra of measurable sets), there is an ideal of atypical subsets defined. To explain how we define $S \models \phi_1 \mapsto \phi_2$, for $S \subseteq W$, first assume that for $i = 1, 2$, there is a largest set $[\phi_i]$ in S such that $[\phi_i] \models \phi_i$. In this case $S \models \phi_1 \mapsto \phi_2$ is defined to be satisfied if $[\phi_1] \cap [\phi_2]^\perp$ is atypical in S ($\perp$ means the complement). That is, the set where ϕ_1 holds but ϕ_2 fails is atypical in S. However, we do not want to restrict our discussion to cases when $[\phi_i]$ can be considered (it may not be well-behaving enough such as measurable to consider etc.). So we essentially define $S \models \phi_1 \mapsto \phi_2$ to hold if for any large enough set $S_2 \subseteq S$ such that $S_2 \models \phi_1$, formula ϕ_2 is also satisfied by S_2 "except maybe on an atypical set". Formally this is expressed such that for any subset S_0 of S with $S_0 \models \phi_1$, there is a subset S_1 of S with $S_0 \subseteq S_1$ and $S_1 \models \phi_1$ and for any subset S_2 of S with $S_1 \subseteq S_2$ (i.e. large enough) and $S_2 \models \phi_1$, for any non-atypical subset S_3 of S_2, there is a further non-atypical subset S_4 of S_2 with $S_4 \models \phi_2$. The semantics of propositional connectives and the quantifiers are defined through Fitting's embedding. Fitting embedding then allows us to "zoom in" on elements of W through non-atypical sets (for every such set there is a further subset where satisfaction is required) rather than defining satisfaction on individual worlds.

Related Works. As we mentioned, the main difference from [7] is that we focus on satisfaction over subsets and zoom in on individual worlds via Fitting's embedding. This way we can give meaning to the satisfaction of conditional implication (or typical implication) on subsets of W, such as the set on which x is a bird. The lottery paradox, as well as the crooked lottery paradox remain satisfiable in our semantics.

Burgess' algebraic definition in [5] is similar to ours if we translate his definition to our setting with atypical subsets: we obtain that for him, $S \models_B \phi_1 \mapsto \phi_2$ holds if for any large enough S_2 subset of S such that $S_2 \models_B \phi_1$, we also have $S_2 \models_B \phi_2$. This property is satisfied by our formulas of the form $\top \mapsto \phi$, that is for things that typically hold. Furthermore, it is satisfied by our formulas for a restricted class of semantics.

The novelty of our work lies in combining Burgess's basic pattern for the semantics of $\mapsto$ with Friedman's et al. idea of having an underlying set W, but avoiding the necessity of defining satisfaction of formulas on each element of W by utilizing Fitting's embedding. In this we developed further our earlier work [4] where we used Fitting's embedding for the case when atypical sets are negligible, and hence at that time there was no need to introduce an additional implication. Here however atypical is not negligible and hence we need both $\mapsto$ and $\rightarrow$. This way we obtain a semantics that satisfies the usual KLM axioms [10].

2 Notions We Combine

2.1 Two Embeddings of First-Order Logic in First-Order Modal Logic

We recall two embeddings of classical first-order logic in classical modal logic that have relevance to our discussion. One is embedding in first-order S5 such that each subterm of a first-order formula obtains a $\Box$ in front of it: For any atomic formula ϕ, let $\phi^+ \equiv \Box\phi$; let $(\phi_1 \vee \phi_2)^+ \equiv \Box(\phi_1^+ \vee \phi_2^+)$; let $(\neg\phi)^+ \equiv \Box\neg\phi^+$; let $(\phi_1 \rightarrow \phi_2)^+ \equiv \Box(\phi_1^+ \rightarrow \phi_2^+)$; let $(\exists x\phi)^+ \equiv \Box\exists x\phi^+$; let $(\phi_1 \wedge \phi_2)^+ \equiv \Box(\phi_1^+ \wedge \phi_2^+)$; and let $(\forall x\phi)^+ \equiv \Box\forall x\phi^+$. It is a rather trivial theorem that $\vdash_{\mathrm{S5}} \phi^+$ if and only if $\vdash_{\mathrm{FOL}} \phi$.

The other embedding is the rather non-trivial Fitting-embedding in first-order S4 [6] putting $\Box\Diamond$ in front of each subformula: $\phi^* \equiv \Box\Diamond\phi$ for atomic ϕ; $(\phi_1 \vee \phi_2)^* \equiv \Box\Diamond(\phi_1^* \vee \phi_2^*)$; $(\neg\phi)^* \equiv \Box\Diamond\neg\phi^*$; $(\phi_1 \rightarrow \phi_2)^* \equiv \Box\Diamond(\phi_1^* \rightarrow \phi_2^*)$; $(\exists x\phi)^* \equiv \Box\Diamond\exists x\phi^*$; $(\phi_1 \wedge \phi_2)^* \equiv \Box\Diamond(\phi_1^* \wedge \phi_2^*)$; and $(\forall x\phi)^* \equiv \Box\Diamond\forall x\phi^*$. Then it can be proven that $\vdash_{\mathrm{S4}} \phi^*$ if and only if $\vdash_{\mathrm{FOL}} \phi$. In this work we assume single domain, hence we consider only S4 models that satisfy the Barcan formulas. It is worth noting that in this setting the $\Box\Diamond$ can be dropped in front of conjunction and universal quantification, and it can be replaced by $\Box$ in front of negation and implication.

In both cases, it is the if part that is important for us: first-order inference is sound with respect to these embeddings.

2.2 Conditional Logic and Typically Implies

Consider now some signature $(\mathfrak{f}, \mathfrak{p})$ of function and predicate symbols, and consider first-order formulas extended with the binary modal connective $\phi \mapsto \psi$, which the reader can think of meaning "ϕ typically implies ψ". Accordingly, let $\mathrm{FOCF}_{(\mathfrak{f},\mathfrak{p})}$ be the set of formulas defined by

$$\phi ::= \phi_A \mid \neg\phi \mid \phi \vee \phi \mid \phi \wedge \phi \mid \phi \rightarrow \phi \mid \phi \mapsto \phi \mid \exists x\phi \mid \forall x\phi$$

where $\phi_A \in \mathrm{AF}_{(\mathfrak{f},\mathfrak{p})}$ are obtained by applying predicates on terms. We shall also use parentheses. Note that it would be possible to use De Morgan identities and conditional-disjunction equivalence to reduce the number of classical connectives. In particular, $\phi \rightarrow \psi$ could be defined as an abbreviation of $\neg\phi \vee \psi$.

The most important feature of conditional implication is that it is non-monotonic: $\phi \mapsto \psi$ does not imply $\phi \wedge \phi' \mapsto \psi$.

Example 1. A usual example presented in the literature to illustrate how implications that typically hold can be violated in atypical situations is the case of birds, flying, and penguins. If ϕ says "x is a bird" and ψ says "x can fly", then $\phi \mapsto \psi$ expresses that a bird can typically fly. However, with ϕ' expressing that "x is a penguin", even if $\phi \mapsto \psi$ is true, $\phi \wedge \phi' \mapsto \psi$ is not, as penguins do not typically fly. A usual idea (as in [7]) to give semantics to these statements is to use a possible world semantics the following way:[1] For a valuation of x, "x is a bird" corresponds to some set of possible worlds (say W_b) while "x is a penguin" corresponds to a set of possible worlds (say W_p) that is atypical within W_b. When something fails only on an atypical set, then it is deemed to be typically satisfied. Then "x is a bird" $\mapsto$ "x can fly" can be satisfied on W together with "x is a bird" $\wedge$ "x is a penguin" $\mapsto$ "x cannot fly".   □

There are various such non-monotonic systems running under the names of default reasoning, defeasibe logic, conditional logic, and so forth. Here we focus on conditional logic, and our starting point is the line of research from Lewis [12] through Adams [1] and Burgess [5] to Kraus et al. [10] and Friedman et al. [7] on conditional implication and its use in default reasoning. This line of research uses a possible world semantics framework, with a hierarchical structure on sets of possible worlds. Most of them are for propositional formulas only, but [7] presents a first-order approach.

The authors of [7] give a good summary of other attempts to define semantics for first-order conditional logic as well as a criticism of all those attempts before proposing theirs. We agree with their criticism, but we also argue that the semantics of [7] has shortcomings as well. This stems from the fact that the authors of [7] were implicitly following the S5 embedding with the □ pattern (mentioned in Sect. 2.1) for their first-order semantics. Here we argue that using the □◊ pattern of the Fitting twist gives a more general, and a better semantics. With the Fitting twist, conditional implication can be considered "locally" on sets of possible worlds. We do not do this here using plausibility measures as is done in [7], instead, we use an equivalent formulation, distinguishing atypical and non-atypical sets. In Sect. 4 we review the semantics of Friedman et al. and raise some issues with it.

3   Atypical and Non-atypical Sets

The following notion of atypical sets will be central in our discussions.

Definition 1 (Hierarchy of atypical and non-atypical sets). *Let W be a set of possible worlds, let $\mathcal{L} \subseteq 2^W$ be some convenient ortholattice of sets (that is, a lattice closed under complementation, and hence containing $\emptyset$ and W, such as measurable sets). Let* atyp *be a relation on $\mathcal{L}$ with the following properties, where for each $S \in \mathcal{L}$, we call*

$$\mathcal{L}_{\mathrm{a}}^S := \{S' \in \mathcal{L} : (S', S) \in \mathtt{atyp}\}$$

the atypical sets of S:

- *$\mathcal{L}_{\mathrm{a}}^S$ is an ideal of $\mathcal{L}$ that is,*

---

[1] This kind of semantics is called "subjective conditionals" in [7], as a hierarchy on the sets of possible worlds indicate what typical is and what atypical is, as opposed to "statistical conditional" where the hierarchy is defined on the domain of interpretation.

- $\emptyset \in \mathcal{L}_{\mathrm{a}}^S$
- if $S' \in \mathcal{L}_{\mathrm{a}}^S$, and $S'' \in \mathcal{L}$ and $S'' \subseteq S'$, then $S'' \in \mathcal{L}_{\mathrm{a}}^S$;
- if $S' \in \mathcal{L}_{\mathrm{a}}^S$, and $S'' \in \mathcal{L}_{\mathrm{a}}^S$, then $S' \cup S'' \in \mathcal{L}_{\mathrm{a}}^S$;
- $\mathcal{L}_{\mathrm{a}}^S \neq \mathcal{L}^S$.

  – for $S, S' \in \mathcal{L}$, if $S' \subseteq S$, then $\mathcal{L}_{\mathrm{a}}^{S'} \subseteq \mathcal{L}_{\mathrm{a}}^S$
  – for $S \in \mathcal{L}$, if $S' \subseteq S$ and $S' \notin \mathcal{L}_{\mathrm{a}}^S$, then $\mathcal{L}_{\mathrm{a}}^{S'} = \{S'' | S'' \in \mathcal{L}_{\mathrm{a}}^S \wedge S'' \subseteq S'\}$

Let $\mathcal{L}^S := \{S' | S' \in \mathcal{L} \wedge S' \subseteq S\}$ and $\mathcal{L}_{\mathrm{na}}^S := \mathcal{L}^S \setminus \mathcal{L}_{\mathrm{a}}^S$ be the set of non-atypical sets in S.

Example 2. Let W be a topological space and $\mathcal{L}$ be the Borel algebra on W. For $S \in \mathcal{L}$, we can define $\mathcal{L}_{\mathrm{a}}^S$ as the subsets of S that have empty interior with respect to the induced topology on S.

Example 3. Let W be a set of elementary events with $\mathcal{L} \subseteq 2^W$ a σ-algebra on W. For each $i \in \mathbb{N}$, let P_i be a (σ-additive) probability measure on $\mathcal{L}$, and let $\mathcal{P}$ denote the sequence $(P_i)_{i \in \mathbb{N}}$. We call $(W, \mathcal{L}, \mathcal{P})$ a parameterized probability space. Parametrized probability spaces are used to consider asymptotic properties for example in computability or in conditional logic. Parameterized probability spaces together with a convergence class $\mathcal{C}$ allow us to distinguish sets that have asymptotically small, insignificant probabilities.

We call $\mathcal{C}$, a set of $\mathbb{N} \to \mathbb{R}^+$ sequences a *convergence class*, if (i) for each $s \in \mathcal{C}$, all subsequences of s are also in $\mathcal{C}$, namely, for each $(s_i)_{i \in \mathbb{N}} \in \mathcal{C}$ and $J : \mathbb{N} \to \mathbb{N}$ strictly increasing, $(s_{J(i)})_{i \in \mathbb{N}} \in \mathcal{C}$; (ii) for all $s \in \mathcal{C}$, $\lim_{i \to \infty} s_i = 0$; (iii) if $s \in \mathcal{C}$, and $s' : \mathbb{N} \to \mathbb{R}^+$, and for all $i \in \mathbb{N}$, $s'_i \leq s_i$, then $s' \in \mathcal{C}$; (iv) if $s, s' \in \mathcal{C}$, then $s + s' \in \mathcal{C}$.

Let $\mathcal{C}$ be a convergence class, and let $(W, \mathcal{L}, \mathcal{P})$ be a parameterized probability space. For $S \in \mathcal{L}$, we call a set $S' \in \mathcal{L}^S$ $\mathcal{C}$-asymptotically possible in S if $(P_i(S'|S))_{i \in \mathbb{N}} \notin \mathcal{C}$ and we call it a $\mathcal{C}$-asymptotically impossible in S if the sequence $(P_i(S'|S))_{i \in \mathbb{N}} \in \mathcal{C}$. The $\mathcal{C}$-asymptotically impossibility relation is an atypicality relation. When the probability of S is 0, one can just set the conditional to 1.

4   The Semantics of Friedman et al.

We denote with $\models_{\mathrm{FHK}}$ the first-order semantics proposed in [7], which goes essentially the following way (they use plausibility measures, but it is equivalent with the following "parameterized probability distribution" formulation due to Goldszmidt et al. [8] for the propositional case): Let $(W, \mathcal{L}, \mathcal{P})$ be a parametric probability space, and let $\mathcal{C}$ be the set of sequences converging to 0. Let $(\mathfrak{f}, \mathfrak{p})$ be a first-order signature. Suppose for each $w \in W$ and $\phi \in \mathsf{AF}_{(\mathfrak{f}, \mathfrak{p})}$ and valuation V of variables in ϕ, the satisfaction relation $w, V \models_{\mathrm{FHK}} \phi$ is defined. Then for each V and $w \in W$, satisfaction of conjunction, disjunction, negation, implication, existential and universal quantifiers by w, V are defined the usual Tarsky way. Then $W, V \models_{\mathrm{FHK}} \phi$ defined to hold iff for all $w \in W$, $w, V \models_{\mathrm{FHK}} \phi$. If we introduce the S5 accessibility relation that is the diagonal on $W \times W$, then

$W, V \models_{FHK} \phi$ is equivalent with $W, V \models_{S5} \phi^+$. For conditional implication, they define

$$V, w \models_{FHK} \phi \mapsto \psi \Leftrightarrow 1 - P_n([\psi]_V|[\phi]_V) \in \mathcal{C} \qquad (1)$$

where $[\phi]_V$ denotes the set of possible worlds that satisfy ϕ:

$$[\phi]_V := \{w|w \in W \wedge V, w \models_{FHK} \phi\}$$

and $P_n([\psi]_V|[\phi]_V) := 1$ if $P_n([\phi]_V) = 0$). The idea here is that the likeliness of the satisfaction of ψ given ϕ can be brought arbitrarily close to 1. It is easy to check that $V, w \models_{FHK} \phi \mapsto \psi$ does not imply $V, w \models_{FHK} \phi \wedge \phi' \mapsto \psi$, hence $\mapsto$ is non-monotonic. That may happen when $P_n([\phi']_V|[\phi]_V) \in \mathcal{C}$, that is, when $[\phi']_V \cap [\phi]_V$ is *atypical* in $[\phi]_V$.

While the first-order semantics of Friedman et al. has a number of good properties, it also has some others that may be inconvenient in certain situations we think. Here we mention three points:

1. It has to be assumed (as Friedman et al. point out) that $[\phi]_V \in \mathcal{L}$ for all ϕ. This is actually a strong assumption, even if it holds for atomic formulas, it does not necessarily hold for compound formulas, even without $\mapsto$.

2. The FHK satisfaction of $\mapsto$ is defined to be the same for all w: the definition in (1) does not have w on the right-hand side of $\Leftrightarrow$. Conditional implication is something that cannot be defined only on each single w, so Friedman et al. define it on W. But for first-order inference the pattern of having a $\Box$ in front has to be kept, so with that, it is necessary to have identical satisfaction of the conditional implication for all w. That is, it is either satisfied for all $w \in W$, or for none. This has some serious implications. For example, if ϕ_1 is FHK-satisfied by V, w_1 for some w_1, then $\phi_1 \rightarrow (\phi_2 \mapsto \phi_3)$ is FHK-satisfied by V, w_1 only if $\phi_2 \mapsto \phi_3$ holds on the entire W that is, if FHK-satisfied by V, w for all $w \in W$. Consequently, if ("x is an animal" $\mapsto$ "x can fly") fails on W, the statement ("x is a bird" $\rightarrow$("x is an animal" $\mapsto$ "x can fly")) also fails unless "x is a bird" is not satisfied on any w, even if ("x is a bird" $\mapsto$ "x can fly") holds. That is a bit strange given that when "x is a bird", "x is an animal" does not add further restriction. Arguably, for $\phi_1 \rightarrow (\phi_2 \mapsto \phi_3)$ to be satisfied, $\phi_2 \mapsto \phi_3$ should be allowed to fail where ϕ_1 fails, or at least on a part of it. Intuitively, the condition "x is a bird" should restrict W to those elements in W that satisfy this condition, and then satisfaction of "x is an animal" $\mapsto$ "x can fly" should be considered there, but that is not how the semantics of Friedman et al. works. To make rigorous sense of this idea, the satisfaction of $\phi_2 \mapsto \phi_3$ should be somehow defined locally as opposed to globally on the whole W.

3. Furthermore, in the semantics of Friedman et al., $\exists x(\phi[x] \mapsto \psi[x])$ is FHK-valid, if there is a single interpretation a of x in the domain for which $V, w \models_{FHK} \phi[a] \mapsto \psi[a]$ holds for all $w \in W$. This is in sharp contrast with $\exists x \phi'[x]$ where ϕ' has no $\mapsto$, because in this case, for FHK-validity, the valuation of x can change from world to world. We can however do something in between, for all formulas: intuitively, that $\exists x \phi$ holds in the semantics we shall

suggest, if there is a valuation for x such that ϕ holds on "neighborhoods" covering W with that valuation of x.

The first point above can be solved by switching from talking about sets of the kind $[\phi]_V$ to talking about sets on which ϕ is satisfied. We will see that this way we naturally obtain a semantics similar to what Burgess defined. The second point is completely resolved by moving to Fitting's embedding, while the third point is also softened by moving to Fitting's embedding as we will see in the next section.

5   Semantics for Conditional Logic with Fitting's Embedding

In this section we present our semantics and some specific examples. We first move from the possible-world-wise satisfaction of Friedman's et al. [7] to satisfaction on sets of possible worlds, and hence obtain a satisfaction notion similar to Burgess [5]. Then we explain how to carry out the Fitting twist, using Fitting's embedding, which makes it possible to define the semantics of $\mapsto$ on subsets as well, instead of the full W. Then we consider some sound axioms, some important special cases, and some examples.

5.1   Moving to Satisfaction on Sets

If for some ϕ and ψ formulas $[\phi]_V, [\psi]_V \in \mathcal{L}$, then for any $S \in \mathcal{L}$, it is natural to define $S, V \models \phi \mapsto \psi$ such that

$$S, V \models \phi \mapsto \psi \iff S \cap [\phi]_V \cap [\psi]_V^\perp \in \mathcal{L}_{\mathrm{a}}^{S \cap [\phi]_V} \text{ or } S \cap [\phi]_V = \emptyset \quad (2)$$

meaning that in S, either ϕ is not satisfied, or the set of possible worlds where ϕ is satisfied but ψ is not is atypical relative to $S \cap [\phi]_V$. This is essentially what Friedman et al. do for $S = W$.

Suppose now that it is not necessarily true that $[\phi]_V \in \mathcal{L}$, and hence we have to avoid the usage of such sets. On the other hand suppose also that for ϕ and ψ formulas, and for any $S, V \in \mathcal{L}$, the truth values of ϕ and ψ for S are defined, that is, either $S, V \models \phi$ or $S, V \not\models \phi$, and the same for ψ. How can we define $S, V \models \phi \mapsto \psi$ in such a situation? Clearly, $S, V \models \phi \mapsto \psi$ should allow $S', V \models \phi$ and $S', V \not\models \psi$ for too small $S' \subseteq S$. However, when S' is large enough, then $S', V \models \phi$ should imply that ψ is satisfied on S', except maybe on an atypical subset of S'. So we have to resolve two things: how to formalize that "S' is large enough", and how to formalize that "ψ is satisfied on S', except maybe on an atypical set".

Large enough can easily be formalized such that for any $S_0 \in \mathcal{L}^S$ with $S_0, V \models \phi$ there is an $S_1 \in \mathcal{L}^S$ with $S_0 \subseteq S_1$ and $S_1, V \models \phi$ such that S' has to be larger than S_1.

"ψ true on S' except maybe on an atypical set of S'" can be formalized such that for any $S_3 \in \mathcal{L}_{\mathrm{na}}^{S'}$, there is an $S_4 \in \mathcal{L}_{\mathrm{na}}^{S'}$ with $S_4 \subseteq S_3$ such that $S_4, V \models \psi$.

The reader may object that it could also be such that there is an $S'' \subseteq S'$ with $S' \setminus S'' \in \mathcal{L}_{\mathrm{na}}^{S'}$ and $S'', V \models \psi$, but this definition does not behave well essentially because patching together sets on which ψ is satisfied may not result in such a set in $\mathcal{L}$. It is better to avoid asking for existence of global sets, and opt for the existence of local sets.

Putting the above two together, we obtain that $S, V \models \phi \mapsto \psi$ should hold if for any $S_0 \in \mathcal{L}^S$ with $S_0, V \models \phi$ there is an $S_1 \in \mathcal{L}^S$ with $S_0 \subseteq S_1$ and $S_1, V \models \phi$ such that whenever $S_2 \in \mathcal{L}^S$ with $S_1 \subseteq S_2$ and $S_2, V \models \phi$, then for any $S_3 \in \mathcal{L}_{\mathrm{na}}^{S_2}$, there is an $S_4 \in \mathcal{L}_{\mathrm{na}}^{S_2}$ with $S_4 \subseteq S_3$ such that $S_4, V \models \psi$.

This definition is similar to that of Burgess [5], which says x satisfies $\phi \mapsto \psi$ iff

$$\forall y \in W_x \cap \llbracket \phi \rrbracket_V \exists z \in W_x \cap \llbracket \phi \rrbracket_V (Rxzy \wedge \forall t \in W_x \cap \llbracket \phi \rrbracket_V (Rxtz \Rightarrow t \in \llbracket \psi \rrbracket_V)) \quad (3)$$

If $x \in \mathcal{L}$, and W_x denotes $\mathcal{L}^x$, and $Rxzy$ denotes that $y, z \in \mathcal{L}^x$ and $y \subseteq z$, and $\llbracket \phi \rrbracket_V$ are all those sets in $\mathcal{L}$ that satisfied ϕ with the valuation V, then Burgess' definition translates to ours, except that we require ψ to be satisfied except on an atypical set. We will come back to this later. This is essentially how we define the semantics of $\mapsto$, presented in Sect. 5.2 rigorously.

5.2   Fitting-Twisted Semantics of First-Order Conditional Logic

Let W be a set of possible worlds, let $(\mathfrak{f}, \mathfrak{p})$ be a signature and $\mathcal{X}$ be a set of variables. Let $\mathtt{FOF}_{(\mathfrak{f},\mathfrak{p})}$ be the set of first-order formulas built on $(\mathfrak{f}, \mathfrak{p})$ and $\mathcal{X}$. Let $\mathtt{FOMF}_{(\mathfrak{f},\mathfrak{p})}$ denote the set of first-order modal formulas over $(\mathfrak{f}, \mathfrak{p})$ and $\mathcal{X}$ with the usual modal operators $\square$ and $\lozenge$. As before, let $\mathtt{FOCF}_{(\mathfrak{f},\mathfrak{p})}$ denote the first-order formulas extended with conditional implication $\mapsto$ (any nestedness allowed), and let $\mathtt{FOCMF}_{(\mathfrak{f},\mathfrak{p})}$ denote the first-order modal formulas with $\mapsto$. Let $\mathcal{D}$ be a single domain on which function symbols are interpreted (rigidly, independently of possible worlds). Suppose for a valuation $V : \mathcal{X} \to \mathcal{D}$, the truth value of each formula on each $w \in W$ is defined: $w, V \models \phi$ or $w, V \not\models \phi$. If we define an accessibility relation $\mathcal{R}_{\mathrm{S5}}$ relation on W such that $w_1 \mathcal{R}_{\mathrm{S5}} w_2$ holds iff $w_1 = w_2$, then the first order semantics extends the usual way to S5 semantics $\models_{\mathrm{S5}}$ of $\mathtt{FOMF}_{(\mathfrak{f},\mathfrak{p})}$. Let us define

$$W, V \models_{\mathrm{S5E}} \phi \Longleftrightarrow W, V \models_{\mathrm{S5}} \phi^+.$$

It is easy to see that $W, V \models_{\mathrm{S5E}} \phi$ iff $w, V \models \phi$ for all $w \in W$. That is, it is exactly what Friedman et al. consider so for formulas without $\mapsto$, $\models_{\mathrm{S5E}}$ is the same as $\models_{\mathrm{FHK}}$. Then $W, V \models_{\mathrm{FHK}} \phi \mapsto \psi$ is defined by formula (1) (or, more generally, (2)), and to be able to consider nested implications, for each $w \in W$, $w, V \models_{\mathrm{FHK}} \phi \mapsto \psi$ is set to hold iff $W, V \models_{\mathrm{FHK}} \phi \mapsto \psi$.

To tackle the problems we mentioned in the previous section, we suggest something different that allows us to define satisfaction of $\phi \mapsto \psi$ over regions of W. First, we need an abstraction of 0-measure sets, which we call *insignificant sets*, and which will allow $\mapsto$ in formula (2) (and in fact other formulas too) to fail not just on the empty set but on insignificant sets. We need this to be able to cover sufficiently general situations:

Definition 2 (Ideal of Insignificant Sets, Significant Sets). *Let W be a set, let $\mathcal{L} \subseteq 2^W$ be an ortholattice of sets. Let $\mathcal{L}_i$ be an ideal of $\mathcal{L}$, namely:*

- *$\emptyset \in \mathcal{L}_i$*
- *if $S \in \mathcal{L}_i$, and $S' \in \mathcal{L}$, and $S' \subseteq S$, then $S' \in \mathcal{L}_i$;*
- *if $S \in \mathcal{L}_i$, and $S' \in \mathcal{L}_i$, then $S \cup S' \in \mathcal{L}_i$;*
- *$\mathcal{L}_i \neq \mathcal{L}$.*

We call $\mathcal{L}_i$ the set of insignificant sets and we call $\mathcal{L}_s := \mathcal{L} \setminus \mathcal{L}_i$ the set of significant sets. We shall refer to elements of $\mathcal{L}$ as events. For a significant set S, let $\mathcal{L}_s^S$ denote the significant sets that are subsets of S, and let $\mathcal{L}_i^S$ denote the insignificant sets that are subsets of S.

$\mathcal{L}_s$ has a natural transitive accessibility relation $\mathcal{R}$, the inclusion: $S_1 \mathcal{R} S_2$ iff $S_2 \subseteq S_1$.

Further assume that satisfaction of formulas in $\texttt{FOF}_{(\mathfrak{f},\mathfrak{p})}$ is defined for each $S \in \mathcal{L}_s$ and V valuation in $\mathcal{D}$. This might come from a point-wise satisfaction (i.e. $S, V \models \phi$ iff for all $w \in S$, $w, V \models \phi$), but not necessarily. Then again this extends the usual way to an S4 semantics $\models_{S4}$ of modal formulas $\texttt{FOMF}_{(\mathfrak{f},\mathfrak{p})}$ over $\mathcal{L}_s$ (note, we only have single domain). We call the the semantics induced by the equivalence

$$S, V \models_{FT} \phi \Longleftrightarrow S, V \models_{S4} \phi^*$$

Fitting-twisted semantics. By Fitting's embedding theorem, first-order inference is sound for $\models_{FT}$. If $\mathcal{L} = 2^W$ and $\mathcal{L}_i = \{\emptyset\}$, then $\models_{FT}$ coincides with $\models_{S5E}$ on W. So $\models_{FT}$ is a generalization of $\models_{S5E}$.

The above Fitting-twisted semantics of first-order formulas defines negation of ϕ to be satisfied on an S if ϕ is not satisfied on any significant subset of S. Furthermore, the semantics of disjunction on an S is very close to being true if S can be split into two parts S_1 and S_2 such that one disjunct is satisfied on S_1, the other on S_2, but with avoiding the necessity of the existence of such global sets. Finally, the semantics of the existential quantifier is close to being true if S can be split into significant parts on each of which there is a witness, but again formulated locally. Interested reader is advised to consult [4] for more detail.

We further need a consistency property between insignificant and atypical sets, namely that *insignificant sets are also atypical*:

- for all $S \in \mathcal{L}_s$, the insignificant subsets of S are atypical in S: $\mathcal{L}_i^S \subseteq \mathcal{L}_a^S$

For defining the semantics of $\mapsto$ we need to overcome an additional difficulty. The dichotomy for FHK between defining the semantics of the classical connectives and the quantifiers on w while the semantics of $\mapsto$ on W cannot be entirely removed, only relaxed. We define the former on small sets (that are significant), while the latter on large sets (that are non-atypical). Accordingly, over W, we define the following set of S4 possible worlds on which we are going to define satisfaction, and each element of which is a pair of a large set and a small set:

$$\mathfrak{S} := \{\mathfrak{s} \mid \mathfrak{s} = (\mathfrak{s}_\top, \mathfrak{s}_\perp) \text{ where } \mathfrak{s}_\top, \mathfrak{s}_\perp \in \mathcal{L}_s \land \mathfrak{s}_\top \supseteq \mathfrak{s}_\perp\}$$

together with a transitive accessibility relation $\geq$ on $\mathfrak{S}$ satisfying

- $\mathfrak{s}^1 \geq \mathfrak{s}^2 \implies \mathfrak{s}^2_\top \in \mathcal{L}^{\mathfrak{s}^1_\top}_{\mathrm{na}} \wedge \mathfrak{s}^2_\bot \subseteq \mathfrak{s}^1_\bot$
- $\mathfrak{s}^1 \geq \mathfrak{s}^2 \implies \mathfrak{s}^1 \geq (\mathfrak{s}^1_\top, \mathfrak{s}^2_\bot)$.
- For $S, S_1, S_2 \in \mathcal{L}_\mathfrak{s}$ with $S_1 \subseteq S$ and $S_2 \subseteq S$ and $S_1 \cap S_2 \in \mathcal{L}_\mathfrak{s}$, we require that there is an $S' \in \mathcal{L}^{S_1 \cap S_2}_{\mathrm{na}}$ such that $(S, S_1) \geq (S, S')$ and $(S, S_2) \geq (S, S')$.

That is, while $\mathfrak{s}^2_\bot$ can be any small subset of $\mathfrak{s}^1_\bot$, non-atypical subsets of $\mathfrak{s}^1_\top$ are carried over to $\mathfrak{s}^2_\top$.

Example 4. Continuing our Example 2, setting $\mathcal{L}_\mathfrak{i} := \{\emptyset\}$, one way to introduce $\geq$ is such that $\mathfrak{s}^1 \geq \mathfrak{s}^2$ if and only if $\mathfrak{s}^2_\top$ is open in $\mathfrak{s}^1_\top$ and $\mathfrak{s}^2_\bot \subseteq \mathfrak{s}^1_\bot$. The reason we require $\mathfrak{s}^2_\top$ is open in $\mathfrak{s}^1_\top$ is to disallow $\mathfrak{s}^1_\top$ to have intersections with non-atypical sets of $\mathfrak{s}^2_\top$ that are atypical, which could cause problems in certain situations that we illustrate later.

We can define a Kripke-semantics $\models_{\mathrm{KC}}$ on $\mathfrak{S}$ for formulas in $\mathrm{FOCMF}_{(\mathfrak{f},\mathfrak{p})}$ by setting

- for any $\phi \in \mathrm{FOMF}_{(\mathfrak{f},\mathfrak{p})}$, $\mathfrak{s}, V \models_{\mathrm{KC}} \phi \iff \mathfrak{s}_\bot, V \models \phi$
- for any $\phi, \psi \in \mathrm{FOCMF}_{(\mathfrak{f},\mathfrak{p})}$, $\mathfrak{s}, V \models_{\mathrm{KC}} \phi \mapsto \psi$ iff for all $\mathfrak{s}'$ with $\mathfrak{s} \geq \mathfrak{s}'$ and all $S_0 \in \mathcal{L}^{\mathfrak{s}'_\top}$ such that $(\mathfrak{s}'_\top, S_0), V \models \phi$, there is an $S_1 \in \mathcal{L}^{\mathfrak{s}'_\top}$ such that $S_0 \subseteq S_1$ and $(\mathfrak{s}'_\top, S_1), V \models \phi$, and forall $S_2 \in \mathcal{L}^{\mathfrak{s}'_\top}$ such that $S_1 \subseteq S_2$ and $(\mathfrak{s}'_\top, S_2), V \models \phi$, it is true that for all $S_3 \in \mathcal{L}^{S_2}_{\mathrm{na}}$, there is an $S_4 \in \mathcal{L}^{S_2}_{\mathrm{na}}$ such that $S_4 \subseteq S_3$ and $(\mathfrak{s}'_\top, S_4), V \models \psi$.

Here for $\mathfrak{s}, V \models_{\mathrm{KC}} \phi \mapsto \psi$, we followed the pattern explained in Sect. 5.1. But before that, we have to require it for all accessible $\mathfrak{s}'$. That is necessary to make it behave well, as the soundness proofs later make it clear. On the other hand, we see now why we needed in Example 2 that in the first argument only open sets are accessible: otherwise $\phi \mapsto \psi$ would be required to be satisfied even when atypical sets are cut out from the part where ϕ is satisfied.

The above recursively generates a Kripke semantics for all formulas in $\mathrm{FOCMF}_{(\mathfrak{f},\mathfrak{p})}$, even those with nested conditional implication. Then $\phi \mapsto \phi^*$ can be extended to $\mathrm{FOCF}_{(\mathfrak{f},\mathfrak{p})}$ the same way by putting $\Box\Diamond$ in front of each subformula (i.e. $(\phi \mapsto \psi)^* = \Box\Diamond(\phi^* \mapsto \psi^*)$), and we can define

$$\mathfrak{s}, V \models_{\mathrm{FTC}} \phi \iff \mathfrak{s}, V \models_{\mathrm{KC}} \phi^*.$$

We further write $S, V \models_{\mathrm{FTC}} \phi$ for $S \in \mathcal{L}_\mathfrak{s}$ if $(S, S), V \models_{\mathrm{FTC}} \phi$.

We will discuss it in the next section in more detail, but it is easy to see that $\models_{\mathrm{FHK}}$ is a special case of $\models_{\mathrm{FTC}}$: When $\mathcal{L}_\mathfrak{i} = \emptyset$, and $[\phi]_V \in \mathcal{L}$ for all ϕ and V, and $(\mathfrak{s}^1_\top, \mathfrak{s}^1_\bot) \geq (\mathfrak{s}^2_\top, \mathfrak{s}^2_\bot)$ if and only if $\mathfrak{s}^1_\top = \mathfrak{s}^2_\top$ and $\mathfrak{s}^1_\bot \supseteq \mathfrak{s}^2_\bot$, then for any $\phi \in \mathrm{FOCF}_{(\mathfrak{f},\mathfrak{p})}$, V valuation, and $w \in W$, we have

$$(W, \{w\}), V \models_{\mathrm{FTC}} \phi \iff w, V \models_{\mathrm{FHK}} \phi.$$

Theorem 1 (Soundness). *The inference rules of first-order classical logic are sound with respect to $\models_{\mathrm{FTC}}$ for the connectives $\wedge$, $\vee$, $\neg$, $\rightarrow$, and the quantifiers $\exists$, $\forall$. For $\mapsto$, we further have the following sound axioms of Burgess for conditional logic:*

- *A0:* $\phi \longmapsto \phi$
- *A1:* $\big((\phi \longmapsto \psi_1) \wedge (\phi \longmapsto \psi_2)\big) \to \big(\phi \longmapsto (\psi_1 \wedge \psi_2)\big)$
- *A2:* $\big(\phi \longmapsto (\psi_1 \wedge \psi_2)\big) \to \big(\phi \longmapsto \psi_1\big)$
- *A3:* $\big((\phi \longmapsto \psi_1) \wedge (\phi \longmapsto \psi_2)\big) \to \big((\phi \wedge \psi_1) \longmapsto \psi_2\big)$

We also have

- *A4':* $\big(((\chi_1 \longmapsto \phi_1) \longmapsto \psi) \wedge ((\chi_2 \longmapsto \phi_2) \longmapsto \psi)\big) \to \big(((\chi_1 \longmapsto \phi_1) \vee (\chi_2 \longmapsto \phi_2)) \longmapsto \psi\big)$

Furthermore we have the following further properties of Kraus et al.:

- *LLE:* $(\phi_1 \leftrightarrow \phi_2) \wedge (\phi_1 \longmapsto \psi) \to (\phi_2 \longmapsto \psi)$
- *RW:* $(\psi_1 \to \psi_2) \wedge (\phi \longmapsto \psi_1) \to (\phi \longmapsto \psi_2)$

Proof. The first-order part of this theorem follows from Fitting's embedding. The rest is quite straightforward from the definitions:

- A0: $\mathfrak{s}, V \models_{\mathrm{FTC}} \phi \longmapsto \phi$ is equivalent with $\mathfrak{s}, V \models_{\mathrm{KC}} \Box \Diamond (\phi^* \longmapsto \phi^*)$. Take any $\mathfrak{s}'$ with $\mathfrak{s} \geq \mathfrak{s}'$. Then $\mathfrak{s}', V \models_{\mathrm{KC}} \phi^* \longmapsto \phi^*$ holds, because on any $\mathfrak{s}''$ with $\mathfrak{s}' \geq \mathfrak{s}''$ and $S \in \mathcal{L}_T^{\mathfrak{s}''}$, $(\mathfrak{s}'', S), V \models_{\mathrm{KC}} \phi^*$ implies $(\mathfrak{s}'', S), V \models_{\mathrm{KC}} \phi^*$.
- A1 and A3: We show that for any V and $\mathfrak{s}$, we have $\mathfrak{s}, V \models_{\mathrm{FTC}} \big((\phi \longmapsto \psi_1) \wedge (\phi \longmapsto \psi_2)\big) \to \xi$, which is equivalent with $\mathfrak{s}, V \models_{\mathrm{KC}} \Box \big(((\phi \longmapsto \psi_1) \wedge (\phi \longmapsto \psi_2))^* \to \xi^*\big)$, where ξ is $\phi \longmapsto (\psi_1 \wedge \psi_2)$ in A1 and $(\phi \wedge \psi_1) \longmapsto \psi_2$ in A3. Take an $\mathfrak{s}'$ with $\mathfrak{s} \geq \mathfrak{s}'$ such that $\mathfrak{s}', V \models_{\mathrm{KC}} \big((\phi \longmapsto \psi_1) \wedge (\phi \longmapsto \psi_2)\big)^*$, which is the same as $\mathfrak{s}', V \models_{\mathrm{KC}} \Box \Diamond (\phi^* \longmapsto \psi_1^*) \wedge \Box \Diamond (\phi^* \longmapsto \psi_2^*)$, and so for all $\mathfrak{s}''$ with $\mathfrak{s}' \geq \mathfrak{s}''$, there is an $\mathfrak{s}'''$ with $\mathfrak{s}'' \geq \mathfrak{s}'''$ such that $\mathfrak{s}''', V \models_{\mathrm{KC}} \phi^* \longmapsto \psi_1^*$ and $\mathfrak{s}''', V \models_{\mathrm{KC}} \phi^* \longmapsto \psi_2^*$.
  - A1: We have to show that $\mathfrak{s}', V \models_{\mathrm{KC}} \big(\phi \longmapsto (\psi_1 \wedge \psi_2)\big)^*$, which is the same as $\mathfrak{s}', V \models_{\mathrm{KC}} \Box \Diamond \big(\phi^* \longmapsto (\psi_1^* \wedge \psi_2^*)\big)$. Take any $\mathfrak{s}''$ with $\mathfrak{s}' \geq \mathfrak{s}''$, and then take $\mathfrak{s}'''$ as above. We claim that $\mathfrak{s}''', V \models_{\mathrm{KC}} \phi^* \longmapsto (\psi_1^* \wedge \psi_2^*)$. For any $\mathfrak{s}''''$ with $\mathfrak{s}''' \geq \mathfrak{s}''''$, we have $\mathfrak{s}'''', V \models_{\mathrm{KC}} \phi^* \longmapsto \psi_1^*$ and $\mathfrak{s}'''', V \models_{\mathrm{KC}} \phi^* \longmapsto \psi_2^*$. If $S_0 \in \mathcal{L}_T^{\mathfrak{s}''''}$ is such that $(\mathfrak{s}'''', S_0), V \models_{\mathrm{KC}} \phi^*$, there is an $S_1 \in \mathcal{L}_T^{\mathfrak{s}''''}$ such that $S_0 \subseteq S_1$ and $(\mathfrak{s}'''', S_1), V \models_{\mathrm{KC}} \phi^*$, and forall $S_2 \in \mathcal{L}_T^{\mathfrak{s}''''}$ such that $S_1 \subseteq S_2$ and $(\mathfrak{s}'''', S_2), V \models_{\mathrm{KC}} \phi^*$, it is true that for all $S_3 \in \mathcal{L}_{\mathrm{na}}^{S_2}$, there is an $S_4 \in \mathcal{L}_{\mathrm{na}}^{S_2}$ such that $S_4 \subseteq S_3$ and $(\mathfrak{s}'''', S_4), V \models_{\mathrm{KC}} \psi_1^*$ and $(\mathfrak{s}'''', S_4), V \models_{\mathrm{KC}} \psi_2^*$, hence $(\mathfrak{s}'''', S_4), V \models_{\mathrm{KC}} \psi_1^* \wedge \psi_2^*$.
  - A3: We have to show that $\mathfrak{s}', V \models_{\mathrm{KC}} \big((\phi \wedge \psi_1) \longmapsto \psi_2\big)^*$, which is the same as $\mathfrak{s}', V \models_{\mathrm{KC}} \Box \Diamond \big((\phi^* \wedge \psi_1^*) \longmapsto \psi_2^*\big)$. Take any $\mathfrak{s}''$ with $\mathfrak{s}' \geq \mathfrak{s}''$, and then take $\mathfrak{s}'''$ as above. We claim that $\mathfrak{s}''', V \models_{\mathrm{KC}} (\phi^* \wedge \psi_1^*) \longmapsto \psi_2^*$. For any $\mathfrak{s}''''$ with $\mathfrak{s}''' \geq \mathfrak{s}''''$, we have $\mathfrak{s}'''', V \models_{\mathrm{KC}} \phi^* \longmapsto \psi_1^*$ and $\mathfrak{s}'''', V \models_{\mathrm{KC}} \phi^* \longmapsto \psi_2^*$. If $S_0 \in \mathcal{L}_T^{\mathfrak{s}''''}$ is such that $(\mathfrak{s}'''', S_0), V \models_{\mathrm{KC}} \phi^* \wedge \psi_1^*$, then $(\mathfrak{s}'''', S_0), V \models_{\mathrm{KC}} \phi^*$ and there is an $S_1 \in \mathcal{L}_T^{\mathfrak{s}''''}$ such that $S_0 \subseteq S_1$ and $(\mathfrak{s}'''', S_1), V \models_{\mathrm{KC}} \phi^*$, and there is an $S_4 \in \mathcal{L}_{\mathrm{na}}^{S_1}$ such that $(\mathfrak{s}'''', S_4), V \models_{\mathrm{KC}} \psi_1^*$. Take $S_1' := S_0 \cup S_4$. Clearly, $S_1' \in \mathcal{L}_{\mathrm{na}}^{S_1}$. We have $S_1' \in \mathcal{L}_T^{\mathfrak{s}''''}$ and $S_0 \subseteq S_1'$ and $(\mathfrak{s}'''', S_1'), V \models_{\mathrm{KC}} \phi^* \wedge \psi_1^*$ Take an $S_2' \in \mathcal{L}_T^{\mathfrak{s}''''}$ such that $S_1' \subseteq S_2'$ and $(\mathfrak{s}'''', S_2'), V \models_{\mathrm{KC}} \phi^* \wedge \psi_1^*$, and further take an $S_3' \in \mathcal{L}_{\mathrm{na}}^{S_2'}$. The set S_2' may

not include S_1, so let us define $S_2 := S_1 \cup S_2'$. Then $(\mathfrak{s}_\top''''', S_2), V \models_{\text{KC}} \phi^*$. Furthermore, $S_2' \in \mathcal{L}_{\text{na}}^{S_2}$ also holds because otherwise $S_1 \in \mathcal{L}_{\text{na}}^{S_2}$, but then $S_1' \in \mathcal{L}_{\text{na}}^{S_2}$ as $S_1' \in \mathcal{L}_{\text{na}}^{S_1}$, however, $S_1' \subseteq S_2'$ so $S_2' \in \mathcal{L}_{\text{na}}^{S_2}$. Consequently, $S_3' \in \mathcal{L}_{\text{na}}^{S_2}$, and therefore by the choice of S_1, there is an $S_4' \in \mathcal{L}_{\text{na}}^{S_2}$ such that $S_4' \subseteq S_3'$ and $(\mathfrak{s}_\top''', S_4'), V \models_{\text{KC}} \psi_2$. But as $S_2' \in \mathcal{L}_{\text{na}}^{S_2}$, we also have $S_4' \in \mathcal{L}_{\text{na}}^{S_2}$, which completes the proof.

- A4': We show that for any V and $\mathfrak{s}$, we have $\mathfrak{s}, V \models_{\text{FTC}} \left(((\chi_1 \mapsto \phi_1) \mapsto \psi) \wedge ((\chi_2 \mapsto \phi_2) \mapsto \psi) \right) \rightarrow \left(((\chi_1 \mapsto \phi_1) \vee (\chi_2 \mapsto \phi_2)) \mapsto \psi \right)$, which is equivalent with $\mathfrak{s}, V \models_{\text{KC}} \Box \left((((\chi_1 \mapsto \phi_1) \mapsto \psi) \wedge ((\chi_2 \mapsto \phi_2) \mapsto \psi))^* \rightarrow (((\chi_1 \mapsto \phi_1) \vee (\chi_2 \mapsto \phi_2)) \mapsto \psi)^* \right)$. Take an $\mathfrak{s}'$ with $\mathfrak{s} \geq \mathfrak{s}'$ and $\mathfrak{s}', V \models_{\text{KC}} \left(((\chi_1 \mapsto \phi_1) \mapsto \psi) \wedge ((\chi_2 \mapsto \phi_2) \mapsto \psi) \right)^*$, which is the same as $\mathfrak{s}', V \models_{\text{KC}} \Box \Diamond ((\chi_1 \mapsto \phi_1)^* \mapsto \psi^*) \wedge \Box \Diamond ((\chi_2 \mapsto \phi_2)^* \mapsto \psi^*)$, and so for all $\mathfrak{s}''$ with $\mathfrak{s}' \geq \mathfrak{s}''$, there is an $\mathfrak{s}'''$ with $\mathfrak{s}'' \geq \mathfrak{s}'''$ such that $\mathfrak{s}''', V \models_{\text{KC}} (\chi_1 \mapsto \phi_1)^* \mapsto \psi^*$ and $\mathfrak{s}''', V \models_{\text{KC}} (\chi_2 \mapsto \phi_2)^* \mapsto \psi^*$. We have to show that $\mathfrak{s}', V \models_{\text{KC}} \left(((\chi_1 \mapsto \phi_1) \vee (\chi_2 \mapsto \phi_2)) \mapsto \psi \right)^*$, which is the same as $\mathfrak{s}', V \models_{\text{KC}} \Box \Diamond ((\Box \Diamond ((\chi_1 \mapsto \phi_1)^* \vee (\chi_2 \mapsto \phi_2)^*)) \mapsto \psi^*)$. Take any $\mathfrak{s}''$ with $\mathfrak{s}' \geq \mathfrak{s}''$, and then take $\mathfrak{s}'''$ as above. We claim that $\mathfrak{s}''', V \models_{\text{KC}} (\Box \Diamond ((\chi_1 \mapsto \phi_1)^* \vee (\chi_2 \mapsto \phi_2)^*)) \mapsto \psi^*$. Note that for any $\mathfrak{s}''''$ with $\mathfrak{s}''' \geq \mathfrak{s}''''$, we still have $\mathfrak{s}'''', V \models_{\text{KC}} (\chi_1 \mapsto \phi_1)^* \mapsto \psi^*$ and $\mathfrak{s}'''', V \models_{\text{KC}} (\chi_2 \mapsto \phi_2)^* \mapsto \psi^*$. Let $S_0 \in \mathcal{L}^{\mathfrak{s}_\top''''}$ be such that $(\mathfrak{s}_\top'''', S_0), V \models_{\text{KC}} \Box \Diamond ((\chi_1 \mapsto \phi_1)^* \vee (\chi_2 \mapsto \phi_2)^*)$. Then since the satisfaction of $\mapsto$ only depends on the first component of the possible world, we also have $(\mathfrak{s}_\top'''', \mathfrak{s}_\top''''), V \models_{\text{KC}} \Box \Diamond ((\chi_1 \mapsto \phi_1)^* \vee (\chi_2 \mapsto \phi_2)^*)$. For the same reason, we also have $(\mathfrak{s}_\top'''', \mathfrak{s}_\top''''), V \models_{\text{KC}} (\chi_1 \mapsto \phi_1)^* \mapsto \psi^*$ and $(\mathfrak{s}_\top'''', \mathfrak{s}_\top''''), V \models_{\text{KC}} (\chi_2 \mapsto \phi_2)^* \mapsto \psi^*$. Take a set $S_3 \in \mathcal{L}_{\text{na}}^{\mathfrak{s}_\top''''}$. By the properties of $\geq$, there exists a further $S_3' \in \mathcal{L}_{\text{na}}^{\mathfrak{s}_\top''''}$ subset of S_3 such that $(\mathfrak{s}_\top'''', \mathfrak{s}_\top'''') \geq (\mathfrak{s}_\top'''', S_3')$. So there is $\mathfrak{s}'$ with $(\mathfrak{s}_\top'''', S_3') \geq \mathfrak{s}'$ such that $\mathfrak{s}', V \models_{\text{KC}} (\chi_i \mapsto \phi_i)^*$ for one of $i = 1$ or $i = 2$. Consequently, there is $S_4 \in \mathcal{L}_{\text{na}}^{\mathfrak{s}'_\top}$ and so $S_4 \in \mathcal{L}_{\text{na}}^{\mathfrak{s}_\top''''}$ such that $(\mathfrak{s}'_\top, S_4), V \models_{\text{KC}} \psi^*$. We show that also $(\mathfrak{s}_\top'''', S_4), V \models_{\text{KC}} \psi^*$ by showing the equivalent $(\mathfrak{s}_\top'''', S_4), V \models_{\text{KC}} \Box \Diamond \psi^*$. Take any $\mathfrak{s}''$ accessible from $(\mathfrak{s}_\top'''', S_4)$. Then there is an $\mathfrak{s}'''$ that is accessible both from $\mathfrak{s}''$ and $(\mathfrak{s}'_\top, S_4)$, and this latter implies $\mathfrak{s}''', V \models_{\text{KC}} \psi^*$.

- Burgess's A2 is a special case of RW, and both LLE and RW are very easy immediate consequences of our definitions, so we omit them for the lack of space.

A3 is called caucious monotonicity. Axioms A0-A3 are from the axiomatization of propositional conditional logic in Burgess [5], LLE and RW are additional axioms from [10]. A4' is a modified modified from Burgess's A4, which says

- A4: $\left((\phi_1 \mapsto \psi) \wedge (\phi_2 \mapsto \psi) \right) \rightarrow \left((\phi_1 \vee \phi_2) \mapsto \psi \right)$.

This is not sound in this generality in our semantics, but, as we will see in the next section, it is sound for some subclasses of our semantics. At this moment we do not know how to give a general characterization of those cases when it is sound. Our next remark shows why it is not sound.

Remark 1. Here we explain why formula A4 is not valid for our semantics. That is because it is possible that both ϕ_1 and ϕ_2 are satisfied on an S only on atypical subsets, but $\phi_1 \vee \phi_2$ may still be satisfied on all of S. Consider for example the following: let $W := [0,1]$ with $\mathcal{L}$ be the Lebesgue measurable sets, and $\mathcal{L}_i = \{\emptyset\}$. Let $\mathcal{L}_a^W$ be the Lebesgue zero-measure sets. Let $(\mathfrak{s}_\top^1, \mathfrak{s}_\perp^1) \geq (\mathfrak{s}_\top^2, \mathfrak{s}_\perp^2)$ if only if $\mathfrak{s}_\top^1 = \mathfrak{s}_\top^2$ and $\mathfrak{s}_\perp^2 \subseteq \mathfrak{s}_\perp^1$. Let ϕ_1 denote a property that holds on S_{ϕ_1}, which is the union of $[0, 0.25]$, and a subset of $[0.5, 1]$ that has only measure zero measurable subsets. Let ϕ_2 denote an atomic formula that holds on S_{ϕ_2}, which is the union of $[0.25, 0.5]$, and a subset of $[0.5, 1]$ that has only measure zero measurable subsets. Suppose further that $S_{\phi_1} \cup S_{\phi_2} = [0,1]$. Such sets are possible to construct in measure theory. That is, the non-measurable parts of S_{ϕ_1} and S_{ϕ_2} in $[0.5, 1]$ complement each other to all of $[0.5, 1]$. Let ψ be a property for which $(0, 0.5) \models_{\text{FTC}} \psi$ and $[0.5, 1] \models_{\text{FTC}} \neg\psi$. In this case, $W \models_{\text{FTC}} \phi_1 \mapsto \psi$ and $W \models_{\text{FTC}} \phi_2 \mapsto \psi$, because on the "largest" sets on which ϕ_1 and ϕ_2 are satisfied, both part of $[0, 0.5]$, ψ is also satisfied except atypically. However, $\phi_1 \vee \phi_2$ is satisfied on the entire $[0, 1]$ set, while ψ only on $(0, 0.5)$. So $W \not\models_{\text{FTC}} \phi_1 \vee \phi_2 \mapsto \psi$. □

Remark 2. Note that although $\mapsto$ is not monotonic in general, in some cases we do have monotonicity. Namely, if $\phi \mapsto \psi$ is satisfied, and $\phi \wedge \phi'$ is satisfied on non-atypical sets and the accessibility relation does access sets in the first argument on which $\phi \wedge \phi'$ is satisfied, then $\phi \wedge \phi' \mapsto \psi$ is also satisfied. Further, if $\phi_1 \vee \phi_2 \mapsto \psi$ is satisfied and ϕ_1 is satisfied on non-atypical sets and the accessibility relation reaches sets in the first argument on which ϕ_1 is satisfied, then $\phi_1 \mapsto \psi$ is also satisfied. Similarly for ϕ_2. □

Next we come back to the example mentioned in the introduction and show that $\texttt{Bird}(\text{Tweety}) \rightarrow (\texttt{Animal}(\text{Tweety}) \mapsto \texttt{Fly}(\text{Tweety}))$ can be satisfied in our example even when $\texttt{Animal}(\text{Tweety}) \mapsto \texttt{Fly}(\text{Tweety})$ is not satisfied.

Example 5. When defining the accessibility relation $\geq$, we have to be careful to define it so that the semantics gives what we expect from it, especially how it behaves on $\mathfrak{s}_\top$. Let us revisit the example from the introduction

$$\texttt{Bird}(\text{Tweety}) \rightarrow (\texttt{Animal}(\text{Tweety}) \mapsto \texttt{Fly}(\text{Tweety}))$$

Depending on how we define $\geq$, we make this satisfied or not. For this case let $\mathcal{D}$ be a set of individuals. Let W be such that each possible world specifies what kind of organisms the individuals in $\mathcal{D}$ are: penguin, human etc. Hence for each possible world $w \in W$, and V valuation, $w \models \texttt{Bird}(\text{Tweety})$ is defined the obvious way: it holds when Tweety is a bird. Similarly for $w \models \texttt{Animal}(\text{Tweety})$ and $w \models \texttt{Fly}(\text{Tweety})$. Let $\mathcal{L} = 2^W$ and $\mathcal{L}_i = \{\emptyset\}$.

Suppose that $[\texttt{Bird}(\text{Tweety})]$, $[\texttt{Animal}(\text{Tweety})]$, $[\texttt{Fly}(\text{Tweety})]$ are not atypical in W and that $[\texttt{Bird}(\text{Tweety})] \cap [\texttt{Fly}(\text{Tweety})]^\perp$ is atypical in $[\texttt{Bird}(\text{Tweety})]$. Suppose further that from (W, W), any $(\mathfrak{s}_\top, \mathfrak{s}_\perp)$ is accessible when $\mathfrak{s}_\top$ is non-atypical in W and $\mathfrak{s}_\top$ does not have atypical intersections with the sets $[\texttt{Bird}(\text{Tweety})]$ and $[\texttt{Animal}(\text{Tweety})]$ (we we saw in Example 4), and further we have $\mathfrak{s}_\perp \in \mathcal{L}_s$. We postulate that $(\mathfrak{s}_\top, \mathfrak{s}_\perp) \models_{\text{FTC}}$

$P(\text{Tweety})$ if $w \models P(\text{Tweety})$ for all $w \in \mathfrak{s}_\perp$. For this note that $(\mathfrak{s}_\top, \mathfrak{s}_\perp) \models_{\text{KC}} \square \lozenge P(\text{Tweety})$ iff $[P(\text{Tweety})]^\perp \cap \mathfrak{s}_\perp \in \mathcal{L}_i$. In this case it is not hard to check that $W \models_{\text{FTC}} \text{Bird}(\text{Tweety}) \to (\text{Animal}(\text{Tweety}) \mapsto \text{Fly}(\text{Tweety}))$ holds. That is because for any $(W, W) \geq (\mathfrak{s}_\top, \mathfrak{s}_\perp)$, if $(\mathfrak{s}_\top, \mathfrak{s}_\perp) \models_{\text{FTC}} \text{Bird}(\text{Tweety})$ (that is, we have $[\text{Bird}(\text{Tweety})]^\perp \cap \mathfrak{s}_\perp \in \mathcal{L}_i$), there is a $(\mathfrak{s}_\top, \mathfrak{s}_\perp) \geq (\mathfrak{s}'_\top, \mathfrak{s}'_\perp)$ such that $(\mathfrak{s}'_\top, \mathfrak{s}'_\perp) \models_{\text{FTC}} \text{Animal}(\text{Tweety}) \mapsto \text{Fly}(\text{Tweety})$, when $\mathfrak{s}'_\top \subseteq [\text{Bird}(\text{Tweety})]$. In this case, for large enough S_2 with $\mathfrak{s}'_\perp \subseteq S_2 \subseteq \mathfrak{s}'_\top$, $S_2 \cap [\text{Fly}(\text{Tweety})]^\perp$ is atypical in $\mathfrak{s}'_\top$, and hence $(\mathfrak{s}'_\top, \mathfrak{s}'_\perp) \models_{\text{FTC}} \text{Animal}(\text{Tweety}) \mapsto \text{Fly}(\text{Tweety})$. Note that it was necessary to assume that $\mathfrak{s}'_\top$ cannot cut too small sets from $[\text{Bird}(\text{Tweety})]$, because that might be the set of penguins, where $\text{Animal}(\text{Tweety}) \mapsto \text{Fly}(\text{Tweety})$ does not hold.

5.3 Interesting Special Cases When A4 is Satisfied

As we have already mentioned, $\models_{\text{FHK}}$ is a special case of $\models_{\text{FTC}}$: Assume that W and $\mathcal{L}$ are given so that $\{w\} \in \mathcal{L}$ for any $w \in W$, and set $\mathcal{L}_i = \{\emptyset\}$. Friedman et al. start by assuming that for each $w \in W$ and V valuation in some fixed domain $\mathcal{D}$, for any $\phi \in \text{FOF}_{(f,p)}$ the satisfaction of a $w, V \models \phi$ is given, and $[\phi]_V \in \mathcal{L}$. Let us define our accessibility relation $\geq$ as $(\mathfrak{s}^1_\top, \mathfrak{s}^1_\perp) \geq (\mathfrak{s}^2_\top, \mathfrak{s}^2_\perp)$ if and only if $\mathfrak{s}^1_\top = \mathfrak{s}^2_\top$ and $\mathfrak{s}^1_\perp \supseteq \mathfrak{s}^2_\perp$, then for any $\phi \in \text{FOCF}_{(f,p)}$, valuation V, and $w \in W$. Then $(W, W) \geq (W, \{w\})$ holds for any $w \in W$. As a result, $(W, W) \models_{\text{KC}} \square \lozenge \phi$ is equivalent with $(W, \{w\}) \models_{\text{KC}} \phi$ for all $w \in W$. It is also easy to see that

$$(W, \{w\}), V \models_{\text{FTC}} \phi \mapsto \psi \iff [\phi]_V = \emptyset \lor [\phi]_V \cap [\psi]^\perp \in \mathcal{L}_a^{[\phi]_V}$$

Consequently, we have

$$(W, \{w\}), V \models_{\text{FTC}} \phi \iff w, V \models_{\text{FHK}} \phi.$$

This class of semantics satisfies the axiom A4 of Burgess as well as Friedman et al. show.

Another special case is when we have W, some $\mathcal{L}$ and $\mathcal{L}_i$ and atyp, and our accessibility relation $\geq$ is defined such that $(\mathfrak{s}^1_\top, \mathfrak{s}^1_\perp) \geq (\mathfrak{s}^2_\top, \mathfrak{s}^2_\perp)$ only if $\mathfrak{s}^2_\perp \in \mathcal{L}_{\text{na}}^{\mathfrak{s}^1_\perp}$. That is, only non-atypical sets are accessible in the second argument. Remember, A4 could fail because it is possible that $(\mathfrak{s}^1_\top, \mathfrak{s}^1_\perp), V \models_{\text{FTC}} \phi_1 \lor \phi_2$ while ϕ_1 and ϕ_2 are only satisfied on $(\mathfrak{s}^2_\top, \mathfrak{s}^2_\perp)$ where $\mathfrak{s}^2_\perp$ is atypical in $\mathfrak{s}^1_\perp$ and hence where ψ might fail as we discussed in Remark 1. However, when only non-atypical sets are accessible, then this is not possible and A4 is valid for this class of semantics. In fact in this case, since accessibility does not go beyond atypicality, it is possible to show that $(\mathfrak{s}_\top, \mathfrak{s}_\perp), V \models_{\text{FTC}} \phi$ hods if and only if for all $S \in \mathcal{L}_{\text{na}}^{\mathfrak{s}_\perp}$ there is an $S' \in \mathcal{L}_{\text{na}}^{\mathfrak{s}_\perp}$ with $S' \subseteq S$ and $(\mathfrak{s}_\top, S'), V \models_{\text{FTC}} \phi$. Consequently, in this case $(\mathfrak{s}_\top, \mathfrak{s}_\perp), V \models_{\text{FTC}} \phi \mapsto \psi$ if and only if for all $S_0 \in \mathcal{L}^{\mathfrak{s}_\top}$ such that $(\mathfrak{s}_\top, S_0), V \models \phi$, there is an $S_1 \in \mathcal{L}^{\mathfrak{s}_\top}$ such that $S_0 \subseteq S_1$ and $(\mathfrak{s}_\top, S_1), V \models \phi$, and forall $S_2 \in \mathcal{L}^{\mathfrak{s}_\top}$ such that $S_1 \subseteq S_2$ and $(\mathfrak{s}_\top, S_2), V \models \phi$, we have $(\mathfrak{s}_\top, S_2), V \models \psi$. And this is the exact analogy of Burgess' definition formula (3).

Finally, limiting further the situation in the previous paragraph, assume that $(\mathfrak{s}^1_\top, \mathfrak{s}^1_\perp) \geq (\mathfrak{s}^2_\top, \mathfrak{s}^2_\perp)$ if $\mathfrak{s}^2_\top \in \mathcal{L}_{\text{na}}^{\mathfrak{s}^1_\top}$ and only if $\mathfrak{s}^2_\perp \in \mathcal{L}_{\text{na}}^{\mathfrak{s}^1_\perp}$. In other words, in the second argument only non-atypical sets are accessible (although deeper accessibility is possible), and in the first argument all non-atypical sets are accessible (although shallower accessibility is allowed there). So in this case accessibility in the first and second argument are the same, they meet. In this case $\mapsto$ and $\rightarrow$ have exactly the same semantics. In particular, in this case $\mapsto$ is monotonic, and satisfies first-order inference. This corresponds the situation when atypical possibilities are not considered: for example, in measure theory, almost everything is formulated almost everywhere, with the exception of 0-measure sets. Or, in the so-called provable security direction of computer security, most of the time only properties that are satisfied with non-negligible probability are interesting. This is the case corresponding to the work in [3,4] applying it to computer security, though not including explicitly $\mapsto$ as $\rightarrow$ was producing exactly the conditional implication in this case. This transition is impossible to carry out with the semantics of Friedman et al., and hence we disapprove Halpern's introduction of it in computer security [9], as the loss of monotonicity has no clear benefit for computer security.

Because of the above possibility to transform the semantics of $\mapsto$ into $\rightarrow$ as an extremal case, it is possible to introduce properties that make $\mapsto$ closer to $\rightarrow$ but still different: For example, one can require $\neg(\phi \mapsto \psi) \rightarrow (\phi \mapsto \neg\psi)$ by making sure that $\geq$ can access sets in the first argument on which $\neg\psi$ is satisfied.

5.4 Further Examples

As we discussed in the previous section, the FHK semantics is a special case of our semantics, so the lottery paradox and the crooked lottery paradox are satisfiable in our semantics as well. To provide some intuition, we discuss these examples nevertheless.

Example 6. The lottery paradox has the following form:

$$\forall x(\mathsf{T} \mapsto \neg\mathtt{Winner}(x)) \wedge (\mathsf{T} \mapsto \exists x\mathtt{Winner}(x))$$

That is, everyone typically loses, and typically someone wins. Classical implication cannot satisfy this property. With our semantics, set W to be the union of atypical sets, and on each atypical set someone wins; then the second conjunct is satisfied. For the satisfaction of the first conjunct, make sure that everyone wins on at most an atypical set. This can be done even with A4 satisfied. □

Example 7. The crooked lottery is the lottery paradox together with the following:

$$\neg\exists x\big(\mathtt{Winner}(x) \mapsto \bot\big) \wedge \exists y\forall x\Big(x \neq y \rightarrow \big((\mathtt{Winner}(x) \vee \mathtt{Winner}(y)) \mapsto \mathtt{Winner}(y)\big)\Big)$$

The meaning of the first conjunct is that there is no player who cannot win at all. The second conjunct means that there is a y such that y typically wins against any other x, that is there is a y whose winning is more likely than all the other's.

Besides the conditions of the previous example, the first conjunct can be satisfied by making sure that all domain elements win on some atypical set. The second conjunct can simply be satisfied by making sure that there are two levels of atypical sets.   □

Example 8. As we allow nested conditional implication, let us see an example how $(\phi_1 \mapsto \phi_2) \mapsto \phi_3$ can make sense, consider the following example: Let ϕ_1 be the formula saying that "x has a headache in the morning". Let ϕ_2 say that "x takes painkiller in the morning", and let ϕ_3 mean that "x feels well at noon". $\phi_1 \mapsto \phi_2$ says that "if x has a headache in the morning, then typically x takes painkiller in the morning". On the other hand, $(\phi_1 \mapsto \phi_2) \mapsto \phi_3$ says that "as long as x typically takes painkiller in the morning when x has headache, x typically feels well at noon". That is, $\phi_1 \mapsto \phi_2$ may be satisfied on a part of W, and on that part, ϕ_3 has to typically hold. On the part where $\phi_1 \mapsto \phi_2$ fails to hold, that is, x does not take painkiller right away, x may still have headache at noon. In the FHK treatment these distinctions cannot be made, as $\phi_1 \mapsto \phi_2$ either fails or holds for the entire W.   □

6   Conclusions

We showed a new semantics for first-order conditional logic that is a generalization of the semantics of Friedman et al. We used Fitting's embedding of classical first-order logic in first-order S4. We showed that except for one, the axioms of Burgess and of Kraus et al. are sound for our semantics. We explained with an example why that one axiom might in general fail, and we also showed a number of special cases of our semantics when that remaining axiom is also sound. We illustrated the flexibility of our definition: Friedman's et al. definition is an extremal special case, while another extremal case is when conditional implication agrees with material implication. It can also be made to correspond to Burgess' definition. We also showed several examples. In particular, we considered how "typically-implies" interpretation of conditional implication works in ways that are not applicable in former work, and presented how our semantics is suitable to accommodate them. We showed how nested implications are better represented in this new semantics. We have not yet investigated completeness, which is the next item on our agenda concerning this topic. Another possible future work is to investigate the relationship between formal semantics for "typically" and "typical" of natural language, including a possible reduction of a certain range of the meaning of the adjective "typical" to that of our adverb "typically".

References

1. Adams, E.W.: The Logic of Conditionals. Springer, Dordrecht (1975). https://doi.org/10.1007/978-94-015-7622-2
2. Bana, G., Comon-Lundh, H.: Towards unconditional soundness: computationally complete symbolic attacker. In: Degano, P., Guttman, J.D. (eds.) POST 2012. LNCS, vol. 7215, pp. 189–208. Springer, Heidelberg (2012). https://doi.org/10.1007/978-3-642-28641-4_11
3. Bana, G., Hasebe, K., Okada, M.: Computationally complete symbolic attacker and key exchange. In: Proceedings of the 20th ACM SIGSAC Conference on Computer and Communications Security (CCS 2013), pp. 1231–1246. ACM (2013)
4. Bana, G., Okada, M.: Semantics for "Enough-Certainty" and fitting's embedding of classical logic in S4. In: 25th EACSL Annual Conference on Computer Science Logic (CSL 2016). LIPIcs, vol. 62, pp. 34:1–34:18. Schloss Dagstuhl (2016)
5. Burgess, J.P.: Quick completeness proofs for some logics of conditionals. Notre Dame J. Formal Logic **22**(1), 76–84 (1981)
6. Fitting, M.: An embedding of classical logic in S4. J. Symb. Logic **35**(4), 529–534 (1970)
7. Friedman, N., Halpern, J.Y., Koller, D.: First-order conditional logic for default reasoning revisited. ACM Trans. Comput. Log. **1**(2), 175–207 (2000)
8. Goldszmidt, M., Morris, P., Pearl, J.: A maximum entropy approach to nonmonotonic reasoning. IEEE Trans. Pattern Anal. Mach. Intell. **15**(3), 220–232 (1993)
9. Halpern, J.Y.: From qualitative to quantitative proofs of security properties using first-order conditional logic. J. Comput. Secur. **25**(1), 1–19 (2017)
10. Kraus, S., Lehmann, D., Magidor, M.: Nonmonotonic reasoning, preferential models and cumulative logics. Artif. Intell. **44**(1–2), 167–207 (1990)
11. Kyburg Jr., H.E.: Probability and the Logic of Rational Belief. Wesleyan University Press, Middletown (1961)
12. Lewis, D.: Counterfactuals. Basil Blackwell Ltd. (1973). Revised addition by Blackwell Publishers (2001)

On Dialogue Modeling: A Dynamic Epistemic Inquisitive Approach

Maria Boritchev and Philippe de Groote$^{(\boxtimes)}$

LORIA, UMR 7503, Université de Lorraine, CNRS, Inria, 54000 Nancy, France
degroote@loria.fr

Abstract. This paper introduces a formal model of dialogue based on insights and ideas developed by Jonathan Ginzburg in [11]. This model, which is logic based, takes advantage of inquisitive semantics [4], which allows to model both declarative and interrogative sentences in a uniform way. It appeals to ideas derived from classical epistemic logic in order to model the knowledge states of the dialogue participants, and includes a context-updating mechanisms based on the type-theoretic dynamic logic developed in [15].

1 Introduction

Dialogues are build in a dynamic way. An utterance follows another and may contain references to concepts and language constructions introduced by previous utterances, but also by the context of the conversation. This dialogue context is constantly updated as the dialogue unrolls, both for each dialogue participant, privately, and in a public way, building the *common ground* [18], composed of information that is available to everyone equally (participants and possible audience). Consider the following piece of dialogue (part of the example we present Sect. 6):

(1) [CONTEXT: Albert and Bernard would like to know when is Cheryl's birthday. She gives them some clues that might help them guess the date.]

    a.   Cheryl (to Albert): *Can you figure it out now?*
    b.   Albert (to Cheryl): *I don't know when your birthday is, but I know Bernard doesn't know, either.*

This simple excerpt illustrates several features that are characteristic of dialogue. It stresses the importance of the context, and in particular, of keeping track of the issues that are being raised, of what questions are under discussion. This allows, for instance, the pronominal anaphoric "it" in (1-a) to be resolved. It also demonstrates that a dialogue is not only made of declarative sentences, but also of interrogative ones (direct, as in (1-a), or embedded under a propositional attitude verb, as in (1-b)). Consequently, the development of a logic-based formal model of dialogue requires a logic that can express the semantic content

© Springer Nature Switzerland AG 2021
N. Okazaki et al. (Eds.): JSAI-isAI 2020 Workshops, LNAI 12758, pp. 21–36, 2021.
https://doi.org/10.1007/978-3-030-79942-7_2

of both declaratives and interrogatives. Inquisitive logic [4] is such a logic, see Sect. 3 for a presentation.

Example (1) also demonstrates the need for a dialogue model to integrate epistemic modalities. In (1-b), Albert mentions his (private) knowledge about Bernard's (private) knowledge. Therefore, we need to model the knowledge states of the dialogue participants; see Sect. 4. The whole dialogue is then modeled using a *dialogue gameboard*, see Sect. 2 for a presentation of the gameboard and Sect. 5 for the formal model. We showcase the way our model works on an example in English, *Cheryl's birthday problem*, a logical puzzle that went viral on the internet of few years ago,[1] see Sect. 6. We then discuss and compare our work to related approaches such as [8] and [5] in Sect. 7.

2 Negotiation Phases and Dialogue Gameboard

Dialogue semantics is radically context-dependent. Following [11], we model the dialogues and dialogue context in particular using *dialogue gameboards* (DGB). We use one DGB per participant in order to model their private contexts, plus one DGB for the public context. A dialogue gameboard is composed of different fields:

$$
\begin{bmatrix}
speaker: & Individual \\
addressee: & Individual \\
FACTS: & set\ of\ propositions \\
QUD: & partially\ ordered\ set\ of\ questions
\end{bmatrix}
$$

Several are used to store information about the indexicals, typically, the speaker and the addressee. *FACTS* is used to store the propositions that have been agreed on by the dialogue participants in the case of *public dialogue gameboards* (the ones that model a shared view of the dialogue), and propositions that are personal to the participant in the case of *private dialogue gameboards*. *QUD*, which stays for *questions under discussion*, stores the issues that have to be solved by the dialogue participants. These issues are raised by questions asked by the dialogue participants, but also by other types of utterances, as any proposition has to be discussed before being accepted by all the participants. The *QUD* is a partially ordered set where the order is used to decide which issue has to be solved first if several issues are raised at the same time.

A simple dialogue gameboard representation of (1-b) would be then look as follows:

$$
\begin{bmatrix}
speaker: & Albert \\
addressee: & Cheryl \\
FACTS: & \{Albert\ doesn't\ know\ when\ Cheryl's\ birhday\ is, \\
& Albert\ knows\ Bernard\ doesn't\ know\ either\} \\
QUD: & \{When\ is\ Cheryl's\ birthday?\}
\end{bmatrix}
$$

---

[1] https://www.nytimes.com/2015/04/15/science/a-math-problem-from-singapore-goes-viral-when-is-cheryls-birthday.html.

Consider Fig. 1, which represents a dynamic view of a dialogue divided in *negotiation phases*. A negotiation phase corresponds to the discussion by the participants of one issue; it begins with the introduction of this issue and ends when an agreement has been reached (while this agreement can be to drop the issue, to disagree). The result of the negotiation phase is then stored in the dialogue context and can be referenced in the utterances build inside future negotiation phases. In terms of dialogue gameboards, a negotiation phase begins when a new question is added to the *QUD* and ends when it has been solved. In this paper, we focus on modeling the dialogue interactions at the level of a negotiation phase; we do not discuss the way negotiation phases articulate with one another.

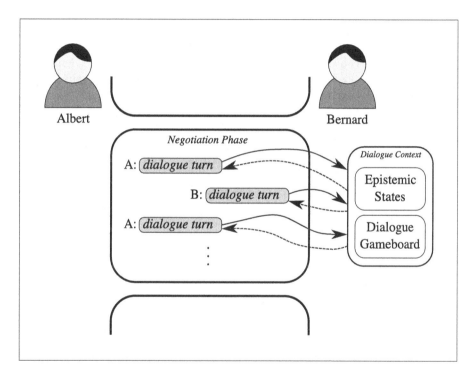

Fig. 1. Subdivision of dialogue in negotiation phases, adapted from [2].

We use inquisitive semantics to model both interrogative and declarative sentences (see the `grey rectangles` around the utterances). `Dotted lines` represent dynamic phenomena between dialogue context and utterances, as dynamicity allows to reference previously stored information. `Full lines` represent the dialogue context's updates, both in terms of epistemic states and dialogue gameboard, as each new utterance brings new information about the participant's epistemic states, but also about the *FACTS* and the *QUD*.

3   Inquisitive Semantics

As pointed out in the introduction, developing a logic-based formal model of dialogue requires a logic that can express the semantic content of both declarative and interrogative sentences. This need motivates the use of inquisitive logic, which is a logic that allows for a uniform treatment of both kinds of sentences.

As opposed to traditional modal logic, where a proposition is interpreted as a set of possible worlds, inquisitive semantics interprets a proposition as a set of sets of possible worlds. Intuitively, an inquisitive proposition may therefore be seen as a set of classical (modal) propositions. This allows questions to be assigned semantics akin to Hamblin's alternative semantics [14]. Inquisitive semantics, however, differs from Hamblin's alternative semantics in several respects.

Technically, in inquisitive logic, a *proposition* is defined to be a non-empty set of sets of possible worlds that is downward-closed with respect to set inclusion. As a consequence, conjunction, disjunction, and entailment can be defined in a standard way, i.e., as intersection, union, and inclusion, respectively. Let us illustrate this by an example.

Suppose it is known that Cheryl's birthday is either May 15, June 17, or July 14. Accordingly, we define a set of possible worlds, $W = \{w_{5.15}, w_{6.17}, w_{7.14}\}$, where each possible world corresponds respectively to one of Cheryl's possible birthdates. Then, the proposition φ_1 that *Cheryl is born on May 15* is interpreted as follows:

$$\llbracket \varphi_1 \rrbracket = \{\{w_{5.15}\}, \varnothing\} \tag{2}$$

The proposition φ_2 that *she is born on June 17* is interpreted in a similar way:

$$\llbracket \varphi_2 \rrbracket = \{\{w_{6.17}\}, \varnothing\} \tag{3}$$

Then, the inquisitive disjunction of φ_1 and φ_2 is interpreted as the union of their interpretations:

$$\llbracket \varphi_1 \vee_i \varphi_2 \rrbracket = \{\{w_{5.15}\}, \{w_{6.17}\}, \varnothing\} \tag{4}$$

This disjunction does not correspond to a proposition asserting that Cheryl's birthday is either May 15 or June 17, it rather corresponds to the question *whether Cheryl's birthday is May 15 or June 17*, assuming that she is born at one of these two dates. The mere assertion that *her birthday is either May 15 or June 17* is interpreted in a different way:

$$\{\{w_{5.15}, w_{6.17}\}, \{w_{5.15}\}, \{w_{6.17}\}, \varnothing\} \tag{5}$$

Intensional logic can be defined by embedding it in Gallin's Ty2 [10]. We provide here below a similar embedding for first-order inquisitive logic:[2]

$$\mathbf{R}_i\, t_1 \ldots t_n \; := \; \mathscr{P}(\mathbf{R}\, t_1 \ldots t_n)$$
$$\text{where } \mathscr{P}a = \lambda b^{\mathbf{s}\to\mathbf{t}}.\,\forall w^{\mathbf{s}}.\,(b\,w) \to (a\,w)$$
$$\varphi \wedge_i \psi \quad := \; \lambda a^{\mathbf{s}\to\mathbf{t}}.\,(\varphi\,a)\wedge(\psi\,a)$$
$$\varphi \vee_i \psi \quad := \; \lambda a^{\mathbf{s}\to\mathbf{t}}.\,(\varphi\,a)\vee(\psi\,a)$$
$$\varphi \to_i \psi \quad := \; \lambda a^{\mathbf{s}\to\mathbf{t}}.\,\forall b^{\mathbf{s}\to\mathbf{t}}.\,((\forall w^{\mathbf{s}}.\,(b\,w)\to(a\,w)) \to ((\varphi\,b)\to(\psi\,b)))$$
$$\neg_i\varphi \quad := \; \lambda a^{\mathbf{s}\to\mathbf{t}}.\,\forall w^{\mathbf{s}}.\,(a\,w) \to \neg(\exists b^{\mathbf{s}\to\mathbf{t}}.\,(\varphi\,b)\wedge(b\,w))$$
$$\forall_i x^{\mathbf{e}}.\,\varphi\,x \quad := \; \lambda a^{\mathbf{s}\to\mathbf{t}}.\,\forall x^{\mathbf{e}}.\,\varphi\,x\,a$$
$$\exists_i x^{\mathbf{e}}.\,\varphi\,x \quad := \; \lambda a^{\mathbf{s}\to\mathbf{t}}.\,\exists x^{\mathbf{e}}.\,\varphi\,x\,a$$

Inquisitive logic also features two *projection operators*, ! and ?. The first one transforms any proposition into a purely informative one by cancelling its inquisitive content. Conversely, the second one transforms any proposition into a purely inquisitive one by cancelling its informative content. These projection operators may be defined as follows:

$$!\varphi \; := \; \neg_i\neg_i\varphi$$
$$?\varphi \; := \; \varphi \vee_i \neg_i\varphi$$

These two operators are useful to turn a question into an assertion, and vice versa. For instance, by applying ! to (4), one obtains the proposition asserting that *Cheryl's birthday is either May 15 or June 17*:

$$[\![!(\varphi_1 \vee_i \varphi_2)]\!] = \{\{w_{5.15}, w_{6.17}\}, \{w_{5.15}\}, \{w_{6.17}\}, \varnothing\} \tag{6}$$

On the other hand, by applying ? to (2), one obtains an inquisitive proposition that corresponds to the issue *whether Cheryl is born on May 15 or not*:

$$[\![?\varphi_1]\!] = \{\{w_{6.17}, w_{7.14}\}, \{w_{5.15}\}, \{w_{6.17}\}, \{w_{7.14}\}, \varnothing\} \tag{7}$$

Inquisitive propositions being downward-closed sets, they are completely characterized by their maximal elements. In the sequel of this paper, we will use the notation $[a, b, c, \ldots]$ to denote the downward-closure of the set $\{a, b, c, \ldots\}$. With this convention, Example (7) may rewritten as follows:

$$[\![?\varphi_1]\!] = [\{w_{6.17}, w_{7.14}\}, \{w_{5.15}\}] \tag{8}$$

Example (4) illustrates that an inquisitive proposition has both an informative and an inquisitive content. It is even the fact that every inquisitive proposition may be defined as the conjunction of a purely informative proposition with a purely inquisitive one. It is indeed not difficult to establish that every proposition φ is such that:

$$\varphi = !\varphi \wedge ?\varphi$$

---

[2] Where $\mathbf{s}$ is the type of possible worlds, $\mathbf{t}$ is the type of truth values, $\mathbf{e}$ is the type of individuals, following [16].

This fact has an interesting consequence with respect to dialogue-gameboard modeling: it allows the *QUD* and the *FACTS* to be expressed by a unique proposition, say φ, such that:

$$\text{QUD} = ?\varphi \quad \text{and} \quad \text{FACTS} = !\varphi$$

We end this quick review of inquisitive semantics by showing how it can be used to provide a Montague-like compositional semantics to questions. To this end, we consider the question *when Cheryl's birthday is* (as it occurs in the sentence *Albert does not know when Cheryl birthday is*). The abstract syntax of the sentence is specified by means of the term:

$$\text{WHEN} \, (\lambda x^{NP}. \, \text{IS} \, x \, (\text{POSSESSIVE CHERYL BIRTHDAY})) \tag{9}$$

which is built upon the following signature:

$$\text{CHERYL} : NP$$
$$\text{BIRTHDAY} : N$$
$$\text{POSSESSIVE} : NP \to N \to NP$$
$$\text{IS} : NP \to NP \to S$$
$$\text{WHEN} : (NP \to S) \to S$$

We define $\mathbf{p}$ to be the type of inquisitive propositions, i.e., $\mathbf{p} = (\mathbf{s} \to \mathbf{t}) \to \mathbf{t}$. Then, the semantic interpretation of the syntactic categories is as follows:

$$[\![NP]\!] := (\mathbf{e} \to \mathbf{p}) \to \mathbf{p}$$
$$[\![N]\!] := \mathbf{e} \to \mathbf{p}$$
$$[\![S]\!] := \mathbf{p}$$

In order to express the semantic interpretation of (9), we use the following non-logical constants:

$$\mathbf{cheryl} : \mathbf{e}$$
$$\mathbf{birthday} : \mathbf{e} \to \mathbf{s} \to \mathbf{t}$$
$$\mathbf{of} : \mathbf{e} \to \mathbf{e} \to \mathbf{s} \to \mathbf{t}$$

Following the inquisitive interpretation of an atomic proposition, we raise the types of the relation symbols:

$$\mathbf{birthday}_i := \lambda x^{\mathbf{e}}. \, \mathscr{P}(\mathbf{birthday} \, x)$$
$$\mathbf{of}_i := \lambda x^{\mathbf{e}} y^{\mathbf{e}}. \, \mathscr{P}(\mathbf{of} \, x \, y)$$

We also raise the equality relation between entities:

$$(x =_i y) \; := \; \mathscr{P}(\lambda w^{\mathbf{s}}. \, x = y)$$

Finally, we provide the lexical entries with the following interpretations:

$$[\![\text{CHERYL}]\!] := \lambda p^{\mathbf{e} \to \mathbf{P}}. \, p \, \mathbf{cheryl}$$
$$[\![\text{BIRTHDAY}]\!] := \mathbf{birthday}_i$$
$$[\![\text{POSSESSIVE}]\!] := \lambda p^{(\mathbf{e} \to \mathbf{P}) \to \mathbf{P}} q^{\mathbf{e} \to \mathbf{P}} r^{\mathbf{e} \to \mathbf{P}}. \, p \, (\lambda x^{\mathbf{e}}. \, !(\exists_i y^{\mathbf{e}}. \, (q \, y) \wedge_i (\mathbf{of}_i \, x \, y) \wedge_i (r \, y)))$$
$$[\![\text{IS}]\!] := \lambda p^{(\mathbf{e} \to \mathbf{P}) \to \mathbf{P}} q^{(\mathbf{e} \to \mathbf{P}) \to \mathbf{P}}. \, q \, (\lambda x^{\mathbf{e}}. \, p \, (\lambda y^{\mathbf{e}}. \, x =_i y))$$
$$[\![\text{WHEN}]\!] := \lambda p^{((\mathbf{e} \to \mathbf{P}) \to \mathbf{P}) \to \mathbf{P}}. \, \exists_i x^{\mathbf{e}}. \, p \, (\lambda q^{\mathbf{e} \to \mathbf{P}}. \, q \, x)$$

Then, applying the above semantic recipes to term (9) yields the following results:

$$\exists_i x^{\mathbf{e}}.\,!(\exists_i y^{\mathbf{e}}.\,(\mathbf{birthday}_i\, y) \wedge_i (\mathbf{of}_i\, \mathbf{cheryl}\, y) \wedge_i (y =_i x))$$

4 Dialogue Participant's Epistemic State

As explained in the introduction, the short exchange between Cheryl and Albert in (1) exemplifies the epistemic nature of a (cooperative) dialogue, and demonstrates the need to represent the knowledge states of the dialogue participants. Consequently, we must add to the dialogue context some information that models the private knowledge of each agent (i.e., each dialogue participant).[3]

Following Ciardelli's and Roelofsen's [5], we associate to each agent $\mathbf{a}$ and each possible world w an inquisitive proposition $\Sigma_{\mathbf{a},w}$ that models the epistemic and inquisitive state of agent $\mathbf{a}$ at world w. In type-theoretic terms, this may be modeled by a function Σ of type $\mathbf{e} \to \mathbf{s} \to \mathbf{p}$. The epistemic modality associated to agent $\mathbf{a}$ is then defined as follows:

$$\mathsf{K}\,\mathbf{a}\,\varphi \;:=\; \lambda q^{\mathbf{s}\to\mathbf{t}}.\,\forall w^{\mathbf{s}}.\,(q\,w) \to (\varphi\,(\bigcup(\Sigma\,\mathbf{a}\,w))) \tag{10}$$

where $\bigcup S = \lambda x.\,\exists a.\,(S\,a) \wedge (a\,x)$.

Let us now continue the example started in the previous section by showing how to interpret the sentence *Albert does not know when Cheryl birthday is*. Its abstract syntax is given by the term:

$$\text{NOT}\,(\text{KNOW}\,(\text{WHEN}\,(\lambda x^{NP}.\,\text{IS}\,x\,(\text{POSSESSIVE CHERYL BIRTHDAY}))))\,\text{ALBERT} \tag{11}$$

where in addition to the already defined abstract syntactic constants, we have:

$$\text{ALBERT} : NP$$
$$\text{KNOW} : S \to NP \to S$$
$$\text{NOT} : (NP \to S) \to NP \to S$$

The semantic interpretations of these new lexical entries is then as follows:

$$[\![\text{ALBERT}]\!] := \lambda p^{\mathbf{e}\to\mathbf{P}}.\,p\,\mathbf{albert}$$
$$[\![\text{KNOW}]\!] := \lambda p^{\mathbf{P}} q^{(\mathbf{e}\to\mathbf{P})\to\mathbf{P}}.\,q\,(\lambda x^{\mathbf{e}}.\,\mathsf{K}\,x\,p)$$
$$[\![\text{NOT}]\!] := \lambda p^{((\mathbf{e}\to\mathbf{P})\to\mathbf{P})\to\mathbf{P}} q^{(\mathbf{e}\to\mathbf{P})\to\mathbf{P}}.\,q\,(\lambda x^{\mathbf{e}}.\,\neg_i(p\,(\lambda r^{\mathbf{e}\to\mathbf{P}}.\,r\,x)))$$

With these entrie interpretations, we obtain the expected interpretation of (11):

$$\neg_i(\mathsf{K}\,\mathbf{albert}\,(\exists_i x^{\mathbf{e}}.\,!(\exists_i y^{\mathbf{e}}.\,(\mathbf{birthday}_i\, y) \wedge_i (\mathbf{of}_i\, \mathbf{cheryl}\, y) \wedge_i (y =_i x))))$$

---

[3] In [11], the dialogue context includes, in addition to the common dialogue gameboard, private dialogue gameboards, one for each agent. Our approach is slightly different. What we model is not quite the private knowledge of each agent but rather what is commonly known about this private knowledge.

5 Dialogue Dynamics and Context Updating

As we have seen, inquisitive logic allows one to assign a formal semantics to each dialogue turn in a compositional way akin to Montague's [6]. The next step is to provide our model with some dynamics that will allow a dialogue turn to update the current dialogue context. For this purpose, we adapt the type-theoretic dynamic logic introduced in [7] and further developed in [15]. This approach has several advantages. It allows several dynamic phenomena to be integrated in a same framework (typically, discourse dynamic, as in [9,13], and epistemic dynamic as in [5,8]). It also allows for a treatment of dynamics at a subsentential level (as in [17]).[4]

The first question to settle is how to model dialogue contexts. We have seen that a typical dialogue gameboard consists of the *speaker*, the *addressee*, the *FACTS*, and the *QUD*. We have also seen that both the *FACTS* and the *QUD* may be encoded as a single inquisitive proposition. In addition, a dialogue context must also contain information about the private knowledge of the dialogue participants. Accordingly, we define a *dialogue context* to be a 4-tuple (s, a, Q, K) where:

- s, which is of type $\mathbf{e}$, is the speaker;
- a, which is of type $\mathbf{e}$, is the addressee;
- Q, which is of type $\mathbf{p}$, is an inquisitive proposition that models both the *FACTS* and the *QUD*;
- K, which is of type $\mathbf{e} \to \mathbf{s} \to \mathbf{p}$, is the function that associates to each agent their epistemic state at a given possible world.

Let $\mathbf{d} = \mathbf{e} \times \mathbf{e} \times \mathbf{p} \times (\mathbf{e} \to \mathbf{s} \to \mathbf{p})$ be the type of dialogue contexts. We posit the existence of four context accessing functions:

$$\mathbf{speaker} : \mathbf{d} \to \mathbf{e}$$
$$\mathbf{addressee} : \mathbf{d} \to \mathbf{e}$$
$$\mathbf{qud} : \mathbf{d} \to \mathbf{p}$$
$$\Sigma : \mathbf{d} \to \mathbf{e} \to \mathbf{s} \to \mathbf{p}$$

which simply correspond to *projection operators*.

Given the notion of a dynamic context, a *dynamic proposition* is defined to be an inquisitive proposition depending upon such a context. Hence, we define $\mathbf{P} = \mathbf{d} \to \mathbf{p}$ to be the type of dynamic propositions. The interpretation of the logical connectives and quantifiers must then be changed in order to accommodate dynamic propositions. The new interpretation is as follows:

---

[4] For the sake of conciseness and simplicity, in this paper, we give a simplified version that does not allow for anaphora resolution. This simplification dispenses one from modeling the so-called right context using a continuation. Taking anaphora resolution into account is feasible but involves a lot of technical details that are orthogonal to our main concern.

$$\mathbf{R_d}\, t_1 \ldots t_n := \lambda c^\mathbf{d}.\, (\mathbf{R_i}\, t_1 \ldots t_n) \wedge_\mathrm{i} !(\mathbf{qud}\, c)$$
$$\varphi \wedge_\mathrm{d} \psi \quad := \lambda c^\mathbf{d}.\, (\varphi\, c) \wedge_\mathrm{i} (\psi\, c)$$
$$\varphi \vee_\mathrm{d} \psi \quad := \lambda c^\mathbf{d}.\, (\varphi\, c) \vee_\mathrm{i} (\psi\, c)$$
$$\varphi \rightarrow_\mathrm{d} \psi \quad := \lambda c^\mathbf{d}.\, (\varphi\, c) \rightarrow_\mathrm{i} (\psi\, c)$$
$$\neg_\mathrm{d} \varphi \quad := \lambda c^\mathbf{d}.\, \neg_\mathrm{i}(\varphi\, c)$$
$$\forall_\mathrm{d} x^\mathbf{e}.\, \varphi\, x \quad := \lambda c^\mathbf{d}.\, \forall_\mathrm{i} x^\mathbf{e}.\, \varphi\, x\, c$$
$$\exists_\mathrm{d} x^\mathbf{e}.\, \varphi\, x \quad := \lambda c^\mathbf{d}.\, \exists_\mathrm{i} x^\mathbf{e}.\, \varphi\, x\, c$$
$$!_\mathrm{d}\, \varphi \quad := \lambda c^\mathbf{d}.\, !(\varphi\, c)$$
$$?_\mathrm{d}\, \varphi \quad := \lambda c^\mathbf{d}.\, ?(\varphi\, c)$$
$$\mathsf{K_d}\, \mathbf{a}\, \varphi \quad := \lambda c^\mathbf{d}.\, \lambda q^{\mathbf{s}\to\mathbf{t}}.\, (\forall w^\mathbf{s}.\, (q\, w) \rightarrow (\varphi\, c\, (\bigcup(\Sigma\, c\, a\, w)))) \wedge (!(\mathbf{qud}\, c)\, q)$$

Note how the interpretation of an atomic proposition is now sensitive to the context because it is intersected with the current *FACTS*. Thus, if the context establishes that Cheryl's birthday is either May 15 or June 17, the question of *when is Cheryl's birthday* will be equivalent to the question of *whether Cheryl's birthday is May 15 or June 17*. Remark that the interpretation of the epistemic modality is also sensitive to the context.

Using the dynamic logic, it is now possible to provide an interpretation to the sentence *I don't know when your birthday is*. To this end, we interpret the syntactic categories dynamically:

$$\llbracket NP \rrbracket := (\mathbf{e} \to \mathbf{P}) \to \mathbf{P}$$
$$\llbracket N \rrbracket := \mathbf{e} \to \mathbf{P}$$
$$\llbracket S \rrbracket := \mathbf{P}$$

The lexical entries are kept unchanged except that the atomic propositions and the logical connectives are interpreted dynamically. For instance, we now have:

$$\llbracket \text{BIRTHDAY} \rrbracket := \mathbf{birthday}_\mathrm{d}$$
$$\llbracket \text{WHEN} \rrbracket := \lambda p^{((\mathbf{e}\to\mathbf{P})\to\mathbf{P})\to\mathbf{P}}.\, \exists_\mathrm{d} x^\mathbf{e}.\, p\, (\lambda q^{\mathbf{e}\to\mathbf{P}}.\, q\, x)$$

Then, we may extend our semantic lexicon as follows:

$$\llbracket \text{I} \rrbracket := \lambda p^{\mathbf{e}\to\mathbf{P}}.\, \lambda c^\mathbf{d}.\, p\, (\mathbf{speaker}\, c)\, c$$
$$\llbracket \text{YOU} \rrbracket := \lambda p^{\mathbf{e}\to\mathbf{P}}.\, \lambda c^\mathbf{d}.\, p\, (\mathbf{addressee}\, c)\, c$$

It remains to show how a dialog turn acts on the dialogue context. To this end, we define the following updating functions:

$$\mathbf{sets} := \lambda c^\mathbf{d} x^\mathbf{e}.\, (x, \mathbf{addressee}\, c, \mathbf{qud}\, c, \Sigma\, c) \quad \text{sets the speaker}$$
$$\mathbf{seta} := \lambda c^\mathbf{d} x^\mathbf{e}.\, (\mathbf{speaker}\, c, x, \mathbf{qud}\, c, \Sigma\, c) \quad \text{sets the addressee}$$
$$\mathbf{upd} := \lambda c^\mathbf{d} a^\mathbf{P}.\, (\mathbf{speaker}\, c, \mathbf{addressee}\, c, (\mathbf{qud}\, c) \wedge_\mathrm{i} (a\, c), \lambda x^\mathbf{e} w^\mathbf{s}.\, (\Sigma\, c\, x\, w) \wedge_\mathrm{i} (a\, c))$$

We then define a *dialogue turn* to be a triple (s, a, φ), of type $\mathbf{e} \times \mathbf{e} \times \mathbf{P}$, where s is the speaker, a is the addressee, and φ is a dynamic proposition that expresses the semantics of the dialogue turn. Finally, we define the action on a dialogue context C of such a dialogue turn as follows:

$$C \circ (s, a, \varphi) = \mathbf{upd}\, (\mathbf{seta}\, (\mathbf{sets}\, C\, s)\, a)\, \varphi$$

6   A Complete Example: Cheryl's Birthday

Let us illustrate the way our model works by applying it to the logical puzzle known as *"When is Cheryl's Birthday"*. Here is the wording of the problem as it appeared on the New York Times website in April 2015 (see Footnote 1).

(2)   [CONTEXT: Albert and Bernard just met Cheryl. "When's your birthday?" Albert asked Cheryl. Cheryl thought a second and said, "I'm not going to tell you, but I'll give you some clues." She wrote down a list of 10 dates:

May 15,   May 16,   May 19,
June 17,   June 18
July 14,   July 16
August 14, August 15, August 17

"My birthday is one of these," she said. Then Cheryl whispered in Albert's ear the month—and only the month—of her birthday. To Bernard, she whispered the day, and only the day.]

a.   Cheryl (to Albert): *Can you figure it out now?*
b.   Albert: *I don't know when your birthday is, but I know Bernard doesn't know, either.*
c.   Bernard: *I didn't know originally, but now I do.*
d.   Albert: *Well, now I know, too!*

When is Cheryl's birthday?

In order to solve the problem, the first task is to formalize the initial dialogue context. To this end, we could first define a first-order object language. This language would include atomic propositions such as $\mathbf{May15}, \mathbf{Jun17}, \mathbf{Jul14}, etc.$ (with the obvious intended meanings). Then, we would have to posit meaning postulates such as $\neg_i(\mathbf{May15} \wedge_i \mathbf{Jun17})$, $\neg_i(\mathbf{May15} \wedge_i \mathbf{Jul14}), etc.$ By following such an approach, we would model the *QUD* as a formula expressing the inquisitive disjunction of the possible birthdate:

$$\mathbf{May15} \vee_i \mathbf{Jun17} \vee_i \mathbf{Jul14} \vee_i \ldots$$

With the objective of making our explanation simpler by not overcharging it with too much syntactic details, we prefer to leave the object language implicit and reason in semantic terms with possible worlds. The set of possible worlds is defined in such a way that each world corresponds to a possible birthdate:

$$W = \{w_{5.15}, w_{5.16}, w_{5.19}, w_{6.17}, w_{6.18}, w_{7.14}, w_{7.16}, w_{8.14}, w_{8.15}, w_{8.17}\}$$

Then the initial *QUD*, in its semantic version, corresponds to the following inquisitive proposition:

$$Q_0 = \big[\{w_{5.15}\}, \{w_{5.16}\}, \{w_{5.19}\}, \{w_{6.17}\}, \{w_{6.18}\}, \\ \{w_{7.14}\}, \{w_{7.16}\}, \{w_{8.14}\}, \{w_{8.15}\}, \{w_{8.17}\} \big]$$

Let us now concentrate on the modeling of the knowledge of the agents. Consider, for instance, world $w_{5.15}$. In this world, the month of Cheryl's birthdate is May, and Albert knows it. Albert is therefore in an inquisitive state where he wonders what is the day of Cheryl's birthdate, knowing that it is either the 15th, the 16th, or the 19th. This inquisitive state is represented by the following proposition:

$$[\{w_{5.15}\}, \{w_{5.16}\}, \{w_{5.19}\}]$$

Continuing this line of reasoning, we obtain that Albert's knowledge is modeled by the following map:

$$K_0 \, \textbf{albert} \; = \; \begin{cases} w_{5.15} \mid w_{5.16} \mid w_{5.19} \; \mapsto \; \big[\{w_{5.15}\}, \{w_{5.16}\}, \{w_{5.19}\}\big] \\ w_{6.17} \mid w_{6.18} \qquad\;\; \mapsto \; \big[\{w_{6.17}\}, \{w_{6.18}\}\big] \\ w_{7.14} \mid w_{7.16} \qquad\;\; \mapsto \; \big[\{\{w_{7.14}\}, \{w_{7.16}\}\big] \\ w_{8.14} \mid w_{8.15} \mid w_{8.17} \; \mapsto \; \big[\{w_{8.14}\}, \{w_{8.15}\}, \{w_{8.17}\}\big] \end{cases}$$

Similarly for Bernard:

$$K_0 \, \textbf{bernard} \; = \; \begin{cases} w_{7.14} \mid w_{8.14} \; \mapsto \; \big[\{w_{7.14}\}, \{w_{8.14}\}\big] \\ w_{5.15} \mid w_{8.15} \; \mapsto \; \big[\{w_{5.15}\}, \{w_{8.15}\}\big] \\ w_{5.16} \mid w_{7.16} \; \mapsto \; \big[\{w_{5.16}\}, \{w_{7.16}\}\big] \\ w_{6.17} \mid w_{8.17} \; \mapsto \; \big[\{w_{6.17}\}, \{w_{8.17}\}\big] \\ w_{6.18} \qquad\quad\; \mapsto \; \big[\{w_{6.18}\}\big] \\ w_{5.19} \qquad\quad\; \mapsto \; \big[\{w_{5.19}\}\big] \end{cases}$$

As for Cheryl, her knowledge (which is irrelevant for the example) corresponds to the map that assigns to each world w the proposition $[\{w\}]$. Our initial context is therefore $C_0 = (Q_0, K_0)$.[5] Let us now consider the dialogue turns. The first one, (2-a), simply restates the QUD and does not affect the context. We therefore have $C_1 = C_0$. The second turn, (2-b), is more interesting. It is interpreted as the dynamic proposition

$$\neg_\mathsf{d}(\mathsf{K_d} \, \textbf{albert} \, \varphi) \wedge_\mathsf{d} (\mathsf{K_d} \, \textbf{albert} \, \neg_\mathsf{d}(\mathsf{K_d} \, \textbf{bernard} \, \varphi)) \tag{13}$$

where φ corresponds to a dynamic proposition that amounts to the QUD when evaluated with respect to the current context. Then, according to the definition of the dynamic connectives, evaluating proposition (13) with respect to the current context consists in evaluating the following term:

$$\neg_\mathsf{i}(\mathsf{K_d} \, \textbf{albert} \, \varphi \, C_1) \wedge_\mathsf{i} (\mathsf{K_d} \, \textbf{albert} \, (\lambda c'. \, \neg_\mathsf{i}(\mathsf{K_d} \, \textbf{bernard} \, \varphi \, C_1)) \, C_1) \tag{14}$$

Let us focus on the subterm $\mathsf{K_d} \, \textbf{bernard} \, \varphi \, C_1$. We have:

$\mathsf{K_d} \, \textbf{bernard} \, \varphi \, C_1$
$\quad = \lambda q^{\mathsf{s} \to \mathsf{t}}. \, (\forall w^\mathsf{s}. \, (q \, w) \to (\varphi \, C_1 \, (\bigcup(\Sigma \, C_1 \, \textbf{bernard} \, w)))) \wedge (!(\textbf{qud} \, C_1) \, q)$
$\quad = \lambda q^{\mathsf{s} \to \mathsf{t}}. \, (\forall w^\mathsf{s}. \, (q \, w) \to \bigcup(K_1 \, \textbf{bernard} \, w) \in Q_1) \wedge q \in \, !Q_1$
$\quad = \lambda q^{\mathsf{s} \to \mathsf{t}}. \, (\forall w^\mathsf{s}. \, (q \, w) \to \bigcup(K_1 \, \textbf{bernard} \, w) \in Q_1) \wedge q \in \mathscr{P}(W)$
$\quad = \lambda q^{\mathsf{s} \to \mathsf{t}}. \, \forall w^\mathsf{s}. \, (q \, w) \to \bigcup(K_1 \, \textbf{bernard} \, w) \in Q_1$

---

[5] We leave the speaker and the addressee implicit.

Now, all the maximal elements of Q_1 are singletons, and the only worlds w such that

$$\bigcup(K_1 \text{ bernard } w)$$

yields a singleton (or possibly the empty set) are $w_{6.18}$ and $w_{5.19}$. Accordingly,

$$\mathsf{K_d} \text{ bernard } \varphi\, C_1$$

is interpreted as $\left[\{w_{6.18}, w_{5.19}\}\right]$. Hence,

$$\neg_i(\mathsf{K_d} \text{ bernard } \varphi\, C_1)$$

is interpreted as $\left[\{w_{5.15}, w_{5.16}, w_{6.17}, w_{7.14}, w_{7.16}, w_{8.14}, w_{8.15}, w_{8.17}\}\right]$. Then, in order to compute the interpretation of

$$\mathsf{K_d} \text{ albert } \neg_d(\mathsf{K_d} \text{ bernard } \varphi)\, C_1, \tag{15}$$

we use a similar reasoning and seek the worlds such that:

$$\bigcup(K_1 \text{ albert } w) \in (\neg_i(\mathsf{K_d} \text{ bernard } \varphi\, C_1))$$

These worlds are $w_{7.14}$, $w_{7.16}$, $w_{8.14}$, $w_{8.15}$, and $w_{8.17}$. Accordingly, proposition (15) is interpreted as

$$\left[\{w_{7.14}, w_{7.16}, w_{8.14}, w_{8.15}, w_{8.17}\}\right] \tag{16}$$

As for the first conjunct of (14), we have that $\mathsf{K_d} \text{ albert } \varphi\, C_1$ is interpreted as the empty set. Consequently, $\neg_i(\mathsf{K_d} \text{ albert } \varphi\, C_1)$ is interpreted as the everywhere true proposition, i.e., $\mathscr{P}(W)$. Therefore, the interpretation of proposition of (14) is given by (16). Then, updating the context C_1 (which mainly consists in intersecting it with (16)) yields a context $C_2 = (Q_2, K_2)$ where:

$$Q_2 = \left[\{w_{7.14}\}, \{w_{7.16}\}, \{w_{8.14}\}, \{w_{8.15}\}, \{w_{8.17}\}\right]$$

$$K_2 \text{ albert } = \begin{cases} w_{7.14} \mid w_{7.16} & \mapsto \left[\{\{w_{7.14}\}, \{w_{7.16}\}\}\right] \\ w_{8.14} \mid w_{8.15} \mid w_{8.17} & \mapsto \left[\{w_{8.14}\}, \{w_{8.15}\}, \{w_{8.17}\}\right] \\ - & \mapsto \left[\varnothing\right] \end{cases}$$

$$K_2 \text{ bernard } = \begin{cases} w_{7.14} \mid w_{8.14} & \mapsto \left[\{w_{7.14}\}, \{w_{8.14}\}\right] \\ w_{5.15} \mid w_{8.15} & \mapsto \left[\{w_{8.15}\}\right] \\ w_{5.16} \mid w_{7.16} & \mapsto \left[\{w_{7.16}\}\right] \\ w_{6.17} \mid w_{8.17} & \mapsto \left[\{w_{8.17}\}\right] \\ - & \mapsto \left[\varnothing\right] \end{cases}$$

The content of the third dialogue turn is captured by the following proposition:[6]

$$\mathsf{K_d} \text{ bernard } \varphi \tag{17}$$

---

[6] For the sake of simplicity, we discard the first part of this dialogue turn, i.e., *I didn't know originally*, for it is not informative.

where φ again is a dynamic proposition that yields the current QUD when applied to the current context. Proposition (17) is then evaluated according to the current context as follows:

$\mathsf{K_d\,bernard}\,\varphi\,C_2$
$= \lambda q^{\mathsf{s}\to\mathsf{t}}.\,(\forall w^{\mathsf{s}}.\,(q\,w) \to (\varphi\,C_2\,(\bigcup(\Sigma\,C_2\,\mathbf{bernard}\,w)))) \wedge (!(\mathbf{qud}\,C_2)\,q)$
$= \lambda q^{\mathsf{s}\to\mathsf{t}}.\,(\forall w^{\mathsf{s}}.\,(q\,w) \to \bigcup(K_1\,\mathbf{bernard}\,w) \in Q_2) \wedge q \in !Q_2$
$= \big[\{w_{5.15}, w_{5.16}, w_{5.19}, w_{6.17}, w_{6.18}, w_{7.16}, w_{8.15}, w_{8.17}\}\big]$
$\hspace{4cm} \cap \big[\{w_{7.14}, w_{7.16}, w_{8.14}, w_{8.15}, w_{8.17}\}\big]$
$= \big[\{w_{7.16}, w_{8.15}, w_{8.17}\}\big]$

Updating the current context C_2 yields a new context $C_3 = (Q_3, K_3)$ where:

$$Q_3 = \big[\{w_{7.16}\}, \{w_{8.15}\}, \{w_{8.17}\}\big]$$

$$K_3\,\mathbf{albert} = \begin{cases} w_{7.14}\,|\,w_{7.16} & \mapsto \big[\{\{w_{7.16}\}\}\big] \\ w_{8.14}\,|\,w_{8.15}\,|\,w_{8.17} & \mapsto \big[\{w_{8.15}\}, \{w_{8.17}\}\big] \\ - & \mapsto \big[\varnothing\big] \end{cases}$$

$$K_3\,\mathbf{bernard} = \begin{cases} w_{5.15}\,|\,w_{8.15} & \mapsto \big[\{w_{8.15}\}\big] \\ w_{5.16}\,|\,w_{7.16} & \mapsto \big[\{w_{7.16}\}\big] \\ w_{6.17}\,|\,w_{8.17} & \mapsto \big[\{w_{8.17}\}\big] \\ - & \mapsto \big[\varnothing\big] \end{cases}$$

Finally, by applying the same analysis to the last dialogue turn, one obtains the following interpretation:

$$\mathsf{K_d\,albert}\,\varphi\,C_3 = \big[\{w_{7.16}\}\big]$$

Then, a last updating to the current context yields the final context $C_4 = (Q_4, K_4)$ where:

$$Q_4 = \big[\{w_{7.16}\}\big]$$

$$K_4\,\mathbf{albert} = \begin{cases} w_{7.14}\,|\,w_{7.16} & \mapsto \big[\{\{w_{7.16}\}\}\big] \\ - & \mapsto \big[\varnothing\big] \end{cases}$$

$$K_4\,\mathbf{bernard} = \begin{cases} w_{5.16}\,|\,w_{7.16} & \mapsto \big[\{w_{7.16}\}\big] \\ - & \mapsto \big[\varnothing\big] \end{cases}$$

This final context is such that the QUD is no longer inquisitive, which means that the originl issue is settled, In addition, the epistemic states of both Albert and Bernard are such that they both know that Cheryl's is July 16.

7 Comparision with Previous Work

We conclude our paper by discussing our model and comparing it to related approaches. [8] presents Dynamic Epistemic Logic (DEL). In DEL, situations are described through sets of agents, each with individual available states of information. Then, as agents perform actions, DEL gives a way to describe the changes in the state of available information, for each agent.

Growing on DEL with an inquisitive take, [5] introduces Inquisitive Dynamic Epistemic Logic (IDEL), a framework designed to provide tools that can be used to model the information exchange between a set of agents as a dynamic process through raising and solving of issues. The approach taken in the paper chooses a bi-categorial presentation of Inquisitive Semantics, with a strict separation between interrogatives and declarative sentences. The authors reference [3] for a meaning-preserving translation between this presentation and the one we use, where interrogatives and declarative sentences are modeled as the same type of objects. In IDEL, issues are raised when the agents ask questions and resolved when they make assertions. This is quite orthogonal to the vision of dialogue defended by Ginzburg in KoS framework [12] and that we follow here, where every speech act gives rise to a QUD, which corresponds to an issue.

IDEL is designed "under the assumption that an agent's information is always truthful". Though the example we show here does not illustrate this, our model is designed with the clear objective of working with real-life data and therefore in settings where disagreements can and do occur. Participants may reject an asserted fact. The negotiation phases model adds a protective additional step in the computation of the dialogue representations that bypasses this issue in a direct way. [5] suggests to try using weaker epistemic modalities such as belief and allowing disagreement to occur in order to address this difficulty.

The last section of [5] draws a comparison between IDEL and Dynamic Epistemic Logic with Questions (DELQ), as presented in [1]. DELQ is based on epistemic models enriched with a set of issues, one per agent. Then, dynamicity is added through several actions, of which we focus on two: public announcement "that ϕ is the case" and public asking "whether ϕ is the case".

Thus, in DELQ all the sentences are considered to be declarative, none are treated as syntactically interrogative or semantically inquisitive [5]. The difference between questions and assertions is drawn through dynamic actions, at the speech act level. In IDEL, the difference between questions and assertions exists at the syntactic level through the form of interrogative sentences. In our approach, the difference between questions and assertions is acknowledged at the syntactic level but is smoothed in the semantics, as we represent issues and propositions as the same type of objects.

[5] concludes on the need to investigate a dynamic epistemic version of [4], the version of Inquisitive Semantics we presented in Sect. 3. This article presents our take on this investigation. We do not claim here that our model works better than IDEL, our idea actually comes from a different perspective: starting from dialogue studies and taking an orientation towards real-life data modeling.

8   Conclusion

Our approach grows from linguistic considerations of interrogative and declarative sentences as speech acts. We take roots in [11] but also in the syntactic parses of the speech acts in order to build our representations. The model presented in this paper addresses phenomena related to context-managing but also to dialogue management, through the way utterances influence public knowledge of private contexts. We harmonically combine several frameworks in order to model complex dialogical interactions in a logically sound way. Solving Cheryl's birthday puzzle gives us a proof of concept for the possibilities of logical reasoning through dialogue modeling. Inquisitive Semantics provides a uniform way of modeling interrogative and declarative sentences, which we think to be of the greatest importance when dealing with dialogue modeling, especially in a real-life data perspective. Next, our model needs to be scaled up in order to be applied to bigger and more complex dialogues. We hope to achieve that through the articulation of negotiation phases. In this paper, we bypassed several linguistic and logical problems related to tense and modality; future work should take these into account. Another interesting research direction would be to compare the way our model behaves on English with other, especially non-Indo-European, languages.

References

1. Van Benthem, J., Minică, Ş.: Toward a dynamic logic of questions. J. Philos. Log. **41**(4), 633–669 (2012)
2. Boritchev, M., Amblard, M.: Picturing questions and answers - a formal approach to SLAM. In: (In)coherence of Discourse - Formal and Conceptual issues of Language. Springer (2019). Language, Cognition and Mind
3. Ciardelli, I., Groenendijk, J., Roelofsen, F.: On the semantics and logic of declaratives and interrogatives. Synthese **192**(6), 1689–1728 (2013). https://doi.org/10.1007/s11229-013-0352-7
4. Ciardelli, I., Groenendijk, J., Roelofsen, F.: Inquisitive Semantics. Oxford Surveys in Semantics and Pragmatics. Oxford University Press, Oxford (2018)
5. Ciardelli, I.A., Roelofsen, F.: Inquisitive dynamic epistemic logic. Synthese **192**(6), 1643–1687 (2014). https://doi.org/10.1007/s11229-014-0404-7
6. Ciardelli, I., Roelofsen, F., Theiler, N.: Composing alternatives. Linguist. Philos. **40**, 1–36 (2017)
7. de Groote, Ph.: Towards a Montagovian account of dynamics. In: Proceedings of Semantics and Linguistic Theory XVI, pp. 1–16. Cornell University, Ithaca (2006)
8. Van Ditmarsch, H., van Der Hoek, W., Kooi, B.: Dynamic Epistemic Logic. Synthese Library, vol. 337. Springer, Heidelberg (2008). https://doi.org/10.1007/978-1-4020-5839-4
9. Dotlačil, J., Roelofsen, F.: Dynamic inquisitive semantics: anaphora and questions. In: Espinal, M.T., Castroviejo, E., Leonetti, M., McNally, L., Real-Puigdollers, C. (eds.) Proceedings of Sinn und Bedeutung 23, vol. 1, pp. 365–382. Universitat Autònoma de Barcelona, Bellaterra (Cerdanyola del Vallès (2019)
10. Gallin, D.: Intensional and Higher-Order Modal Logic. Mathematics Studies, vol. 19 North-Holland (1975)

11. Ginzburg, J.: The Interactive Stance. Oxford University Press, Oxford (2012)
12. Ginzburg, J.: Semantics of Dialogue. The Cambridge Handbook of Formal Semantics (2016)
13. Groenendijk, J., Stokhof, M.: Dynamic predicate logic. Linguist. Philos. **14**(1), 39–100 (1991)
14. Hamblin, C.L.: Questions in Montague English. Found. Lang. **10**(1), 41–53 (1973)
15. Lebedeva, E.: Expressing discourse dynamics through continuations. Université de Lorraine, Thèse de doctorat (2012)
16. Montague, R.: The proper treatment of quantification in ordinary English. In: Hintikka, K.J.J., Moravcsik, J.M.E., Suppes, P. (eds.) Approaches to Natural Language, vol. 49, pp. 221–242. Springer, Heidelberg (1973). https://doi.org/10.1007/978-94-010-2506-5_10
17. Muskens, R.: Combining Montague semantics and discourse representation. Linguist. Philos. **19**, 143–186 (1995)
18. Stalnaker, R.: Common ground. Linguist. Philos. **25**(5–6), 701–721 (2002)

Knowledge Acquisition from Natural Language with Treebank Semantics and $\mathcal{F}$LORA-2

Alastair Butler[✉]

Faculty of Humanities and Social Sciences, Hirosaki University,
Bunkyo-cho 1, Hirosaki-shi 036-8560, Japan
ajb129@hirosaki-u.ac.jp

Abstract. Knowledge acquisition in this paper concerns converting raw natural language input into database entries. This is achieved by linking two systems: Treebank Semantics and $\mathcal{F}$LORA-2. Treebank Semantics (Butler 2021) is an implemented grammar system that converts parsed constituency trees from a treebank parser into logic based representations that capture sentence and discourse dependencies. Further postprocessing produces content for $\mathcal{F}$LORA-2, "a sophisticated object-based knowledge representation and reasoning system" (Kifer et al. 2020). A running example illustrates capabilities and use of the combined systems.

Keywords: Knowledge representation · Treebank annotation · Analysis conversion · Discourse dependencies · Clause local dependencies

1 Introduction

This paper links Treebank Semantics to the $\mathcal{F}$LORA-2 database system to achieve a knowledge acquisition pipeline. Treebank Semantics (Butler 2021) is an implemented grammar system that converts constituency tree annotations into the structures of a formal language which are then processed against a locally constrained global (discourse level) calculation. Outputs of the calculation are logic based representations that capture sentence and discourse dependencies. To achieve knowledge acquisition, a further postprocessing component is added to produce content for $\mathcal{F}$LORA-2, "a sophisticated object-based knowledge representation and reasoning system" (Kifer et al. 2020). The paper is structured as follows. Section 2 illustrates the process of reaching database content with a running example. Section 3 demonstrates use of the $\mathcal{F}$LORA-2 system with the database content obtained from Sect. 2. Section 4 discusses alternatives to the techniques of this paper. Section 5 concludes the paper.

This paper benefited from the comments of two anonymous reviewers, and from the participants of LENLS17, all of whom are gratefully acknowledged. This research was supported by the NINJAL Parsed Corpus of Modern Japanese (NPCMJ) project funded by the National Institute for Japanese Language and Linguistics (NINJAL), and by the Japan Society for the Promotion of Science (JSPS), Kakenhi Project 19K00541.

N. Okazaki et al. (Eds.): JSAI-isAI 2020 Workshops, LNAI 12758, pp. 37–49, 2021.
https://doi.org/10.1007/978-3-030-79942-7_3

2   Reaching Database Content

To illustrate the approach of reaching database content, let's consider giving analysis to (1).

(1) MrMcGregor was on his hands and knees, but he jumped up and ran after Peter, waving a large rake.

Example (1) raises a number of challenges for the establishment of dependencies:

– *MrMcGregor* and *his* need to corefer, a case of binding within the syntactic scope of *MrMcGregor*;

– *MrMcGregor* and *he* need to corefer, a case of binding outside the syntactic scope of *MrMcGregor*;

– *MrMcGregor* (via *he*) needs to be the subject of both *jumped_up* and *ran*, instances of across-the-board binding; and

– *MrMcGregor* (via *he*) needs to be the subject of *waving*, an instance of subject control.

To meet these challenges with an implemented system, we first obtain a syntactic parse for (1) that conforms to the annotation scheme of the Treebank Semantics Parsed Corpus (TSPC; Butler 2021). This annotation scheme was created as a consolidation of other widely used schemes for English: the SUSANNE Corpus and Analytic Scheme (Sampson 1995), the ICE Parsing Scheme (Nelson et al. 2002), the Penn Treebank Scheme (Marcus, Santorini and Marcinkiewicz 1993), and the Penn Historical Parsed Corpora Scheme (Santorini 2010).

Construction analysis with functional and grammatical information largely follows the SUSANNE scheme, which is closely related to the English grammars of Quirk et al. (1972, 1985). The ICE Parsing Scheme similarly follows the Quirk et al. grammars. The Penn Historical Corpora scheme, which itself draws on the bracketed approach of the Penn Treebank scheme, informs the 'look' of the annotation. This includes adoption of the bracketed encoding, choice of tag labels, and the presentation of conjunction structure with CONJP layers. However, IML and NML, used with CONJP layers below, are innovations of the TSPC scheme.

The resulting TSPC annotation scheme is notable because it channels wide coverage analysis towards a high degree of normalised structure, particularly with respect to: the projection of structure, the adjunction of structure, the coordination of structure, and the presentation of function information. Having normalised structure eases the processing task.

Automatic creation of parsed data from raw text input is possible with wide coverage parsers, e.g., the RASP system (Briscoe et al. 2006), the Stanford CoreNLP system (Manning et al. 2014), or the Berkeley Neural Parser (Kitaev et al. 2019). The gained output is supplemented by post-processing to reach the TSPC tree format, as described in Butler (2020). With (1) as input, the parse result of (2) is reached.

(2)

```
1   (IP-MAT (IML (IML (NP-SBJ;{PERSON} (NPR MrMcGregor))
2                    (BED was)
3                    (PP-LOC (P-ROLE on)
4                            (NP (NP-GENV;{PERSON} (PRO his))
5                                (NML (NP (NS hands))
6                                     (CONJP (CONJ and)
7                                            (NP (NS knees)))))))
8               (PU ,)
9               (CONJP (CONJ but)
10                     (IML (NP-SBJ;{PERSON} (PRO he))
11                          (IML (IML (VBD jumped_up))
12                               (CONJP (CONJ and)
13                                      (IML (VBD ran)
14                                           (PP-DIR (P-ROLE after)
15                                                   (NP;{PERSON} (NPR Peter)))
16                                           (PU ,)
17                                           (IP-PPL-CNT (VAG waving)
18                                                       (NP-OB1 (D a)
19                                                               (ADJP (ADJ large))
20                                                               (N rake)))))))))))
```

The syntactic parse of (2) has:

- word class information: ADJ = adjective, BED = past tense *be*, CONJ = coordinating conjunction, D = determiner, NPR = singular proper name, N = singular noun, NS = plural noun, P-ROLE = preposition, PRO = pronoun, PU = punctuation, VAG = present participle (*-ing*) form of lexical verb, and VBD = past tense form of lexical verb;

- constituency structure information: ADJP = adjective phrase, CONJP = conjunction phrase, IML = intermediate clause layer, present for clause internal conjunction, IP-MAT = matrix clause, IP-PPL = participle clause, NML = intermediate noun phrase layer, NP = noun phrase, and PP = preposition phrase;

- functional information: CNT = continuative, DIR = direction, GENV = genitive/possessive, LOC = location, OB1 = object, and SBJ = subject; and

- ';{PERSON}' = type information to aid with pronominal resolution.

With the syntactic parse information of (2) as input, we can automatically obtain from the Treebank Semantics calculation (Butler 2021) the formula of (3), presented with TPTP syntax (Sutcliffe 2009). This formula has the form of a Discourse Representation Structure (DRS; Kamp and Reyle 1993), first introducing all widely scoped discourse existentially bound variables (discourse referents) followed by the body of the expression consisting of conditions on the discourse referents. Note that links to the original text (1) are achieved with word numbering that also follows the line numbering of the syntactic parse in (2).

(3)

```
1  fof(example1,axiom,
2    ? [ATTRIBX10,FACTX8,PERSONX12,PERSONX4,ENTITYX2,ENTITYX3,
3       ENTITYX5,ENTITYX11,EVENTX1,EVENTX6,EVENTX9,EVENTX7]:
4    ( isA(ATTRIBX10,large19)
5    & ( isA(FACTX8,fact3)
6      & emb(FACTX8) = EVENTX9
7      & ( isA(EVENTX9,waving17)
8        & arg1(EVENTX9) = ENTITYX11
9        & arg0(EVENTX9) = PERSONX12 ) )
10   & ( isA(ENTITYX11,rake20)
11     & attribute2(ENTITYX11) = ATTRIBX10 )
12   & ( PERSONX12 = cPERSONSortMrMcGregor1 )
13   & isA(ENTITYX2,hands5)
14   & isA(ENTITYX3,knees7)
15   & ( PERSONX4 = cPERSONSortMrMcGregor1 )
16   & ( isA(ENTITYX5,and6)
17     & genv(ENTITYX5) = PERSONX4
18     & conj2(ENTITYX5) = ENTITYX3
19     & conj1(ENTITYX5) = ENTITYX2 )
20   & ( isA(cCONJSortbut9,but9)
21     & conj1(cCONJSortbut9) = EVENTX1
22     & ( isA(EVENTX1,was2)
23       & loc_on3(EVENTX1) = ENTITYX5
24       & arg0(EVENTX1) = cPERSONSortMrMcGregor1 )
25     & conj2(cCONJSortbut9) = cCONJSortand12
26     & ( isA(cCONJSortand12,and12)
27       & conj1(cCONJSortand12) = EVENTX6
28       & ( isA(EVENTX6,jumped_up11)
29         & arg0(EVENTX6) = PERSONX12 )
30       & conj2(cCONJSortand12) = EVENTX7
31       & ( isA(EVENTX7,ran13)
32         & arg0(EVENTX7) = PERSONX12
33         & dir_after14(EVENTX7) = cPERSONSortPeter15
34         & cnt4(EVENTX7) = FACTX8 ) ) ) )
35 ).
```

Prefixes added to the created discourse referents indicate their contribution, thus:

– ATTRIBX takes an attribute value, e.g., a value to integrate attribute large19;

– ENTITYX takes an entity value, e.g., used for values of hands5, knees7, and rake20;

– EVENTX takes an event value as part of a neo-Davidsonian representation for linking event predicates (jumped_up11, ran13, etc.) to arguments via argument roles: `arg0` (subject/doer), `arg1` (object/done to), `dir_after14` (direction), etc.;

- `PERSONX` takes a typed person entity value, e.g., restricting the pronominal reference seen with the equations in lines 12 and 15 of (3); and

- `FACTX` is a bridge for linking an event to an embedded or subordinate event via an argument role, e.g., `cnt4` (continuative function) is used to link the event of "waving a large rake" to the event of MrMcGregor's running after Peter.

In addition to the discourse referents captured as bound variables, there are discourse referents that show up as constants in (3): `cPERSONSortMrMcGregor1` and `cPERSONSortPeter15`. These serve as accessible discourse referents for the instances of proper names in (2) during the process of calculation for reaching (3).

The process of calculation and a Prolog based implementation are described in Butler (2021). In essence, this involves making two passes over an input term that is a processed version of the TSPC syntactic parse. With the first pass, the calculation collects discourse referents. During the second pass over the input term, the collected discourse referents are released following rules of accessibility from Dynamic Semantics (Dekker 2012): From the discourse level of total collection, the discourse referents filter through to local sentence/clause internal binding levels, where they form the arguments of the predicates that populate the resulting logical expression.

The exact makeup of arguments essentially remains unspecified by the input, as there is no reference to additional information, like dictionary information to establish predicate valencies, that is beyond the content of the syntactic parse input. At the point in the calculation when a predicate is reached, the availability of discourse referents as local bindings is established. The predicate's sensitivity to what is available as a potential binding determines the arguments. With this setup, a syntactic parse like (2) has sufficient overall information to determine a calculation result.

There are also the constants of `cCONJSortbut9` and `cCONJSortand12` in (3). These are not discourse referents because they are never available as accessible antecedents during the calculation. Rather they are created to link the conjunct content of the conjunctions `but9` and `and6`, respectively. This serves to preserve the dependency information of the source sentence.

With (3) semantic relations are captured, but there isn't yet content suitably arranged for a database. We get a huge step closer with conversion to clause normal form, which can be achieved by sending (3) through the CNF translation procedure of FLOTTER (Nonnengart et al. 1998), resulting in (4). With (4), all instances of quantification are eliminated with the skolemization of the translation, but what is especially attractive is that the resulting skolemization relates all content through terms that are essentially paths to `cCONJSortbut9`, or paths to content that can then be equated to a path to `cCONJSortbut9`, possibly via further equivalences. The constant cCONJSortbut9 is the value used for gathering the conjunct content of the connective instance but9. but9 is the top-most element in the dependency structure derivable from (1). This is not an artifact of this one example, but rather this is a general property of the rooted nature of natural language sentences.

(4)

```
list_of_clauses(axioms, cnf).
clause( || -> isA(cCONJSortbut9,but9),1).
clause( || -> isA(cCONJSortand12,and12),2).
clause( || -> isA(conj1(cCONJSortbut9),was2),3).
clause( || -> equal(conj2(cCONJSortbut9),cCONJSortand12),4).
clause( || -> isA(conj1(cCONJSortand12),jumped_up11),5).
clause( || -> isA(conj2(cCONJSortand12),ran13),6).
clause( || -> isA(cnt4(conj2(cCONJSortand12)),fact3),7).
clause( || -> isA(loc_on3(conj1(cCONJSortbut9)),and6),8).
clause( || -> equal(arg0(conj1(cCONJSortbut9)),cPERSONSortMrMcGregor1),9).
clause( || -> equal(dir_after14(conj2(cCONJSortand12)),cPERSONSortPeter15),10).
clause( || -> isA(emb(cnt4(conj2(cCONJSortand12))),waving17),11).
clause( || -> isA(conj1(loc_on3(conj1(cCONJSortbut9))),hands5),12).
clause( || -> isA(conj2(loc_on3(conj1(cCONJSortbut9))),knees7),13).
clause( || -> equal(genv(loc_on3(conj1(cCONJSortbut9))),cPERSONSortMrMcGregor1),14).
clause( || -> isA(arg1(emb(cnt4(conj2(cCONJSortand12)))),rake20),15).
clause( || -> equal(arg0(emb(cnt4(conj2(cCONJSortand12)))),cPERSONSortMrMcGregor1),16).
clause( || -> isA(attribute2(arg1(emb(cnt4(conj2(cCONJSortand12))))),large19),17).
clause( || -> equal(arg0(emb(cnt4(conj2(cCONJSortand12)))),arg0(conj1(cCONJSortand12))),18).
clause( || -> equal(arg0(emb(cnt4(conj2(cCONJSortand12)))),arg0(conj2(cCONJSortand12))),19).
end_of_list.
```

With (4) there is information to map word content to the dependency information of the entire sentence. We can use this to connect word content to other word content via single relations derived from the outermost layers of the path terms left by skolemization (conj2 (second conjunct), arg0 (subject/doer), genv (possessive), cnt (continuative), etc.), as in the (Prolog) terms of (5).

(5)

```
arc(was2,cPERSONSortMrMcGregor1,arg0).
arc(was2,and6,loc_on3).
arc(and6,cPERSONSortMrMcGregor1,genv).
arc(and6,hands5,conj1).
arc(and6,knees7,conj2).
arc(but9,was2,conj1).
arc(but9,and12,conj2).
arc(jumped_up11,cPERSONSortMrMcGregor1,arg0).
arc(and12,jumped_up11,conj1).
arc(and12,ran13,conj2).
arc(ran13,cPERSONSortPeter15,dir_after14).
arc(ran13,cPERSONSortMrMcGregor1,arg0).
arc(ran13,waving17,cnt4).
```

```
arc(waving17,cPERSONSortMrMcGregor1,arg0).
arc(waving17,rake20,arg1).
arc(rake20,large19,attribute2).
```

The dependency information of (5) can be visualised as in Fig. 1.

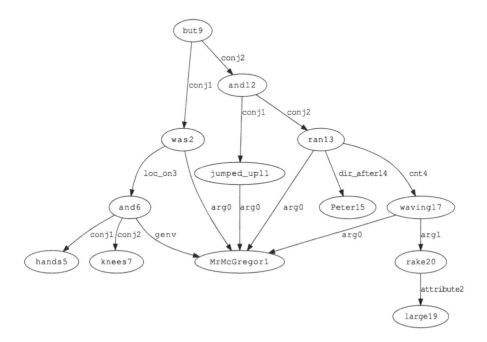

Fig. 1. Graph visualisation of (5)

From (5) we can collate the word connections to realise the $\mathcal{F}$LORA-2 database entries of (6).

(6)

```
was2[arg0->MrMcGregor1:PERSON, loc_on3->{hands5, knees7}].
hands5[genv->MrMcGregor1:PERSON].
knees7[genv->MrMcGregor1:PERSON].
but9[conj1->was2, conj2->and12].
jumped_up11[arg0->MrMcGregor1:PERSON].
and12[conj1->jumped_up11, conj2->ran13].
ran13[arg0->MrMcGregor1:PERSON, cnt4->waving17, dir_after14->Peter15:PERSON].
waving17[arg0->MrMcGregor1:PERSON, arg1->rake20].
rake20[large19].
```

The declarations of (6) specify objects in the form of frame entries of F-logic (Kifer, Lausen and Wu 1995), with symbols beginning with upper or lowercase letters denoting constants. Objects can have single-valued, set-valued, or Boolean attributes.

In the last frame entry `large19` is a Boolean attribute that is set to the value of true for object `rake20`.

A single frame entry is able to assert multiple facts simultaneously. For example, the frame concerning event object `ran13` has a single-valued attribute `arg0` (the runner) with object `MrMcGregor1` as the attribute value. Moreover `MrMcGregor1` is asserted to have type PERSON. Also, `ran13` has a single-valued attribute `dir_after14` (the thing run after) with object `Peter15` as the attribute value.

Among the attributes asserted with the `was2` event object is `loc_on3` which takes the set-value {hands5, knees7} which contains two objects: `hands5` and `knees7`. In separate frame entries, it is also asserted that both these objects belong to (genv) the person object `MrMcGregor1`.

3   Using the Obtained Database Content

With $\mathcal{F}$LORA-2, objects can be queried by entering object frame calls at the 'flora2 ?-' prompt. Queries analogous to constituent questions are created by placing variables at appropriate syntactic positions of an object frame call, where a variable is a symbol preceeded by a question mark. Additional operations can further process retrieved information. For example, we can use the `setof` aggregate operation in the query of (7) to find all objects of type PERSON.

(7)

```
flora2 ?- ?Objects = setof{?O | ?O^^PERSON[] }.

?Objects = [MrMcGregor1, Peter15]

1 solution(s) in 0.002 seconds; elapsed time = 0.002
```

An occurrence of '?' without an accompanying symbol stands for a don't-care variable. This is used in query (8) to find all objects that either have attributes or are the values of attributes. That is, (8) returns the domain of discourse—the entities and events—derived from processing (1).

(8)

```
flora2 ?- ?Objects = setof{?O | ?O[?->?] ; ?[?->?O] }.

?Objects = [MrMcGregor1, Peter15, and12, but9, hands5, jumped_up11,
            knees7, rake20, ran13, was2, waving17]

1 solution(s) in 0.000 seconds; elapsed time = 0.002
```

We can further use the `setof` aggregate in query (9) to find all the single-valued and set-valued attributes (methods) of objects, which gives a list of the argument roles or dependency roles that connect objects and also inform what objects are (e.g., an event is an object with typically a single-valued or set-valued `arg0` attribute, linked to the event's 'doer' value(s)).

(9)

```
flora2 ?- ?Methods = setof{?M | ?[?M->?]}.
```

```
?Methods = [arg0, arg1, cnt4, conj1, conj2, dir_after14, genv, loc_on3]
```

```
1 solution(s) in 0.000 seconds; elapsed time = 0.001
```

With (10), we ask a query to find objects that have a Boolean attribute and to report the attribute.

(10)

```
flora2 ?- ?O[?A].
```

```
?O = rake20
?A = large19
```

```
1 solution(s) in 0.001 seconds; elapsed time = 0.000
```

In (11), a (Prolog) rule is defined that is able to find objects based on the object symbol matching some string.

(11)

```
instance(?String,?Object) :-
  ?Object[], match(?String, ?Object, ?_Match, one)@\prolog(pcre), ?_Match \= [].
```

Having (11), we can now ask about the details of any waving event without needing to know a full object id.

(12)

```
flora2 ?- instance('waving', ?X), ?X[?M->?Y].
```

```
?X = waving17
?M = arg0
?Y = MrMcGregor1
```

```
?X = waving17
?M = arg1
?Y = rake20
```

```
2 solution(s) in 0.007 seconds; elapsed time = 0.010
```

```
Yes
```

From the query responses, we find out that there has been one waving event instance, namely waving17, which involves MrMcGregor1 as the waver and rake20 as the waved object.

With the query of (13), we ask to report on MrMcGregor.

(13)

```
flora2 ?- instance('MrMcGregor', ?Y), ?X[?A->?Y].

?Y = MrMcGregor1
?X = hands5
?A = genv

?Y = MrMcGregor1
?X = jumped_up11
?A = arg0

?Y = MrMcGregor1
?X = knees7
?A = genv

?Y = MrMcGregor1
?X = ran13
?A = arg0

?Y = MrMcGregor1
?X = was2
?A = arg0

?Y = MrMcGregor1
?X = waving17
?A = arg0

6 solution(s) in 0.004 seconds; elapsed time = 0.013

Yes
```

From the returned results, we can see that all the challenges for the establishment of dependencies mentioned in Sect. 2 are met, and now carried over to database content that can be queried, aggregated, etc.

3.1 Path Expressions

In addition to the basic frame syntax, F-logic also supports path expressions to facilitate navigation along single-valued and set-valued attributes. A single-valued path expression, O.M, refers to the unique object R for which O[M -> R] holds.

Path expressions and F-logic formulas can be arbitrarily nested in a manner analogous to an XPath query. This offers a way to query dependency structure. For example, (14) demonstrates the longest dependency path extractable from the analysis of (1), which starts with but9 as the topmost element and ends with object rake20 that has attribute large19.

(14)

```
flora2 ?- ?A.?B.?C.?D[?E->?F[?G]].

?A = but9
?B = conj2
?C = conj2
?D = cnt4
?E = arg1
?F = rake20
?G = large19


1 solution(s) in 0.000 seconds; elapsed time = 0.001

Yes
```

4   A Note to Consider Alternatives

As mentioned in the discussion of the TSPC annotation scheme, there are widely used alternative annotation schemes available for English. Already mentioned schemes are constituent tree based, but there are also alternative parsing methods with properties shaped by particular grammatical theories/formalisms such as HPSG (Flickinger et al. 2012), LFG (Dyvik et al. 2016), CCG (Hockenmaier and Steedman 2005), and TLG (Moot 2015). There are also dependency based grammar formalisms, with Universal Dependencies (Schuster and Manning 2016) as the popular option for this approach.

All these alternative methods can provide syntactic information to feed the described Treebank Semantics calculation, while offering varying degrees of awareness for grammatical distinctions. Such alternative approaches can also render the Treebank Semantics calculation unnecessary by providing their own methods for constructing a semantic base from which ℱLORA-2 database entries could be derived, or indeed entries for some other database system.

In regard to alternatives for the semantic base, Abstract Meaning Representation (AMR; Banarescu et al. 2013) is a notable choice. The rooted nature of natural language sentences that was observed above lies at the foundation of the AMR approach. However this key strength also leaves AMR analysis limited to whole sentence analysis, while the approach advocated in this paper is fundamentally discourse oriented, with its dependency allocation driven by a calculation of accessibility from Dynamic Semantics.

Alternative discourse semantics based methods include the Boxer implementation of Discourse Representation Theory (Basile et al. 2012), but here the level of internal sentence dependencies is lost. Arguably, the current approach is exceptional for unifying both discourse and sentence dependency perspectives.

5   Conclusion

To sum up, this paper has linked Treebank Semantics to the $\mathcal{F}$LORA-2 database system to achieve a knowledge acquisition pipeline. From raw natural language input, the pipeline was shown to lead to database content. Furthermore, there was illustration of how the resulting database content could be utilised through query formation to extract objects (corresponding to the events and entities mentioned in the natural language input) together with object type information and the argument and dependency relations that connect the objects and inform what the objects are.

This paper focused only on information that was directly collected from the natural language input. If this were combined with ascribing default properties to object types, and the further specification of lexical information, e.g., through rules of synonymy and entailment, then the information contribution extracted from the natural language would go further still.

This paper has shown how going to a semantic representation that retains dependency information from the input natural language is helpful for then structuring the resulting information as object based database information.

References

Banarescu, L., et al.: Abstract meaning representation for sembanking. In: Proceedings of the 7th Linguistic Annotation Workshop and Interoperability with Discourse, pp. 178–186 (2013)

Basile, V., Bos, J., Evang, K., Venhuizen, N.: Developing a large semantically annotated corpus. In: Proceedings of the 8th International Conference on Language Resources and Evaluation, Istanbul, Turkey (2012)

Briscoe, T., Carroll, J.A., Watson, R.: The second release of the RASP system. In: Proceedings of the COLING/ACL 2006 Interactive Presentation Sessions, Sydney, Australia, pp. 77–80 (2006)

Butler, A.: From discourse to logic with stanford CoreNLP and treebank semantics. In: Sakamoto, M., Okazaki, N., Mineshima, K., Satoh, K. (eds.) JSAI-isAI 2019. LNCS (LNAI), vol. 12331, pp. 182–196. Springer, Cham (2020). https://doi.org/10.1007/978-3-030-58790-1_12

Butler, A.: Meaning representations from treebanks. The Treebank Semantics Web Site (2021). http://www.compling.jp/ajb129/ts.html

Dekker, P.: Dynamic Semantics. Studies in Linguistics and Philosophy, vol. 91. Springer, Dordrecht (2012). https://doi.org/10.1007/978-94-007-4869-9

Dyvik, H., et al.: NorGramBank: a 'Deep' treebank for Norwegian. In: Proceedings of the Tenth International Conference on Language Resources and Evaluation (LREC 2016), pp. 3555–3562. European Language Resources Association (ELRA), Paris (2016)

Flickinger, D., Zhang, Y., Kordoni, V.: DeepBank: a dynamically annotated treebank of the wall street journal. In: Proceedings of TLT-11, Lisbon, Portugal (2012)

Hockenmaier, J., Steedman, M.: CCGbank: user's manual. Technical report MS-CIS-05-09, Department of Computer and Information Science, University of Pennsylvania, Philadelphia (2005)

Kamp, H., Reyle, U.: From Discourse to Logic: Introduction to Model-theoretic Semantics of Natural Language, Formal Logic and Discourse Representation Theory. Kluwer, Dordrecht (1993)

Kifer, M., Lausen, G., James, W.: Logical foundations of object-oriented and frame-based languages. J. ACM (JACM) **42**, 741–843 (1995)

Kifer, M., Yang, G., Wan, H., Zhao, C.: ERGO Lite (a.k.a. Flora-2): user's manual, Version 2.0. Technical report, Department of Computer Science, Stony Brook University, Brook, NY 11794–4400, U.S.A (2020)

Kitaev, N., Cao, S., Klein, D.: Multilingual constituency parsing with self-attention and pre-training. In: Proceedings of the 57th Annual Meeting of the Association for Computational Linguistics (ACL 2019), Florence, Italy, pp. 3499–3505 (2019)

Manning, C.D., Surdeanu, M., Bauer, J., Finkel, J.R., Bethard, S., McClosky, D.: The stanford CoreNLP natural language processing toolkit. In: Proceedings of the 52nd Annual Meeting of the Association for Computational Linguistics: System Demonstrations, pp. 55–60 (2014)

Marcus, M., Santorini, B., Marcinkiewicz, M.A.: Building a large annotated corpus of English: the penn treebank. Comput. Linguist. **19**(2), 313–330 (1993)

Moot, R.: A type-logical treebank for French. J. Lang. Modell. **3**(1), 229–265 (2015)

Nelson, G., Wallis, S., Aarts, B.: Exploring Natural Language: Working with the British Component of the International Corpus of English. John Benjamins, Amsterdam (2002)

Nonnengart, A., Rock, G., Weidenbach, C.: On generating small clause normal forms. In: Kirchner, C., Kirchner, H. (eds.) CADE 1998. LNCS, vol. 1421, pp. 397–411. Springer, Heidelberg (1998). https://doi.org/10.1007/BFb0054274

Quirk, R., Greenbaum, S., Leech, G., Svartvik, J.: A Grammar of Contemporary English. Longman, London (1972)

Quirk, R., Greenbaum, S., Leech, G., Svartvik, J.: A Comprehensive Grammar of the English Language. Longman, London (1985)

Sampson, G.R.: English for the Computer: The SUSANNE Corpus and Analytic Scheme. Clarendon Press/Oxford University Press, Oxford (1995)

Santorini, B.: Annotation manual for the penn historical corpora and the PCEEC (Release 2). Technical report, Department of Computer and Information Science, University of Pennsylvania, Philadelphia (2010). http://www.ling.upenn.edu/histcorpora/annotation

Schuster, S., Manning, C.D.: Enhanced English universal dependencies: an improved representation for natural language understanding tasks. In: Proceedings of the Tenth International Conference on Language Resources and Evaluation (LREC 2016), pp. 2371–2378. European Language Resources Association (2016)

Sutcliffe, G.: The TPTP problem library and associated infrastructure: the FOF and CNF Parts, v3.5.0. J. Autom. Reason. **43**(4), 337–362 (2009)

The Explicated Addressee: A (Mainly) Pragmatic Account of Japanese *ka*-Questions

Regine Eckardt[1]([✉]) and Eva Csipak[2]

[1] Konstanz University, Konstanz, Germany
Regine.Eckardt@uni-konstanz.de
[2] University of British Columbia, Vancouver, Canada
Eva.Csipak@uni-konstanz.de, eva.csipak@ubc.ca

Abstract. Japanese *ka*-questions have been described in the literature as always requesting honorific markers, unless they are used as self-addressed questions. Self-addressed questions are marked with the evidential modal *daroo*. This evidential has a polite counterpart *desyoo* which is used in declaratives and questions if the addressee is of higher rank or addressed formally. This is surprising at first sight, as the notion of addressing another person with a self-addressed question seems paradox. We argue that (a) *daroo* questions are not just questions to oneself, and that (b) *ka*-questions are not just polite questions. Instead, we propose that *ka* introduces a requirement that the addressee of the utterance must be explicated, i.e., explicitly mentioned in the utterance, and that honorific morphemes are one way of explicating the addressee. This correctly predicts that anti-honorific pronouns can also license *ka*-questions. Finally, we show how the grammatical marking of *ka*-questions coheres with the question prosody (final fall or rise).

Keywords: Self-addressed question · Evidentials · Honorification · Antihonorifics · Explicated addressee · Prosody

1 Introduction

Questions are typically directed to an addressee as requests for information. Yet, interrogatives can also be used in non-canonical questions, such as rhetorical questions, self-addressed questions or exam questions. Independently, many languages use honorification to express the social relation between speaker and addressee. In Japanese *ka*-questions, however, these two pragmatic phenomena are interrelated in a complex system of question type and addressee honorification. Japanese is a *wh-in-situ* language where questions are marked by sentence final particles. The particle *ka* marks polar and constituent interrogative clauses. Miyagawa (2012) draws attention to the fact that information seeking questions require honorification (HON) marking.

© Springer Nature Switzerland AG 2021
N. Okazaki et al. (Eds.): JSAI-isAI 2020 Workshops, LNAI 12758, pp. 50–65, 2021.
https://doi.org/10.1007/978-3-030-79942-7_4

(1)   Taro-wa   sushi-o   tabe-mas-u   ka
       Taro-TOP sushi-ACC eat.HON.PRES ka
       'Does Taro eat sushi?' Information seeking question (IsQ)

(2)   *Taro-wa   sushi-o   taberu   ka
       Taro-TOP sushi-ACC eat.PRES ka
       unavailable: 'Does Taro eat sushi?' (IsQ)

The verbal morpheme *mas* conveys that the speaker and addressee are engaged in distanced discourse or that the addressee is socially superior to the speaker.[1] While the "polite" information seeking question in (1) is acceptable, leaving out the honorific *mas* renders the question ungrammatical.

Yokoyama (2013) points out that *ka*-interrogatives without HON marking is felicitous in non-information-seeking utterances, for example in rhetorical or self-addressed questions. His example (3) shows a rhetorical *ka*-question without HON marker.

(3)   (Konna tokoro-ni) dare-ga   kuru ka
       like.this place-to   who-NOM come ka
       'Who would come (to a place like this)?' (= 'Nobody would come.')

Sentence (3) is a felicitous rhetorical question in a context where the speaker can assume that all interlocutors agree on the answer. Lacking *mas*, it is unacceptable as an information seeking question. Yokoyama lists seven possible interpretations for *ka*-interrogatives without honorification, which he labels as +assertive, as opposed to information seeking questions (IsQ) which he labels -assertive.

Oguro (2017) focuses on self-addressed questions marked with the evidential modal *daroo* and its polite counterpart *desyoo*. The following questions can be interpreted as self-addressed questions.

(4)   Taro-wa   sushi-o   taberu   daroo ka
       Taro-TOP sushi-ACC eat.PRES daroo ka
       'I wonder whether Taro eats sushi.' (talking to oneself)

(5)   Taro-wa   sushi-o   taberu   desyoo   ka
       Taro-TOP sushi-ACC eat.PRES daroo-HON ka
       'I wonder whether Taro eats sushi.' (conjecturing in the presence of a higher person)

Example (4) confirms the observation that self-addressed *ka*-questions do not require honorification, but (5) demonstrates that self-addressed questions can still acknowledge the presence of higher-ranked interlocutors. Moreover, Oguro diagnoses a second, IsQ interpretation for (5) but not for (4). In sum, Japanese *ka*-questions exhibit complex correlations of syntactic and pragmatic factors that

---

[1] We use the terms 'socially inferior' and 'superior' and 'distanced' vs. 'informal' discourse to refer to the social relations triggering the use of honorifics. See McCready (2019) for the complex social facts mirrored by the use of honorifics in Japanese.

we aim to analyse. Specifically, we want to model how *ka* triggers HON-marking in ISQ but not in other speech acts, how *daroo* forces questions to be interpreted as self-addressed questions, and how the two factors interact in the uses of *desyoo*.

In earlier literature, Miyagawa, Yokoyama and Oguro pursue an analysis of these data in syntactic terms, building on the extended speech act phrase (SAP) first proposed in Speas and Tenny (2003). While their idea – that a question in the absence of an addressee must be self-addressed – has some plausibility, the semantic underpinnings remain unclear. The present paper aims to cast the basic ideas in a semantic/pragmatic account. We agree with earlier authors that the presence of HON marking makes the addressee 'visible' in the sentence, but argue that this visibility can be captured in semantic terms. Specifically, we claim that the property of being an *explicated addressee* is crucial in understanding the nature of information seeking and self-addressed *ka*-questions.

The paper is structured as follows: Sect. 2 presents the data, and Sect. 3 briefly recapitulates earlier theories. Section 4 presents our analysis, and Sect. 5 concludes.

2   The Data

2.1   Japanese *ka*-Questions and Honorification

Japanese questions with the question marker *ka* can express information-seeking questions (ISQs), as in the following example. In this speech act type, they require the presence of a honorification marker.

(6)   Taro-wa   sushi-o   tabe-mas-u   ka
      Taro-TOP sushi-ACC eat.HON.PRES ka
      'Does Taro eat sushi?' Information seeking question (ISQ)

(7)   *Taro-wa   sushi-o   taberu   ka
      Taro-TOP sushi-ACC eat.PRES ka
      unavailable: 'Does Taro eat sushi?' (ISQ)

While (6) is HON-marked by the verbal morpheme *mas*, (7) lacks HON marking. As a consequence, native speakers judge (7) as unacceptable in the ISQ reading (Miyagawa 2012: 87). The requirement is dismissed when the question is intended as a rhetorical question, as (8-a) illustrates.

(8)   Context: Some Japanese teens agree that Italian style food is better than anything else, in particular better than traditional Japanese dishes. One of them says:
      a.   Dare-ga   sushi-o   taberu   ka
           who-NOM sushi-ACC eat.PRES ka
           'Who eats sushi, after all?' (implied: Nobody does.)

(8) can be interpreted as a rhetorical question, whereas an ISQ interpretation is unavailable.[2]

Yokoyama (2013) lists seven possible interpretations for *ka*-interrogatives without honorification: rhetorical questions, conjectural questions (marked with *ka naa* or *daroo*, often also with a nominalizer -*no*), wh-exclamatives, polar interrogatives as self-addressed confirmatives, polar interrogatives as strong resistives ('I will not do X'), polar imperatives and embedded questions (see Sect. 2.2). He moreover points out that **prosody** correlates with question type: While ISQ are pronounced with a final rise as *ka*↗, all other question types require a final fall *ka*↘. Yokoyama therefore proposes two homonyms *ka*: In ISQ we find *ka*↗, which he terms -assertive, as opposed to *ka*↘ in all other interrogatives, which he terms +assertive. His findings cohere with the prosodic study in Hara (2012), where she demonstrates a correlation between ISQs and final rising accent, as opposed to self-addressed questions and falling accent (see Sect. 2.3.). We adopt Yokoyama's homonyms and annotate examples with rise/fall in the following. We leave aside for now the question whether a general theory of final rise and fall can be given for Japanese. Likewise, we will focus on *ka*-questions with *daroo*/ *desyoo*, disregarding Yokoyama's full range of non-questioning acts with unspecific *ka*.[3]

Oguro (2017) finally observes that *ka*-questions can be ISQs without a HON marker if the addressee is expressed elsewhere in the sentence, for instance by using a pronoun.

(9)   Omae-wa sushi-o   taberu ka↗
       You-TOP sushi-ACC eat   ka
       'Do you eat sushi?' possible ISQ

(10)   Omae-wa nani(-o)   taberu ka↗
       you-TOP what(-ACC) eat   ka
       'what do you eat?' possible ISQ

The pronoun *omae* is an anti-honorific form of 'you', used for instance by school teachers to pupils, pet owners to their pets, male adults to kids, and also by boyfriends to girlfriends, husbands to wives. The examples suggest that *ka* in ISQs cannot be a politeness marker, as *omae* is only used in very informal, colloquial register. The use of *omae* alone suffices to satisfy the requirement imposed by *ka* that the addressee must be visible. If the informal pronoun *omae* is replaced by formal *anata* 'you', HON marking is also required on the verb. Yokoyama (2013: 7) offers the following example.

(11)   Anata-wa   shutubasi-mas-u   ka ↗
       you.HON-TOP run.for.election-HON ka
       'Will you run for the election?', ISQ

---

[2] More restrictions obtain for felicitous rhetorical questions, and we observe that not every *mas*-free *ka*-question can be used in a rhetorical sense. This deserves further investigation.

[3] As each of these speech act types is marked by further cues, we conclude that *ka* alone doesn't suffice to specify the intended sense of a non-HON clause.

While the doubly HON marked question (11) is acceptable, the sentence without *mas* is ungrammatical. This shows that the formal *anata* 'you' imposes its own independent requirement that the verb must be HON marked. The correlation is confirmed by the use of copula *des-u* vs. *da* ('be'). (12-a) repeats Yokoyama's (2017, ex.20).[4]

(12) a. Anata-wa   isha   des-u   ka ↗
          you.HON-TOP doctor Cpl.HON ka
          'Are you a doctor?' ISQ
      b. *Omae-wa isha   des-u   ka
          you-TOP doctor Cpl.HON ka
      c. *Omae-wa isha   da ka
          you-TOP doctor Cpl ka
          unavailable: 'Are you a doctor?'

Formal *anata* requires the use of the formal copula *desu*, which would be incompatible with *omae*. The neutral copula *da* imposes its own restrictions on the kind of speech acts in which it can be used – the ISQ (12-b) cannot be rendered grammatical by replacing *des-u* by *da*. We have to leave this part of the data to be investigated in the future. Yet, we take (9) and (10) as evidence that the requirements of ISQ *ka* – that the addressee be visible in the sentence – can be satisfied by the use of a second person pronoun without honorification.

2.2 Honorification is a Root Clause Phenomenon

Languages with a *tu/vous* system use pronouns as carrier of social information. For example, German *Du* is used to address friends or family, whereas *Sie* is chosen in many workplace contexts, between interlocutors of social distance or in official discourse. Formal pronouns can (and indeed must) be used in all syntactic positions. Japanese exhibits a different system, in that the use of honorific morphemes on the verb is restricted to root clauses. This restriction includes embedded *ka*-questions.

(13) Hanako-wa   Taro-ga   nani-o   taberu ka(-o)   shitteiru.
      Hanako-TOP Taro-NOM what-ACC eat   ka(-ACC) know
      'Hanako knows what Taro eats'

(14) *Hanako-wa   Taro-ga   nani-o   tabe-mas-u ka shitteiru.
      Hanako-TOP [Taro-NOM what-ACC eat-HON   ka] know
      ungrammatical: 'Hanako knows what Taro eats'

(15) Hanako-wa   Taro-ga   sushi-o   taberu ka shitteiru.
      Hanako-TOP [Taro-NOM sushi-ACC eat   ka] know
      'Hanako knows whether Taro eats sushi'

(16) *Hanako-wa   Taro-ga   sushi-o   tabe-mas-u ka shitteiru.
      Hanako-TOP [Taro-NOM sushi-ACC eat-HON   ka] know
      ungrammatical: 'Hanako knows whether Taro eats sushi'

---

[4] We don't annotate prosody whenever either version of the question would be ungrammatical.

As (14) and (16) show, Hon marking in embedded clauses is prohibited for any matrix predicate and independently of whether the embedded clause is case marked with *-o* (ACC). It is also independent of the pragmatic point of the utterance: indirect questions or directives cannot use mas in embedded contexts even if the speaker intends to request information from the addressee. This is shown in (17)–(19).

(17)   [Dare-ga   race-ni   ka-tta(*-mas)-ka] mite-mi-yoo!
       [who-NOM race-OBJ win-PST-KA]   find.out-try.to.MOD
       Let's find out who won the race!

(18)   [Dare-ga   race-ni   ka-tta(*-mas)-ka] oshie-te!
       [who-NOM race-OBJ win-PST-KA]   tell-IMP
       Tell me who won the race!

(19)   [Dare-ga   race-ni   ka-tta(*-mas)-ka] gimon-ni-omou/shiri-tai.
       [who-NOM race-OBJ win-PST-KA]   question-DAT-think/know-want.to
       I wonder/want to know who won the race

These data challenge Oguro's judgement that *-mas-* is sometimes possible in embedded contexts, illustrated by (20) (Oguro 2017:195, (18a)).

(20)   Dare-ga   ki-masu   ka sirabemasyoo
       who-NOM come-Hon ka check.let's
       'Let's check who will come.'

Without aiming at a comprehensive syntactic discussion of this type of example, we conjecture that (20) might be a bi-clausal structure, consisting of a matrix *ka* question ('Who comes?') and a subjectless second clause ('let's check.'). The prosodic structure remains to be investigated, including the issue whether the rising accent on *ka* in (20) might be missing for phonological reasons, thus leading Oguro to assume a mono-clausal structure.

We follow earlier syntactic analyses of root clause phenomena and assume that the prohibition of Hon morphemes in embedded clauses is regulated in syntax. A minimal way to implement root clause restrictions has been proposed in Bayer and Obenauer 2011) who assume that the highest CP level is dominated by ForceP. Honorific morphemes must be sufficiently syntactically close to ForceP to be licensed. We do not assume that ForceP makes an independent contribution to meaning. In Sect. 4, we assume that *ka* takes highest scope at LF, which is compatible with the assumption that it gets interpreted in ForceP at LF.

2.3   *Daroo/Desyoo* in Declaratives and Questions

The evidential modal *daroo/desyoo* can be used both in declaratives and interrogatives. *Ka*-interrogatives with *daroo* or its +Hon counterpart *desyoo* are one important type of self-addressed questions in Japanese. In order to understand the interaction of question type and honorification, we first illustrate the use of *daroo/desyoo* in declaratives.

(21)   Taro-wa sushi-o   taberu daroo.
        Taro.wa sushi.acc eat   daroo
        decl: 'I assume that Taro eats sushi.' (in informal discourse)

(22)   Taro-wa sushi-o   taberu desyoo.
        Taro.wa sushi.acc eat   desyoo
        decl: 'I assume that Taro eats sushi.' (in formal discourse)

Daroo combines with a proposition p and indicates that the speaker believes p but doesn't have first-hand knowledge. Oguro (2017); Uegaki and Roelofsen (2018) use $ASSUME(x,p)$ to paraphrase the contribution of *daroo* and we use their paraphrase in the translations above. Hara and Davis (2013) delineate the semantic content of *daroo* more precisely. *daroo* p conveys that speaker x infers p from general expectations about the world. The authors contrast this to *youda* p which expresses that the speaker has direct evidence which leads her to infer p. To give an example, *Taro-wa sushi-o taberu daroo* is appropriate when the speaker believes that Taro generally loves sushi so much that he almost always eats sushi. *Taro-wa sushi-o taberu youda*, in contrast, expresses that the speaker has specific direct evidence that suggests Taro eating sushi – e.g., a sushi delivery box in front of Taro's door.

These observations align *daroo/youda* with evidentials in other languages (Aikhenvald 2004; Faller 2006; Korotkova 2017; SanRoque et al. 2017). In particular, *daroo*, like other evidentials, is oriented to the speaker: the assertion p is justified by the speaker's beliefs and inferences. We use $ASSUME(x,p)$ as a suitable cover term for the content of *daroo*, as it explicates speaker orientedness.

Daroo in questions triggers a reading as self-addressed question. Speakers report the intuition that the question is uttered in the absence of an addressee (Oguro 2017; Hara 2012) and observe that the question doesn't request an answer or is conjectural. The question us uttered with a fall accent on sentence-final *ka*.

(23)   Taro-wa   sushi-o   taberu daroo ka↘
        Taro-TOP sushi-ACC eat   daroo ka
        'I wonder whether Taro eats sushi.' (SAQ)

(24)   Dare-ga   sushi-o   taberu daroo ka↘.
        who-NOM sushi-ACC eat   daroo ka
        'I wonder who eats sushi.' (SAQ)

(25)   Taro-wa   nani-o   taberu daroo ka↘.
        Taro-TOP what-ACC eat   daroo ka
        'I wonder what Taro eats.' (SAQ)

Daroo can be used in polar and constituent questions with the same pragmatic effect, as illustrated in (25)–(25). The same questions can also be used with honorific *desyoo*. At first sight, this seems at odds with the fact that (25)–(25) are self-addressed questions. Yokoyama diagnoses that such questions indeed have two readings, while their *daroo* counterpart is unambiguous.

(26)   Taro-wa   sushi-o   taberu desyoo ka\.
        Taro-TOP sushi-ACC eat   desyoo ka
        a. 'I wonder whether Taro eats sushi.' (SAQ)
        b. 'Does Taro eat sushi? What do you think?' (FlipQ)

Uttering (26), the speaker could ask a self-addressed question and at the same time acknowledge the presence of a socially superior interlocutor. Alternatively, she can pose the question to a socially superior interlocutor, granting them that the answer may rest on assumptions instead of secure knowledge. The (b) interpretation corresponds to the 'flip-reading' of evidentials in questions that has been described for many other languages (SanRoque et al. 2017; Eckardt 2020). We abbreviate it as FlipQ. The ambiguity also arises in constituent questions.

(27)   Dare-ga   sushi-o   taberu desyoo ka\.
        who-NOM sushi-ACC eat   desyoo ka
        a. 'I wonder who eats sushi.' (SAQ)
        b. 'Who eats sushi? What do you think?' (FlipQ)

The speaker in (27) can either wonder who eats sushi, at the same time indicating that she is aware of the presence of an interlocutor. Or she can intend the FlipQ reading and invite the interlocutor to volunteer their assumptions about Q.

In summary, we see that *ka*-questions can be true questions iff some morpheme explicates the addressee – be it a honorific, or an anti-honorific. According to our informant, vocatives can also serve this purpose. ISQ *ka* carries a rising accent. Questions with *ka* that lack an explicated addressee can be self-addressed or code other speech acts. In this case, *ka* carries a falling accent. *Daroo-ka* questions are always self-addressed, and *desyoo-ka* questions can be self-addressed or ask for the addressee's opinion. These are the data we aim to account for.

3   Earlier Theories

Syntax Based Accounts. Miyagawa, Yokoyama and Oguro pursue an analysis of these data in syntactic terms, building on the extended speech act phrase (SAP) first proposed in Speas and Tenny (2003). The presence or absence of a SpeakerPhrase as part of the SAP is assumed to correspond to the presence or absence of HON marking. This structural contrast is proposed to have repercussions on the grammaticality of *ka* in questions (in an ISQ sense), the interpretation of *daroo/desyoo* and the choice of *ka* in the +assertive sense (Yokoyama 2013).

While we grant that the authors can correctly predict the data in question, this type of approach leaves several foundational issues unaddressed. For one, the connection between speech act type and honorification seems essentially a pragmatic phenomenon which should be treated in terms of a pragmatic theory. While there are excellent general accounts of honorification in Japanese and other Asian languages (McCready 2014, 2019; Potts and Kawahara 2004), the link between question type and honorification has so far only been discussed in Korean (Jang 1999; Eckardt and Disselkamp 2019). Eckardt and Disselkamp show that the Korean data can be captured in a purely pragmatic analysis. While Japanese poses a more complex case, it would still be interesting to see whether a pragmatic analysis is also possible.[5]

Speas and Tenny suggest that the presence or absence of Speaker Phrase and Hearer Phrase is somehow rooted in pragmatics, or corresponds somehow to facts about the utterance context. Jang (1999) assumes that the absence of a Hearer Phrase "leads to" the interpretation as self-addressed question. Yokoyama (2013) stipulates in passing that the use of a second person pronoun in the clause triggers the presence of a Hearer Phrase in syntactic structure. Oguro presupposes that Hearer Phrase is semantically interpreted, referring to the addressee in context. Yet, while the idea that a question in the absence of an addressee must be self-addressed certainly has some plausibility, it is by no means trivial to put these remarks on solid semantic ground.

An Interface Theory. Portner et al. (2019) propose a treatment of Korean honorifics at the syntax-semantics interface, which potentially extends to Japanese. Their account codes speaker-addressee relations in two ways. For one, they represent sentence meanings by centered propositions, i.e., sets of tuples of speaker, addressee, time and possible world, as illustrated below.

(28) $[[$ I love you $]]^u$
$$= \{< x, y, t, w >: x = sp(u) \wedge y = ad(u) \wedge t = time(u) \wedge x \; loves \; y \; in \; w\}.$$

This replaces the standard set of possible worlds, and allows to track speaker and addressee as part of the meaning of the sentence. Secondly, sentence and discourse meanings include a participant structure to code honorification. In a discourse between two interlocutors P1, P2, the participant structure contains the tuple <P1, P2> of interlocutors, an ordered set $<M, \leq >$ and a function h that maps {P1, P2} into M. In each utterance, honorifics specify the function h_u in u. For instance, if u includes a honorific to express that P1 is socially higher than P2, then h_u maps {P1, P2} into M accordingly $(h_u(P2) \leq h_u(P1))$. The function h can change from utterance to utterance when speakers in Korean re-calibrate the social signals over discourse.

As we saw in Sect. 2, *ka*-questions are not just "polite" questions but questions that require an explicated addressee. Portner et al.'s account keeps a record of Hon marking but doesn't trace whether the addressee is explicated in the present utterance u. If there are no new Hon morphemes, the participant structure of the previous utterance is maintained. Therefore, the account does not extend to the case of *ka*-questions straightforwardly.

---

[5] We acknowledge that Hon marking can have syntactic repercussions, such as subj-verb agreement or restrictions to root clauses.

Semantic Theories. Starting with Hara (2006), Yurie Hara explores various semantic/pragmatic accounts for *daroo*. Closest to our analysis is Hara and Davis (2013), which we will apply below. Her most recent approach in Hara (2018) treats the data in terms of inquisitive semantics. She assumes that 'daroo T' expresses that the speaker entertains issue T, which can be a question or an assertion. For questions T, this predicts the SAQ interpretation, but fails to leave room for the Flip interpretation we see in honorific *desyoo* questions like (26). Building on her work, the present paper aims to fill this gap. Another attractive feature of Hara (2012) is the independent pragmatic contribution of a final rise accent, which is treated as a meaningful unit in its own right. We however do not fully understand how final rise can be blocked for *desyoo* questions (which can address a second person), nor whether the ideal analysis should predict this blocking, We comment on relevant data at the end of Sect. 4.4.

4   Analysis

Our analysis rests on the idea that *ka*-questions can only request an answer if the addressee is explicitly mentioned in the clause. And this is the case iff a honorific marker, or a pronoun have been used. Self-addressed $ka\searrow$ questions are not requesting this. In particular *daroo*-questions are necessarily interpreted as self-addressed for this reason, while *desyoo*-question, with an explicated addressee, allow for more readings.

4.1   The Explicated Addressee

We assume that honorifics and pronouns have the effect that the addressee of utterance u, made in context c, is explicitly mentioned. This is part of the denotations of *omae(-wa)* and HON in (29), which introduce the non-at-issue meaning $\text{EXPAD}(ad(c), u)$. We use $\bullet$ to notate two-dimensional meaning as $\langle$ at-issue content $\bullet$ non-at-issue content $\rangle$ (Potts 2005). We moreover use $x < y$ as a shorthand for "x is in a socially lower or distanced relation to y", in the sense that warrants the use of HON, and inverse anti-honorifics.

(29)   a. If interpreted as part of utterance u in context c,
            $[[\text{HON } p]]^c = \langle p \bullet \text{EXPAD}(ad(c), u) \rangle$. Presupposition: $sp(c) < ad(c)$.
            b. If interpreted as part of utterance u in contect c,
            $[[omae]]^c = \langle ad(c) \bullet \text{EXPAD}(ad(c), u) \rangle$.
            Presupposition: $ad(c) < sp(c)$.

We build on Potts' immediacy property for expressive content (Potts 2007). He observes that expressive content is not "asserted" in the sense that the assertion could also be false. Instead, saying so makes it so (Austin 1962), and the use of honorifics or anti-honorifics suffices to make the non-at-issue content true, as repeated in (30).

(30) $\text{EXPAD}(x, u)$ is true iff there is at least one morpheme in the sentence uttered in u that contributes the non-at-issue content $\text{EXPAD}(x, u)$.

The ExpAd relation is thus a meta-linguistic relation between persons and utterance events in the real world. If Mizuki asks question (1) to Yuzu, then Yuzu acquires a new property ExpAd(Yuzu,u), in addition to the properties that she had before. If Mizuki didn't ask the question, Yuzu would not have this property. Likewise if Mizuki asks the rhetorical question (3) instead, Yuzu does not have the property of being an explicated addressee. Given that ExpAd relates persons to specific utterances u, we predict that the property of being explicated in u is short-lived and must be re-established in every new assertion or question u. This also seems correct. The next subsection spells out how information seeking questions with $ka \nearrow$ rely on an explicated addressee, and in what respect non-information-seeking questions $ka \searrow$ are different.

4.2   Asking a *ka* question

We propose that the morpheme $ka \nearrow$ takes highest scope over questions Q. If the question is uttered u in context c, $ka \nearrow$ expresses the speaker intention that $sp(c)$ requests $ad(c)$ to give an answer. $ka \nearrow$ presupposes that the addressee is an explicated addressee in the ongoing utterance u. If used in utterance u, uttered in context c:

(31)   If used in utterance u, uttered in context c:
$[[ka \nearrow]]^c = \lambda Q.\langle Q \bullet sp(c) \text{ requests } x \text{ to answer } Q\rangle.$
Presupposition: $\text{ExpAd}(x, u)$.

The presupposition of $ka \nearrow$ cannot be accommodated. This is a reasonable assumption, as the presupposition is about the linguistic form of the question uttered. If the question does not contain HON, a pronoun or a vocative, the hearer cannot be requested to accommodate that it did.[6] This entry (31) thus ensures that the use of $ka \nearrow$ is only semantically warranted in a sentence where the addressee is explicated. Given the short-livedness of 'being ExpAd', we make sure that explicated addressees of previous utterances are not available. We follow Yokoyama in assuming that ka in embedded questions does not convey a request for an answer. Given that $ka \nearrow$ must take highest scope over the sentence (e.g. by interpreted in ForceP at LF), syntactic structure prohibits the use of $ka \nearrow$ in embedded sentences.

We propose that the counterpart $ka \searrow$ is a question marker that does not contribute further pragmatic or semantic content.

(32) $[[ka \searrow]]^c = \lambda Q.\langle Q \bullet \phi\rangle$ where ϕ are the speaker intentions that are contributed by other cues.

We leave the possibility unexplored whether $ka \searrow$ together with other cues can be a complex pragmatic marker and might contribute speaker intentions, as described in Yokoyama (2013).

---

[6] Similarly strict presuppositions have been described e.g. for additive markers *too*, *also*.

4.3 *Daroo*: Orientation and Honorification

We propose that *daroo* takes scope over the prejacent S and contributes the non-at-issue meaning that x assumes S. In declaratives, x must be the speaker, as well as in self-addressed questions. And we must ensure that *desyoo*-questions allow for the second, FLIP interpretation. This second reading is obviously triggered by the explicated addressee (i.e. an utterance u with $\text{ExpAd}(ad(c), S, w)$) but unavailable otherwise. This is captured by the following definitions.

(33)   If used in utterance u and context c
         $[[daroo]]^c = \lambda p.\langle p \bullet ASSUME(x, p, w)\rangle$
         Presupposition: $x = sp(c) \vee \text{ExpAd}(x, u)$.
         The value of x is determined by anaphor resolution. It must either be the speaker or an explicated addressee in the ongoing utterance.

Moreover, we adopt Korotkova (2014)'s AUTHORITY PRINCIPLE for evidential *daroo*. Korotkova uses the principle for reports of taste experiences, building on Kaufmann's Authority principle in the semantics of imperatives.

(34)   AUTHORITY PRINCIPLE for the evidential ASSUME: Only the holder of the attitude A has the authority to assert the relation $ASSUME(A, p, w)$.

In declarative sentences S, *daroo* composes with $[[S]]^c$. The subject of ASSUME must be the speaker $sp(c)$, as the speaker would not be authorized to make assertions about the addressee's mental attitudes.

For questions Q we adopt a Hamblin semantics and assume the standard point-wise composition of *daroo* with the propositions in $[[Q]]$. In questions, then, the instantiation of A in $ASSUME(A, p, w)$ depends on (a) whether the question is self-addressed and (b) whether the addressee has been explicated (*desyoo*), the pronoun *omae*, other pronouns, vocatives) or not. The predicted readings are listed in the next subsection.

4.4 Predictions

Firstly, we predict the contrast in (6)/(7). In a question with HON marking the addressee has the property $\text{ExpAd}(ad(c), u)$ presupposed by *ka* $\nearrow$ and the question is well-formed. Due to *ka*, it requests an answer. Alternatively, the presuppositions of *ka* $\nearrow$ can be satisfied by the use of *omae* (9) (10) or a vocative. Without any item to explicate the addressee, *ka* $\nearrow$-questions are ill-formed due to presupposition failure as in (7).

We did not spell out a full analysis of rhetorical questions like (3), (8-a). Yet we do predict that *ka* $\searrow$ does not impose a presupposition that the addressee be explicated. Hence the analysis is open to be extended by cues that mark rhetorical *ka* questions.

Next let us turn to the predictions for *daroo*. In declaratives *daroo S*, like (21), the evidential modal adds the non-at-issue content $ASSUME(x, p, w)$, where x remains to be specified. In a declarative, we must choose the speaker, and the overall sentence in context c denotes: $\langle [[S]]^c \bullet \text{ASSUME}(sp(c), [[S]]^c, w)\rangle$. We cannot choose $ad(c)$, as this would violate the authority principle. The same holds true for *desyoo* in declaratives, as in (22).

What happens if *daroo* is used in a $ka \searrow$-question as in (23), (24)? For one, there is no presupposition that the addressee be explicated, so the question is not ruled out due to presupposition failure. We first compute the Hamblin semantics of question Q and then combine point-wise with the evidential modal.

(35) $[[daroo\ Q\ ka \searrow]]^c = \{\langle p \bullet \text{ASSUME}(sp(c), p, w)\rangle : p \in [[Q]]^c\}.$

We predict that the only choice for the subject of ASSUME is $sp(c)$. The lexical entry for *daroo* requests that any subject x of ASSUME that is not the speaker can only be an explicated addressee. In result, then, the questions in (35) put up a set of possible answers p, each one with the non-at-issue comment that the speaker $sp(c)$ assumes that p be true. But only the speaker is authorized to provide that specific non-at-issue comment, due to the authority principle. We argue that this entails that the speaker can only pose this question to herself. It would be irrational to request answers from addressees that they are not authorized to give.[7]

We finally turn to *desyoo* in questions Q with $ka \searrow$, as in (26), (27). We assume that *desyoo* is composed of *daroo* and the HON morpheme, which compose with Q in turn. We thus get the following question denotation in utterance u and context c.

(36) $[[daroo\ HON\ Q\ ka \searrow]]^c =$
         $\{\langle p \bullet \text{ASSUME}(x, p, w), sp(c) < ad(c), \text{EXPAD}(ad(c), u)\rangle : p \in [[Q]]^c\}.$

Note that the subject of ASSUME, x has to be instantiated yet. In the present case, there are two possible choices. We can have $\text{ASSUME}(sp(c), p, w)$ by default, or else we can choose $\text{ASSUME}(ad(c), p, w)$, as the addressee is explicated in (36). This leads us to the following two readings for (26), (27).

(37) $[[daroo\ HON\ Q\ ka \searrow]]^c =$
         $\{\langle p \bullet \text{ASSUME}(sp(c), p, w), sp(c) < ad(c), \text{EXPAD}(ad(c), u)\rangle : p \in [[Q]]^c\}.$

(38) $[[daroo\ HON\ Q\ ka \searrow]]^c =$
         $\{\langle p \bullet \text{ASSUME}(ad(x), p, w), sp(c) < ad(c), \text{EXPAD}(ad(c), u)\rangle : p \in [[Q]]^c\}.$

The denotation in (37) expresses a self-addressed question, by the same reasoning as the denotation in (35). The denotation in (38), however, puts up a set of possible answers which only the addressee is authorized to answer. Only the addressee can felicitously put up the non-at-issue content that s/he has evidence to assume p, for any of the possible answers p to Q. The content of this kind of question can therefore be felicitously paraphrased as "what is the answer to

---

[7] We leave it open for now whether $ad(c)$ is not a possible source for a self-oriented speech act of $sp(c)$, or whether we should, more conservatively, class it as assertions without authority.

Q, what do you think?", which matches with the paraphrases for the second reading provided by Oguro (2017). This reading moreover corresponds to the Flip-question interpretation for questions with evidentials described elsewhere in the literature (SanRoque et al. 2017). We observe that questions like (26), (27) invite the addressee to answer, even though they are marked with $ka \searrow$, the non-demanding version of ka. We assume that its unspecific content is compatible with a speech act that invites an answer, but does not force one.

Interestingly, some authors mention that the use of $ka \nearrow$ in $daroo$-questions is possible, if they are intended as quiz questions, exam questions or socratic questions (Hara 2012; Oguro 2017). In discussions with native speakers, we got mixed comments on these. Some agree that $desyoo$-ka questions with a final rise can be used in these kinds of context. Others object that the rise in quiz questions differs prosodically from the rise in ISQs. We therefore have to leave these data aside for the moment. Yet our theory predicts that a question $desyoo$ Q with $ka \nearrow$ should instantiate the subject x in $ASSUME(x, p, w)$ with $ad(c)$ – given that $ka \nearrow$ requests the addressee to answer, and the addressee is an authority only on her own assumptions. Indeed it would be adequate to nuance quiz, Socratic and exam questions as "questions about the belief of the addressee". In contexts of this kind, the speaker knows the answer already and wants to find out whether the addressee maintains the correct belief. Using a Flip question is therefore rational. Admittedly, however, the pattern is in part arbitrary as not all speakers necessarily answer every exam or quiz question on basis of their inferential evidence. We thus conjecture that quiz questions exhibit a conventionalized pattern rather than being fully compositional.

5   Summary

We propose an analysis of Japanese ka ISQ and SAQ in terms of semantics and pragmatics. We assume that HON morphemes make the addressee of the utterance visible, which we capture with the relation EXPAD. Answer-requesting $ka \nearrow$ requires an explicated addressee, whereas neutral $ka \searrow$ does not. Neutral $ka \searrow$ is however compatible with an explicated addressee, which can pave the way for additional readings. Specifically, we predict that $desyoo$-ka questions can have a reading that invites the addressee to answer (Flip-reading) whereas $daroo$-ka questions cannot. Thus, linking the orientation of the modal evidential to speaker or explicated addressee, we successfully predict the data reported in the literature. Given that our lexical entries make heavy use of indexicals and non-at-issue meaning, we label the analysis as "pragmatic". We hedge it as "mainly" pragmatic, as we must leave some aspects of honorifics in questions to syntax (Sect. 2.2.). However, our account shows how the syntactic stipulation of Speaker Phrase and Hearer Phrase as part of the Speech Act Phrase Tenny (2003) can be replaced by the semantic/pragmatic property of being an explicated addressee.

Acknowledgements. Research for this paper was funded by the DFG in project P05 'Self-Addressed Questions', part of the RU 2111 'Questions at the Interfaces', Konstanz. We want to thank Katsuko Yatsushiro, Naoya Fujikawa, Chen-An Chang,

Ryan Bochnak and the audience of the SPAGAT workshop at Berlin 2020 for valuable comments and advice. Particular thanks are due to Mizuki Satoh for sharing her native intuitions and providing data without ever loosing her good mood.

References

Aikhenvald, A.Y.: Evidentiality. Oxford University Press, Oxford (2004)

Austin, J.: How to do Things with Words, 2nd edn. In: Urmson, J.O., Sbisá, M. (eds.) Cambridge MA, Harvard University Press (1962)

Bayer, J., Obenauer, H.G.: Discourse particles, clause structure, and question types. Linguist. Rev. **28**(4), 449–491 (2011). https://doi.org/10.1515/tlir.2011.013

Eckardt, R.: Conjectural questions: the case of German verb-final 'wohl' questions. Semant. Pragmatics **13**(9), 1–47 (2020)

Eckardt, R., Disselkamp, G.: Self-addressed questions and indexicality: the case of Korean. In: Proceedings of SUB, Barcelona, vol. 23, pp. 383–398 (2019)

Faller, M.: Evidentiality below and above speech acts. Semantics Archive (2006)

Hara, Y.: Non-propositional modal meaning. Semanticsarchive (2006). https://www.semanticsarchive.net/Archive/WUxZjFiM/darou_hara.pdf. Accessed July 2018

Hara, Y.: On the interaction among sentence types, bias, and intonation: a rating study. In: Proceedings of GLOW in AsiaIX, Poster Session (2012)

Hara, Y.: Daroo as an entertain modal: an inquisitive approach. Japanese/Korean Linguist. **25**, 1–13 (2018)

Hara, Y., Davis, C.: Darou as a deictic context shifter. In: Yatsushiro, K., Sauerland, U. (eds.) Formal Approaches to Japanese Linguistics 6, pp. 41–56. MIT, Boston (2013)

Jang, Y.: Two types of question and existential quantification. Linguistics **37**(5), 847–869 (1999). https://doi.org/10.1515/ling.37.5.847

Korotkova, N.: Evidentials in attitudes: do's and don'ts. In: Csipak, E., Zeijstra, H. (eds.) Proceedings of SuB 19, pp. 320–337 (2014)

Korotkova, N.: Diagnosing the semantic status of evidentials. In: Talk at the Workshop Questioning Speech Acts, University of Konstanz (2017). http://nkorotkova.net/files/korotkova2017-qsa-abstract.pdf

McCready, E.: A semantics for honorifics with reference to Thai. In: Proceedings of PALIC, vol. 28, pp. 503–512 (2014)

McCready, E.: The Semantics and Pragmatics of Honorification. Register and Social Meaning. Oxford University Press, Oxford (2019)

Miyagawa, S.: Agreements that occur mainly in the main clause. In: Aelbrecht, L., Haegeman, L., Nye, R. (eds.) Main Clause Phenomena, Benjamins, Amst., pp. 79–111 (2012)

Oguro, T.: Speech act phrase, conjectural questions, and hearer. In: Proceedings of the 40th Annual Penn Linguistics Conference (2017)

Portner, P., Pak, M., Zanuttini, R.: The speaker-addressee relation at the syntax-semantics interface. Language **95**(1), 1–36 (2019)

Potts, C., Kawahara, S.: Japanese honorifics as emotive definite descriptions. In: Young, R. (ed.) Proceedings of SALT 14, pp. 253–270 (2004)

Potts, C.: The expressive dimension. Theor. Linguist. **33**(2), 165–198 (2007)

SanRoque, L., Floyd, S., Norcliffe, E.: Evidentiality and interrogativity. Lingua **186**(187), 120–143 (2017)

Speas, P., Tenny, C.: Configurational properties of point of view roles. In: DiScullio, A. (ed.) Asymmetry in Grammar I, Benjamins, Amst., pp. 315–344 (2003)

Uegaki, W., Roelofsen, F.: Do modals take propositions or sets of propositions? Evidence from Japanese darou. In: Proceedings of SALT, vol. 28, pp. 809–829 (2018)

Yokoyama, T.: Re-evaluating the 'question' marker ka in Japanese. In: Proceedings of the 2013 Annual Conference, Canadian Linguistic Association, pp. 1–15 (2013)

Superlative Modifiers as Concessive Conditionals

Shun Ihara[1]([✉])[iD] and Kenta Mizutani[2][iD]

[1] Graduate School of Intercultural Studies, Kobe University, Kobe, Japan
[2] Department of British and American Studies, Aichi Prefectural University,
Nagakute, Japan

Abstract. This paper offers a new compositional semantics of the superlative modifier *sukunakutomo* 'at least' in Japanese. The notable feature of this expression is that it does not utilize a superlative morpheme. How does *sukunakutomo* derive the superlative meaning, then? The main goal of this paper is to provide the answer to this question, while capturing the diverse behavior of superlative modifiers. Focusing on the decompositionality of *sukunakutomo*, we suggest that the meaning of this expression is essentially a concessive conditional with a focus to a contextually supplied degree. The analysis supports the view that *at least*-expressions have only one denotation, and moreover contributes to providing a strategy for deriving the superlative meaning.

Keywords: Superlative modifiers · Ignorance inference · At least · Concessive conditionals · Japanese

1 Introduction

Sentences with superlative expressions such as *at least* are known to give rise to *ignorance inferences* of the speaker. In (1), for example, the speaker asserts that it is the case that John came to the party, but is uncertain as to who else came besides John.

(1) A: Who came to the party?
     B: At least John came.
        ⤳ the speaker is uncertain as to who else came besides John.

To explain the behavior of superlative modifiers, previous studies have proposed a variety of approaches. The modal analysis proposed by Geurts and Nouwen [13] utilizes a modal operator which is encoded in the lexical semantics of *at least*. Büring [5] alternatively proposes the disjunction analysis that

We would like to thank Eri Tanaka, Hideharu Tanaka, Yusuke Kubota, and the audience at LENLS17 for providing us valuable comments. This work was supported by JSPS KAKENHI (Grant Number 20J00175). All errors are of course our own.

N. Okazaki et al. (Eds.): JSAI-isAI 2020 Workshops, LNAI 12758, pp. 66–81, 2021.
https://doi.org/10.1007/978-3-030-79942-7_5

attributes ignorance inferences of *at least* to a pragmatic reasoning: the inference could arise via Gricean reasoning from the disjunctive semantics of the expression (cf. Cummins and Katsos [10], Biezma [4]). Building on the idea of Büring, Coppock & Brochhagen [9] also offer the disjunctive semantics to the semantics of *at least* in terms of inquisitive semantics (Ciardelli, Groenendijk & Roelofsen [7]). Nouwen [23] classifies modified numerals into two separate classes (class A and B), and superlatives are in class B that denote a lower-bound degree, e.g., *from, minimally*.

Despite the existence of such a wide variety of approaches, we will not adopt any of the directions for our analysis. Alternatively, we offer a compositional approach of superlative modifiers by focusing on the Japanese *sukunakutomo*, which is sometimes considered to be the counterpart of *at least* (cf. Hirayama & Brasoveanu [16]).

(2) Sukunakutomo Taro-ga kita   yo.
     at.least   T-NOM   came DP
     'At least Taro came to the party'.

The notable feature of this expression is that, unlike *at least* (which is considered to be the spell-out of '*at [little+est]*'), it does not utilize a superlative morpheme or inflection.[1] What does the superlative meaning of *sukunakutomo* stem from, then?

The goal of this paper is to provide the answer to this question, while capturing the diverse empirical facts of the superlative modifiers. Our analysis based on the compositional nature of *sukunakutomo* indicates that the meaning of *sukunakutomo* is essentially a concessive conditional in the sense that it contains *even* as its conditional antecedent. We argue that this proposal provides the most empirically successful account of *sukunakutomo* to date.

The rest of this paper is structured as follows. Section 2 provides an overview of existing studies on superlative modifiers and presents data on their empirical issues that arise when they are applied to *sukunakutomo*. Section 3 introduces the ingredients to be used in our analysis and then illustrates how the meaning of *sukunakutomo* is derived in a compositional way. Section 4 attempts to capture the core data at issue, and Sect. 5 provides further predictions that support our claim. Section 6 is the conclusion with theoretical and empirical implications for the study of superlative modifiers.

2   Previous Approaches

In this section, we provide brief backgrounds of the theories of superlative modifiers, which we believe are necessary to support our proposal. Here, for the

---

[1] To the best of our knowledge, Chen [6] and Coppock [8] are the only works that attempt to offer a detailed decompositional analysis of English *at least*. In particular, Chen proposes that *at least* can be structurally decomposed into three morphological pieces: a quantity adjective *much*, a superlative *-est* and an existential operator (See also Coppock's [8] treatment). Refer to Chen ([6], 238–243) to see how the composition goes on.

purpose of this study, we mainly focus on two approaches: the modal approach and the disjunction approach. We evaluate these two approaches in view of what they predict with regard to the data of *sukunakutomo*, and show that neither theory alone is sufficient to explain these data in a unified way.

2.1   Modal Approach

Geurts and Nouwen [13] give two lexical entries for *at least*: one modifies a proposition, and one modifies a modifier.

(3)   a. If α is of type t (a propositional argument),
$[\![$ at least $\alpha\,]\!] = \Box\alpha \wedge \exists\beta\,[\,\beta \rhd \alpha \wedge \Diamond\beta\,]$,
where $\rhd$ is a precedence relation.

b. If α is of type $\langle a, t\rangle$ where a is any type (a predicative argument),
$[\![$ at least $\alpha\,]\!] = \lambda X\,[\,\Box\alpha(X) \wedge \exists\beta\,[\,\beta \rhd \alpha \wedge \Diamond\beta(X)\,]\,]$ ([13]: 543)

(4)   *Taro had at least three beers.*
$\Box\exists x\,[\,\#(x) = 3 \wedge \mathsf{beer}(x) \wedge \mathsf{had}(T, x)\,] \wedge \Diamond\exists x\,[\,\#(x) > 3 \wedge \mathsf{beer}(x) \wedge \mathsf{had}(T, x)\,]$

Crucially, they treat the ignorance effect of *at least* as part of its lexical semantics. The presence of an epistemic possibility modal explains the fact that sentences with *at least* (and *at most*) convey ignorance on the part of the speaker. On their theory, comparative modifiers, unlike superlative modifiers, do not signal epistemic possibility, which explains the contrast between superlative and comparative modifiers with respect to the ignorance inference.

Let us first suppose that *sukunakutomo* has the same semantics as *at least* proposed in Geurts & Nouwen, $[\![$ at least $]\!] = [\![$ sukunakutomo $]\!]$. As Geurts & Nouwen themselves admit, this line of analysis fails to account for conditionalized and negated examples, as shown in (5) and (6).

(5)   Sukunakutomo san-hai biiru-o   nonde-tara, Hanako-wa
at.least   3-CL   beer-ACC drink-then H-TOP
yottei-ta.
get.drunk-PAST
'If Hanako had had at least three beers, she would have been drunk.'

(6)   Hanako-wa biiru-o   sukunakutomo san-hai(-wa) nom-anakat-ta.
H-TOP   beer-ACC at.least   3-CL(-TOP)   drink-NEG-PAST
'Hanako didn't have at least three beers.'

The reading that Geurts & Nouwen's theory predicts for (5) is "if it *must* be the case that Hanako had three beers, and it *may* be that she had more than three, then she would have been drunk", which is not what the sentence means. Moreover, what the sentence in (6) implies is "it's not the case that Hanako had three beers, and the amount was *at most* two beers". However, the reading that their theory predicts for (6) is "it's not the case that Hanako must have had three beers, and (at the same time) it's not the case that she may have had more than three beers". Again, this goes against our intuition, and there is no way this line of analysis will capture the correct reading ([13], §10).

It is worth noting that in Geurts & Nouwen, the necessity operator is posited mainly in order to feed a process of modal concord. However, the need of such a process has been questioned in Büring [13] and Nouwen [23]. Geurts & Nouwen also motivate the necessity operator with a symmetry argument referring to *at least*'s negative partner *at most*, but Japanese *sukunakutomo* lacks such an explicit partner.[2]

Another study that makes use of a modal as the interpretation of superlative modifiers is the work of Nouwen [23], who proposes that *at least* stands for the lower bound modifier. He argues that an epistemic possibility modal for the speaker is introduced into the interpretation of sentences with superlative modifiers through a "reinterpretation" process. As Coppock & Brochhagen [9] point out, however, it is not clear how this reinterpretation process works or under what circumstances it applies. Moreover, since his analysis only deals with the numerical cases, it does not account for the non-numerical case like (2).

2.2   Disjunction Approach

Büring [13], building on Krifka [20], proposes that *at least* is interpreted as a disjunction operator over scalar alternatives. According to his proposal in (7), *at least* amounts to a disjunction between the prejacent and its higher-ranked alternatives.

(7)   a. $[\![\text{at least } \alpha]\!] = [[\![\alpha]\!] - \bigcup \text{ABOVE}(\alpha)] \vee \bigcup \text{ABOVE}(\alpha)$

   b. $\text{ABOVE}(\alpha) = \bigcup\{O' \mid \langle \alpha, O' \rangle \in [\![\alpha]\!]^A\}$,
        where $[\![\alpha]\!]^A$ is the alternative semantic value of α.

(8)   *Taro had at least three beers.*
     $[[\![\text{had}(T, 3\,beers)]\!] - \bigcup \text{ABOVE}([\![\text{had}(T, 3\,beers)]\!])] \vee$
     $\bigcup \text{ABOVE}([\![\text{had}(T, 3\,beers)]\!])]$

Informally speaking, the example in (8) means "Taro had exactly three beers OR Taro had more than three beers".

---

[2] At first glance, *ookutomo* 'at most' in Japanese appears to be the counterpart to *sukunakutomo*, but it differs from *sukunakutomo* in that while *sukunakutomo* can be used in non-numerical contexts, *ookutomo* can be used only in the numerical contexts:

(i)   Sukunakutomo   kare-wa   isha-da.   (Dakara kanemoti-da.)
     at.least   he-TOP   doctor-COP   so   rich-COP
     'He is at least a doctor. (So he is rich.)'

(ii) *Ookutomo   kare-wa   tada-no   isha-da.   (Meii-de-wa   nai.)
     at.most   he-TOP   only-GEN doctor-COP   a.highly.skilled.doctor-COP-TOP NEG
     'He is only a doctor at best. (He's not a highly skilled doctor.)'

The contrast may be derived from the difference in the lexical semantics of *sukunai* 'little' and *ooi* 'many' in Japanese, which will be a subject for future study.

Büring's proposal differs crucially from the one of Geurts & Nouwen in that his analysis derives all modal aspects of the meaning of *at least* from pragmatic implicatures. According to Büring, the particular conversational implicature in (9) arises when uttering sentences with *at least*. (9) expresses the Gricean intuition that one doesn't use a disjunction if one is certain of the truth of any individual conjunct.

(9)   If a speaker utters p or q, it is implied that (i) in all of the speaker's doxastic alternatives $p \vee q$ and (ii-a) not in all p, and (ii-b) not in all q. Büring ([5]: 114)

Take the sentence in (8) for example. According to the schema in (9), the sentence implies that (i) the speaker is certain that Taro had three beers, and (ii-a) she is not certain that Taro had exactly three beers, and (ii-b) she is not certain that Taro had more than three beers.

A problem of Büring's approach is that sentences containing *at least* expressions are obviously not disjunctive on the level of surface form.[3] For instance, the disjunction theory is problematic in a context where the speaker has perfect knowledge about the truth of alternatives.

(10)   (The speaker does not want the addressee to know exactly how many points the speaker scored, because she knows that the addressee is likely to have scored more than her.)

A: What was your score on yesterday's exam?

B: Sukunakutomo gookakuten-no   rokuju-ten-wa tot-ta   yo.
    at.least   passing.score-GEN 60-CL-TOP   get-PAST DP
    'I got at least a passing score of 60.'

B′#Gookakuten-no   rokuju-ten-wa tot-ta   ka, aruiwa motto
    passing.score-GEN 60-CL   get-PAST or either   more
    tot-ta   ka da   yo.
    get-PAST or COP DP
    'I scored a passing score of 60 or higher than that.'

If a sentence with *sukunakutomo* is interpreted as a disjunction in a surface level, the utterance by B′ in (10) should be accepted, contrary to the fact that they are not. Then, what does it mean to say that *at least* amounts to a disjunction?

Coppock & Brochhagen [9] point out that it is not at the level of *denotation* that the sentence with *at least* is disjunctive for some conceptual reasons. While keeping the idea of Büring that disjunction is a core of the meaning of sentences with *at least* and that the ignorance effect is a pragmatic inference, Coppock & Brochhagen propose that a solution for the problems is to treat *at least* as *a proposition* including the prejacent and the higher-ranked possibilities in terms of inquisitive semantics (Ciardelli, Groenendijk & Roelofsen [7]). That

---

[3] Coppock & Brochhagen [9], too, are aware of this problem ([9]: 18), but do not provide clear counterexamples.

is, they argue that *at least* sentences have something in common with disjunctions, without resorting to the claim that there is any level of representation at which they *are* disjunctions. Technically, *at least(p)* denotes the set containing all possibilities p' such that p' is at least as strong as p according to the pragmatic strength ranking over answers to the QUD (Question under Discussion; Roberts [24]).[4] The denotation of *At least Ann snores* based on their analysis is represented as follows. (The detailed framework/notations and calculation process are discarded here).

(11) $[\![$ At least $[\text{Ann}]_\text{F}$ snores $]\!]^s = \{a, ab\}$,
       where s is a state, a is 'Ann snores', b is 'Bill snores', and ab is 'Ann and Bill snore'.

In (11), since the focus-marking on *Ann* ensures that the QUD concerns who snores, we can assume that the possible answers are a, b, and $a\&b$. Here, the *at least* sentence entails 'Ann snores', because both a and $a\&b$ share the same informational content 'Ann snores'. At the same time, the sentence is inquisitive in that it has a possibility of $a\&b$, which explains why the sentence gives rise to the ignorance implicature that it is possible that b.

The problem with their analysis is that they do not make clear how to distinguish between *at least* sentences and sentences containing disjunction expressions (e.g., *or, either*). More specifically speaking, the framework of inquisitive semantics translates the sentence with disjunctions "Ann snores OR both Ann and Bill snore" as $\{a, ab\}$, which is exactly the same as the one in (11), which ends up predicting that "At least Ann snores" and "Ann snores or both Ann and Bill snore" have the same meaning. Thus, their analysis requires a further explanation of how sentences with disjunctions can be analyzed in terms of inquisitive semantics, and how that analysis can capture the difference in behavior between *at least* sentences and sentences containing disjunctions.

2.3   Summary

From the discussion above, we conclude that the meaning of *sukunakutomo* should not be represented in terms of neither modals nor disjunctions. Let us summarize the fact to be accounted for in this paper as follows. (i) Ignorance inference: *sukunakutomo* gives rise to the ignorance inference, but the meaning should be represented without making use of modals. (ii) Embedding under conditionals and negations: again, the modalized interpretation of *sukunakutomo* goes against our intuition when embedded under conditionals and negations. (iii) Distribution: *sukunakuotmo* can modify a range of expressions, not just numerals, and are acceptable in contexts in which a speaker knows the truth

---

[4] We will not cover their detailed analysis here for reasons of space. Refer to Coppock & Brochhagen ([9], §3) for the relevant discussion.

of all relevant alternatives. Our proposal to be put forth in the next section is empirically successful in capturing these facts.[5]

3   Proposal

In this section, we propose a new analysis from a perspective that has not received much attention in previous studies on superlative modifiers. Instead of treating the Japanese superlative modifier *sukunakutomo* as a fully lexicalized expression, we highlight a decompositionality of this expression and offer a compositional semantics which derives its meaning. Specifically, the denotation of *sukunakutomo* is morphologically broken down into *sukunai* 'little', a conditional morpheme *to*, and *mo* 'even': $[\![\text{sukunakutomo}]\!] = [\![\text{sukunai}_{little}]\!] + [\![\text{to}_{conditional}]\!] + [\![\text{mo}_{even}]\!]$. In this line of analysis, the core meaning of *sukunakutomo* is no longer the modal or the disjunctive semantics, but rather is a *concessive conditional* that composes of a conditional morpheme and *even*. We show in this section that the notion of concessive presupposition is the key of deriving the superlative meaning without superlative morphemes.

3.1   Ingredients

This section introduces the semantics of the individual pieces that compose *sukunakutomo* for the analysis.

First, *sukunai* is simply interpreted as *few* or *little* as in (12). For concreteness, we represent the interpretation of *sukunai* in the system of Kennedy [18], according to which the exact interpretation (here, *exactly* a 'small' amount) involves a degree quantifier incorporating the MAX-operator.

(12) $[\![\text{sukunai}]\!]^{c,w} = \lambda D_{\langle d,t \rangle}.\text{MAX}_d(D) = \mathbf{d}_\Delta$,
       where D is a set of degrees and $\mathbf{d}_\Delta$ is a small value relative to a context
       c.

(13)   a.   *Taro-ga non-da sake-no ryoo-wa sukunai.*
            'The amount of sake that Taro drunk is "small".'

---

[5] Büring [13] and Coppock & Brochhagen [9] argue that (what they call) the speaker insecurity readings and the authoritative readings are also the data which should be explain. As Büring points out, the sentence with *at least* under deontic necessity modal is ambiguous:

(i)   The paper has to be at least 10 pages long.

The sentence has both the authoritative reading, on which it informs the interlocutor what the acceptable page lengths are, speaking as the authority on the subject, and the speaker insecurity reading, on which the speaker does not know what the required length of the paper is, but believes it to be over 10 pages. Looking at the data in Japanese, however, it is doubtful whether these readings are really a matter of the interaction between the superlative modifier and the modal. (We will not present a relevant example for the sake of space, but sentences with necessity modals seem to give both readings without *sukunakutomo*.) For this reason, we will not treat the data regarding to the two readings in this paper.

b. $[\![(13a)]\!]^{c,w} = [\![\,\mathsf{sukunai}\,]\!]^{c,w}([\![\,\text{the amount of beer that Taro drunk}\,]\!]^{c,w})$
   $= [\lambda D.\mathrm{MAX}_d(D) = \mathbf{d}_\Delta](\lambda d.\exists x.[\mathsf{beer}(x) \wedge \mathsf{drunk}_w(T, x) \wedge \mu(x) = d])$
   $= \mathrm{MAX}_d(\lambda d.\exists x.[\mathsf{beer}(x) \wedge \mathsf{drunk}_w(T, x) \wedge \mu(x) = d]) = \mathbf{d}_\Delta$

According to the semantics that we have in (12), the sentence in (13) conveys the meaning that the (maximal) amount of beer that Taro drunk is equal to the amount that we judge to be "small" in that context.

We assume a *to*-conditional as a prototypical conditional construction (Akatsuka [1]). Following the Kratzerean analysis of conditionals (Kratzer [19]), *to* introduces a covert necessity operator to derive the conditional meaning. The definition in (14) amounts to saying that in all the worlds (according to the conversational background f_c) in which p is true, q is true.

(14) a. $\mathsf{to}_{conditional}(p)(q) \rightsquigarrow \mathrm{NEC}_w[p][q]$
   b. $[\![\,\mathrm{NEC}_{to}\,]\!]^{c,w} = \lambda p.\lambda q.\forall w' \in \bigcap f_c^*(w) : q(w')$,
      where $f_c^*(w) = f_c(w) \cup \{[\![\,p\,]\!]\}$

(15) a. *Sake-o nomu to, Taro-wa yopparau.*
      'If Taro drinks, he gets drunk.'
   b. $[\![(15a)]\!]^{c,w}$
      $= [\lambda p.\lambda q.\forall w' \in \bigcap f_c^*(w) : q(w')]([\![\,\text{Taro drinks}\,]\!])([\![\,\text{Taro gets drunk}\,]\!])$,
         where $f_c^*(w) = f_c(w) \cup \{[\![\,p\,]\!]\}$
      $= \forall w' \in \bigcap f_c^*(w) : [\![\,\text{Taro gets drunk}\,]\!](w')$,
         where $f_c^*(w) = f_c(w) \cup \{[\![\,\text{Taro drinks}\,]\!]\}$

What the example in (15a) says is that in all the best worlds in which 'Taro drinks' is true, 'he gets drunk' is true. Roughly speaking, when it is the case that Taro drinks, it must be the case that he gets drunk.

Following Nakanishi [21], the focus particle *mo* is assumed to be *even*, which ranks the alternatives by correlating them with a graded property which is salient in the context (Gianakidou [14]).[6] *Mo* as *even*, which is defined as (16), is used to claim that the associated graded property w.r.t. the context holds to a degree that is lower than those of the alternatives.

(16) $[\![\,\mathsf{mo}_{even}\,]\!]^{c,w} = \lambda p.p(w) \wedge \partial[\forall q \in \mathit{Alt}_p : q \neq p \rightarrow p \prec_c q]$,
      where ∂ is a presupposition operator (Beaver [3]) and $\prec_c$ stands for 'less than' relation with respect to the contextually given scale.

(17) a. $[Roku\text{-}nin]_F$-*mo kita*. 'Even six people came.'
   b. $[\![(17a)]\!]^{c,w}$
      $= [\lambda p.\,p(w) \wedge \partial[\forall q \in \mathit{Alt}_p : q \neq p \rightarrow p \prec_c q]]([\![\,\text{six people came}\,]\!]^{c,w})$
      $= [\mathsf{came}_w(six\,people)](w) \wedge$
      $\partial[\forall q \in \mathit{Alt}_p : q \neq [\mathsf{came}_w(six\,people)] \rightarrow$
      $\hspace{6cm} [\mathsf{came}_w(six\,people)] \prec_c q\,]$,
      where $\prec_c = \prec_{likelihood}$.

---

[6] Note that *mo* also corresponds to additive particles like *also* or *too*. This study exclusively assumes that *sukunakutomo* is a case where *mo* plays a role as *even*.

c. $\mathcal{A}lt_p = \{\, \mathsf{came}_w(six\,people), \mathsf{came}_w(five\,people),$
$\mathsf{came}_w(four\,people), \mathsf{came}_w(three\,people), ...\}$

In (17), the relation $\prec_c$ is resolved to the unlikelihood relation in terms of the number of people coming. (17) is true iff (i) it is the case that six people came, and (ii) it is presupposed that six people's coming is less likely than { five people's, four people's, three people's, ... } coming.

3.2 Deriving *At Least* Without Superlative Morpheme

Given the semantic ingredients introduced in the last section, we are now in the position to derive the superlative meaning of *sukunakutomo*. We assume the simplified LF structure for the sentence with *sukunakutomo* in (18).

Before explaining the interpretation of this structure, it is necessary to add the following assumptions. First, *mo* is assumed to be a sentential operator that takes an entire sentence as its scope. This is motivated by the general fact that while a focus particle in Japanese (e.g., *mo, dake* 'only', *sae* 'even') appears as a postposition attached to a focused NP, the focus site can be wider than that NP (Aoyagi [2]).[7]

(18) Simplified LF of "*Taro-wa sukunakutomo san-hai sake-o non-da.*" 'Taro had at least three sakes.'

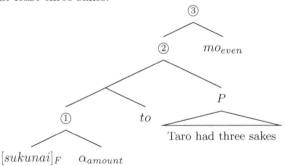

Second, the predicative *sukunai* in *sukunakutomo* takes a contextually determined (unpronounced) scalar anaphor α_{amount}, in (18), $\alpha_{amount} =$ 'the amount of sake that Taro had'. This assumption may seem strange at first glance, but it is reasonable in light of the analysis of relevant previous studies. For instance, Kayne [17] proposes that the English minimizer *little* is an expression that modifies an unpronounced AMOUNT. In this account, "John has a little money" is interpreted as "John has a little AMOUNT of money". Sawada [25] adopts this

---

[7] There would be at least two possible ways to explain this discrepancy between the interpretation in LF and the surface compositionality. One is to allow a LF-movement of focus particles (e.g., Futagi [12]). Another possibility is to assume that certain focus particles are associated with an alternative generating operator independently, and to assume that this operator takes a sentential scope (e.g., Tomioka [26]). Since what is important in this paper is that *mo* makes an alternatives with respect to the entire sentence of *sukunakutomo*, the reader may adopt either option.

view and proposes that the Japanese *sukoshi*, the adverbial counterpart of *suku-nai*, modifies an invisible AMOUNT predicate.

The derivations represented in ①–③ in (18) are as follows. The intuition that we have for (18) is as follows. Suppose that we are considering how much sake Taro had and taking into account various cases where the amount of sake that he had is "the least", "small", "neither small nor large", "large", "the largest", and so on. What (18) expresses is that in the case that the amount of sake that Taro had is 'the least', he had three sakes.

(19) a. $[\![①]\!]^{c,w} = [\![\,\mathsf{sukunai}\,]\!]^{c,w}([\![\,\alpha\,]\!]^{c,w})$
    $= [\lambda D_{\langle d,t\rangle}.\mathrm{MAX}_d(D) = \mathbf{d}_\Delta](\lambda d.\exists x.[\mathsf{sake}(x) \wedge \mathsf{had}_w(T,x) \wedge \mu(x) = d])$
    $= \mathrm{MAX}_d(\lambda d.\exists x.[\mathsf{sake}(x) \wedge \mathsf{had}_w(T,x) \wedge \mu(x) = d]) = \mathbf{d}_\Delta,$
    where $[\![\,\alpha\,]\!]^{c,w} = \lambda d.\exists x.[\mathsf{sake}(x) \wedge \mathsf{had}_w(T,x) \wedge \mu(x) = d].$

  b. $[\![②]\!]^{c,w} = [\![\,\mathsf{to}\,]\!]^{c,w}([\![①]\!]^{c,w})([\![\,P\,]\!]^{c,w})$
    $= \mathrm{NEC}_w \begin{bmatrix} [\mathrm{MAX}_d(\lambda d.\exists x.[\mathsf{sake}(x) \wedge \mathsf{had}_w(T,x) \wedge \mu(x) = d]) = \mathbf{d}_\Delta] \\ [\exists x.[\mathsf{sake}(x) \wedge \mathsf{had}_w(T,x) \wedge |x| = 3]] \end{bmatrix}$

  c. $[\![③]\!]^{c,w} = [\![\,\mathsf{mo}\,]\!]^{c,w}([\![②]\!]^{c,w})$
    $= [\lambda p.\, p(w) \wedge \partial[\forall q \in Alt_p : q \neq p \to p \prec_c q]]$

    $\left(\mathrm{NEC}_w \begin{bmatrix} [\mathrm{MAX}_d(\lambda d.\exists x.[\mathsf{sake}(x) \wedge \mathsf{had}_w(T,x) \wedge \mu(x) = d]) = \mathbf{d}_\Delta] \\ [\exists x.[\mathsf{sake}(x) \wedge \mathsf{had}_w(T,x) \wedge |x| = 3]] \end{bmatrix}\right)$
    $= \mathrm{NEC}_w \begin{bmatrix} [\mathrm{MAX}_d(\lambda d.\exists x.[\mathsf{sake}(x) \wedge \mathsf{had}_w(T,x) \wedge \mu(x) = d]) = \mathbf{d}_\Delta] \\ [\exists x.[\mathsf{sake}(x) \wedge \mathsf{had}_w(T,x) \wedge |x| = 3]] \end{bmatrix}$
    $\wedge\, \partial[\forall q \in Alt_② : q \neq [\![②]\!] \to [\![②]\!] \prec_c q],$
    where $\prec_c$ is resolved to less-than relation.

  d. $Alt_② = \left\{\begin{array}{l} \vdots \\ \text{[If the max-amount of sake that Taro had is } d_1 \prec_c \mathbf{d}_\Delta, \\ \qquad\qquad\qquad\qquad\text{then he had three sakes],} \\ \text{[If the max-amount of sake that Taro had is } d_2 = \mathbf{d}_\Delta, \\ \qquad\qquad\qquad\qquad\text{then he had three sakes],} \\ \text{[If the max-amount of sake that Taro had is } d_3 \succ_c \mathbf{d}_\Delta, \\ \qquad\qquad\qquad\qquad\text{then he had three sakes],} \\ \vdots \end{array}\right\}$

As an assertion, (19c) conveys that "if the amount of sake that Taro had is $\mathbf{d}_\Delta$, which is a small value to the context c, he had three sakes". Here, the truth of the consequent P "Taro had three sakes" is entailed; assuming that the antecedent exhausts all relevant possibilities, the assertion $\ulcorner mo_{even}$ if $[p]_F,\ P\urcorner$ will implicate the truth of the consequent P (von Fintel [11]: 147). At the same time, (19c) presupposes that "$\mathbf{d}_\Delta$ is the 'least' value among the focus alternatives". Since the focused element here is *sukunai*, the set of possible alternatives are calculated with respect to the amount of sake that Taro had, (19d). Putting the asserted and the presupposed meaning together, (19c) expresses that "if the amount of sake that Taro had is the least value, he had three sakes". This successfully captures our intuition about the sentence with *sukunakutomo*. The crucial point here is that, thanks to the existence of *mo*, we can ensure that the amount of sake that Taro had is not merely 'small' but 'the least' amount, without using the superlative morpheme.

In our analysis, the ignorance inference is generated pragmatically via a typical rule of conversation (Grice [15]).[8] For instance, in (19): (i) the speaker asserted that if the amount of sake that Taro had is the 'least' = 'small' amount, then he had three sakes; (ii) there are possible alternatives that the speaker could have made, i.e., [If the amount of sake that Taro had is more than the least (= small) amount, he had three sakes]. This intuitively means "we are considering some possibilities that Taro had more than the least amount, but in any case what the speaker is sure of is that he had three sakes"; (iii) from this, we can make an inference that there must be a reason for the speaker's asserting only one of the possible alternatives and not asserting the remaining. For example, the reason could be "she does not know the truth about how much more sake Taro drank than that amount", or "she just does not want to mention the other possibilities for personal reasons", etc.

It should be noted that while this analysis has in common with Büring [13] and Coppock & Brochhagen [9] in that it derives the ignorance effect of superlative modifiers at the level of pragmatics, it departs from their analysis in that the starting point that signals the inference is not the disjunctive semantics but the conditional semantics.

4   Explaining the Data

Let us first illustrate how to derive the data of *sukunakutomo* in conditionals and negations that we have identified as problematic for the modal analysis.

As for the conditional example in (5), since our analysis does not assume the modal meaning to be encoded in the semantics of *sukunakutomo*, it does not cause the problem in the interpretation that occurs under the modal analysis. That is, the truth conditions of *sukunakutomo* are simply added to the truth conditions of the antecedent part of the conditional. Technically, (5) is true when in all the worlds (according to the conversational background) in which the antecedent "Hanako had *sukunakutomo* three beers" is true, the consequent "she would have been drunk" is true. More intuitively, (5) expresses "If it is the case that Hanako had drunk three beers, and the amount was considered to be 'the least', then she would have been drunk".

The analysis also captures our intuition about the negated example in (6), whose interpretation is "the amount of beer that Hanako had is *at most* two".

(20)   a. *Hanako-wa biiru-o sukunakutomo san-hai nomanakat-ta.*
           'Hanako didn't have at least three beers.'

       b. LF: *mo* [$_P$ *to* [*sukunai$_F$* α], $\neg$[Hanako had three beers]],
           where $[\![\alpha]\!]^{c,w} = \lambda d.\exists x.[\mathsf{beer}(x) \wedge \mathsf{had}_w(H,x) \wedge \mu(x) = d]$.

---

[8] The analysis here is inspired by Tomioka [26], who argues that the ignorance inference of sentences with the contrastive topic *wa* in Japanese is pragmatically derived by Gricean rules of conversation.

c. $[\![(20a)]\!]^{c,w}$

$$= \mathrm{NEC}_w \begin{bmatrix} [\mathrm{MAX}_d(\lambda d.\exists x.[\mathsf{beer}(x) \wedge \mathsf{had}_w(H,x) \wedge \mu(x)=d]) = \mathbf{d}_\Delta] \\ [\neg \exists x.[\mathsf{beer}(x) \wedge \mathsf{had}_w(H,x) \wedge |x|=3]] \end{bmatrix}$$

$$\wedge \, \partial[\forall q \in \mathcal{A}lt_P : q \neq [\![P]\!] \rightarrow [\![P]\!] \prec_c q],$$

where $\prec_c$ is resolved to the less-than relation with respect to the amount of beer that one **does not** drink.

d. $\mathcal{A}lt_P = \left\{ p \,\middle|\, p = \begin{array}{l} \text{if the max-amount of beer that Hanako had is } d, \\ \text{she did not have three beers} : d \end{array} \right\}$

As represented above, the interpretation that our analysis predicts for (20a) is as follows. As an at-issue meaning, it conveys the conditional meaning that "if the amount of beer that Hanako had is 'small', she did not have three beers".[9] This implicates the truth of the consequent "Hanako did not have three beers", which implies that she did not have *more than* three beers. That is, the amount of beer that Hanako had is *at most* two beers. By the contribution of *mo*, the presupposition of the sentence ensures that the amount of beer that Hanako had is the least amount in terms of the amount of beer that one does not drink.

What about the cases of the example where the speaker has a perfect knowledge about the truth of alternatives (cf. (10))? Crucially, in our analysis, the ignorance inference induced by a sentence with *sukunakutomo* is not limited to the epistemic inference that the speaker does not know about the truth of the alternatives, which captures the fact that the use of *sukunakutomo* is fine in (10). In (10), the conversational inference that we can obtain from the utterance is that the speaker might have some personal reason for not mentioning about the alternative scores; here, she just does not want to tell the addressee the exact score that she got.

Thus far, we have dealt with examples with numerals. Consider the basic case in (21a) below, which dose not involve numerals. The interpretation here is that the speaker is certain that Taro came but is uncertain about whether people other than Taro came or not. The proposed analysis can easily derive this interpretation.

(21) a. *Sukunakutomo Taro-ga kita.* 'At least Taro came to the party.'

b. LF: *mo* [$_P$ *to* [*sukunai$_F$* α], [Taro came]]

---

[9] Under our analysis, since *sukunakutomo* is semantically a conditional and its prejacent (e.g., in (20a) 'Hanako didn't have three beers') is assumed to be the consequent clause, a negation in *sukunakutomo(p)* must apply to the consequent part in parallel with ordinary conditionals:

(i) Asu-ga   ame nara, soto-de   asoba-**nai**.   (ordinary conditional)
     tomorrow-NOM rain then outside-at play-NEG
     'If it rains tomorrow, I won't spend my time outside.'
     ⤳ if it rains tomorrow, ¬(I will spend my time outside)
     ⤳̸ ¬(if it rains tomorrow, I will spend my time outside)

c. $[\![(21a)]\!]^{c,w} = \text{NEC}_w \begin{bmatrix} [\text{MAX}_d(\lambda d.\exists x.[\text{came}_w(T) \wedge |x| = d]) = \mathbf{d}_\Delta] \\ [\,\text{came}_w(T)\,] \end{bmatrix}$

$\qquad \wedge \, \partial[\forall q \in \mathcal{A}lt_P : q \neq [\![P]\!] \rightarrow [\![P]\!] \prec_c q\,],$

where $\prec_c$ is the less-than relation in terms of the number who came.

d. $\mathcal{A}lt_P = \left\{ \lambda p \, \middle| \, p = \begin{array}{l} \text{if the max-amount of people who came is } d, \\ \hfill \text{Taro came} : d \end{array} \right\}$

As shown in the truth conditions in (21c), (21a) asserts that if the amount of people who came is d_Δ, Taro came. In addition, d_Δ is presupposed to be the least among its alternatives. This in turn means that even when the amount of people who came is "1", Taro came, which is equivalent to saying that the speaker is certain that Taro came. Hence, the current analysis can successfully generate the correct truth conditions of cases with proper nouns.

5   Further Predictions

5.1 *Sukunakutomo* with ∀

Let us turn to some predictions of the current analysis. As we have argued above, *sukunakutomo* expresses that if the amount in question is the least, the consequent is true. This predicts that if the amount expressed by the matrix clause cannot be considered to be the least, the sentence become unacceptable. As shown below, this prediction is borne out.

(22) #Sukunakutomo zenin-ga   kita.
     at.least   everyone-NOM came
     '[Int.] At least everyone came.'

(22) involves the universal quantifier *zenin* 'everyone', which denotes the largest value in the quantity scale, and this example is unacceptable as expected. The reason is clear from the truth conditions below.[10]

(23) $[\![(22)]\!]^{c,w} = \text{NEC}_w \begin{bmatrix} [\text{MAX}_d(\lambda d.\exists x.[\text{people}(x) \wedge \text{came}_w(x) \wedge |x| = d]) = \mathbf{d}_\Delta] \\ [\,\forall x.[\text{people}(x) \rightarrow \text{came}_w(x)]\,] \end{bmatrix}$

$\qquad \wedge \, \partial[\forall q \in \mathcal{A}lt_{p^0} : q \neq [\![p]\!]^0 \rightarrow [\![p]\!]^0 \prec_c q\,]$

---

[10] Note that the sentence (22) is acceptable when the associated scale is not numerical/plural, i.e. the context is "concessive":

(i) Yuushou-wa nogashita ga sukunakutomo zenin-ga   kesshou   made
     victory-TOP missed   but at.least   everyone-NOM final.game to
     kita.
     came
     'We couldn't win, but at least we all made it to the final.'

In this case, the relevant set of alternative is represented with respect to the degree of success, rather than to the amount of people who came. Thus, the truth condition does not require that "if the amount of people who came is the least, everyone came", but rather that "if the the degree of success is the least, everyone came", which is possible to be true.

As shown above, the truth conditions require that if the amount of people who came is the least, everyone came. However, this is impossible, since the amount of people who came is the greatest if everyone came. Hence, these truth conditions cannot be satisfied, and the unacceptability arises.

5.2 *Mo* and Superlativity

Another empirical prediction is related to the presence of *mo* 'even'. In our analysis, the existence of *mo* ensures that we are considering the least case among alternatives even when there is no superlative morpheme. An anonymous reviewer, however, points out that *sukunakute* 'little + if', which lacks *mo*, can also express the same meaning as *at least*, as shown in (24). Based on this, the reviewer doubt that *mo* plays a crucial role in deriving the superlative meaning.

(24) Sukunakute san-nin-ga kita.
      little.if   3-CL-NOM came
      '[Int.] At least three people came.'

Although we agree with the reviewer's view that *sukunakute* can express a similar meaning with *sukunakutomo*, there is still evidence in favor of our claim. As the following example indicates, the superlative expression *ichiban* 'the most' can be used with *sukunakute* but not with *sukunakutomo*:

(25) Ichiban { sukunakute / #sukunakutomo } san-nin-ga kita.
      the.most { little.if   /   at.least   } 3-CL-NOM came
      'At least three people came.'

The above contrast can be captured if *sukunakutomo* has the least meaning thanks to the existence of *mo* and the superlative expression *ichiban* is redundant.[11]

---

[11] A problem with this line of analysis (in which *mo* 'even' contributes to adding the superlative meaning) is that another Japanese superlative expression *saitei-demo*, which consists of a superlative *sai*, *tei* 'low', and *demo* 'even if', may end up having a redundant meaning, since *saitei* 'lowest' itself denotes the superlative meaning (Yusuke Kubota, p.c.). Then the challenge for our account is to figure out the semantic contribution of *mo* in *saitei-demo*. We should identify, for instance, what difference there is between (i-a) and (i-b), namely *saitei* with and without *mo*:

(i) a. Saitei-de-mo san-nin kuru.
         lowest-if-even 3-CL will come
         'At least three people came.'

     b. Saitei(-de) san-nin kuru.
         lowest-(if) 3-CL come
         'At least three people will come.'

For us, intuitively (i-a) seems to have a stronger meaning than (i-b), but we don't have any linguistic evidence for this intuition at this moment. We hope readers can help us figure out what is going on here.

6   Conclusion

Unlike English *at least*, Japanese *sukunakutomo* is morphologically broken down into *little*, a conditional morpheme, and *even*, which contribute to providing a strategy for deriving the meaning of superlative modifiers.

Much work is still needed to determine factors affecting the availability of the different readings. As is well known, Nakanishi & Rullmann [22] observe that sentences containing *at least* have not only an epistemic reading, but also a concessive reading (e.g., "Mary didn't win a gold medal, but *at least* she won a silver medal"). The analysis of the concessive reading of *sukunakutomo* will be our future task, but since our framework assumes that scales and alternatives related to the interpretation of *mo* are context/discourse dependent, it would not be difficult to capture the relevant data by utilizing the flexibility, although some refinement may be required.

If our analysis of *sukunakutomo* is on the right track, it would support the view of Biezma [4] that 'at least' expressions have only one denotation, not two different denotations (cf. Nakanishi & Rullmann [22]). We take this as an indication that the next interesting/crucial question about superlative modifiers is not simply "What do they denote?", but rather "What are their semantic variations, and how are those variations distributed among natural languages?" (cf. Chen [6]).

References

1. Akatsuka, N.: Japanese modals are conditionals. In: Brentari, D., Larson, G.N., MacLeod, L.A. (eds.) The Joy of Grammar: A Festschrift in Honor of James D. McCawley, pp. 1–10. John Benjamins, Amsterdam (1992)
2. Aoyagi, H.: On association with focus and scope of focus particles in Japanese. In: Koizumi, M., Ura, H. (eds.) Formal Approaches to Japanese Linguistics, vol. 1, pp. 23–44. MITWPL, Cambridge (1994)
3. Beaver, D.I.: Presupposition and Assertion in Dynamic Semantics. CSLI Publications, Stanford (2001)
4. Biezma, M.: Only one at least: refining the role of discourse in building alternatives. In: University of Pennsylvania Working Papers in Linguistics, vol. 19. Penn Linguistics Club. (2013)
5. Büring, B.: The least at least can do. In: Chang, C.B., Haynie, H.J. (eds.) Proceedings of the 26th West Coast Conference on Formal Linguistics, pp. 114–120. Cascadilla Proceedings Project, Somerville (2008)
6. Chen, Y.-H.: Another look at superlative modifiers as modified superlatives. In: Espinal, M.T, Castroviejo, E., Leonetti, M., McNally, L., Real-Puigdollers, C. (eds.) Proceedings of Sinn und Bedeutung, vol. 23, no. 1, pp. 231–248 (2019)
7. Ciardelli, I., Groenendijk, J., Roelofsen, F.: Inquisitive Semantics. Oxford University Press, Oxford (2018)
8. Coppock, E.: Superlative modifiers as modified superlatives. In: Moroney, M., Little, C.-R., Collard, J. and Burgdorf, D. (eds.) Proceedings of Semantics and Linguistic Theory, vol. 26, pp. 471–488. University of Texas at Austin (2016)
9. Coppock, E., Brochhagen, T.: Raising and resolving issues with scalar modifiers. Semant. Pragmat **6**(3), 1–57 (2013)

10. Cummins, C., Katsos, N.: Comparative and superlative quantifiers: pragmatic effects of comparison type. J. Semant. **27**, 271–305 (2010)
11. von Fintel, K.: Restrictions on quantifier domains. Ph.D. Dissertation. University of Massachusetts (1994)
12. Futagi, Y.: Japanese focus particles at the syntax-semantics interface. Ph.D. Dissertation. Rutgers University (2004)
13. Geurts, B., Nouwen, R.: At least et al.: The Semantics of scalar modifiers. Language **83**, 533–559 (2007)
14. Gianakidou, A.: The landscape of even. Nat. Lang. Linguist. Theory **25**, 39–81 (2007)
15. Grice, P.: Logic and conversation. In: Cole, P., Morgan, J.L. (eds.) Syntax and Semantics 3: Speech Acts, pp. 41–58. Academic Press, New York (1975)
16. Hirayama, H., Brasoveanu, A.: Expressing ignorance in Japanese: contrastive wa versus sukunakutomo. J. Cogn. Sci. **19**, 331–355 (2018)
17. Kayne, R.S.: Movement and Silence. Oxford University Press, Oxford (2005)
18. Kennedy, C.: A "de-Fregean" semantics (and neo-Gricean pragmatics) for modified and unmodified numerals. Semant. Pragmat. **8**(10) (2015)
19. Kratzer, A.: Conditionals. Chicago Linguist. Soc. **22**, 1–15 (1986)
20. Krifka, M.: At least some determiners aren't determiners. In: Turner, K. (ed.) The Semantics/Pragmatics Interface from Different Points of View, pp. 257–291. Elsevier, Oxford (1999)
21. Nakanishi, K.: The semantics of even and negative polarity items in Japanese. In: Baumer, D., Montero, D., Scanlon, M. (eds.) Proceedings of WCCFL, vol. 25, pp. 288–296. Cascadilla Proceedings Project, Somerville (2006)
22. Nakanishi, K., Rullmann, H.: Epistemic and concessive interpretation of at least. In: CLA 2009 (2009)
23. Nouwen, R.: Two kinds of modified numerals. Semant. Pragmat. **3**(3), 1–41 (2010)
24. Roberts, C.: Information structure in discourse: towards an integrated formal theory of pragmatics. In: OSU Working Papers in Linguistics 49: Papers in Semantics, pp. 91–136. (1996)
25. Sawada, O.: Varieties of positive polarity minimizers in Japanese. Manuscript, Mie University (2016)
26. Tomioka, S.: Contrastive topics operate on speech acts. In: Zimmermann, M., Fèry, C. (eds.) Information Structure: Theoretical, Typological, and Experimental Perspectives, pp. 115–138. Oxford University Press, Oxford (2009)

Polynomial Event Semantics: Negation

Oleg Kiselyov(✉) [iD]

Tohoku University, Sendai, Japan
oleg@okmij.org

Abstract. Polynomial event semantics is an interpretation of Neo-Davidsonian semantics in which the thorny event quantification problem does not even arise. Denotations are constructed strictly compositionally, from lexical entries up, and quantifiers are analyzed in situ. All advantages of event semantics, in particular, regarding entailment, are preserved. The previous work has dealt only with positive polarity phrases involving universal, existential and counting quantification.

We now extend the polynomial event semantics to sentences with negation and negative quantification, including adverbial quantification, with attendant ambiguities. The analysis remains compositional, and does not require positing of non-existing entities or events.

1 Introduction

Quantification in (Neo-) Davidsonian event semantics has been the subject of many debates; we remind the so-called 'event quantification problem' in Sect. 2 and review the proposed resolutions, or postulates, in Sect. 6. The problem becomes especially acute with negation.

We propose an interpretation of Neo-Davidsonian semantics in which the event quantification problem does not even arise. The previous work has [5] laid the foundation and described the compositional but non-Montagovian treatment of universal, existential and counting quantification. Denotations are constructed strictly compositionally, from lexical entries up, and quantifiers are analyzed in situ, with no need for lifting. The underlying machinery is not of lambda-calculus but of much simpler relational algebra, with the straightforward set-theoretic interpretation.

The first key idea, strongly reminiscent of the BHK interpretation of intuitionistic logic [4], is viewing the truth value of a sentence not as the simple true/false but as a set of *evidence* for it: e.g., transpired events that witness for the sentence. Entailment is decided by set inclusion. The denotation then is a *query*, of a database of events. The query, expressed in a relational algebra, is constructed following the structure of the sentence, i.e., compositionally. One query entails another if the result of the former is contained in the result of the latter, for any event database. Queries have no event variable (or any variables for that matter); therefore, the problem of the scope of event quantification does not arise.

N. Okazaki et al. (Eds.): JSAI-isAI 2020 Workshops, LNAI 12758, pp. 82–95, 2021.
https://doi.org/10.1007/978-3-030-79942-7_6

The present paper extends the approach of [5] to sentences with negation and negative quantification, including adverbial quantification, with attendant ambiguities. The analysis remains compositional, and does not require positing of non-existing entities or events. The key extension is viewing the truth value of a sentence as a set of evidence as well as *counter-evidence*. The denotation now is a query both for the supporting and the contradicting evidence.

The structure of the paper is as follows. We remind the event quantification problem in Sect. 2 and the polynomial event semantics in Sect. 3, detailing the treatment of existential quantification in Sect. 3.2 and the corresponding entailments in Sect. 3.3. Negation is dealt with in Sect. 4; in particular, the ambiguity in the presence of quantified adverbial modifiers is analyzed in Sect. 4.1. Double-negation is briefly described in Sect. 4.2. Section 5 presents a set-theoretical model of the polyconcept algebra. Section 6 discusses related work.

The presented approach is not just a pen-and-paper analysis: it has been implemented so to analyze sentences mechanically and compute their models and counter-models. The implementation, which includes all the example in the paper plus many more, is available at http://okmij.org/gengo/poly-event/poly.ml.

2   Event Quantification Problem

We start by recalling the event quantification problem and its particular acute case of negation.

Neo-Davidsonian event semantics [9] (see [8] for a survey) is attractive because of the uniform treatment of VP adverbials, among other things, which explains entailments among sentences without ad hoc meaning postulates. To take the canonical example,

(1)   Brutus stabbed Caesar

(2)   Brutus stabbed Caesar violently

are given in the Neo-Davidsonian semantics the following denotations (logical formulas), resp.

(3) $\exists e.\, \mathsf{stabbed}(e) \wedge \mathsf{th}(e) = \mathsf{caesar} \wedge \mathsf{ag}(e) = \mathsf{brutus}$

(4) $\exists e.\, \mathsf{stabbed}(e) \wedge \mathsf{th}(e) = \mathsf{caesar} \wedge \mathsf{ag}(e) = \mathsf{brutus} \wedge \mathsf{violent}(e)$

Here $\mathsf{stabbed}(e)$ and $\mathsf{violent}(e)$ are predicates on the event e (telling if e is a stabbing or violent event, resp); th and ag are thematic functions, which return the theme (resp., agent) for their event argument. Characteristically for the (Neo-) Davidsonian semantics, the event variable e is bound by the existential quantifier at the sentence level. This so-called existential closure lets us interpret the sentence as the proposition: whether an event with the described properties exists. Clearly (4) entails (3) by first-order logic, thus reproducing the entailment from (2) to (1).

There is already a problem when substituting 'every senator' for Caesar:

(5)   Brutus stabbed every senator

(6) $\exists e. \forall x.\, \mathsf{senator}(x) \implies \mathsf{stabbed}(e) \land \mathsf{th}(e){=}x \land \mathsf{ag}(e){=}\mathsf{brutus}$

whose denotation (6) asserts the existence of a single event of the stabbing spree – 'collective', so to speak, reading of the universal quantifier. This denotation hence cannot reproduce the reading of (5) with stabbing spread over time.

The biggest problem however comes from substituting 'no senator' for Caesar in (1)–(2):

(7)   Brutus stabbed no senator

(8)   Brutus stabbed no senator violently

If we keep applying the existential closure at the sentence level as before we obtain the following logical formula for (7):

(9) $\exists e. \lnot\exists x.\, \mathsf{senator}(x) \land \mathsf{stabbed}(e) \land \mathsf{th}(e){=}x \land \mathsf{ag}(e){=}\mathsf{brutus}$

which is true if there is any event other than Brutus stabbing some senator (that is, for almost any event). Although the sentences (1) and (7) are contradictory,[1] the denotations (3) and (9) are not: both denotations are true of ancient Rome, for example.

The two problems are instances of what is called the event quantification problem [2,3]: the problem of scoping of the existential closure with respect to other quantificational phrases, which arises when combining Montagovian semantics and event semantics. Landman [7] suggested so-called scope domain principle, that the existential quantifier for the event variable obligatory takes the lowest scope. The implementations of this postulate are reviewed in Sect. 6.

We avoid the problem altogether. The story about quantifiers such as 'everyone' was told in [5]. Here we deal with negative-polarity sentences like (7), and also

Brutus did not stab Caesar
Brutus never stabbed Caesar
Brutus did not accuse Caesar for one hour
It is not the case that Brutus never stabbed a senator

3   Polynomial Event Semantics

We now recall the polynomial event semantics from [5], but present it algebraically. Our running example is the earlier (1)–(2), repeated below:

(1)   Brutus stabbed Caesar

(2)   Brutus stabbed Caesar violently

---

[1] keeping in mind that Caesar was a senator.

Suppose we have a record – a database – of events of ancient times. To see if (1) is true, we would query the database for the events of stabbing whose agent/subject is Brutus and theme is Caesar. In the language of set theory, this query may be written as

(10)   subj′/brutus ∩ Stabbed ∩ ob1′/caesar

Here, Stabbed is the set of stabbing events. As in description logic [1], we call a set of events or individuals a *concept* and typeset in san-serif and capitalized. If subj′ is a binary relation (thematic role) between events and their subjects, subj′/brutus are those events that are related by subj′ to the individual brutus:

$$\text{subj}'/\text{brutus} = \{e \mid \text{subj}'(e, \text{brutus})\} = \{e \mid \text{ag}(e) = \text{brutus}\}$$

ob1′/caesar is similar.

Query (10) gives a set of events: each event in this set can act as an *evidence* that Brutus indeed stabbed Caesar – in other words, as a witness for the proposition of (1). This evidence set, or 'support set', may then be regarded as the truth value for the sentence – and the query itself as the denotation.

For (2), the query is

(11)   subj′/brutus ∩ Stabbed ∩ ob1′/caesar ∩ Violently

where Violently is the set of violent events. Clearly, (11) is a subset of (10), from the very meaning of set intersection. Therefore, if the former is non-empty so is the latter, establishing the entailment from (2) to (1).

3.1   Polyconcepts

In the polynomial event semantics [5] queries are actually written in a more general form, to accommodate quantification. Instead of concepts we will be dealing with polyconcepts – which are also sets, but with more structure (see Sect. 5). A concept can be turned into a polyconcept by an injective operator $\mathcal{P}$. The empty polyconcept is written $\bot$, and the polyconcept intersection (a symmetric associative operation) is denoted by $\sqcap$. These operations have the following properties

(12) $\mathcal{P}(c_1 \cap c_2) = \mathcal{P}c_1 \sqcap \mathcal{P}c_2$ $\mathcal{P}c = \bot$ iff $c = \varnothing$

where the meta-variable c stands for an arbitrary concept. Using polyconcepts, the queries (10) and (11) are written as

(13) $\mathcal{P}$ (subj′/brutus) $\sqcap \mathcal{P}$ Stabbed $\sqcap \mathcal{P}$(ob1′/caesar)
                    $= \mathcal{P}$(subj′/brutus ∩ Stabbed ∩ ob1′/caesar)

(14) $\mathcal{P}$(subj′/brutus) $\sqcap \mathcal{P}$ Stabbed $\sqcap \mathcal{P}$(ob1′/caesar) $\sqcap \mathcal{P}$ Violently
                    $= \mathcal{P}$(subj′/brutus ∩ Stabbed ∩ ob1′/caesar ∩ Violently)

where the equated expressions in (13) and (14) are obtained using (12). Property (12) also lets us conclude that if (14) is non-empty then so must be (13), justifying the entailment. The polyconcept queries are hence an equivalent, but more complicated way of writing the earlier set-theoretic queries. The need for polyconcept comes when we turn to quantification.

We should stress the overt absence of the existential closure. To decide entailments, which is one of the main goals of semantics, working with 'support sets' as they are – or the queries that symbolize them – is enough. The queries are expressed in the form of a relational algebra (description logic [1], to be precise) and have no variables; in particular, no event variable.

Finally, we stress that queries (13) and (14) (as (10) and (11)) look quite like the original sentences (1) and (2). Therefore, the queries (denotations) can be systematically, compositionally constructed from the (parsed tree) of a sentence. As we shall see, this property still holds in the presence of quantification.

3.2 Quantification

The paper [5] extends the query-based semantics to sentences with quantified phrases such as the earlier (5) as well as the following:

(15)   Brutus stabbed a senator

We systematically apply the principle that the truth value of a sentence is the set of witnesses for it. A witness for (15) would be a stabbing event with Brutus as the agent and any senator as the theme. A query to search for these events would be a generalization of (13) – or, one may say, a relaxation of (13), where the theme of stabbing events is not just Caesar but any senator:[2]

(16) $\mathcal{P}$ subj$'$/brutus $\sqcap$ $\mathcal{P}$ Stabbed $\sqcap$ $\mathcal{P}$ ob1$'$/Senator

Here we have extended the rel$'$/x notation to x being not an individual but a set of individuals (i.e., a concept):

$$\text{ob1}'/\text{Senator} = \{e \mid \text{ob1}'(e,i), i \in \text{Senator}\} = \{e \mid \text{th}(e) \in \text{Senator}\}$$

There is another way to look for the evidence of Brutus' stabbing a senator: query the events database to see if Brutus stabbed Caesar or if Brutus stabbed Antonius, or Cicero, etc. Such 'union' query can be written as

$$(\mathcal{P}\,\text{subj}'/\text{brutus} \sqcap \mathcal{P}\,\text{Stabbed} \sqcap \mathcal{P}\,\text{ob1}'/\text{Caesar})\ \oplus$$
$$(\mathcal{P}\,\text{subj}'/\text{brutus} \sqcap \mathcal{P}\,\text{Stabbed} \sqcap \mathcal{P}\,\text{ob1}'/\text{Antonius}) \oplus \ldots$$

(17) $= \bigoplus_{i \in Senator} \mathcal{P}\,\text{subj}'/\text{brutus} \sqcap \mathcal{P}\,\text{Stabbed} \sqcap \mathcal{P}\,\text{ob1}'/i$

if we introduce the $\oplus$ operation to build a 'union' polyconcept out of polyconcept alternatives (pace alternative semantics [11]). One may feel that (16) and (17)

---

[2] We often drop the parentheses in $\mathcal{P}(\text{subj}'/\text{brutus})$, etc. if no confusion results.

ought to be equivalent: indeed, an event of Brutus stabbing a senator would be found by either query. However, as was observed in [5], if the sentence contained a universal quantifier, e.g., 'Every guard stabbed a senator', the corresponding two queries would no longer give the same result. Hence we need to consider both ways to query for the existential evidence.

The operation $\oplus$ is meant to feel like set-union. We likewise regard it as associative and commutative, and let $\sqcap$ distribute similarly to set-intersection distributing through set-union:

$$(18) \qquad (x_1 \oplus x_2) \sqcap y = (x_1 \sqcap y) \oplus (x_2 \sqcap y) \qquad\qquad x \oplus x = x$$

Then (17) may be written simpler as

$$\mathcal{P}\,\mathsf{subj}'/\mathsf{brutus} \sqcap \mathcal{P}\,\mathsf{Stabbed} \sqcap \left(\bigoplus_{i \in Senator} \mathcal{P}\,\mathsf{ob1}'/i\right)$$

To simplify the notation even further, we introduce the operator $\mathcal{A}$ turning a concept into a polyconcept:

$$\mathcal{A}c = \bigoplus_{i \in c} \mathcal{P}\{i\}$$

Unlike $\mathcal{P}c$, the polyconcept $\mathcal{A}c$ treats each element of c as its own alternative. Extending the notation rel'/x one more time, to x being a polyconcept:

$$\mathsf{rel}'/(\mathcal{P}c) = \mathcal{P}\,\mathsf{rel}'/c \qquad\qquad \mathsf{rel}'/(\mathcal{A}c) = \bigoplus_{i \in c} \mathsf{rel}'/i$$

lets us finally write the two queries expressing the meaning of (15) as:

$$(19) \qquad\qquad \mathcal{P}\,\mathsf{subj}'/\mathsf{brutus} \sqcap \mathcal{P}\,\mathsf{Stabbed} \sqcap \mathsf{ob1}'/\mathcal{P}\mathsf{Senator}$$
$$(20) \qquad\qquad \mathcal{P}\,\mathsf{subj}'/\mathsf{brutus} \sqcap \mathcal{P}\,\mathsf{Stabbed} \sqcap \mathsf{ob1}'/\mathcal{A}\mathsf{Senator}$$

One may have noticed that (17) did not look compositionally constructed. On the other hand, queries (19) and (20) both clearly match the structure of sentence (15) and are constructed compositionally. One may then conclude that $\mathcal{P}$ Senator and $\mathcal{A}$ Senator are two ways to denote 'a senator'. (If we had more quantifiers, we would have observed that the former is the narrow-scope existential and the latter is wide-scope: see [5] for discussion.) In polynomial semantics, existentials (and other quantifiers, for that matter) are analyzed in situ, with no movements.

3.3 Existential Quantification and Entailment

Deciding entailment in the polynomial event semantics is hardly any different from the ordinary Neo-Davidsonian semantics, even in the presence of (existential) quantification. For example, consider (15) (repeated below) and (21)

$$(15) \qquad\qquad \text{Brutus stabbed a senator}$$

$$(21) \qquad\qquad \text{Brutus stabbed a senator violently}$$

Similarly to (19) and (20), the meaning of (21) is expressed by:

(22) $\mathcal{P}\,\mathsf{subj}'/\mathsf{brutus} \sqcap \mathcal{P}\,\mathsf{Stabbed} \sqcap \mathsf{ob1}'/\mathcal{P}\mathsf{Senator} \sqcap \mathcal{P}\,\mathsf{Violently}$

(23) $\mathcal{P}\,\mathsf{subj}'/\mathsf{brutus} \sqcap \mathcal{P}\,\mathsf{Stabbed} \sqcap \mathsf{ob1}'/\mathcal{A}\mathsf{Senator} \sqcap \mathcal{P}\,\mathsf{Violently}$

In our evidence-based approach, one sentence is said to entail another if any evidence for the former is, or gives, the evidence for the latter, for any event database. More formal, and useful for polyconcepts, definition is that a sentence denoted by the polyconcept x entails another, denoted by y, just in case $y \neq \bot$ whenever $x \neq \bot$ – for any event database. It is easy to see, from (12) and (18) that $x \sqcap y \neq \bot$ always implies $x \neq \bot$. Therefore, (21) entails (15).

With a bit more work one can show that if $(\mathcal{P}c_1 \oplus \mathcal{P}c_2) \sqcap x$ is not $\bot$ then neither is $\mathcal{P}(c_1 \cup c_2) \sqcap x$. That is, that the wide-existential reading, such as (23), entails the narrow-existential reading, such as (22) (in the sentences without negation).

4   Negation

Our principle has been that the truth value of a sentence is a (poly-)set of witnessing events. Applying it to sentences like (7) and (8), repeated below

(7)   Brutus stabbed no senator

(8)   Brutus stabbed no senator violently

is a challenge: how can one witness something that has not occurred? Our resolution is to consider 'counter-witnesses': events that testify against the sentence. The truth value of a sentence hence becomes a set of witnesses and a set of counter-witnesses (or, refutations). To evaluate (7) we would query the database of events for senator stabbings done by Brutus. The empty result would mean (7) is *non-refuted* by the available evidence.

Formally, we extend the previously introduced polynomial event semantics by assigning polarity: Positive polyconcepts characterize supporting, and negative polyconcepts—refuting events. The empty polyconcepts are also polarized: $\bot$ resp. $\bar{\bot}$, which are distinct. The operations $\mathcal{P}$ and $\mathcal{A}$ create positive polyconcepts. For negative ones we introduce negation $\neg x$, with the property

(24) $\neg x \sqcap y = \neg(x \sqcap y) \quad \neg(x \oplus y) = \neg x \oplus \neg y \quad \mathsf{rel}'/\neg x = \neg\,\mathsf{rel}'/x$

where x and y are assumed of positive polarity. (For double-negation, see Sect. 4.2.)

We have seen in Sect. 3.2 that 'a senator' may be represented either by $\mathcal{A}\mathsf{Senator}$ or $\mathcal{P}\mathsf{Senator}$. In the former, 'wide-scope' reading, the polyconcept contains $\oplus$-collected alternatives for each particular senator. The 'narrow-scope' reading collapses them. Since 'no senator' does not focus (pun intended) on individual people, it seems reasonable to give it only one interpretation: $\neg\mathcal{P}\,\mathsf{Senator}$. Thus, 'no senator' is adversarially testifying narrow-scope 'a senator'.

The meaning of (7) is hence the query

(25) $\mathcal{P}\,\text{subj}'/\text{brutus}\sqcap\mathcal{P}\,\text{Stabbed}\sqcap\text{ob1}'/\neg\mathcal{P}\text{Senator}$

(26) $=\neg\mathcal{P}(\text{subj}'/\text{brutus}\cap\text{Stabbed}\cap\text{ob1}'/\text{Senator})$

where (26) is obtained by applying the properties of polyconcept operations. The result, if not $\bar{\bot}$, carries an event of Brutus stabbing a senator: the evidence refuting (7).

For (8) we obtain

(27) $\mathcal{P}\,\text{subj}'/\text{brutus}\sqcap\mathcal{P}\,\text{Stabbed}\sqcap\text{ob1}'/\neg\mathcal{P}\text{Senator}\sqcap\mathcal{P}\,\text{Violently}$

(28) $=\neg\mathcal{P}(\text{subj}'/\text{brutus}\cap\text{Stabbed}\cap\text{ob1}'/\text{Senator}\cap\text{Violently})$

From (12) and the properties of set-intersection we obtain that if (26) is $\bar{\bot}$, then so must be (28) – meaning that (7) entails (8). In general, one may observe that the operator $\sqcap$ is upwards monotone. Therefore, dropping ($\sqcap\mathcal{P}\,\text{Violently}$) does not reduce supporting or refuting evidence – letting us decide entailments such as 'no guard stabbed Caesar' entailing 'no guard stabbed Caesar violently' without any meaning postulates, just by monotonicity of $\sqcap$.

Negated verbs such as 'do not stab' are represented by applying $\neg$ to the verb's concept. (Adverbs like 'never' are treated similarly, as the negated concept 'ever'; we look at time-period–related concepts in Sect. 4.1). Thus the meaning of (29) is (30)

(29)   Brutus did not stab Caesar

(30) $\mathcal{P}\,\text{subj}'/\text{brutus}\sqcap\neg\mathcal{P}\,\text{Stabbed}\sqcap\mathcal{P}\,\text{ob1}'/\text{caesar}$

                $=\neg\mathcal{P}(\text{subj}'/\text{brutus}\cap\text{Stabbed}\cap\text{ob1}'/\text{caesar})$

as expected. Likewise, for (31) we obtain the query (32)

(31)   Brutus did not stab a senator

(32) $\mathcal{P}\,\text{subj}'/\text{brutus}\sqcap\neg\mathcal{P}\,\text{Stabbed}\sqcap\text{ob1}'/\mathcal{P}\text{Senator}$

The paper [5] described in detail how ambiguities in sentences like "A soldier stabbed everyone" are reflected in the polynomial event semantics. The just shown treatment of 'do not stab' predicts that "A soldier did not stab everyone" will be just as ambiguous. We deal with ambiguous negative sentences in more detail next.

4.1 Scope Ambiguities with Quantified Adverbial Modifiers

It has long been observed (see [2] for references and detailed discussion) that negative sentences with for-adverbials like 'for one hour' are ambiguous. For example,

(33)   Brutus did not accuse Caesar for one hour

may be paraphrased either as (34) or (35), 'for one hour' taking scope above or under the negation.

(34)   There was an one-hour period during which Brutus

                                did not accuse Caesar

(35)   It was not the case that Brutus accused Caesar for one hour

The first comprehensive treatment of this phenomenon in event semantics was done by Krifka [6]. The source of much of the complexity in his very complicated treatment was the desire to avoid having for-adverbials necessarily take the sentence-wide scope (otherwise, overgeneration occurs). Later Champollion [2] delivered a much simpler and compelling analysis in his compositional event semantics, still avoiding the sentence-wide scope of for-adverbials and accounting for tense and sub-interval quantification, as in [6].

Yet another event-based analysis is proposed in [3], using abstract categorial grammar. However, that analysis [3, eq. (36)], makes significant simplifying assumptions: it lets for-adverbials take the sentence-wide scope, and also disregards tense. Also it does not quite convey the meaning of (their version of) (34), which states that there was one hour period during which Brutus did not accuse Caesar, even for a moment. The analysis of [3] however assumed that an accusation action necessarily spans the entire one-hour period.

For-adverbials have the inherently complex semantics, referring not just to an interval of time but also to all sub-intervals of that interval (or all (sub)events that occurred during that interval). Since we eschewed universal quantification in this paper, we will not analyze (34) in all its complexity, assuming, like [3], that the accusation spans the entire period. We do avoid the need for sentence-wide scoping of 'for one hour', and can account for tense (along the lines of [2,6]). We also exhibit the ambiguity.

We take the concept 'for one hour', denoted as 1hr, to be a set of events that lasted for one hour, within some reference time frame. We implicitly assume that all queries search for events within the reference time frame determined from tense markers – following the anaphoric treatment of tense in the style of [10], also used in [6] and [2]. The concept 1hr can be turned into a polyconcept in two distinct ways: as $\mathcal{P}$1hr or $\mathcal{A}$1hr Then (36) is the query representing the meaning of (34), and (37) representing the meaning of (35).

(36) $\mathcal{P}\, \mathsf{subj}'/\mathsf{brutus} \sqcap \neg\mathcal{P}\, \mathsf{Accused} \sqcap \mathcal{P}\, \mathsf{ob1}'/\mathsf{caesar} \sqcap \mathcal{A}\, \mathsf{1hr}$

(37) $\mathcal{P}\, \mathsf{subj}'/\mathsf{brutus} \sqcap \neg\mathcal{P}\, \mathsf{Accused} \sqcap \mathcal{P}\, \mathsf{ob1}'/\mathsf{caesar} \sqcap \mathcal{P}\, \mathsf{1hr}$

Indeed, (37) looks for any event of Brutus' accusing Caesar for a one-hour period within the reference time frame, delivering the result as the single alternative. If it is $\bar{\bot}$, then no such events are found and (35) is non-refuted. On the other hand, (36) delivers the refutation events as multiple alternatives, one per each 1hr period. An alternative $\bar{\bot}$, if present, would then non-refute (34).

4.2   Double Negation

Standard English generally does not allow multiple negations, at least overtly. (Although combining negation with verbs like 'deny' is grammatical, the meaning is not easy to grasp. Native speakers are routinely confused: see the extensive 'Archive of Misnegation' maintained by Language Log.[3])

Yet there is the construction "It is not the case that S" in which the clause S may already be negated. In that case, the construction performs the classical double negation. For example:

(38)   Brutus never stabbed a senator

(39)   It is not the case that Brutus never stabbed a senator

Here, (38) denies but (39) affirms a stabbing.

Our treatment of negation easily explains such behavior. Recall our earlier example:

(15)   Brutus stabbed a senator

In Sect. 3.2 we derived the polyconcept for its meaning; let us call it y_{bss}. The meaning of (38) then works out to be $\neg y_{bss}$ (similarly to the derivation of (32)). If (39) is deemed to be the negation of (38), its meaning then is represented by $\neg\neg y_{bss}$. If y_{bss} is not $\perp$ it carries an event of Brutus' stabbing some senator, which supports (15). Then $\neg y_{bss}$ is not $\bar{\perp}$, which means (38) is refuted – by the same event, in fact. The very same event witnesses (39). If, however, $\neg y_{bss}$ is $\bar{\perp}$ (that is, (38) is non-refuted), then y_{bss} must be empty: there are no events to support (15), nor (39). All in all, we see that the negation of $\neg y_{bss}$ is indeed tantamount to y_{bss}.

5   A Model of Polyconcepts

So far we have used polyconcepts as abstract entities with operations $\mathcal{P}$, $\sqcap$, $\oplus$, $\neg$. We postulated desired properties of these operations, and intuitively justified them by analogy with operations on sets. One cannot help but ask: does such polyconcept algebra really exist? Is there a concrete mathematical structure on which we can define $\oplus$, etc. that actually possess the postulated properties? In other words, is there a model of polyconcepts?

This section exhibits a set-theoretic model. It is based on the model introduced in [5], with one simplification and one extension. Paper [5] dealt with the universal and counting quantification (out of scope for the present paper); omitting it gives a simpler model. The extension is the polarity, to deal with negation.

Following the terminology of [5], we call events, humans and other entities *individuals*, and use the meta-variable i to refer to an individual. We call a

---

[3] https://languagelog.ldc.upenn.edu/nll/?cat=273.

possibly empty set of individuals a *concept*, referred to by the meta-variable c. A *factor* is a polarized concept.[4] A positive factor is written just as the corresponding concept, using the meta-variable c. A negative factor is written as $\bar{c}$. A polyconcept then is a set of factors, for which we use the meta-variables x and y.

The operations on polyconcepts are defined as follows.

$$
\begin{aligned}
\mathcal{P}c &:= \{c\} & &= \{\textstyle\bigcup_{i \in c}\{i\}\} \\
\mathcal{A}c &:= \textstyle\bigoplus_{i \in c}\{\{i\}\} & &= \textstyle\bigcup_{i \in c}\{\{i\}\} \\
\bot &:= \{\varnothing\} \\
\bar{\bot} &:= \{\bar{\varnothing}\} \\
\mathbf{0} &:= \varnothing \\
x \oplus y &:= x \cup y \\
x \sqcap y &:= \{c_1 \cap c_2 \mid c_1 \in x, c_2 \in y\} \\
\neg x &:= \{\bar{c} \mid c \in x\} \\
\mathsf{rel}'/x &:= \{\mathsf{rel}'/c \mid c \in x\}
\end{aligned}
$$

$\mathcal{P}c$ is thus a polyconcept made of a single positive factor. In contrast, $\mathcal{A}c$ is a set of positive singleton factors. Clearly, $\bot$ and $\bar{\bot}$ are distinct, and both are different from $\mathbf{0}$. (We have not used $\mathbf{0}$ before: it is the unit of $\oplus$, see below.) The operation $\oplus$ unions the factors of its polyconcept arguments. When computing $x \sqcap y$ and intersecting factors, if one factor is negative the resulting factor is also negative. The intersection of two negative factors is not defined (it can be permitted in languages with negative concord). If rel' is a binary relation, the sectioning notation rel'/x applies to each factor of x (keeping its polarity).

Below is the summary of the properties of the polyconcept operations; most of them have already been mentioned earlier. It is easy to see that the just defined operations do have all these properties.

$$\oplus, \sqcap \text{ are associative and commutative}$$

$$
\begin{aligned}
\mathcal{P}(c_1 \cap c_2) &= \mathcal{P}c_1 \sqcap \mathcal{P}c_2 \\
\mathcal{P}c &= \bot \text{ iff } c = \varnothing \\
x \sqcap \mathbf{0} &= \mathbf{0} \\
x \sqcap \bot &= \bot & &\text{if all factors of } x \text{ are positive} \\
x \sqcap \bar{\bot} &= \bar{\bot} & &\text{if all factors of } x \text{ are positive} \\
(x_1 \oplus x_2) \sqcap y &= (x_1 \sqcap y) \oplus (x_2 \sqcap y) \\
x \oplus x &= x \\
\neg x \sqcap y &= \neg(x \sqcap y) & &\text{if all factors of } x, y \text{ are positive} \\
\neg(x \oplus y) &= \neg x \oplus \neg y & &\text{if all factors of } x, y \text{ are positive} \\
\mathsf{rel}'/\neg x &= \neg\, \mathsf{rel}'/x & &\text{if all factors of } x \text{ are positive}
\end{aligned}
$$

---

[4] To witness universal quantification, [5] introduces a so-called group of events. A factor is then a set of groups. We do not deal with the universal or counting quantification in this paper, and so elide groups, and the related operation $\otimes$ for clarity.

6   Related Work

The problems of quantification and negation in event semantics are well-known and well-described; see [2,3] for the recent detailed discussion. The proposed resolutions all (except for Krifka's [6] unusual and controversial treatment of negation) center around making the existential quantifier that binds the event variable obligatorily take the lowest scope. The postulate of existential closure having the lowest scope is the generalization of the 'scope domain principle' by Landman [7].

The approaches also effect this lowest scope taking in the same way: existential closure is postulated at the sentence (sometimes VP) level, and other scope-taking operators are *moved* over it. The approaches differ in how exactly this movement happens. So-called syntactic approaches (see [7] for an overview) posit this movement by fiat, as a covert movement or other such operation on the parsed form of the sentence. The abstract categorial grammar approaches [3] postulate abstract types in such a way so that the scope taking operators have no choice but to take scope over existential closure in the so-called abstract form of the sentence. Semantic approaches, rather than postulating a movement upfront, postulate type shifting (or, type-lifting), whose result is the same sort of movement but accomplished during normalizing the denotation.

Of these semantic approaches, Champollion's [2] is notable for using the movement also for existential closure. On his account, the existential quantifier that binds the event variable is included in the lexical entry of a verb, and moved into the sentence or VP scope by the continuation-taking/scope-taking mechanism underlying all semantic approaches. Champollion arranges for stacking-up continuations (in other words, for stacking-up type lifting) in such a way so that the existential closure comes always in the lowest scope with respect to other scope-taking operators.

Positing the existential quantifier for an event in a lexical entry for a verb is a rather strong assumption, as Tomita [12] demonstrated in the analysis of infinitival complements. It commits one to the existence of an event even in sentences such as "Mary forbade every student to leave", where no event related to leaving is ever asserted to take place. Tomita [12] proposes non-existing eventualities to deal with this problem. Applying polynomial semantics to perception reports and infinitival complements is the subject of the future work.

Polynomial event semantics was first introduced in [5] (see that paper also for an overview of related work.) That paper thoroughly employed model-theoretic approach, in the explicit set-theoretic notation similar to that in Sect. 5. The present paper pursues the algebraic treatment.

7   Conclusions

We described the extension of the polynomial event semantics to deal with negation and negative quantification. We thus demonstrated how upwards and downwards entailments and quantification ambiguities can be analyzed without resorting to existential closure. As befits the event semantics, the entailments involving verbal modification (such as 'violently') come out set-theoretically, from the properties of set intersection, without resorting to any meaning postulates.

The key idea is defining the truth value of a sentence in terms of events that support or refute it. The denotation of a sentence is represented by a query, which searches for supporting and refuting events in a 'world events' database. The sentence meaning hence becomes fine-grain: a sentence may be supported or unsupported, and also refuted or non-refuted.

A sentence like 'Exactly two people came to the party', treated as the conjunction 'At least two but no more than two people came to the party' can be both supported (in part) and refuted (in part) by an event of three people coming. It is the subject of future work to analyze such conjunctions, and coordination in general, as well as modality.

The grouping and distributing events through factors, which underlies our treatment of quantificational phrases, holds the promise for the uniform approach to collective and distributive quantification. That is one of our ultimate goals.

Acknowledgments. I am grateful to anonymous reviewers for very helpful comments and suggestions. I thank Daisuke Bekki for insightful and stimulating questions. This work was partially supported by a JSPS KAKENHI Grant Number 17K00091.

References

1. Baader, F.: Description logics. In: Tessaris, S., et al. (eds.) Reasoning Web 2009. LNCS, vol. 5689, pp. 1–39. Springer, Heidelberg (2009). https://doi.org/10.1007/978-3-642-03754-2_1
2. Champollion, L.: The interaction of compositional semantics and event semantics. Linguist. Philos. **38**(1), 31–66 (2014). https://doi.org/10.1007/s10988-014-9162-8
3. de Groote, P., Winter, Y.: A type-logical account of quantification in event semantics. In: Murata, T., Mineshima, K., Bekki, D. (eds.) JSAI-isAI 2014. LNCS (LNAI), vol. 9067, pp. 53–65. Springer, Heidelberg (2015). https://doi.org/10.1007/978-3-662-48119-6_5 https://hal.inria.fr/hal-01102261
4. Iemhoff, R.: Intuitionism in the Philosophy of Mathematics. In: Zalta, E.N. (ed.) The Stanford Encyclopedia of Philosophy. Metaphysics Research Lab, Stanford University, fall 2020 edn. (2020)
5. Kiselyov, O.: Polynomial event semantics - non-montagovian proper treatment of quantifiers. In: Kojima, K., Sakamoto, M., Mineshima, K., Satoh, K. (eds.) JSAI-isAI 2018. LNCS (LNAI), vol. 11717, pp. 313–324. Springer, Cham (2019). https://doi.org/10.1007/978-3-030-31605-1_23
6. Krifka, M.: Nominal reference, temporal consitution, and quantification in event semantics. In: Bartsch, R., van Benthem, J., van Emde Boas, P. (eds.) Semantics and Contextual Expression, pp. 75–111. Foris Publications, Dordrecht (1989)
7. Landman, F.: Events and Plurality. Kluwer Academic Publishers, Dordrecht (2000)
8. Maienborn, C.: 8. Event semantics, pp. 232–266. De Gruyter Mouton (2019). https://doi.org/10.1515/9783110589245-008
9. Parsons, T.: Events in the Semantics of English: A Study in Subatomic Semantics. The MIT Press, Cambridge (1990)

10. Partee, B.H.: Some structural analogies between tenses and pronouns in English. J. Philos. **70**(18), 601–609 (1973). https://doi.org/10.2307/2025024
11. Rooth, M.: Alternative Semantics. Oxford University Press, Oxford (2016). https://doi.org/10.1093/oxfordhb/9780199642670.013.19
12. Tomita, Y.: Event quantification in infinitival complements: a free-logic approach. In: Kojima, K., Sakamoto, M., Mineshima, K., Satoh, K. (eds.) JSAI-isAI 2018. LNCS (LNAI), vol. 11717, pp. 372–384. Springer, Cham (2019). https://doi.org/10.1007/978-3-030-31605-1_27

Experiential Imagination and the Inside/Outside-Distinction

Kristina Liefke$^{(\boxtimes)}$ and Markus Werning

Department of Philosophy II, Ruhr-University Bochum, 44780 Bochum, Germany
{kristina.liefke,markus.werning}@rub.de
https://www.rub.de/phil-inf/
https://www.rub.de/phil-lang/

Abstract. Gerundive imagination reports with an embedded reflexive subject (e.g. *Zeno imagines himself swimming*) are ambiguous between an 'inside' and an 'outside' reading: the inside reading captures the imaginer's directly making the described experience (here: swimming); the outside reading captures the imaginer's having an experience of an event, involving his own counterpart, from an out-of-body point of view (watching one's counterpart swim). Our paper explains the inside/outside-ambiguity through the observation (i) that imagining can referentially target different phenomenal experiences – esp. proprioception (i.e. bodily feeling) and visual perception (seeing, watching) – and (ii) that imagining and its associated experience can both be *de se*. Inside/outside readings then arise from intuitive constraints in the lexical semantics of verbs like *feel*, *see*.

Keywords: Inside/outside readings · Imagistic perspective · Experiential imagining · Self-imagining · Counterfactual parasitism

1 Introduction

Imagination reports like (1) are generally taken to have two different kinds of *de se*-reading (see e.g. [2,39–41]): an *inside* (*subjective*, or *experiential*) reading,[1] which captures what it would be like for the imaginer to undergo the described

---

[1] In philosophy and psychology, the inside and the outside reading are commonly associated with a first-person *field perspective* on the experienced event, respectively with a third-person *observer perspective* on this event (see e.g. [2,17,18,22,29,30, 35]).

We thank two reviewers for LENLS 17 for valuable comments on the précis of this paper. The paper has profited from discussions with Alex Grzankowski and Ede Zimmermann. Kristina Liefke's contribution was supported by the German Research Foundation (DFG) through grant no. ZI 683/13-1 (to Ede Zimmermann). Markus Werning's contribution is supported by DFG grants no. 419038924 and no. 419040015 as part of the DFG research group *Constructing Scenarios of the Past* (FOR 2812).

© Springer Nature Switzerland AG 2021
N. Okazaki et al. (Eds.): JSAI-isAI 2020 Workshops, LNAI 12758, pp. 96–112, 2021.
https://doi.org/10.1007/978-3-030-79942-7_7

experience; and an *outside* (*objective*, or *imagistic*) reading, which captures what it would be like for the imaginer to witness an event, that involves his own counterpart, from an out-of-body point of view. The inside reading of (1), i.e. (1a), reports a relation towards the bodily experiences of Zeno's swimming counterpart (e.g. the salty taste of the water, the tug of the current, the feeling of cold). The outside reading, (1b), reports a relation towards the target of Zeno's (counterfactual) visual perception that has Zeno's swimming counterpart as its object (e.g. an observer view of Zeno being tossed about, his body bobbing up and down in the foamy waste; [39, p. 161]).

(1)   Zeno imagines himself swimming in the rough ocean
    a.   Zeno imagines *what it would feel like* to swim in the rough ocean
    b.   Zeno imagines *seeing/watching himself* swimming in the rough ocean

Recent work on self-imagination reports (esp. Anand [2] and Ninan [24]) explains the ambiguity in (1) through the *de dicto/de se*-distinction [24] (see [13]) or through the particular way in which we set up imaginative projects [2] (see [46]). However, this work either fails to capture the experiential character of imagining (in Anand's case) or the perceptival nature of the outside reading (in Ninan's case). Specifically, Ninan's account (dubbed the *Simple View* in [24]) counterintuitively treats the outside reading of (1) as equivalent to (2):

(2)   Zeno imagines *that* he is (doing/experiencing a) swimming in the ocean

Our paper seeks to compensate for the above shortcoming. To do so, it uses a variant of Blumberg's [5] observation (see also [25,34,40]) that imagining can be referentially dependent – or *parasitic* – on experiences. Our variant involves the <u>inverse</u> of Blumberg's referential dependency relation, viz. the dependency of some counterfactual experiences (e.g. counterfactual proprioception or visual perception) on imagining. The ambiguity in (1) can then be explained through the fact that imagining and its dependent experience(s) can <u>both</u> be ascribed *de se*. It arises from the existence of intuitive constraints in the lexical semantics of proprioception and perception verbs.

The paper is structured as follows: we start (in Sect. 2.2, 3.1) by describing two properties of imagining that are particularly relevant for the inside/outside-ambiguity, viz. experiential parasitism and *de se*-ness, and argue that these properties can be co-instantiated in a single imagination report. We then show that the formal-semantic tools that are commonly used to capture these properties, viz. world-variables in syntax (see [27]) and centered worlds [13], can be straightforwardly combined into a single formalism (Sect. 3.2). Section 4 uses the content- and act-specific properties of proprioception and perception to reduce the many possible LFs of (1) that our formalism predicts to the inside- and the outside reading. Section 5 identifies the grounds for Vendler and Walton's disagreement about outside readings of gerundive imagination reports with a PRO subject and explains the non-availability of an outside reading of Williams' [46] *imagine being Napoleon*. The paper closes by pointing out that the linguistic inside/outside-distinction may reflect a real psychological and neurobiological difference.

2   Experiential and Parasitic Imagining

Before we discuss the properties of imagining that are relevant for the inside/outside-distinction, it is important to identify the particular kind of imagining that this paper is about:

2.1   Experientiality

We have suggested above that our considerations in this paper focus on *experiential* imagining (esp. imagining feeling/seeing). The latter is an event-directed attitude – similar to experiential [= episodic] remembering (see [36,37,43]) – that requires the attitudinal agent's personal (counterfactual) experience of the target event or scene (see [8,34]). For the memory report in (3a) and a variant, (4a), of the imagination report in (1), the satisfaction of this requirement is evidenced by the validity of the inferences in (3) and (4):

(3)   a.   Anna remembers [a woman being chased by a squirrel]
     ⇒ b.   Anna has veridically (visually) experienced [a woman being chased. . .]

(4)   a.   Zeno imagines [Ken swimming in the ocean]
            (≡ Zeno imagines <u>seeing</u> [Ken swimming in the ocean])   (Sect. 2.2)
     ⇒ b.   Zeno counterfactually experiences (= has a visual/experiential simulation of) [Ken swimming in the ocean]

As is suggested by our use of the verb *experience* in (4b), we assume that *experience* does not entail or presuppose the truth of its complement (i.e. *experience* is neither veridical nor factive; see [9]). To still explain the factivity of *remember* in (3a) (attested, e.g., in [12,45]), we observe that *remember* is derivative on the particular <u>mode</u> of the remembered experience (e.g. visual [see (3b)], proprioceptive, agentive, emotional; see Sect. 2.2). The relevant occurrence of *remember* then inherits the veridicality and factivity properties of this mode.

Importantly, in contrast to episodic remembering, experiential imagining can also be reported through *that*-clause complements (see [15,23]; *pace* [34]).[2] This is reflected in the fact that *that*-clause-taking *imagine* allows modification with event-modifiers like *vividly* (see (5b) and the data in [38]). It has been argued that such modification is not possible for *that*-clause memory reports (see (6b)) and that those are associated with propositional, i.e. semantic, memory (see [34]).

(5)   a.   ✓Zeno vividly imagines [Ken swimming in the ocean]
         b.   ✓Zeno vividly imagines [that Ken is swimming in the ocean]

---

[2] This is not to argue against the possibility of <u>propositional</u> imagining. For an intuitive example, see *Bill imagined [that 4 was a prime number]*.

(6)   a. $^\checkmark$ Anna vividly remembers [a woman being chased by a squirrel]
       b. $^\#$ Anna vividly remembers [that a woman was chased by a squirrel]

The above suggests that the inadequacy of Ninan's paraphrase in (2) (which uses a *that*-clause) is not due to the syntactic form of its complement, but to the particular inserted predicate (i.e. *doing/experiencing*). We will return to this point in Sect. 4.

2.2   Counterfactual Parasitism

Recently, Blumberg [5] and Ninan [25] have argued that experiential imagining can be *parasitic* [= referentially dependent] on experiences, in the sense that the 'correct' analysis of experiential imagining requires some imagination contents to take their referents from worlds other than the actual/evaluation world or the agent's imagination alternatives.[3] This analysis is prompted either by the presence of experience predicates (in (7) and (8): *see* resp. *dream*) or by the lack of adequate truth-conditions in the absence of these predicates (thus, (9a) requires the insertion of a *dream*-PP; in (9b)). Examples (7) and (8) are due to Ninan [25, ex. (18)] and Blumberg [5, ex. (102)], respectively. Example (9) is inspired by Blumberg's [4] 'burgled Bill'-case. In what follows, we mark the matrix [= 'parasite'] attitude (here: imagining) with a grey frame. The experience [= 'host'] (i.e. seeing resp. dreaming) is highlighted in grey:

(7)   Ralph is imagining that the man [whom he sees sneaking around on
       the waterfront] is flying a kite in an alpine meadow

(8)   John is imagining that the woman [who threatened him in his dream
       last night] is swimming in the sea

(9)   Context: Ira has been dreaming of a tattooed woman (no particular one
       that he has come across in real life)

       a.   Now, he is imagining her having clear, untattooed skin

       $\not\equiv$ i.   *de re:* There exists a tattooed woman whom Ira is imagining

---

[3] This is in line with Vendler [39, p. 164] who analyzes '*B imagines A's V'ing*' as '*B imagines seeing (or hearing) A's V'ing*':

> [...] imagining being in some situation or other involves not merely fancying tactual, muscular or kinesthetic sensations, but auditory and visual ones as well. Consequently imagining myself swimming in that water, or imagining you running on the field, can be understood in terms of imagining seeing myself swimming in that water, and imagining seeing you running on the field. And what about imagining you (or myself) whistling in the dark? Obviously, what this means is imagining hearing you (or myself) whistling in the dark. If this is true, then [*Imagine yourself swimming in that water*] is nothing but an elliptical product of *Imagine seeing yourself swimming in that water*.

having clear, untattooed skin

$\not\equiv$ ii. *de dicto:* Ira is imagining an inconsistent scene in which a woman simultaneously does and does not have tattoos

$\equiv$ b.   Ira is imagining [the tattooed woman from his dream] having clear, untattooed skin

The parasitic interpretation of *imagine* in (9a) is triggered by the observation that – given the context in (9) – (9a) is false on its *de re*-reading (which gives the DP *her* [= *a tattooed woman*] a specific interpretation; see (9a-i), (10a)) and that (9a) is contradictory on its *de dicto*-reading (see (9a-ii), (10b)). The parasitic interpretation is then prompted by the observation that (9a) has plausible truth-conditions on a reading that evaluates *her* at some other world (different from the actual world and from Ira's imagination alternatives; see (9b), (10c)). Our name for this reading, i.e. *de hospite*, is motivated by the observation that this world is associated with the host experience, on which the matrix attitude (here: Ira's imagining) is parasitic. In (10c), the 'host' world is denoted by X:[4]

(10)   a.   [a woman in **@**] [λt. Ira imagines in @ [λw. t has clear skin in w]]]

        b.   Ira imagines in @ [λw. a woman in w has clear skin in w]

        c.   Ira imagines in @ [λw. a woman-in-$\underline{X}$ has clear skin in w]

To specify the particular world(s) at which the different constituents of the complement in (9a) are evaluated, (10) uses Percus' [27] *Index Variables-approach*. This approach posits possible world-variables in the representation of syntactic structures, and allows intensional (here: attitude/experience) operators to bind these variables. In particular, Percus' approach assumes that all predicates contain an unpronounced variable that saturates their world-argument. It further assumes that intensional operators are associated with a lambda abstractor that can bind a world variable. The ability of the same world variable in a syntactic structure to be bound by different lambdas then accounts for different readings.

The LFs in (10) only assume a single world-variable, w, next to our variable for the actual world, @. To capture our observation that the constituents of the complement in (9a) are dependent on different worlds/alternatives, we follow Blumberg [4] in positing *distinct* variables for the alternatives that are introduced by the parasite attitude [here: imagining] (w_2) and for the alternatives that are introduced by the host experience [here: dreaming] (w_1). The different readings of the imagination report in (9a) (see (10)) are then associated with the LFs in (11). The relevant LF – on which (9a) is true – is given in (11c).

---

[4] Below, the hyphens in 'woman-in-X' indicate that the DP *a woman* is <u>evaluated</u> at the world X. The thus-obtained individual is then imported in the interpretation of the complement (at w, where interpretation is indicated without hyphens). This import can proceed through a rigidifying operator, analogous to Kaplan's [11] *dthat*.

(11)   a. [a woman in @] [$\lambda t.$ Ira $\boxed{\text{imagines}}$ in @

$$[\lambda w_1 \, [\lambda w_2. \; t \text{ has clear skin in } w_2]]]]$$

    b. I. $\boxed{\text{imagines}}$ in @ $[\lambda w_1 \, [\lambda w_2. \text{ a woman in } \boldsymbol{w_2} \text{ has clear skin in } w_2]]]$

    c. I. $\boxed{\text{imagines}}$ in @ $[\lambda w_1 \, [\lambda w_2. \text{ a woman-in-}\boldsymbol{w_1} \text{ has clear skin in } w_2]]]$

We have suggested above that, in (11c), the matrix attitude [= imagining] depends for its reference on the underlying experience [= dreaming]. The direction of this dependence motivates the 'parasite'/'host'-terminology in [5] (see [4], due to [16]). The situation is different for imagination reports like (1): arguably, in such reports, the embedded subject DP (in (1): *himself*) is still interpreted at the imaginer's experience alternatives (viz. at Zeno's proprioception- or perception alternatives). However, in these reports, the referential dependency is the other way around, i.e. the implicit experience is *dependent on the imagining*.[5] In particular – unlike (9) –, (1) does <u>not</u> assume that the imaginer's experience [there: Zeno's feeling or seeing] happens in the same world as his imagining (viz. at @). Rather, it only happens *in his imagination*. To capture the inverse dependency relation of reports like (1) w.r.t. *de hospite*-reports, we describe reports like (1) as *de parasito*. The inverse dependency of the matrix attitude and the experience in (1) validates the equivalence in (12) (see [40]), where 'V' stands proxy for the experience (i.e. V $\in$ {*feel, see*}):

(12)   a.   Zeno $\boxed{\text{imagines}}$ [himself in V swimming in the ocean]

$\equiv$ b.   Zeno $\boxed{\text{imagines}}$ [V'ing himself swimming in the ocean]

The above suggests that (1) should not be analyzed as an analogue of (11c) (i.e. as (13)), but rather as (14a). This LF inverses the order of the lambda abstractors over imagination- and experience alternatives (in comparison to the order of the lambda abstractors over imagination- and dream alternatives in (11c)).

(13)   [Zeno] [$\lambda t. t$ $\boxed{\text{imagines}}$ in @ $[\lambda w_1 \, [\lambda w_2.$

$$t\text{'s counterpart-in-}w_1 \text{ swims in } \boldsymbol{w_2}]]]]$$

(14)   a. [Zeno] [$\lambda t. t$ $\boxed{\text{imagines}}$ in @ $[\lambda w_2. \, [\lambda w_1.$

$$t\text{'s counterpart-in-}w_1 \text{ swims in } \boldsymbol{w_1}]]]]$$

    b. [Zeno] [$\lambda t. t$ $\boxed{\text{imagines}}$ in @ $[\lambda w_2. \; ⓣ\text{Vs in } w_2 \, [\lambda w_1.$

$$ⓣ'\text{s} \text{counterpart-in-}w_1 \text{ swims in } \boldsymbol{w_1}]]]]$$

---

[5] The bi-directional dependence of imagination contents is due to the fact that imagining stands in a *synchronic* relation to its associated experience (see [19]). This differs from the (*diachronic*) referential dependence of episodic memory contents, which is only uni-directional (in the direction of (9a)).

      ($\equiv$ Zeno imagines V'ing his counterpart in an imaginary V'ed scene
      swim in this scene)

Notably, in contrast to (11c), the LF in (14a) interprets the embedded predicate *swim* at the same world as the embedded subject DP *himself*, viz. at the imaginer's experience alternatives, w_1. This is required by the assumption that the described event (here: a swimming) takes place in the same counterfactual world at which the agent of this event (here: the referent of the embedded subject DP; i.e. Zeno's counterpart) is determined. To capture the equivalence in (12), (14b) makes explicit reference to the dependent experience (see the clause 't Vs in w_2'). Since this reference also requires identifying the subject of this experience (here: Zeno['s counterpart], or – as we will see later – the semantic value of the silent pronoun PRO), it facilitates the formal implementation of first person-perspective (see Sect. 3.2). In (14b), the LF-referents of the 'imaginer' and the 'experiencer' are circled in grey (imaginer) resp. in black (experiencer).

    We close this subsection with a remark on the compatibility of (14) with Percus' *Generalization X*. The latter is a constraint on admissible readings of a sentence which demands that the world variable that a verb selects for must be coindexed with the nearest lambda above it [27, p. 201]. This constraint excludes (15a) as an admissible reading of (1). This LF gives a reading that describes Zeno's experience-counterpart as swimming in the actual world, @:

(15)   a.   [Zeno] [$\lambda t. t$ $\boxed{\text{imagines}}$ in @ $\boxed{[\lambda w_2.}$ t Vs in w_2
                                             $[\lambda w_1.$ t-in-w_1 swims in $\boxed{\textbf{@}}$ $]$ $]$ $]$

    b.   [Zeno] [$\lambda t. t$ $\boxed{\text{imagines}}$ in @ $\boxed{[\lambda w_2.}$ t Vs in w_2
                                             $[\lambda w_1.$ t-in-w_1 swims in $\boldsymbol{w_2}$ $]$ $]$ $]$

Since the mere inversion of the order of the lambdas in (13) (see (15b)) evaluates *swim* at the 'middle' world, w_2, *Generalization X* also excludes the reading in (15b). By interpreting the embedded predicate at the same world as the embedded subject DP (along the lines proposed in (14)), we avoid this exclusion. In (14), *swim* is evaluated at the 'lowest' world, w_1, as *Generalization X* demands.

3   Self-Imagination and Experiential Parasitism

With the referential dependence between imagination and experience(s) in place, we turn to the second property of imagining that is relevant for the inside/outside-distinction, viz. *de se*-ness:

3.1   Imagining *de se*

De se- (or self-locating) attitudes are first-personal attitudes that the holders of these attitudes self-ascribe, to the effect that these attitudes "crucially involve the attitude holder's access to [his/her] own 'self'" ([33, p. 411]; see also [13,

34]). In English, *de se*-attitudes are commonly denoted by reports with subject-controlled infinitives or gerundives (e.g. (16b), (17); see [6]) and can be denoted by infinitives and gerundive small clauses with a reflexive subject (e.g. (16); see [28]):

(16)   John wants himself to be famous

    a.   John$_i$ wants John$_i$ to be famous ($\equiv$ [J.][$\lambda t.\, t$ wants t to be famous])

    b.   John$_i$ wants PRO$_i$ to be famous

(17)   Alda$_i$ avoids PRO$_i$ getting a parking ticket

Following Lewis [13] and Chierchia [6], the contents of *de se*-attitudes are standardly modelled as sets of centered worlds. Centered worlds are worlds that are experienced from the perspective of one of the individuals in these worlds (i.e. from the perspective of the *center* of these worlds). Formally, centered worlds are coded as world/individual-pairs $\langle w, y \rangle$, where y is the center of w (see [13,33]).

In attitude reports like (16b) and (17), Chierchia's analysis associates the subject of the control clause, i.e. PRO, with the individual center of the world that is introduced by the matrix attitude verb (above: *want* resp. *avoid*; see [6]). Analogously to the treatment of world-variables in syntax (see Sect. 2.2), variables over individual centers can be bound by a lambda abstractor. To emphasize the 'unity' of centered worlds, we allow abstraction over ordered pairs of world- and individual-variables, resulting in abstracts of the form $\lambda \overline{\langle w, y \rangle}$. Using such abstracts, the reports in (16b) and (17) are then analyzed as (18) and (19), respectively:

(18)   John $\boxed{\text{wants}}$ in @ $\boxed{[\lambda\langle w, y\rangle.\, y \text{ is famous in } w]}$

    ($\equiv$ John stands in a wanting relation to worlds whose center is famous)

(19)   Alda $\boxed{\text{avoids}}$ in @ $\boxed{[\lambda\langle w, y\rangle.\, y \text{ gets a parking ticket in } w]}$

Unsurprisingly, the above analysis is often also applied to imagination reports with subject-controlled gerundive small clauses (e.g. (20a); see [10,34]). On this analysis, the 'non-parasitic' reading of (20a) (which neglects the dependent experience) is taken to report Zeno as standing in the imagining relation to worlds whose center is swimming (see (20b)):

(20)   a.   Zeno$_i$ imagines PRO$_i$ swimming in the ocean

    b.   Zeno $\boxed{\text{imagines}}$ in @ $\boxed{[\lambda\langle w, y\rangle.\, y \text{ is swimming in the ocean in } w]}$

3.2   Experientially Parasitic *de se*-Imagining

The analysis of the subject-controlled imagination report in (20b) can be straightforwardly transferred to the *de parasito*-version of (20a), i.e. (21a). In the resulting LF (see (21b)), the *de se*-center is doubly circled. To avoid overly long LFs, we replace 't's counterpart-in-w_1' by 't-in-w_1':

(21)   a.   Zeno$_i$ imagines **PRO**$_i$ V'ing himself swimming in the ocean

  b.   [Zeno] $[\lambda t.\,t\;\boxed{\text{imagines}}\;\text{in}\;@\;(\!(\,\overline{[\lambda\langle w_2,y\rangle.\;\boxed{y}}\,)\!)\;\text{Vs in}\;w_2\;[\lambda w_1.$
                                                                    $t\text{-in-}w_1\;\text{swims in}\;w_1\,]\,\boxed{]}\,]\,]$

Note that the LFs in (20b) and (21b) identify different centered contents. In particular, while (20b) interprets the complement in (20a) as the set of centered worlds whose center is swimming, (21b) interprets this complement (analyzed as the *imagine*-complement in (21a)) as the set of worlds whose center is $\underline{\text{V'ing}}$ (e.g. visually perceiving) Zeno's counterpart from the imagined scene swimming. We will return to this difference below.

Work on self-imagining (e.g. the kind of imagining reported by (1)) typically follows the above in identifying the *de se*-attitude with the matrix attitude (see e.g. [34, 40]). What has escaped researchers' attention – but what is at work in (1a) *vis-à-vis* (1b) – is that the experience can also be *de se*. This is suggested by our discussion of parasitic imagining in Section 2.2 and is evidenced by (22) (note the silent pronoun PRO in the complement of V):

(22)   Zeno$_i$ imagines PRO$_i$ V'ing **PRO**$_i$ swimming in the rough ocean

The possible *de se*-ness of the matrix attitude [= imagining] and the experience [= V'ing] then predicts four combinatorially possible parametrized LFs for (1) (in (23), where (23a) copies (14b) and where V = {*feel, see*}). Since we assume that names are rigid designators (s.t. evaluating *Zeno* yields the same individual at all worlds), we suppress counterpart relations (writing 't' instead of 't-in-w_1').

(23)   a. [Zeno]$[\lambda t.\,t\;\boxed{\text{imagines}}\;\text{in}\;@\;[\boxed{\lambda w_2.}\;t\;\text{Vs in}\;w_2\;[\lambda w_1.\;t\;\text{swims in}\;w_1\,]\,\boxed{]}\,]$

       b. [Z.]$[\lambda t.\,t\;\boxed{\text{imagines}}\;\text{in}\;@\;[\boxed{\lambda w_2.}\;t\;\text{Vs in}\;w_2\;[\lambda\langle w_1,x\rangle.\;x\;\text{swims in}\;w_1\,]\,\boxed{]}\,]$

       c. [Z.]$[\lambda t.\,t\;\boxed{\text{imagines}}\;\text{in}\;@\;[\boxed{\lambda\langle w_2,y\rangle.}\;y\;\text{Vs in}\;w_2\;[\lambda w_1.\;t\;\text{swims in}\;w_1\,]\,\boxed{]}\,]$

       d. Z. $\boxed{\text{imagines}}\;\text{in}\;@\;[\boxed{\lambda\langle w_2,y\rangle.}\;y\;\text{Vs in}\;w_2\;[\lambda\langle w_1,x\rangle.\;x\;\text{swims in}\;w_1\,]\,\boxed{]}$

In what follows, we call the above LFs 'non-*de se*' (i.e. (23a)), 'experience *de se*' (i.e. (23b)), 'matrix *de se*' (i.e. (23c)), and 'doubly *de se*' (i.e. (23d)), respectively. The LFs in (23) roughly correspond to the English sentences in (24):

(24)   a. Zeno$_i$ imagines [that he$_i$ Vs [that he$_i$ is swimming in the ocean]]
       b. Zeno$_i$ imagines [that he$_i$ Vs [PRO$_i$ swimming in the ocean]]
       c. Zeno$_i$ imagines [PRO$_i$ V'ing [that he$_i$ is swimming in the ocean]]
       d. Zeno$_i$ imagines [PRO$_i$ V'ing [PRO$_i$ swimming in the ocean]]

4   Multiply Parasitic Imagining and Constraints on *de se*-Ascription

We have suggested above that imagining can determine *different* counterfactual experiences – saliently, proprioception [bodily feeling] (see (1a)) and visual perception [seeing/watching] (see (1b)). Given the possible realization of V by *feel* respectively by *see*, the parametrized LFs in (23) then have the (many !) possible readings in (25):

(25)   Zeno imagines himself swimming   (see (1))
        (≡ Zeno imagines [himself V'ing [himself swimming]])

    a. ~~[Zeno][$\lambda t.t$ imagines in @ [$\lambda w_2.t$ feels in w_2 [$\lambda w_1.t$ swims in w_1]]]~~

    b. [Zeno][$\lambda t.t$ imagines in @ [$\lambda w_2.t$ sees in w_2 [$\lambda w_1.t$ swims in w_1]]]

    c. ~~[Z.][$\lambda t.t$ imagines in @ [$\lambda \langle w_2,y\rangle.y$ feels in w_2 [$\lambda w_1.t$ swims in w_1]]]~~

    d. [Z.][$\lambda t.t$ imagines in @ [$\lambda \langle w_2,y\rangle.y$ sees in w_2 [$\lambda w_1.t$ swims in w_1]]]

    e. [Z.][$\lambda t.t$ imagines in @ [$\lambda w_2.t$ feels in w_2 [$\lambda \langle w_1,x\rangle.x$ swims in w_1]]]

    f. ~~[Z.][$\lambda t.t$ imagines in @ [$\lambda w_2.t$ sees in w_2 [$\lambda \langle w_1,x\rangle.x$ swims in w_1]]]~~

    g. Zeno imagines in @ [$\lambda \langle w_2,y\rangle.y$ feels in w_2 [$\lambda \langle w_1,x\rangle.x$ swims in w_1]]

    h. ~~Zeno imagines in @ [$\lambda \langle w_2,y\rangle.y$ sees in w_2 [$\lambda \langle w_1,x\rangle.x$ swims in w_1]]~~

A first restriction on the readings in (25) comes from natural constraints on the content of proprioception resp. of visual perception. These constraints include the obligatory *de se*-nature of proprioceptive content (i.e. the inherently first-personal perspective – or self-directedness – of bodily feeling) and the typically non-*de se* nature of visual perception content (i.e. the observation that our vision is typically directed towards the outside). The first constraint excludes all LFs with non-centered 'feeling'-content, viz. (25a) and (25c) (indicated by a double strikethrough). The second constraint marks as non-salient all LFs with centered visual perception content, viz. (25f) and (25h). Vendler attributes this non-salience to the external perspectivity of visual perception, which "put[s] the perceiver in a spatial relation to the object" [39, p. 165]. In (25), LFs with centered visual perception content are indicated by a single strikethrough.

From the remaining LFs (copied in (26)), the intuitive readings of (1), i.e. (26d) [= (1a)] and (26b) [= (1b)], are then obtained by considering intuitive lexical-semantic constraints on acts of proprioception respectively of (visual) perception. These constraints include the inherently *de se*-nature of bodily feeling and of seeing. This nature excludes non-self-locating feeling and seeing, as is assumed in (26c) and in (26a) (indicated by a single strikethrough):

(26)   a. ~~[Zeno][$\lambda t.t$ imagines in @ [$\lambda w_2.t$ sees in w_2 [$\lambda w_1.t$ swims in w_1]]]~~

    b. [Z.][$\lambda t.t$ imagines in @ [$\lambda \langle w_2,y\rangle.y$ sees in w_2 [$\lambda w_1.t$ swims in w_1]]]

       ≡ [Zeno$_i$][$\lambda t.t$ imagines [PRO$_i$ seeing [t swimming ...]]]

       ≡ Zeno imagines seeing/watching himself swimming ...   ≡ (1b)

    c. ~~[Z][$\lambda t.t$ imagines in @ [$\lambda w_2.t$ feels in w_2 [$\lambda \langle w_1,x\rangle.x$ swims in w_1]]]~~

    d. Z. imagines in @ [$\lambda \langle w_2,y\rangle.y$ feels in w_2 [$\lambda \langle w_1,x\rangle.x$ swims in w_1]]

       ≡ Zeno$_i$ imagines [PRO$_i$ experiencing [PRO$_i$ swimming ...]]

       ≡ Zeno imagines what it would feel like to swim ...   ≡ (1a)

The combination of 'V = *feel*' with centered matrix and experience content – and the attendant identification of the 'experiencer'- with the 'swimmer'-perspective in (26d) – then identifies (26d) with the inside reading of (1). The combination of 'V = *see*' only with centered matrix content – and the attendant separation of the (centered) 'perceiver'- and the 'swimmer'-perspective – identifies (26b) with the outside reading.

5   Applications

We finish our paper by using the proposed analysis to account for some well-known puzzles and debates involving the inside/outside-distinction. These include Vendler and Walton's disagreement about outside readings of gerundive imagination reports with PRO-subjects (see Sect. 5.1), the salience of inside readings of subject-controlled gerundive memory reports, and the non-availability of an outside reading of Williams' [46] *imagine being Napoleon* (both Sect. 5.2):

5.1   Vendler and Walton's Disagreement

Our previous considerations have focused on imagination reports with reflexive complements (i.e. complements that are headed by reflexive pronouns like *himself*). While most researchers agree that such reports are ambiguous along the lines described in Sect. 1, they disagree whether imagination reports with subject-controlled gerundive complements (e.g. (20a), copied in (27)) display an analogous ambiguity: in line with Vendler [39, pp. 162–163], many researchers assume that subject-controlled gerundive imagination reports only allow for an *inside* reading (see e.g. [26,34]), making (27) equivalent with (27a). Following Walton [41, pp. 28–35], researchers in the opposing camp assume that (27) can also be used to report an outside perspective (see e.g. [2,44]), making (27) ambiguous between (27a) and (27b) (with a slight preference for (27a)):

(27)   Zeno$_i$ imagines [PRO$_i$ swimming in the ocean]

    a.   Zeno imagines *what it would feel like* to swim in the ocean ($\equiv$ (1a))

    b. $^{??}$Zeno imagines *watching himself* swimming in the ocean ($\equiv$ (1b))

The acceptance of outside readings like (27b) is typically fuddered by examples like (28), which include the perspective of the spectator (in (28a), due to Walton [41, p. 31]) or which remove the possibility of inside consciousness (in (28b); due to Anand [2, p. 4]; see [39, p. 166]):

(28)   a.   Gregory imagines hitting the home run [in a major league baseball game] from the perspective of a spectator in the stands. [...] his imagination of the field includes Gregory as he slams the ball over the center field fence and rounds the bases

    b.   Mary imagined being buried, unconscious, under a pile of snow inches away from the rescue team

However, upon closer inspection, the examples in (28) do not support the availability of (27b) as an admissible reading for (27). This is due to the fact that, in the scenes that are described by these examples, the familiar interpretation of subject-controlled gerundive complements (= 'inside') is not available. The outside reading of (28a) and (28b) can then be explained through a pragmatic reinterpretation of the complement in these reports. Since (27) – by admission of defenders of Walton's ambiguity – has an inside reading, an analogous explanation of the outside reading is not available for (27).

The above suggests that Walton's predicted ambiguity is due to a flip-flop between a syntactically suggested inside reading and a pragmatically coerced outside reading. Our results from Sects. 2, 3 and 4 suggest an alternative explanation of Vendler and Walton's disagreement about the ambiguity of (27) that does not assume pragmatic coercion. This explanation is based on the existence of two possible referents of PRO in (27), viz. the individual center of the alternatives that are introduced by the matrix verb (s.t. (27) is analyzed as 'matrix *de se*'; see (29a)) or the individual center of the alternatives that are introduced by the silent experience verb V (s.t. (27) is analyzed as 'experience *de se*'; see (29b)):

(29) $Zeno_i$ imagines PRO_i swimming in the ocean

    a. $Zeno_i$ imagines $[PRO_i$ V'ing [himself swimming in the ocean]]

    b. $Zeno_i$ imagines [himself V'ing $[PRO_i$ swimming in the ocean]]

The readings in (29a) and (29b) differ with regard to which LFs they allow for (29): while the matrix *de se*-reading in (29a) – which we associate with Walton – is compatible with both of the LFs in (30) (see (23c), (23d)), the experience *de se*-reading in (29b) – which we associate with Vendler – is only compatible with the LF in (30b) (see (23d)). The unavailability of this LF for 'V = *see*' (see our argument for the exclusion of (25h) in Sect. 4) then explains Vendler's exclusion of an outside reading of (27). The availability of (30a) for 'V = *see*' explains Walton's inclusion of this reading.

(30)   a. $[Z.] [\lambda t. t\ \boxed{\text{imagines}}\ \text{in @}\ \boxed{[\lambda \langle w_2, y \rangle.}\ y\ \text{Vs in } w_2\ [\lambda w_1.\ t\ \text{swims in } w_1]\ \boxed{]}\ \boxed{]}\ ]$

        $(\equiv\ [\text{Zeno}] [\lambda t. t\ \text{imagines } [PRO_i\ \text{V'ing } [t\ \text{swimming} \ldots]]])$

    b. $Z. \boxed{\text{imagines}}\ \text{in @}\ \boxed{[\lambda \langle w_2, y \rangle.}\ y\ \text{Vs in } w_2\ [\lambda \langle w_1, x \rangle.\ x\ \text{swims in } w_1]\ \boxed{]}$

        $(\equiv\ Zeno_i\ \text{imagines } [PRO_i\ \text{V'ing } [PRO_i\ \text{swimming} \ldots]])$

Arguably, the above observations still leave open the question of which one – matrix or experience *de se* – is the 'correct' reading of PRO in (27), i.e. who was right: Vendler or Walton. Since the syntax of iterated attitude reports is still understudied (s.t. we cannot draw any conclusions about matrix or experience *de se* based on the movement and ellipsis behavior of (24)), we try to answer this question by considering a closely related domain, viz. gerundive *remember*-reports:

5.2 Remembering 'From the Outside'

In contrast to gerundive imagination reports (e.g. (20a), (1)), gerundive memory reports are generally taken to have a salient inside reading (see (32a)):

(31)   John$_i$ remembers [PRO$_i$ feeding the cat]   (see [34, ex. (22)])

(32)   John remembers [himself feeding the cat]

      a.   John remembers [what is felt/was like to feed the cat]

      b. $^{??}$John remembers [seeing/watching himself feeding the cat]

The salience of the reading in (32a) is supported by the observation – reflected in corpus data – that memory reports with subject-controlled gerundive complements (e.g. (31)) are strongly preferred[6] over memory reports with reflexive subject-complements (e.g. (32)) in most contexts. This observation is striking since the pronoun *himself* is typically ambiguous between a control and a non-control interpretation (see [28]). As a result, one would expect that the admissible readings of (32) <u>include</u>[7] the reading(s) of (31). Given speakers' general dispreference for (32), this suggests that *remember* semantically marks (as deviant, or 'noteworthy') non-centered alternatives in either matrix or experience position.

    We will see below that our constraints on the content and act of the experience (i.e. V $\in$ {*feel, see*}; see Sect. 4) attribute this marking to non-centered alternatives in <u>experience</u> position. We have already found that these constraints only leave the $\overline{imagine}$-counterparts of (33a) (see (26d)) and (33b) (see (26b)):

(33)   a.   John $\boxed{\text{remembers}}$ in @ $\boxed{[\lambda\langle w_2, y\rangle.\; y\; \boxed{\text{feels}}\; \text{in } w_2\; [\lambda\langle w_1, x\rangle.}$

$$x \text{ feeds the cat in } w_1]\,]$$

        $\equiv$ John$_i$ remembers [PRO$_i$ experiencing [PRO$_i$ feeding the cat]]

    b.   [John] $[\lambda t.\, t\; \boxed{\text{remembers}}\; \text{in } @\; \boxed{[\lambda\langle w_2, y\rangle.\; y\; \boxed{\text{sees}}\; \text{in } w_2\; [\lambda w_1.}$

$$t \text{ feeds the cat in } w_1]\,]\,]$$

        $\equiv$ [John$_i$] $[\lambda t.\, t$ remembers [PRO$_i$ seeing [t feeding the cat]]]

Since, in (33), the only LF that is not doubly *de se* (i.e. (33b)) has its non-centered alternative in experience position, we conclude that *remember* marks non-centered alternatives in this position. This suggests that the explicit PRO in (31) is interpreted in experience position. This is in line with Vendler [40] and with the intuition of most researchers on the inside/outside-distinction (see Sect. 5.1).

    We finish this section by suggesting an explanation for the non-availability of an outside reading of Williams' *imagine being Napoleon*: in [46, p. 43], Bernard Williams observes that, while he can imagine from the inside being Napoleon (s.t. he can hold the attitude that is reported by the reading of (34) in (34a)),

---

[6] This preference disappears in self-reflection contexts, in which the mnemonic subject considers herself as a perceived object (see e.g. [18]).

[7] Whether this inclusion is proper depends on whether PRO denotes the matrix or the experiential center.

he is unable to imagine from the outside that he is Napoleon (s.t. he ca<u>nnot</u> hold the attitude that is reported by the reading in (34b)). Williams backs his observation by referring to the intuitive absence of a self – distinct from (himself *qua*) Napoleon – that could perceive this identity.[8]

(34)   Bernard imagines [PRO$_i$ being Napoleon]

    a.   Bernard imagines [what it would be like if he were Napoleon]

    b.   #Bernard$_i$ imagines [PRO$_i$ seeing [that he$_i$ is Napoleon]]

$$\equiv [\text{Bernard}]\,[\lambda t.\, t \,\boxed{\text{imagines}}\, \text{in} \, @ \, \boxed{[\lambda\langle w_2, y\rangle.\, y \,\textbf{ sees } \text{in } w_2}$$
$$\boxed{[\lambda w_1.\, t \text{ is Napoleon in } w_1]}]]$$

Our framework captures Williams' intuition through another familiar constraint on visual perception: the restriction to what can be visually perceived. Specifically, this constraint includes that perception cannot serve to establish the personal identity of a perceived object (e.g. Napoleon) with the perceiver. However, exactly this would be required for the outside reading of (34). The insufficiency of perception for the establishment of personal identity is reflected in the semantic deviance of (34b).

The above notwithstanding, our identification of PRO in (34) with <u>experience</u> *de se* (see above) even allows for a yet simpler exclusion of (34b). The latter is based on the fact that (34b) involves experience <u>non-</u>*de se* (see the overt [= non-controlled] occurrence of *he* in the complement of *see*). Since this is incompatible with the use of PRO in (34) – as we have argued for (31) –, (34b) is not an admissible reading of (34).

6   Outlook

Our considerations in this paper have focused on the linguistic realization of the inside/outside-distinction. The cross-linguistic robustness[9] of this distinction suggests that there is a real psychological difference between the first-personal (*field*) and the third-personal (*observer*) perspective on a personally experienced event. For imagination, this difference is already suggested in Vendler [39], and has been corroborated by behavioral and imaging studies (see e.g. [7,14]). In particular, in [7], Christian et al. have shown that first-person imagining of painful scenarios elicits greater activity in brain areas associated with interoceptive and emotional awareness, with visual imagery, and with sense of body ownership.

---

[8] see Williams' "images of myself being Napoleon can scarcely merely be images of the physical figure of Napoleon, for they will not in themselves have enough of me in them – an external view would lose the essence of what makes such imaginings so much more compelling about myself than they are about another" [46, p. 43].

[9] The inside/outside-ambiguity is also attested in languages (e.g. German) that do not allow for subject-controlled *imagine*-complements (see (†)):

    (†)   Zeno$_i$ stellt sich vor, wie er$_i$ (selbst) im Ozean schwimmt (translation of (29))

        a.   Zeno stellt sich vor, wie es sich anfühlt, im Ozean zu schwimmen   (s. (1a))

        b.   Zeno$_i$ stellt sich vor, wie er$_i$ sich (selbst) im Ozean schwimmen sieht (s. (1b)).

In their groundbreaking work, Addis et al. [1] and St. Jacques et al. [32] have observed a remarkable overlap in the neural and cognitive mechanisms that underlie episodic memory and imagination. Michaelian [21] even goes so far as to claim that remembering is just a special form of imagining that results from a reliable episodic construction mechanism and is directed towards one's personal past. Pointing out the close connection between the reliability of remembering and its causal dependence on the event remembering, Werning [42] contradicts this view and argues that remembering is distinct in kind from imagining.

Regardless of this controversy, the overlap between neural and cognitive processes underlying remembering and imagining might suggest that the difference between first- and third-person perspective on the experienced event in imagination is equally present in episodic remembering. This suggestion is further supported by the fact that the verbs *remember* and *imagine* have a very similar selection behavior. However, at least for recent events, observer perspective has been found to be less common in episodic remembering [20,31] (see [29,30]). This may be due to the particular importance of self-performed actions for episodic memory, and to the inherently first-personal perspective on such actions. Exceptions to this rule are PTSD patients' memories of traumatic events [3] and memories that involve intense emotional components or high self-awareness [22,30].

Recently, McCarroll [17,18] has claimed that agents can also take a third-personal mnemonic perspective on non-traumatic and emotionally less intense events. McCarroll supports his claim with reference to the epistemic generativity of episodic memory and to the observation that observer memories can be epistemically and emotionally beneficial. We leave the exploration of this claim as a topic for future work.

References

1. Addis, D.R., Wong, A.T., Schacter, D.L.: Remembering the past and imagining the future. Neuropsychologia **45**(7), 1363–1377 (2007)
2. Anand, P.: Suppositional projects and subjectivity. Ms (2011)
3. Berntsen, D., Willert, M., Rubin, D.C.: Splintered memories or vivid landmarks? Appl. Cogn. Psychol. **17**(6), 675–693 (2003)
4. Blumberg, K.: Counterfactual attitudes and the relational analysis. Mind **127**(506), 521–546 (2018)
5. Blumberg, K.: Desire, imagination, and the many-layered mind. Ph.D. thesis, NYU (2019)
6. Chierchia, G.: Anaphora and attitudes de se. Semant. Context. Expr. **11**, 1–31 (1989)
7. Christian, B.M., Parkinson, C., Macrae, C.N., Miles, L.K., Wheatley, T.: When imagining yourself in pain, visual perspective matters. J. Cogn. Neurosci. **27**(5), 866–875 (2015)
8. Debus, D.: Imagination and memory. In: Kind, A. (ed.) Routledge Handbook of the Philosophy of Imagination, pp. 135–148. Routledge (2016)
9. Egré, P.: Question-embedding and factivity. Ms (2008)
10. Higginbotham, J.: Remembering, imagining, and the first person. In: Barber, A. (ed.) Epistemology of Language, pp. 496–533. OUP, Oxford (2003)

11. Kaplan, D.: Demonstratives. In: Almog, J., Perry, J., Wettstein, H. (eds.) Themes from Kaplan, pp. 489–563. Oxford University Press, Oxford (1989)

12. Karttunen, L.: Some observations on factivity. Res. Lang. Soc. Interact. **4**(1), 55–69 (1971)

13. Lewis, D.: Attitudes de dicto and de se. Phil. Rev. **88**(4), 513–543 (1979)

14. Libby, L.K., Eibach, R.P.: Visual perspective in mental imagery. Adv. Exp. Soc. Psychol. **44**, 185–245 (2011)

15. Liefke, K.: Reasoning with an (experiential) attitude. In: Sakamoto, M., Okazaki, N., Mineshima, K., Satoh, K. (eds.) JSAI-isAI 2019. LNCS (LNAI), vol. 12331, pp. 276–293. Springer, Cham (2020). https://doi.org/10.1007/978-3-030-58790-1_18

16. Maier, E.: Parasitic attitudes. Ling. Philos. **38**(3), 205–36 (2015)

17. McCarroll, C.J.: Looking the past in the eye: distortion in memory and the costs and benefits of recalling from an observer perspective. Conscious. Cogn. **49**, 322–332 (2017)

18. McCarroll, C.J.: Remembering from the Outside: Personal Memory and the Perspectival Mind. Oxford University Press, Oxford (2018)

19. McCarroll, C.J.: Remembering the personal past: beyond the boundaries of imagination. Front. Psychol. **11**, 26–52 (2020)

20. McDermott, K.B., Wooldridge, C.L., Rice, H.J., Berg, J.J., Szpunar, K.K.: Visual perspective in remembering and episodic future thought. Q. J. Exp. Psychol. **69**(2), 243–253 (2016)

21. Michaelian, K.: Mental Time Travel: Episodic Memory and our Knowledge of the Personal Past. MIT Press, Cambridge, MA (2016)

22. Nigro, G., Neisser, U.: Point of view in personal memories. Cogn. Psychol. **15**(4), 467–482 (1983)

23. Niiniluoto, I.: Imagination and fiction. J. Semant. **4**(3), 209–222 (1985)

24. Ninan, D.: Imagination, inside and out. Ms (2007)

25. Ninan, D.: Counterfactual attitudes and multi-centered worlds. Semant. Pragmat. **5**(5), 1–57 (2012)

26. Peacocke, C.: Imagination, experience, and possibility: a Berkelein view defended. In: Foster, J., Robinson, H. (eds.) Essays on Berkeley: A Tercentennial Celebration, pp. 19–35. Clarendon Press, Oxford (1985)

27. Percus, O.: Constraints on some other variables in syntax. Nat. Lang. Seman. **8**, 173–229 (2000)

28. Percus, O., Sauerland, U.: On the LFs of attitude reports. Proc. Sinn Bedeutung **7**, 228–242 (2003)

29. Rice, H.J., Rubin, D.C.: I can see it both ways: first-and third-person visual perspectives at retrieval. Conscious. Cogn. **18**(4), 877–90 (2009)

30. Robinson, J.A., Swanson, K.L.: Autobiographical memory: the next phase. Appl. Cogn. Psychol. **4**(4), 321–335 (1990)

31. Schacter, D.L.: Searching for Memory: The Brain, the Mind, and the Past. Basic Books, New York (1996)

32. St. Jacques, P.L., Carpenter, A.C., Szpunar, K.K., Schacter, D.L.: Remembering and imagining alternative versions of the personal past. Neuropsychologia **110**, 170–179 (2018)

33. Stephenson, T.: Control in centred worlds. J. Semant. **27**(4), 409–36 (2010)

34. Stephenson, T.: Vivid attitudes: centered situations in the semantics of remember and imagine. In: Proceedings of SALT, vol. XX, pp. 147–160 (2010)

35. Sutton, J.: Observer perspective and acentred memory: some puzzles about point of view in personal memory. Philoso. Stud. **148**(1), 27–37 (2010)

36. Tulving, E.: Memory and consciousness. Can. J. Psychol. **26**, 1–26 (1985)
37. Tulving, E.: Episodic memory and autonoesis: uniquely human? In: Terrace, H., Metcalfe, J. (eds.) The Missing Link in Cognition, pp. 3–56. OUP (2005)
38. Umbach, C.: Vivid perception: Dewac 1 summary. Ms. Unpublished (2018)
39. Vendler, Z.: Vicarious experience. Rev. Métaphys. Morale **84**(2), 161–173 (1979)
40. Vendler, Z.: Speaking of imagination. In: Simon, T.W., Scholes, R.J. (eds.) Language, Mind, & Brain, pp. 35–43. Lawrence Erlbaum Associates (1982)
41. Walton, K.L.: Mimesis as Make-Believe. Harvard UP, Cambridge (1990)
42. Werning, M.: Predicting the past from minimal traces: episodic memory and its distinction from imagination and preservation. Rev. Philos. Psychol. 1–33 (2020)
43. Werning, M., Cheng, S.: Taxonomy and unity of memory. In: Bernecker, S., Michaelian, K. (eds.) The Routledge Handbook of Philosophy of Memory, pp. 7–20. Routledge, New York (2017)
44. White, A.R.: The Language of Imagination. Basil Blackwell (1990)
45. White, A.S., Rawlins, K.: The role of veridicality and factivity in clause selection. In: Proceedings of NELS 48 (2018)
46. Williams, B.: Imagination and the self. In: Problems of the Self: Philosophical Papers 1956–1972, pp. 26–45. CUP, Cambridge (1973)

Against the Multidimensional Approach to Honorific Meaning: A Solution to the Binding Problem of Conventional Implicature

David Y. Oshima[✉]

Nagoya University, Nagoya 464-8601, Japan
davidyo@nagoya-u.jp
http://www.hum.nagoya-u.ac.jp/~oshima

Abstract. It has been suggested in the literature that the social-deictic meaning contributed by honorific expressions (in Japanese, Korean, Thai, etc.) belong to a dimension isolated from that of proffered (or at-issue) content. This work demonstrates that, like proffered contents and presuppositions, honorific meanings may interact with a proffered content introduced elsewhere in a way that cannot be easily accounted for under the Pottsian multidimensional approach, and develops an alternative analysis using a "pseudo-multidimensional" framework.

Keywords: Honorification · Projection of conventional implicature · The binding problem · Japanese

1 Introduction

In some recent works on the semantics of honorific expressions, including Potts and Kawahara (2004) and McCready (2019), honorific meaning—the social-deictic meaning contributed by honorific expressions in Japanese, Korean, Thai, etc.—is regarded as belonging to a dimension isolated from that of proffered (or at-issue) content. Drawing on data from Japanese, a language known to have an elaborate system of honorifics, this work argues that this multidimensional approach to honorific meaning is problematic in suffering from the "binding problem" familiar from the literature on the projection of non-proffered meaning (Karttunen and Peters 1979; Sudo 2012). As an alternative, a compositional analysis of honorific meaning couched in a "pseudo-multidimensional" framework will be put forth, which circumvents the binding problem concerning honorific meaning as well as other types of non-proffered (projective) meaning.

2 Basic Assumptions

This section illustrates some key assumptions as to how honorific meaning is to be represented, and what kind of non-proffered content it is.

© Springer Nature Switzerland AG 2021
N. Okazaki et al. (Eds.): JSAI-isAI 2020 Workshops, LNAI 12758, pp. 113–128, 2021.
https://doi.org/10.1007/978-3-030-79942-7_8

2.1   The Logical Representation of Honorific Meaning

It has been widely acknowledged in the literature that honorifics contrast with each other not only in terms of *who* they honorify but also *to what degree* they honorify their target. The gradable nature of honorific meaning can be illustrated with a data set like (1).[1] All data sets to be discussed are from standard Japanese.

(1)   Resutoran wa kyuukai ni   {a. **aru**   /b. **arimasu**
       restaurant Th 9th.floor Dat   exist.Prs   exist.AddrHon.Prs
       /c. **gozaimasu**   }.
          exist.AddrHon.Prs
       'The restaurant is on the 9th floor.'

(1a) does not convey any honorific meaning. (1b) and (1c) involve addressee(-oriented) honorifics and convey respect toward the addressee, the latter's honorific meaning being stronger.

Largely based on Oshima (2019), I adopt the following assumptions concerning the logical representation of honorific meaning.[2]

(2)   a.   The range of respectfulness expressible with honorifics is represented as the interval between real numbers 0 and 1. The members of this interval are referred to as "honorific values". The value 0 corresponds to the lack or respect, and the value 1 corresponds to the maximum degree of (linguistically expressible) reverence.

       b.   In any given utterance context, the addressee and potential referents are assigned honorific values within the interval: $[0, 1]$, depending on to what extent the speaker (acknowledges that she) honors them.

       c.   Each honorific expression is associated with an honorific value within the range: $(0, 1]$ (i.e., greater than 0 and equal to or smaller than 1), and conveys that its target's honorability is at least as high as that value.

More elaborate ways to represent the social relation/status that honorifics make reference to (the notion that has been labeled as honorability, honorificity, etc.) have been put forth in the literature; for example, McCready (2019), formulates it in terms of real-number intervals, and Yamada (2019) in terms of probability distributions. The relatively simple representation in terms of real-number values, however, will suffice for the purpose of the current work.

---

[1] The abbreviations in glosses are: Acc = accusative, AddrHon = addressee(-oriented) honorific, ARG1Hon = ARG1 honorific (subject-oriented honorific), ARG2Hon = ARG2 honorific (object-oriented honorific), Attr = attributive, Cop = copula, Dat = dative, DP = discourse particle, Gen = genitive, Ger = gerund, NegAux = negative auxiliary, Nom = nominative, Npfv = non-perfective auxiliary, PossHon = possessor honorific, Prs = present, Pst = past, Th = thematic *wa* (topic/ground marker).

[2] Oshima (2019) discusses that some referents may be assigned, and some honorifics—called negative honorifics or dishonorifics—are associated with, honorific values smaller than 0. The issue of negative honorification is not directly relevant to the purpose of the current work, and will be put aside.

The indexical (i.e., context-sensitive) function **HON** is introduced as the contextual parameter that honorifics look up. This function assigns honorific values to individuals, thus serving as a representation of who the speaker (acknowledges that) she honors to what extent in the utterance context.

(1b) and (1c)'s honorific meanings can be represented as in (3a) and (3b), with the tentative minimum honorific values of 0.3 and 0.7, respectively (for the purpose of the current discussion, it is not the specific honorific values but their relative order that matters).

(3) a. **HON(Addressee)** ≥ 0.3
     b. **HON(Addressee)** ≥ 0.7

For a Japanese conversation to be felicitous, it is required that "due respect" be expressed toward the individuals mentioned or evoked in the utterance as well as toward the addressee, and also that none of these individuals be excessively elevated ("overhonorified"). To account for this, Oshima (2019) introduces the following pragmatic principles (called Reverence Maximization #1/Reverence Maximization #2 there):

(4) a. **Reverence Maximization (Content)**: For any utterance u, each lexical item (word or multi-word unit) i involved in u must be chosen in such a way that i, among its honorific variants, expresses the highest degrees of reverence toward (i) the addressee of u and (ii) the referents mentioned or evoked in u that do not exceed what these individuals deserve.
     b. **Reverence Maximization (Form)**: For any utterance u, each lexical item (word or multi-word unit) i involved in u must be chosen in such a way that i, among its honorific variants, expresses reverence toward (i) the addressee of u and (ii) the referents mentioned or evoked in u with the largest number of honorific feature types without expressing a degree of reverence that exceeds what these individuals deserve.

Two (or more) expressions are said to be honorific variants of each other if they are synonymous or near-synonymous (see Note 4) but differ in the strength (or presence/absence) of honorific meaning. ARU[3], ARIMASU, and GOZAIMASU in (1) are an example of (a tuple of) honorific variants. (4a) dictates that (1a), (1b), and (1c) are the appropriate choice when the addressee's honorific value is within (i) $[0, 0.3)$, (ii) $[0.3, 0.7)$, and (iii) $[0.7, 1]$, respectively. When the addressee is the speaker's child, sibling, or parent, (1a) will be the only natural option; this implies that the Japanese social norms are such that one does not attribute an honorific value of 0.3 or greater to their close blood relatives. When the speaker is a receptionist of a luxury hotel and is talking to a guest, (1c) will be the most

---

[3] Expressions in small capitals refer to lexemes.

natural option; this implies in this setting the speaker is expected to assign an honorific value of 0.7 or greater to the addressee.[4]

(4b), on the other hand, accounts for the pattern illustrated in (5). Here, the meanings of (5a) and (5c), including the honorific components, are expected to be equivalent, the addressee-oriented honorific morpheme *mas* targeting the same individual as the ARG1 (subject-oriented) honorific morpheme *rare* but conveying a weaker (honorific) meaning; compare (6a) and (6c).[5]

(5)   (Tanaka, an office worker, grabs a document on the desk. Eguchi, a younger colleague, says to her:)

    a.   Sore, moo   yomaremashita   yo.
         that already read.ARG1Hon.AddrHon.Pst DP
         'You read it already.'

    b.   Sore, moo   yomimashita   yo.
         that already read.AddrHon.Pst DP
         'idem'

    c.   #Sore, moo   yomareta   yo.
          that already read.ARG1Hon.Pst DP
         (idem)

                                               (Oshima 2019:377)

(6)   a.   (5a) $\mapsto$ $\langle$**read(tanaka, the-document); HON(Addressee)** ≥ 0.3 & **HON(tanaka)** $\geq 0.4\rangle$
       (equivalent in the context to:
       $\langle$**read(tanaka, the-document); HON(tanaka)** ≥ 0.3 & **HON(tanaka)** $\geq 0.4\rangle)$

    b.   (5b) $\mapsto$ $\langle$**read(tanaka, the-document); HON(Addressee)** $\geq 0.3\rangle$
       (equivalent in the context to:
       $\langle$**read(tanaka, the-document); HON(tanaka)** $\geq 0.3\rangle)$

    c.   (5c) $\mapsto$ $\langle$**read(tanaka, the-document); HON(tanaka)** $\geq 0.4\rangle$

(4b) dictates here that two types, rather than one, of honorific features—addressee honorific and ARG1 honorific—be present.

---

[4] McCready (2019) suggests that the effects of (4a) arise from a scale-based pragmatic principle along the lines of Maximize Presupposition. A potentially problematic issue with this idea is the existence of honorific variants which differ not only in honorific meaning but also in some other semantic components. An example of such a tuple of honorific variants is $\langle$KURU, IRASSHARU$\rangle$, where the first is a non-honorific verb meaning 'come', and the second is an ARG1 (subject-oriented) honorific covering the meanings of 'come', 'go', and 'exist, be (located)'. I will not attempt here to settle the issue of whether (4a) can be reduced to a purely pragmatic process.

[5] ARG1 honorifics and ARG2 honorifics refer to those honorific predicates whose target of reverence is the referent of the least oblique (most prominent) argument (i.e., subject) and the second second-least oblique (most prominent) argument (e.g., dative object), respectively.

2.2   The Status of Honorific Meaning

It has also been widely acknowledged that honorific meaning is a kind of "non-proffered" (or "not-at-issue") content. The current work, in line with Oshima (2016), adopts the taxonomy/terminology presented in (7), where the term conventional implicature (CI) is understood broadly, (i) as an equivalent of "non-proffered content" and (ii) as a category subsuming "presupposition" as well as "expressive content".

(7)   **conventionally coded meaning**
   i.   **proffered content**
   ii.   **conventional implicature (CI)** (= non-proffered content ≈ Tonhauser et al.'s (2013) "projective content")
        ii-a.   **non-presuppositional CI** (≈ CI in Potts's (2005) sense)
        ii-b.   **presuppositional CI** (= presupposition ≈ CI in Karttunen and Peters's (1979) sense)

   With McCready (2019), and departing from Oshima (2019), I will take honorific meaning to be non-presuppositional (CI). The non-presuppositionality of honorific meaning can be illustrated with an example like the following, where *ome ni* KAKARU 'meet' (lit., 'be caught in (somebody's) eyes') is a phrasal honorific ARG2 predicate contributing a complex honorific meaning along the lines of (9), which amounts to saying (i) that the referent of its object is honorable and (ii) that the referent of its subject is less honorable than that of its object (Kikuchi 1997:262–267). Observe that the use of this honorific is felicitous despite it not being common ground that interlocutor B (or A) is supposed to show high respect to the woman in question.

(8)   (A and B work for the same company. B is senior to and in a higher position than A. They are attending a banquet in a hotel.)
   A: Mechakucha hade   na   kimono kite
        extremely   flashy Cop.Attr kimono put.on.Ger
        masu   ne, ano hito.
        Npfv.AddrHon.Prs DP that person
        'That person wears a very flashy kimono, doesn't she?'
   B: Kimi wa **ome-ni-kakatta**   koto   ga   nakatta   ka.
        you   Th meet.ARG2Hon.Pst matter Nom not.exist.Pst DP
        Shachoo no   okusama   da.
        president Gen wife.PossHon Cop.AddrHon.Prs
        'So you have not met her. She is the president's wife.'
   B': #Kimi wa atta   koto   ga   nakatta   ka. Shachoo no
         you   Th meet.Pst matter Nom not.exist.Pst DP president Gen
        okusama   da.
        wife.PossHon Cop.AddrHon.Prs
        'So you have not met her. She is the president's wife.'

(9)   **HON(the-woman)** ≥ 0.6 & **HON(the-woman)** > **HON(Addressee)**

3   The Two Approaches

This section illustrates the key features of two recently developed formal models of honorification, McCready (2019) and Oshima (2019), which respectively adopt the multidimensional and monodimensional approaches.

3.1   The Multidimensional Approach

McCready (2019), as well as Potts and Kawahara (2004), considers honorific meaning to be completely isolated from proffered content, being confined in a separate dimension of semantic representation. She adopts a multidimensional framework built on Potts (2005), where generally the meaning of an utterance is understood to be a pair of (i) a proffered content and (ii) a collection of CIs, the latter of which is possibly empty. The semantic representation of (10a–d), for example, will look like (11). For an expository purpose, the specific formulation of honorific meaning is adapted from that in McCready (2019) to the one explained in Sect. 2.1.

(10) a. Yamada-kyooju-ga **mieta**.
          Y.-professor-Nom   come.ARG1Hon.Pst

          'Professor Yamada (who is honorable) came.'
      b. Suzuki-kyooju-ga Ken-o **homerareta**.
          S.-professor-Nom K.-Acc praise.ARG1Hon.Pst

          'Professor Suzuki (who is honorable) praised Ken. '
      c. Ken-ga Suzuki-kyooju-o **otetsudai-shita**.
          K.-Nom S.-professor-Acc help.ARG2Hon.Pst

          'Ken helped Professor Suzuki (who is honorable and is more honorable than Ken).'
      d. Yumi-**san**-ga   Ken-o **homemashita**.
          Y.-HonRT-Nom K.-Acc write.AddrHon.Pst

          'Yumi (who is honorable) praised Ken (and I honor you).'

(11) a. (10a) $\mapsto$ $\langle$**come(yamada)**,
          $\{$**HON(yamada)** ≥ 0.5, **professor(yamada)**$\}\rangle$
      b. (10b) $\mapsto$ $\langle$**praise(suzuki, ken)**,
          $\{$**HON(suzuki)** ≥ 0.4, **professor(suzuki)**$\}\rangle$
      c. (10c) $\mapsto$ $\langle$**help(ken, suzuki)**,
          $\{$**HON(suzuki)** ≥ 0.4 & **HON(suzuki)** > **HON(ken)**$\}\rangle$
      d. (10d) $\mapsto$ $\langle$**praise(yumi, ken)**,
          $\{$**HON(yumi)** ≥ 0.2, **HON(Addressee)** $\geq 0.3\}\rangle$

The lexical meanings of the honorifics involved and the relevant compositional rules (in the form of rules of proofs) will be along the lines of (12) and (13); the names of the rules are those in McCready (2019). The system assumed here has three kinds of types: the at-issue type (σ^a), the CI type (σ^c), and the shunting type (σ^s). The third type occurs in the semantic representation of a natural-language expression with mixed content (such as an honorific), and is converted to the CI type during the compositional process. A logical expression of the form '$\alpha \blacklozenge \beta$' corresponds to the product type of σ^α and σ^β ($\sigma^\alpha \times \sigma^\beta$). '$\blacklozenge$' represents metalogical conjunction.

(12)   a.   mieta 'came' $\mapsto$
$\lambda x[\mathbf{come}(x)] \blacklozenge \lambda y[\mathbf{HON}(y) \geq 0.5] : \langle e, t\rangle^a \times \langle e, t\rangle^s$

   b.   homerareta 'praised' $\mapsto$
$\lambda x[\lambda y[\mathbf{praise}(y, x)]] \blacklozenge \lambda z[\mathbf{HON}(z) \geq 0.4] : \langle e, \langle e, t\rangle\rangle^a \times \langle e, t\rangle^s$

   c.   otetsudai-shita 'helped' $\mapsto$
$\lambda x[\lambda y[\mathbf{help}(y, x)]] \blacklozenge \lambda z[\lambda x_1[\mathbf{HON}(x_1) \geq 0.4 \ \& \ \mathbf{HON}(x_1) > \mathbf{HON}(z)] : \langle e, \langle e, t\rangle\rangle^a \times \langle e, \langle e, t\rangle\rangle^s$

   d.   homemashita 'praised' $\mapsto$
$\lambda x[\lambda y[\mathbf{praise}(y, x)]] \blacklozenge \mathbf{HON}(\mathbf{Addressee}) \geq 0.3 : \langle e, \langle e, t\rangle\rangle^a \times t^s$

   e.   Yamada $\mapsto$ **yamada** $: e^a$
(likewise for any other proper name)

   f.   kyooju $\mapsto \lambda x[\mathbf{professor}(x)] : \langle e, t\rangle^c$

   g.   san $\mapsto \lambda x[\mathbf{HON}(x)] \geq 0.2 : \langle e, t\rangle^c$

(13)   (R2) $\dfrac{\alpha : \langle \sigma^a, \tau^a\rangle, \ \beta : \sigma^a}{\alpha(\beta) : \tau^a}$

   (R4) $\dfrac{\alpha : \langle \sigma^a, \tau^c\rangle, \ \beta : \sigma^a}{\alpha(\beta) : \tau^c \bullet \beta : \sigma^a}$

   (R5) $\dfrac{\alpha : t^c \bullet \beta : \tau^a}{\beta : \tau^a}$

   (R9) $\dfrac{\alpha \blacklozenge \beta : \sigma^a \times t^s}{\alpha : \sigma^a \bullet \beta : t^c}$

These rules alone do not suffice to compose the meanings of (10a–c), which involve a predicative honorific targeting the referent of an argument, as will be discussed below.

3.2   The Unidimensional Approach

In Oshima (2019), honorific meaning is considered to belong to the same dimension as proffered content as well as paradigmatic varieties of presupposition. The framework adopted there can be characterized as "pseudo-multidimensional", and has the following features.

(14)   a.   Proffered content and CI are represented within a single logical expression, but nevertheless contribute to the pragmatic effect of the utterance in distinct ways.

   b.   Two levels of truth values are distinguished. The first is the classic values, 1 and 0, for regular logical formulas; they are called *semantic truth values*. The second is the *pragmatic truth values*, I and II, which are respectively concerned with "truth of proffered content" and "satisfaction of CI". The extension of a root declarative clause will be *a set of* pragmatic truth values, rather than an individual (semantic or pragmatic) value.

c. A natural language clause is translated into a "higher-order" formula involving (a variant of) Oshima's (2016) *transjunction* operator, defined in (15).[6]

(15) *The syntax and semantics of transjunction*
syntax: If ϕ and ψ are expressions of type t ($\mathbf{D}_t = \{1, 0\}$), then $\langle \phi; \psi \rangle$ is an expression of type T ($\mathbf{D}_T = \wp(\{\text{I}, \text{II}\}) = \{\emptyset, \{\text{I}\}, \{\text{II}\}, \{\text{I}, \text{II}\}\}$).
semantics: For any c, w, and g,

a. $\text{I} \in [\![\langle \phi; \psi \rangle]\!]^{c,w,g}$ iff $[\![\phi]\!]^{c,w,g} = 1$;
b. $\text{II} \in [\![\langle \phi; \psi \rangle]\!]^{c,w,g}$ iff $[\![\psi]\!]^{c,w,g} = 1$.

By way of exemplification, (16a), (16b), and (16c), respectively involving no (non-trivial) CI, a non-presuppositional CI (the content of the non-restrictive relative clause), and a presuppositional CI (the existential presupposition induced by *too*), will have logical translations along the lines of (17a–c); "**CG**($^\wedge p$)" is to be read as "It is common ground that p".

(16) a. John is in Chicago.
      b. John, who Mary admires, is in Chicago.
      c. [John]$_\text{F}$ too is in Chicago.

(17) a. $\langle \mathbf{in}(\mathbf{john}, \mathbf{chicago}); \top \rangle$
      b. $\langle \mathbf{in}(\mathbf{john}, \mathbf{chicago}); \mathbf{admire}(\mathbf{mary}, \mathbf{john}) \rangle$
      c. $\langle \mathbf{in}(\mathbf{john}, \mathbf{chicago}); \mathbf{CG}(^\wedge [\exists x[x \neq \mathbf{john}\ \&\ \mathbf{in}(x, \mathbf{chicago})]]) \rangle$

The meanings of (10a–d) can be approximated as in (18a–d), and those of the relevant lexical items as in (19a–g); note that here names (with or without a role term) are treated as generalized quantifiers.

(18) a. (10a) $\mapsto$
         $\langle \mathbf{come}(\mathbf{yamada}); \mathbf{HON}(\mathbf{yamada}) \geq 0.6\ \&\ \mathbf{professor}(\mathbf{yamada}) \rangle$
      b. (10b) $\mapsto$
         $\langle \mathbf{praise}(\mathbf{suzuki}, \mathbf{ken}); \mathbf{HON}(\mathbf{suzuki}) \geq 0.4\ \&\ \mathbf{professor}(\mathbf{suzuki}) \rangle$
      c. (10c) $\mapsto \langle \mathbf{help}(\mathbf{ken}, \mathbf{suzuki})$;
         $\mathbf{HON}(\mathbf{suzuki}) \geq 0.4\ \&\ \mathbf{HON}(\mathbf{suzuki}) > \mathbf{HON}(\mathbf{ken}) \rangle$
      d. (10d) $\mapsto \langle \mathbf{praise}(\mathbf{yumi}, \mathbf{ken})$;
         $\mathbf{HON}(\mathbf{yumi}) \geq 0.2\ \&\ \mathbf{HON}(\mathbf{Addressee}) \geq 0.3 \rangle$

(19) a. mieta $\mapsto$
         $\lambda x[\langle \mathbf{come}(x); \mathbf{HON}(x) \geq 0.5 \rangle]$
      b. homerareta $\mapsto$
         $\lambda x[\lambda y[\langle \mathbf{praise}(y, x); \mathbf{HON}(x) \geq 0.4 \rangle]]$

---

[6] Oshima's (2016) treatment of CIs is based on the model developed in Oshima (2006a,b), where the operator called *preditional* plays a simlar role as transjunction.

c. otetsudai-shita $\mapsto$
$\lambda x[\lambda y[\langle \mathbf{help}(y, x); \mathbf{HON}(x) \geq 0.4 \,\&\, \mathbf{HON}(x) > \mathbf{HON}(y)\rangle]]$

d. homemashita $\mapsto$
$\lambda x[\lambda y[\langle \mathbf{praise}(y, x); \mathbf{HON}(\mathbf{Addressee}) \geq 0.3\rangle]]$

e. Yamada $\mapsto$
$\lambda \mathcal{P}_{\langle e,T \rangle}[\langle \mathbf{F}_p((\mathcal{P})(\mathbf{yamada})); \mathbf{F}_c((\mathcal{P})(\mathbf{yamada}))\rangle]$
(likewise for any other proper name)

f. kyooju $\mapsto$
$\lambda \mathbb{P}_{\langle\langle e,T \rangle,T \rangle}[\lambda \mathcal{P}_{\langle e,T \rangle}[\langle \mathbf{F}_p(\mathbb{P}(\mathcal{P})); \mathbf{F}_c(\mathbb{P}(\mathcal{P}))\,\&\,$
$\mathbf{F}_c(\mathbb{P}(\lambda x[\langle \top; \mathbf{professor}(x)\rangle]))]]$

g. san $\mapsto$
$\lambda \mathbb{P}_{\langle\langle e,T \rangle,T \rangle}[\lambda \mathcal{P}_{\langle e,T \rangle}[\langle \mathbf{F}_p(\mathbb{P}(\mathcal{P})); \mathbf{F}_c(\mathbb{P}(\mathcal{P}))\,\&\,$
$\mathbf{F}_c(\mathbb{P}(\lambda x[\langle \top; \mathbf{HON}(x) \geq 0.2\rangle]))]]$

The function $\mathbf{F}_p$ serves to extract the proffered content of a higher-order formula, while $\mathbf{F}_c$ serves to extract the CI. Their definitions are as follows:

(20) For any c, w, and g,

a. if Φ is an expression of type T, then,
$[\![\mathbf{F}_p(\Phi)]\!]^{c,w,g}$
$= 1$ if $\mathrm{I} \in [\![\Phi]\!]^{c,w,g}$;
$= 0$ otherwise;

b. if Φ is an expression of type T, then,
$[\![\mathbf{F}_c(\Phi)]\!]^{c,w,g}$
$= 1$ if $\mathrm{II} \in [\![\Phi]\!]^{c,w,g}$;
$= 0$ otherwise.

The compositional rules in (21)–(23), built on run-of-the-mill PTQ-style translation rules, will guarantee that any pieces of CI introduced by predicates and arguments are projected (inherited) to the clause level.

(21) **The 'Name + Role Term' Rule**:
Let α be a phrase whose daughters are (i) a name β, and (ii) a role term γ, where β translates into: $\beta'_{\langle\langle e,T \rangle,T \rangle}$ and γ translates into: $\gamma'_{\langle\langle\langle e,T \rangle,T \rangle,\langle\langle e,T \rangle,T \rangle\rangle}$. Then, α translates into: $\gamma'(\beta')$.

(22) **The 'Subj. + Pred.' Rule**:
Let α be a phrase whose daughters are (i) a one-place predicate β, and (ii) its argument NP γ, where β translates into: $\beta'_{\langle e,T \rangle}$ and γ translates into: $\gamma'_{\langle\langle e,T \rangle,T \rangle}$. Then, α translates into: $\gamma'(\beta')$.

(23) **The 'Subj. + Obj. + Pred.' Rule**:
Let α be a phrase whose daughters are (i) a two-place predicate β, (ii) its subject argument NP γ, and (iii) its object argument NP δ, where β translates into: $\beta'_{\langle e,T \rangle}$, γ translates into: $\gamma'_{\langle\langle e,T \rangle,T \rangle}$, and δ translates into: $\delta'_{\langle\langle e,T \rangle,T \rangle}$. Then, α translates into: $\gamma'(\lambda x_2[\delta'(\lambda x_1[\beta'(x_1)(x_2)])])$.

4   The Binding Problem for Honorific Meaning

The multidimensional approach is motivated by the observation that honorific meaning does not interact with such sentential operators as negation and attitude predicates. Oshima's pseudo-multidimensional treatment too is compatible with this feature; a case can be made, however, that if a formal analysis that is more constrained in disallowing—by design—interaction between honorific meaning and other semantic components suffices to account for all facts, it is preferable to a less constrained one.

Honorific meaning, however, does interact with proffered content introduced elsewhere. For one thing, the honorific meaning of an argument honorific predicate has to be applied to the individual referred to by an argument nominal (the least oblique argument (i.e., the subject) in the case of an ARG1 honorific; the second-least oblique argument in the case of an ARG2 honorific), as in (10a–c). As discussed by McCready (2019:64–70) in detail, under the multidimensional analysis it is a tricky task to achieve this compositionally. McCready considers some possible solutions, but finds none of them fully satisfactory.

The problem becomes more prominent when one considers cases involving quantification. Consider the scenario in (24).

(24)   24-year-old Sato works for a humanitarian NGO, and Ando is the president of this organization. They are involved in a joint disaster relief activity with several volunteer groups. Volunteer group A has 20 members. 10 are college students around 20 years old; Sato is close to them, and does not use argument honorifics targeting them when talking with Ando. The other 10 are senior to Sato. He considers them honorable, and specifically assigns honorific values around 0.5, when talking with Ando. Ando is senior to all 20 members, and does not use argument honorifics targeting them when talking with Sato.

In this context, an utterance like (25S) can be felicitously made. The quantificational expression *nannin-ka* here is an adverbial (an instance of what is sometimes called a floating quantifier), and requires their restrictor to be humans. The meaning of *mimashita*, which involves an ARG1 honorific feature and an addressee honorific feature, is assumed to be (26).

(25)   A: A-han-kara-wa   dareka   kita?
          A-group-from-Th somebody come.Pst
          'Did anyone come from Group A?'
        S: Hai, A-han-no   menbaa-wa nannin-ka
          yes   A-group-Gen member-Th several
          miemashita.
          come.ARG1Hon.AddrHon.Pst
          'Yes, several members of Group A came.'

(26)   miemashita ↦
        $\lambda x [\langle \mathbf{come}(x); \mathbf{HON}(x) \geq 0.5\ \&\ \mathbf{HON}(\mathbf{Addressee}) \geq 0.3 \rangle]$

The felicity of the use of the honorific *miemashita* indicates that (25S) does not conventionally implicate that all individuals included in the restrictor (i.e., the members of Group A) are honorable. On the other hand, (25S) does not merely conventionally implicate that several individuals included in the restriction are honorable. If this were the case, (25S) would be true and felicitous when it is some of the junior members who came. In actuality, however, (25S) is understood to mean that several of the senior members—the honorable ones—came.[7]

Since Karttunen and Peters , it has been widely recognized that a multidimensional framework has difficulty accounting for how a natural-language quantifier (especially an existential one) may refer to the same individual(s) at the level of proffered content and at the level of CI (which is taken here to subsume

---

[7] (25S) furthermore conversationally implicates that no junior members came. That is, (25S) would be misleading (though true) if uttered in a situation where, say five senior members and five junior members came. Such a situation, indeed, cannot be easily described—one would have to say something like:

(i)   Nannin-ka nenpai-no   menbaa-ga **miete,**   ato
        several   senior-Cop.Attr member-Nom come.ARG1Hon.Ger and
        nannin-ka wakate-mo   **kimashita.**
        several   young.person-also come.AddrHon.Pst.
        'Several senior members came, and several junior members came, too.'

   Conversely, the variant of (25S) without the referent-honorific feature, (ii), conversationally implicates that no senior members come.

(ii)   A-han-no   menbaa-wa nannin-ka **kimashita.**
        A-group-Gen member-Th several   come.AddrHon.Pst
        'Several members of Group A came.'

   A similar "ineffability" issue arises when an argument denotes a group that is heterogenous in terms of honorability; in my judgment, (iii-a) and (iii-b) sound both deviant, and some sort of rephrasing has to be made to express the same propositional content in a pragmatically felicitous way (cf. (i) above).

(iii)   (The speaker works under Matsui, and Umeno works under the speaker.)
        Matsui-buchoo-to Umeno-ga ni-ji-ni   {a. #**kuru** /b.
        M.-director-and   U.-Nom   two-o'clock-Dat   come.Prs
        #**mieru**}.
        come.ARG1Hon.Prs
        (Matsui, the director, and Umeno will come at two o'clock.)

   Davis (2020) discusses that in a variety of the Yaeyaman language (genetically related to Japanese, belonging to the Japonic family), Kohama, an analog of (iii-a) is felicitous, and in two other varieties, Maezato and Hatoma, an analog of (iii-b) is felicitous. He further remarks that speakers of standard Japanese are divided into three groups: (i) those who reject both (iii-a,b), (ii) those who prefer (iii-a), and (iii) those who prefer (iii-b). Davis develops an account of this kind of cross- and intra-linguistic variation in terms of rankings of competing pragmatic constraints, which might be extendable to sentences like (25S) and its analogs in other dialects/languages.

presupposition), e.g., why sentence (27) conveys something along the lines of (28a), rather than something like (28b)/(28c).

(27)   Several students had [a dessert]$_F$ too.

(28)   a.   Several students had a dessert (proffered content), and *those students who had a dessert* had something other than a dessert (presupposition).

    b.   Several students had a dessert (proffered content), and several students had something other than a dessert (presupposition).

    c.   Several students had a dessert (proffered content), and all students had something other than a dessert (presupposition).

That (27) does not mean (28b) can be confirmed with the observation that (27) cannot be felicitous when (29a) is commmon ground. That (27) does not mean (28c) can be confirmed with the observation that (27) can be felicitous when (29b) is commmon ground.

(29)   a.   There are 20 students in the cafeteria. Five of them had a dessert and nothing else, seven had a sandwich and nothing else, and eight had a hamburger and nothing else.

    b.   There are 20 students in the cafeteria. Five of them ate nothing. Seven had a sandwich, and eight had a hamburger.

The issue posed by (25S) can be seen as a special case of this general "binding problem".

It is also worth noting that the putative semantic independence—the property of exclusively contributing to a dimension distinct from that of the proffered content—of certain kinds of non-presuppositional CI-bearing expressions, including expressive adjectives like *damn* and appositive phrases, have been called into question. Amaral et al. 2007 point out that in (30a) the expressive adjective *friggin'* in the complement clause most naturally reflects negative evaluation by Monty, rather than the speaker, and that in (30b) the appositive phrase is most naturally taken to convey that Sheila, rather than the speaker, is committed to Chuck's potentially being a sweetheart.

(30)   a.   (We know that Bob loves to do yard work and is very proud of his lawn, but also that he has a son Monty who hates to do yard chores. So Bob could say (perhaps in response to his partner's suggestion that Monty be asked to mow the lawn while he is away on business):) Well, in fact Monty said to me this very morning that he hates to mow the friggin' lawn.

    b.   (It is common ground that Chuck is a psychopath.) Sheila believes that Chuck, a sweetheart if she ever met one, is fit to watch the kids.

(adapted from Amaral et al. 2007:736,737)

Such observations imply that the CIs induced by these triggers may interact with the meanings of embedding verbs like *say* and *believe*, thereby suggesting that the multidimensional analysis is not as suitable for the treatment of non-presuppositional CIs, let alone presuppositional ones, as it may initially appear.

Now back to honorifics. To derive the appropriate meaning of (25S), I postulate (31) as the meaning of the quantificational adverb *nannin-ka*. (31a) involves the CI that the restrictor consists of humans; (31b) is a simplified version without this CI, and I will use it hereafter for the ease of exposition.

(31)   nannin-ka $\mapsto$

    a. $\lambda \mathcal{P}_{\langle e,T \rangle}[\lambda \mathcal{Q}_{\langle e,T \rangle}[\textbf{SEVERAL}(\lambda x[\langle \textbf{F}_p(\mathcal{P}(x)); \textbf{F}_c(\mathcal{P}(x))$ & $\forall y[\textbf{F}_p(\mathcal{P}(y)) \rightarrow \textbf{human}(y)]\rangle], \mathcal{Q})]]$

    b. $\lambda \mathcal{P}_{\langle e,T \rangle}[\lambda \mathcal{Q}_{\langle e,T \rangle}[\textbf{SEVERAL}(\mathcal{P}, \mathcal{Q})]]$

The interpretative rule for the logical predicate **SEVERAL**, built on the denotation of *nannin-ka* (or English *several*) assumed in the classical (i.e., transjunction-free) GQ theory, is given in (32); $\textbf{F}_m$, the "merging" function, is defined in (33).

(32)   For any c, w, and g,

    a. $[\![\textbf{SEVERAL}(\mathcal{P}, \mathcal{Q})]\!]^{c,w,g} = \{\text{I, II}\}$ if
        $[\![\textbf{several}(\lambda x[\textbf{F}_m(\mathcal{P}(x))], \lambda y[\textbf{F}_m(\mathcal{Q}(y))])]\!]^{c,w,g} = 1$;

    b.   else,

        (i) $[\![\textbf{SEVERAL}(\mathcal{P}, \mathcal{Q})]\!]^{c,w,g} = \{\text{I}\}$ if
            $[\![\textbf{several}(\lambda x[\textbf{F}_p(\mathcal{P}(x))], \lambda y[\textbf{F}_p(\mathcal{Q}(y))])]\!]^{c,w,g} = 1$; and

        (ii) $[\![\textbf{SEVERAL}(\mathcal{P}, \mathcal{Q})]\!]^{c, w, g} = \{\text{II}\}$ if
            $[\![\textbf{several}(\lambda x[\textbf{F}_c(\mathcal{P}(x))], \lambda y[\textbf{F}_c(\mathcal{Q}(y))])]\!]^{c,w,g} = 1$;

    c.   else, $[\![\textbf{SEVERAL}(\mathcal{P}, \mathcal{Q})]\!]^{c,w,g} = \emptyset$.

(33)   For any c, w, and g, if Φ is an expression of type T, then,
    $[\![\textbf{F}_m(\Phi)]\!]^{c,w,g}$
    $= 1$ if $[\![\Phi]\!]^{c,w,g} = \{\text{I, II}\}$;
    $= 0$ otherwise.
    (i.e., "$\textbf{F}_m(\langle \phi; \psi \rangle)$" is equivalent to "$\phi$ & ψ")

The interpretation of **several** may be approximated as in (34), in accordance with the plain GQ theory.

(34)   For any c, w, and g, $[\![\textbf{several}(P_{\langle e,t \rangle}, Q_{\langle e,t \rangle})]\!]^{c,w,g} = 1$ iff
    the cardinality of $\{a \mid [\![P(x)]\!]^{c,w,g[a/x]} = 1\} \cap \{b \mid [\![Q(x)]\!]^{c,w,g[b/x]} = 1\}$
    is greater than two.

With the additional semantic rule in (35) and the lexical meaning of *A-han-no menbaa* 'members of group A' as postulated in (36), the meaning of (25S) will be computed as (37).

(35)   **The 'Subj. + Q Adv. + Pred.' Rule**:
    Let α be a phrase whose daughters are (i) a one-place predicate β, (ii)

its subject argument NP γ, and (iii) an adverbial quantifier δ, where β translates into: $\beta'_{\langle e,T\rangle}$, γ translates into: $\gamma'_{\langle e,T\rangle}$, and δ translates into: $\delta'_{\langle\langle e,T\rangle,\langle\langle e,T\rangle,T\rangle\rangle}$. Then, α translates into: $(\delta'(\gamma'))(\beta')$.

(36)   A-han-no menbaa $\mapsto \lambda x[\langle(\textbf{member-of}(\textbf{group-a}))(x); \top\rangle]$

(37) $\textbf{SEVERAL}(\lambda x[\langle(\textbf{member-of}(\textbf{group-a}))(x); \top\rangle], \lambda y[\langle\textbf{come}(y);$
$\textbf{HON}(y) \geq 0.5 \ \& \ \textbf{HON}(\textbf{Addressee}) \geq 0.3\rangle])$

What (37) denotes under what conditions can be roughly put as follows. Let P be the set of members of Group A, and Q, Q', and Q'' be the set of "honorable comers", "comers", and "honorable people", respectively. If the cardinality of $P \cap Q$ is greater than two (and the addressee is honorable), then the extension of (37) will be {I, II}—i.e., (37) will be both true and "felicitous" (in the sense that its CI is satisfied). If this condition is not met, then, (i) if "$|P \cap Q'| > 2$" holds, then the extension of (37) will be {I}, and (ii) if "$|P \cap Q''| > 2$" holds (and the addressee is honorable), then the extension of (37) will be {II}.

In this way, the proposed analysis rightly predicts (i) that sentence (25S) is true and felicitous in the specified context, (ii) that (25S) would be true but infelicitous if it were some junior members (or some junior members plus one senior member) who came, (iii) (25S) would be false but felicitous if no member had come, (iv) (25S) would be false and infelicitous if no member had come *and* no member were honorable from Sato's viewpoint.

(32) is formulated in such a way that any CIs in the restrictor and any CIs in the nuclear scope contribute to the felicity conditions of the whole sentence in a symmetric way. (38) is an example of a sentence where the restrictor of *several* involves a non-trivial CI, with its subject having a meaning along the lines of (39) ($^\cap$ is an operator that maps a property of individuals to a kind; Carlson 1980). (32) guarantees that the propositional CI present in (39)—something to the effect that the speaker thinks negatively of astrologers in general—is projected (inherited) to the whole sentence.

(38)   Several damn astrologers left.

(39)   several damn astrologers $\mapsto$
$\lambda \mathcal{P}_{\langle e,T\rangle}[\textbf{SEVERAL}(\lambda x[\langle\textbf{astrologer}(x); \textbf{bad}(^\cap\textbf{astrologer})\rangle], \mathcal{P})]$

The illustrated analysis of how CIs induced by honorifics and other triggers may contribute to the meanings of quantified statements leaves much room for further development and improvement. In particular, it is yet to be seen how the meanings of a full range of quantificational operators (*most, no, exactly three*, etc.) might be handled. I believe, however, the discussion presented above makes a fairly strong case for adopting a system that allows interaction between honorific meaning induced by honorifics and proffered content induced elsewhere.

5   A Note on Sudo's Anaphora-Based Solution of the Binding Problem

Sudo (2012, 2014) proposes a solution to the challenge posed by the binding problem with the multidimensional approach to presupposition. His discussion is concerned with presupposition, but it can straightforwardly be extended to CIs in general.

His key idea is that a presupposition (CI) may involve a discourse referent that may be anaphoric to one introduced and quantified in the proffered dimension. This process of "cross-dimensional anaphora" works essentially in the same way as "cross-sentential anaphora"; in particular, (i) when the "antecedent" is an existential-quantificational nominal, such as *a student* and *two students*, it is the intersection of its restrictor and nuclear scope that is understood as being linked to the relevant referent in the presupposition (*refset* anaphora), (ii) when the antecedent has a positive or negative universal force, as is the case with *no student*, it is its restrictor (*maxset* anaphora), and (iii) when the antecedent is a partitive nominal such as *most of the students*, both *refset* and *maxset* interpretations are available (though one of them may be preferred in context).

Although Sudo's solution seems technically viable, I find the pseudo-multidimensional approach more promising for two reasons. First, Sudo's account implies that presupposition is computed after the update of the context with the proffered takes place. As acknowledged by Sudo himself (2014:8), this goes against the standard assumption as to the order of semantic calculation—that if presupposition and the rest are computed step-wise, it is the former that is computed first.

Second, a full theory of CIs will need to account for a different sort of interaction across putative dimensions—specifically, that between an attitude predicate such as *believe* and the CI of its complement. The following example, and possibly (30a,b) above too, instantiate the phenomenon in question.

(40)   Lucy believes that [Ken]$_F$ sang, too.
         ⤳ 'Lucy believes that somebody other than Ken sang.'

It is not clear how an anaphora-based analysis may deal with this.[8]

6   Summary

The social-deictic meaning conveyed by honorifics is non-presuppositional conventional implicature, and may interact with a semantic operator in the proffered dimension. It was argued that the multi-dimensional approach adopted by McCready (2019) has trouble accounting for the latter feature, and that a pseudo-multidimensional framework in line with Oshima (2016, 2019) is more suitable for the description of honorific meaning.

---

[8] See Oshima (2006a, 2006b) for a pseudo-multidimensional account of the CI projection pattern under attitude predicates.

References

Amaral, P., Roberts, C., Smith, A.: Review of the logic of conventional implicatures by Chris Potts. Linguist. Philos. **30**, 707–749 (2007). https://doi.org/10.1007/s10988-008-9025-2

Carlson, G.: Reference to Kinds in English. Garland, New York (1980)

Davis, C.: Pragmatic constraints on subject-oriented honorifics in Yaeyaman and Japanese. In: Proceedings of Semantics and Linguistic Theory, vol. 30, pp. 674–693 (2020)

Karttunen, L., Peters, S.: Conventional implicature. In: Oh, C.-K., Dinneen, D.A. (eds.) Syntax and Semantics, vol. 11: Presupposition, pp. 1–56. Academic Press, New York (1979)

Kikuchi, Y.: Keigo [Honorifics]. Kodansha, Tokyo. A reprint of a book published in 1994 by Kadokawa Shoten, Tokyo (1997)

McCready, E.: The Semantics and Pragmatics of Honorification: Register and Social Meaning. Oxford University Press, Oxford (2019)

Oshima, D.Y.: Perspectives in reported discourse. Ph.D. dissertation, Stanford University (2006a)

Oshima, D.Y.: Motion deixis, indexicality, and presupposition. In: Proceedings of Semantics and Linguistic Theory, vol. 16, pp. 172–189. CLC Publications, Ithaka (2006b)

Oshima, D.Y.: The meanings of perspectival verbs and their implications on the taxonomy of projective content/conventional implicature. In: Proceedings of Semantics and Linguistic Theory, vol. 26, pp. 43–60. CLC Publications, Ithaka (2016)

Oshima, D.Y.: The logical principles of honorification and dishonorification in Japanese. In: Kojima, K., Sakamoto, M., Mineshima, K., Satoh, K. (eds.) JSAI-isAI 2018. LNCS (LNAI), vol. 11717, pp. 325–340. Springer, Cham (2019). https://doi.org/10.1007/978-3-030-31605-1_24

Potts, C.: The Logic of Conventional Implicatures. Oxford University Press, Oxford (2005)

Potts, C., Kawahara, S.: Japanese honorifics as emotive definite descriptions. In: Proceedings of Semantics and Linguistic Theory, vol. 14, pp. 235–254. CLC Publications, Ithaka (2004)

Sudo, Y.: On the semantics of phi features on pronouns. Ph.D. dissertation, Massachusetts Institute of Technology (2012)

Sudo, Y.: Presupposition projection in quantified sentences and cross-dimensional anaphora. Manuscipt, University College London (2014)

Tonhauser, J., Beaver, D., Roberts, C., Simons, M.: Toward a taxonomy of projective content. Language **89**, 66–109 (2013). https://doi.org/10.1353/lan.2013.0001

Yamada, A.: The syntax, semantics and pragmatics of Japanese addressee-honorific markers. Ph.D. dissertation, Georgetown University (2019)

A Persona-Based Analysis of Politeness in Japanese and Spanish

Akitaka Yamada[1]([envelope]) [ORCID] and Lucia Donatelli[2] [ORCID]

[1] Osaka University, 1-8 Machikaneyama-cho, Toyonaka, Osaka, Japan
a.yamada@lang.osaka-u.ac.jp
[2] Saarland University, Saarbrücken, Germany
donatelli@coli.uni-saarland.de

Abstract. We present descriptive accounts of 'politeness' in Japanese and Spanish by analyzing Japanese subject- and addressee-honorifics and Spanish pronominal addressee forms. Our accounts focus on inter- and intra-speaker variation in the use of these expressions. Observing this variation, we ask the question of how expressive content interacts with context. We develop a model of Bayesian Dynamic Pragmatics [26], and propose an algorithm for how the use of a politeness-oriented marker contributes to the dynamic creation of the speaker's persona or publicized self-image. Our model captures multiple pragmatic factors that impact politeness-usage and persona simultaneously. As such, it is designed to be extended and explain comparable phenomena in other languages that employ politeness-oriented expressions.

Keywords: Bayesian Dynamic Pragmatics · Politeness · Honorifics · Persona · Real Number-based Pragmatics

1 Introduction

The principles governing 'politeness' in social interaction, or the grammatical expressions of social relations between speaker and addressee, are a current research question in formal semantics and pragmatics [17,19,26]. Exploring these principles in Japanese and Spanish—two well-documented languages that grammaticalize social relations and accompanying politeness in distinct manners—we propose a general pragmatic model regarding the way politeness information interacts with the context to create a specific persona of discourse participants.

In particular, our central concern lies in the source of the inter-/intra-speaker variation in usage of politeness-oriented expressions. In Japanese and Spanish, the way the speaker uses these expressions is affected by many different sociolinguistic and pragmatic factors [3,14,16,17,24,26]. Certainly, as a rule of thumb, there is a general tendency regulating the use of politeness expressions. Yet each

This work was supported by Grant-in-Aid for Research Activity Start-up [Grant Number: 20K21957 to Akitaka Yamada].

N. Okazaki et al. (Eds.): JSAI-isAI 2020 Workshops, LNAI 12758, pp. 129–144, 2021.
https://doi.org/10.1007/978-3-030-79942-7_9

time a speaker produces an utterance, they can strategically switch politeness forms, reflecting the multiplicity of the relevant contextual factors. These factors include age-difference, emotional engagement, formality, and psychological distance, among others. As a result, the speaker's use of a 'polite' form is subject to variation. By observing the speaker's tendency to use certain polite forms in place of others, the audience can learn what kind of person the speaker is. Our model intends to capture this dynamism in discourse and, we will argue, can be extended to other languages that make use of similar politeness-oriented expressions.

Our paper is structured as follows. In Sect. 2, we present the relevant data from both Japanese (Sect. 2.1) and Spanish (Sect. 2.2). In Sect. 3, we develop our analysis within the framework of Dynamic Pragmatics and extend it with Bayesian probability modeling to capture the specific dynamics of speaker relations [26]. Section 4 demonstrates how the concept of persona allows us to refine our model in Sect. 3 and capture the speaker intent behind politeness usage. We conclude our discussion in Sect. 5 with remarks on our work's theoretical implications and ideas for future studies.

2   Evidence

2.1   Japanese

Subject-Honorifics and Addressee-Honorifics. Japanese has several honorific markers to encode the speaker's 'politeness.' For example, observe the sentences in (1) .

(1)   Subject-honorifics

    a.   *yamada-san-wa   asita   koogi-o   **sur**-u.*
        Yamada-Ms.-TOP tomorrow lecture-ACC do-PRS
        'Ms. Yamada will have a lecture tomorrow.'

    b.   *yamada-san-wa   asita   koogi-o   **nasar**-u.*
        Yamada-Ms.-TOP tomorrow lecture-ACC do.SH-PRS
        '(i) Ms. Yamada will have a lecture tomorrow;
        (ii) the speaker respects the referent of the subject (= Ms. Yamada).'

Truth-conditionally, these sentences are equivalent. The second sentence, however, differs from the first one in that it uses the predicate *nasar-* 'do.SH,' in place of *sur-* 'do.' As a result, this sentence delivers secondary information that the speaker expresses their respect for the referent of the subject (= *Ms. Yamada*). Since *nasar-* obligatorily targets the subject of the sentence, it is called the SUBJECT-HONORIFIC MARKER (hereafter SH), and there are many different verbs and affixes used for subject-honorification.

Now, consider a different type of honorific marker provided in (2). Again, the sentences in (2) are equivalent in the at-issue dimension of the meaning. But unlike the first sentence, the second sentence contains an additional marker -*mas* 'AH,' with which the speaker shows their respect for the addressee. Since the target of the respect is always fixed to the addressee, it is called the ADDRESSEE-HONORIFIC MARKER (hereafter AH).

(2)   Addressee-honorifics

   a.   *yamada-san-wa   asita   undoo-o   sur-u.*
         Yamada-Ms.-TOP tomorrow exercise-ACC do-PRS
         'Ms. Yamada will do exercise tomorrow'

   b.   *yamada-san-wa   asita   undoo-o   si-**mas**-u.*
         Yamada-Ms.-TOP tomorrow exercise-ACC do-AH-PRS

         '(i) Ms. Yamada will do exercise tomorrow;
         (ii) the speaker respects the addressee.'

Differences. Traditional Japanese linguistics has treated SH and AH as being instances of the same honorific property with their difference only lying in the target of respect. Yet, the detailed honorific meanings they encode seem to be different.

To see how, consider a case where the referent of the subject noun phrase coincides with the addressee. If these politeness meanings are regulated by the same principle, we predict that either SH and AH are both present (= (3-a)), or both absent. However, this prediction is not borne out, as seen in (3).[1] These sentences are both grammatical, and the acceptability of the sentence in (3-b) suggests that the condition in which -*mas* is used is different from the one for the SH.[2]

---

[1] **Avoidance of a pronoun.** In Japanese, using an overt pronoun to refer to the addressee is considered rude, so the sentence in (3) lacks an overt second-person subject pronoun.

[2] **Real use examples.** A reviewer asked us whether there is yet another pattern acceptable in Japanese; that is, a sentence with an SH but not with an AH. Admittedly, such a sentence is not frequently observed. But as shown below, there are indeed some real use examples.

   (i)   *sikasi kyoo-wa sooyatte sugu   muri-o   **nasar**-u.*
          but   lord-TOP like that always impossible thing-ACC do.SH-PRS
          '(i) But you (= the lord) always overwork (= do impossible things) like that;
          (ii) the speaker respects the referent of the subject (= the addressee).'
          (http://matuhisa.doorblog.jp/archives/48889542.html)

   (ii)   *imasara mata   nani-o   **ossyar**-u.*
          this pass oh boy what-ACC say.SH-PRS.
          '(i) Now that things have come to this pass, oh boy, what are you saying?;
          (ii) the speaker respects the referent of the subject (= the addressee).'
          (http://dazai.or.jp/modules/novel/index.php?op=viewarticle&artid=108&page=54)

(3)   a.   *asita   hapyoo-o   **nasai-mas**-u-ka?*
              tomorrow presentation-ACC do.SH-AH-PRS-Q
              '(i) Are you having a presentation tomorrow?;
              (ii) the speaker respects the referent of the subject ($<$ -*nasar*)';
              (iii) the speaker respects the addressee ($<$ -*mas*).
       b.   *asita   happyoo-o   si-**mas**-u-ka?*
              tomorrow presentation-ACC do-AH-PRS-Q
              '(i) Are you having a presentation tomorrow?;
              (ii) the speaker respects the addressee ($<$ -*mas*).'

So, how do they differ? At the most rudimentary level, the following test in (4) serves as a nice criterion for classification. Normally, a teacher does not use the sentence in (3-a) without violating the social expectation, whereas they can use (3-b) felicitously. This suggests that an SH involves the speaker's assumption about the social hierarchy: specifically, that the speaker has a social status lower than the target of the honorification.

(4)   **Teacher-Student Test**
       Can a teacher/president (someone with a higher social status) use the honorific form to a student/employee (someone with a lower social status) without intentionally violating the expectation in the society?

What makes our language description slightly more complicated is that this social convention/assumption can be strategically violated if the speaker has a good reason to do so. For example, for the aforementioned reason, normally, teachers do not use the sentence in (3-a) when talking to their students, because teachers have a social status higher than the students. But when they do, they can give the audience an impression that they are polite to such an extent that they treat the students as having a higher social status. So, teachers who wish to create a superpolite or humble publicized self-image would prefer using the sentence in (3-a).

One may wonder whether (a) the social hierarchy is the only deterministic factor, or (b) it is a dominant factor, but just one of many factors for an SH. We will put forth the argument that (b) is the correct analysis. As far as we are aware, no literature in Japanese linguistics has proposed the former, stronger view. In addition, empirically, it is not necessary for a speaker to keep using SH markers to the same addressee, especially when the difference in social status is very small. If the social hierarchy is the only factor, the speaker obligatorily uses a SH, however small the difference may be. For these reasons, we take the latter view in (b) and elaborate our argument in Sect. 3.

In contrast, the addressee of (3-b) does not have to be someone whose social status is higher than the speaker. A teacher, for example, can utter this sentence to a student without violating the expectation of the social convention. Of course, a social status would be one important factor in deciding whether to use an AH, but there are many more possible motivations. Formality is one such factor. If a teacher is casually talking to a student after the class, they would use the sentence in (5), where no AHs are used.

(5)   *asita   happyoo   sur-u?*
       tomorrow presentation do-PRS
       'Are you having a presentation tomorrow?'

If the same teacher is in a conference, and a similar conversation takes place in a Q and A session, the teacher would use the sentence in (3-b). In both contexts, the social relation remains the same. But the formality of the contexts is different, and when it is formal, the 'probability' of the teacher's using (3-b) is strengthened.

Again, this observation is nothing more than a general tendency, obtained at the rudimentary level. Speakers can violate the social expectation when they strategically create their own self-image, resulting in inter- and intra-speaker variations. Even in an informal context, a teacher can use the sentence in (3-b). Thus, a study of politeness-oriented expressions inevitably touches the issue of pragmatic, sociolinguistic factors and variation, and as will be seen, this is also the case in Spanish.

2.2   Spanish

Pronominal Address Forms. Here we consider the grammaticalization of politeness in Spanish proniminal address forms; cf., Spanish also expresses politeness in the form of intonation [2]; prosody and gesture [5]; and discourse markers [15]. Spanish addressee systems differ in whether they are bipartite or tripartite in nature. Bipartite systems make use of the T-V distinction found in many languages with Latin origins, such that the singular pronoun *tú* conveys familiarity and confidence while *usted* connotes formality and respect [4]. Tripartite systems employ a third singular form, *vos*, which allows speakers to convey more solidarity and/or intimacy in its use to signal more equality and/or horizontality with their interlocutors [1]. In all varieties except for Castillian (Spain) Spanish, the plural address form is invariant and adheres to the V form, *ustedes*; in Spain, the informal variant is present as plural *vosotros*.

Though usage of pronominal address forms in Spanish tends to adhere to factors that distinguish familiar (T) from formal (V) uses, usage in practice can vary depending on geographical area and particular community norms. Contemporary Spanish exhibits a preponderance towards the general usage of *tú* or *vos* (depending on geographical location), in large part due to social and political movements for equality [22]. Thus, settings that previously typically called for the use of formal addressee pronouns such as with parents, grandparents, and professors, now frequently permit the use of familiar pronouns. The use of formal pronouns persist in situations with unknown addressees who are senior in age or profession.

Relevant to our study here, the intraspeaker variation in pronoun usage has been a focus of recent discourse-based studies analyzing how speakers flout known, institutionalized norms and instead create personal identities through their use of pronouns. Fine-grained corpus investigations analyzing discourse makers, pronominal and verbal forms, and intonation patterns have demonstrated that address forms are dynamic discourse tools used to construct relevant, time-specific aspects of speaker identities. Helinks [12] in particular adopts two key theoretical notions related to this: (i) the notion of *face*, or a socially attributed and temporary aspect of self evident for the duration of the interaction based on the speaker's conscious use of politeness; and (ii) *facework*, understood as 'efforts made by the participants in verbal interaction to preserve their own face and the face of others' [25]. In other words, a speaker can choose to play with the personal pronouns they use, given that this variation remains within certain social and conversational constraints.

Variation in Tripartite Address Systems. The ability to manipulate personal identity by varying pronoun usage is particularly evident in tripartite addressee systems such as those found in Chile, Argentina, and Uruguay. The *vos* pronoun used in certain dialects offers speakers an additional dichotomy within T forms to create a more nuanced identity and relationship with the addressee. An example of how a grandmother employs all three forms in the course of talking to her baby granddaughter is below [9]; cf., a comparable performative effect is also reported for Japanese addressee-honorifics [26] and Korean addressee-honorifics [19].

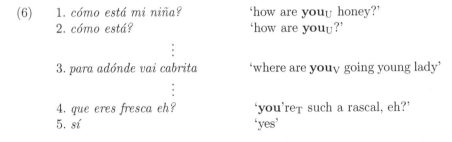

(6)   1. *cómo está mi niña?*   'how are **you**$_U$ honey?'
      2. *cómo está?*   'how are **you**$_U$?'

       ⋮

      3. *para adónde vai cabrita*   'where are **you**$_V$ going young lady'

       ⋮

      4. *que eres fresca eh?*   '**you**'re$_T$ such a rascal, eh?'
      5. *sí*   'yes'

In the example, *vos* is used simultaneously with *tú* and *usted* to navigate authority, respect, and family relations. Gladys, the grandmother, first addresses her infant granddaughter, Gabriela, in the unexpected *usted* form to indicate familial respect; the pronoun is understood as a more affectionate and tender address than the expected *tú*, as indicated by the accompanying possessive expression *mi niña* ('my girl','honey') and use of rising intonation [7,21]. Following the use of *ustedeante* verbal forms, the grandmother switches to *voseante* forms to indicate authority and, possibly, annoyance [23]. This is understood with the lack of possessive pronoun following the verbal form (*cabrita* 'young lady') and the fact that the address form is triggered by the granddaughter crawling away from her grandmother. This invoked authoritative figure then changes to a friskier one closer to that of the loving grandmother: an address shift from *voseante* to *tuteante* forms is evident as the grandmother playfully scolds Gabriela by telling her that she is a *fresca* 'rascal' for crawling away. Additional discursive and interactional resources contribute to this interpretation.

The example above illustrates intraspeaker variation in use of Spanish personal pronouns in a single conversation. Though constrained in a very specific and private domain, institutional contexts where both speaker and addressee actively contribute to the discourse exhibit similar variation in how speakers make use of pronouns to construct identities. For example, a policewoman taking an emergency call from a teenage girl can switch between addressing her as *usted* and *tú* to convey both the seriousness of the matter and the reassurance she hopes to provide [9]. Nevertheless, such institutional demonstrate less variation in pronominal usage, such that speakers are more constrained by public social expectations of pronimal use and do not have as much freedom to stray from these expectations.

2.3   Interim summary

In this section, we have seen the basics of Japanese and Spanish honorific and politeness systems. Certainly, these systems differ in several ways. First, Japanese uses verbal suffixes to encode honorificity, whereas politeness is encoded in the nominal domain in Spanish. Second, unlike in Spanish, Japanese has two distinct honorific systems, which are regulated by different pragmatic and social factors.

But the Japanese and Spanish systems do also have some important commonalities. First, at the coarse-grained level, there is a general consensus regarding when to use a politeness-oriented expression. Generally speaking, the use of an SH involves a social-hierarchy. Likewise, the use of *usted* generally relates to the formality/respect. For referential purposes, let us call this anticipation of expected social norms the PRIOR CONDITION. One may wish to describe this meaning as a kind of presupposition, just as we do for the meaning of phi-features; indeed, in Spanish, these same phi-features are utilized to express differing values of politeness [8]. Some survey- and interview-based methods present a static picture of form usage determined by speaker, interlocutor, and setting that is in line with such an analysis [1].

The static view alone fails to capture the expressive aspect of politeness, which is the second important property of politeness-oriented features: SH, AH and the Spanish pronouns can strategically violate the above-mentioned social anticipation, giving a performative and dynamic change in discourse and this is the source of intra-speaker variation. Since this is an effect triggered by the use of these markers, let us call it the POSTERIOR CONDITION. Returning to the Teacher-Student Test in (4), Spanish allows the same flexibility in that a teacher may use a formal pronoun with a student temporarily to express respect. However, this switch is only a temporary one: it would be infelicitous for a teacher to repeatedly use a formal pronoun with a student if such a relationship were not previously established. On the flip side, if a teacher would like to express a more accessible, even 'hip' version of themselves to their students, the teacher can consciously begin to use a T form in conversation. Informal data collection reveals that this pattern occurs in German, too.

Finally, the use of a politeness-oriented feature is involved with a combination of multiple social and pragmatic factors, e.g., formality, psychological distance, social status, age difference, etc. These many factors are, however, not taken into account with the same weights; some are more prioritized than others, and the distribution of the weights is different from speaker to speaker.

(7)   a.   **Prior condition**: prior to the new utterance, the context expects the speaker to use/not to use a politeness-oriented expression.

     b.   **Posterior condition**: by (not) being produced by the speaker, a politeness-oriented expression changes the context in a certain way.

     c.   **Relation with social/pragmatic factors**: more than one factors contribute to the choice of the politeness-oriented form. When a language has more than two honorific systems, each system may have different weights to these factors.

Importantly, the interaction of the presuppositional and performative uses of politeness is quite distinct in Japanese and Spanish. Thus, we also need to address how a language's grammatical resources (i.e. SH/AH markers versus pronominal address forms) constrain possible interpretation of politeness.

3   A Bayesian Dynamic Pragmatics Account of Politeness

The decision-making process in which politeness-oriented form to use is 'probabilistic,' rather than 'deterministic.' For example, formality is not the only factor regulating the use of the Japanese AH. The choice between (3-b) and (5) cannot be categorically determined, because the speaker may place more weights on factors other than the formality. If the addressee is the speaker's best friend, and the speaker may wish to emphasize this psychological proximity, they may avoid using an AH. This decision process is evident in the Spanish dialogue in (6), too.

For this reason, it is appropriate to consider a combination of several pragmatic factors, following the proposal of Politeness Theory [3] and the recent literature of Dynamic Semantics/Pragmatics [17,26]. Though we leave the exhaustive identification of such factors to future study, here we develop the insights from the aforementioned previous studies and propose a general scheme by assuming p anonymous parameters. Without losing generality, we use $f_i \in \mathbf{R}$ to denote the i-th social/pragmatic factor of our discourse model, and let $w_i \in \mathbf{R}$ be the weight of this i-th element ($i \in \{1, 2, ..., p\}$). Now, our decision making process is dependent upon their linear combination, as shown below.

(8) $w_1 f_1 + w_2 f_2 + \ldots + w_p f_p$

As was previously mentioned, the factors involved in the Japanese SH system and the AH system are different. Thus, it is reasonable to assume that the weight vector for AH, $\mathbf{w}^a = (w_1^a \; w_2^a \; \ldots w_p^a)^T$, is different from the weight vector for SH, $\mathbf{w}^s = (w_1^s \; w_2^s \; \ldots w_p^s)^T$, and the weight parameter for the social hierarchy in $\mathbf{w}^s$ is significantly larger than that in $\mathbf{w^a}$; n.b., here, T indicates that the vector/matrix is transposed.

3.1 Dynamic Pragmatics

In what follows, we develop a model within the framework of Dynamic Pragmatics that meets the desiderata given in (7). Dynamic Pragmatics is a theoretical framework that aims to capture the discourse dynamicity and the communicative effect of an utterance by articulating pragmatic principles [18]. In the recent literature of this paradigm, a discourse context is modeled to be a tuple of different information component. For example, in (9), the context (c) is modeled to be constituted by the common ground (cg), the question set (qs), and the to-do list (tdl). The effect of a command-expressing sentence is, for example, analyzed as the process of replacing an old tdl in the prior context with a new tdl' for the new, posterior context.

(9)   Structured Discourse Context   (Version 1 out of 3)
        $c = < cg, qs, tdl >$

Model 1 (to be improved). While the model in (9) is useful especially when we examine the sentence mood, our main goal is to develop a model for the meaning associated with honorifics. With the formula in (8) in mind, let us consider the following preliminary model, in which a component p is added to (9), which is a set of tuples of a discourse participant, and the estimated weights:

(10)   Structured Discourse Context   (Version 2 out of 3)
        a. $c = < cg, qs, tdl, p >$
        b. $p = \left\{ \begin{array}{l} < alice, \mathbf{w}^a_{alice}, \mathbf{w}^s_{alice} >, < bob, \mathbf{w}^a_{bob}, \mathbf{w}^s_{bob} >, \\ \ldots\ < zelda, \mathbf{w}^a_{zelda}, \mathbf{w}^s_{zelda} > \end{array} \right\}$

For each individual there are weight vectors summarizing their personal idiosyncrasies in their use of honorific markers. These vectors are represented as $\mathbf{w}^a_{alice}$ (for addressee-honorifics) and $\mathbf{w}^s_{alice}$ (subject-honorifics), respectively, and in this regard, the Japanese system is assumed for (10-b). For the Spanish system, we do not need two different vectors; (11) would be used in place of (10-b). Since the Spanish system is seen as a simpler version of the Japanese system, our subsequent discussions are based on the model in (10-b).

(11) $p = \left\{ < alice, \mathbf{w}^{usted}_{alice} >, < bob, \mathbf{w}^{usted}_{bob} >, \ \ldots, \ < zelda, \mathbf{w}^{usted}_{zelda} > \right\}$

To see more clearly what these vectors are, we would benefit from a concrete example. In (12), we give specific values to the weight vectors, where values can be any real number. Smaller values indicate a lesser estimated likelihood of the factor to affect the production of a politeness marker; values of 0 are neutral.

(12) $< alice, \begin{pmatrix} 0.5 \\ 8 \end{pmatrix}, \begin{pmatrix} 1 \\ 1 \end{pmatrix} >$

This represents the situation where the discourse participants all believe that 0.5 and 8 are the right parameter values for $\mathbf{w}^a_{\text{alice}}$ and 1 and 1 for $\mathbf{w}^s_{\text{alice}}$. The first element of the vector corresponds to the weight of the first factor. In this context, Factor 1 (0.5) does not affect her use of addressee-honorifics that much, whereas the effect of Factor 2 (8) is quite substantial. If Factor 1 represents the formality, and Factor 2 the age difference, then Alice is seen as a person who produces addressee-honorific markers towards elder people, but is not too much sensitive to the formality of the context. In this way, the vector $\mathbf{w}^a_{\text{alice}}$, or the tuple $< alice, \mathbf{w}^a_{\text{alice}}, \mathbf{w}^s_{\text{alice}} >$ represents her character (what kind of person she is) inferred by her use of honorific expressions.

Model 2. The model in (10) has a problem in practice, however: discourse participants (except for Alice) would never know the true values in $\mathbf{w}^a_{\text{alice}}$.[3] What the audience can do is to keep estimating what values are appropriate for the weights in $\mathbf{w}^a_{\text{alice}}$. It is thus more appropriate to think that what is stored in the structured discourse context is not the true values, but the estimated values.

The fact that we have to estimate Alice's parameters means that we have some uncertainty about the parameters. In other words, rather than pinning down a single value, we are also open to other many possible candidate values. Following the practice in Bayesian statistics, we use a probability distribution to represent our uncertainty.

To make this idea much clearer, consider how the first element in $\mathbf{w}^a_{\text{alice}}$ (i.e., the weight for Factor 1) is estimated. If we are to estimate the weight of Factor 1, all real numbers are potential candidates, and the audience assigns different probabilities to these real numbers. By relating a real number with its probability, we can draw curves as in Fig. 1. The x-axis represents candidate values for the weight of Factor 1, and the y-axis is for the corresponding probability assigned by the audience on a scale from 0 to 1. Some values are more likely than others. For example, consider the curve in the left panel in Fig. 1. This curve shows that the value 0.5 is most likely. Other values near 0.5 are also possible and are, thus, given a reasonably high probability. For 1.0, we may assign a smaller, and yet relatively high probability. But an even smaller probability is assigned to 2.0. In this way, by drawing a curve (a probability distribution), we can represent the audience's uncertainty state.

With a large amount of exposure to Alice's utterances, her audience will become more confident about certain values. Imagine, for instance, that after a few more utterances, our uncertainty represented by the left panel of Fig. 1 is updated to the one shown by the right panel in Fig. 1. The probability distribution is more narrowly distributed around 0.5, which means that the audience is more confident in this value. This means that the context update for honorific states is now seen as a change of our uncertainty state represented by a probability distribution.

---

[3] **The speaker's ignorance.** Perhaps, Alice herself does not know the true value, either. The model we are developing here does not matter whether Alice knows the exact value or not.

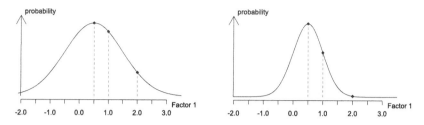

Fig. 1. Modeling uncertainties for a single factor.

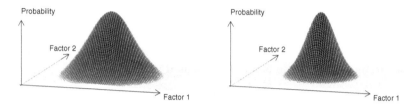

Fig. 2. Modeling uncertainties for two factors.

For simplicity's sake, we have been concerned with the first parameter of $\mathbf{w}^a_{alice}$. But the same argument can be obtained for the other weights. When we track two factors, the uncertainty shift is modeled as a change of a 3-dimensional probability distribution, as shown in Fig. 2. A context change is an update from a particular uncertainty state (e.g., the one in the left panel) to a new state (e.g., the one in the right panel of Fig. 2).

If we take all these into considerations, it is reasonable to have probability distributions for each individual, as shown in (13), unlike the single value approach, as assumed in (12). The update from (a) to (b) in (13) mirrors the update shown in Fig. 2.

(13)　a.　$< alice,$ ⬚ , ⬚ $>$

　　　b.　$< alice,$ ⬚ , ⬚ $>$

(For some distributions) it is possible to identify its profile by parameters. For example, for a Normal distribution, we can uniquely identify its shape of the distribution by providing the values for μ (the parameter for its center) and Σ (the parameter for its variance); the tuples in (13) can be re-written as:

(14)　a.　$< alice, \left(\begin{pmatrix} 0.5 \\ 8 \end{pmatrix}, \begin{pmatrix} 1.5^2 & 0 \\ 0 & 1.3^2 \end{pmatrix} \right), \left(\begin{pmatrix} 0.5 \\ 7.3 \end{pmatrix}, \begin{pmatrix} 0.5^2 & 0 \\ 0 & 0.4^2 \end{pmatrix} \right) >$

　　　b.　$< alice, \left(\begin{pmatrix} 0.5 \\ 8 \end{pmatrix}, \begin{pmatrix} 0.3^2 & 0 \\ 0 & 1.3^2 \end{pmatrix} \right), \left(\begin{pmatrix} 0.3 \\ 7.1 \end{pmatrix}, \begin{pmatrix} 0.2^2 & 0 \\ 0 & 0.1^2 \end{pmatrix} \right) >$

From this view point, the nature of context shift is seen as an update of these vectors and matrices. The proposed model is now formally defined as follows:

(15)   Structured Discourse Context   (Version 3 out of 3)

a. $c = < cg, qs, tdl, p >$

b. $p = \left\{ \begin{array}{c} < alice, (\boldsymbol{\mu}^a_{\text{alice}}, \boldsymbol{\Sigma}^a_{\text{alice}}), (\boldsymbol{\mu}^s_{\text{alice}}, \boldsymbol{\Sigma}^s_{\text{alice}}) >, \\ < bob, (\boldsymbol{\mu}^a_{\text{bob}}, \boldsymbol{\Sigma}^a_{\text{bob}}), (\boldsymbol{\mu}^s_{\text{bob}}, \boldsymbol{\Sigma}^s_{\text{bob}}) >, \\ \vdots \\ < zelda, (\boldsymbol{\mu}^a_{\text{zelda}}, \boldsymbol{\Sigma}^a_{\text{zelda}}), (\boldsymbol{\mu}^s_{\text{zelda}}, \boldsymbol{\Sigma}^s_{\text{zelda}}) > \end{array} \right\}$

From (15-b), we now see that our parameters that store individual profiles for politeness-usage are represented as tuples of the speaker (e.g., *alice*, *bob*, ..., *zelda*), their estimated mean value for all relevant factors represented as a vector ($\boldsymbol{\mu}$), and variance of the same factors represented as a matrix ($\boldsymbol{\Sigma}$).

3.2   Discussion

In Sect. 2.3, we saw three important desiderata for the pragmatics of honorific elements. Let us now articulate how these properties are explained by our proposal.

Multiple factors. The issue of multiplicity of social/pragmatic factors is simply a matter of the length of the vector. For example, when one wishes to propose three-dimensional weight vector for μ^a_{alice}, something like the tuple in 16 would be proposed. Notice first that, although it is impossible for us to draw the probability distribution when we have more than two factors, the algebra extends to represent this naturally. Second, it is also noted that the length of μ^a_{alice} does not necessarily match the length of μ^s_{alice}. Finally, if one wishes to propose a more complicated structure among factors, one can improve the variance-covariance matrix by assuming correlations among factors.

(16) $< alice, \left(\begin{pmatrix} 0.5 \\ 8 \\ 5.2 \end{pmatrix}, \begin{pmatrix} 0.3^2 & 0 & 0 \\ 0 & 1.3^2 & 0 \\ 0 & 0 & 0.2^2 \end{pmatrix} \right), \left(\begin{pmatrix} 0.3 \\ 7.1 \end{pmatrix}, \begin{pmatrix} 0.2^2 & 0 \\ 0 & 0.1^2 \end{pmatrix} \right) >$

Prior Context. The audience's expectation about the speaker's 'politeness' prior to the their utterance is modeled by the calculation of the formula in (8) together with the information, for example, in (16).

For example, suppose Factor 1 represents the difference in social status, Factor 2 the difference in age, and Factor 3 the formality of the given context. When the new person is her new colleague (= no difference in social status), but he is 2 years older than she is, and the conversation is about to take place in a very formal setting, then we can predict the probability of her producing an addressee-honorific marker, despite her new encounter with this addressee. Notice that we can predict how Alice behaves even before she has started talking to a new addressee. This kind of expectation is seen as a type of 'presupposition,' because this predicted probability formally states how the discourse participants expect her to behave.

Posterior Context. Of course, Alice does not have to behave as she is expected to. If she violates the audience's expectation, it is understood that their estimation is not accurate, which, as a consequence, serves as a hint for the newly-updated/estimated values for her parameters. This can be seen in (6), in which the speaker consciously violates the expected norms of pronominal use in a grandmother/infant granddaughter setting. This particular example concerns an addressee who cannot perceive this violation; it thus highlights a speaker-oriented effect of this behavior in that the speaker actively chooses to flout the pre-established conversational parameters. We return to this in our analysis in the next section.

Now consider a case where Alice behaves as expected. A context update still takes place. In this case, the audience's uncertainty is reduced: the probability distribution is more narrowly distributed. Suppose that on the first day Alice met Bob, she heard Bob use two SHs out of his three utterances. At this moment, she would vaguely infer that Bob is a relatively polite person, but she is not so certain about her inference. But a semester later, suppose she has heard 1,999 SHs out of his 2,000 utterances. Now she should be more certain about her estimation. The larger exposure to the utterances, the more certain we are about someone's persona.

4   Dynamic update as Persona learning

For each individual, the posterior mean vectors in (15-b), e.g., μ^a_{bob} and μ^s_{bob}, reflect how the give person is analyzed by discourse participants. Let the vector μ_{bob} represent the combined vector made of μ^a_{bob} and μ^s_{bob}; e.g., for (14-b), $\mu_{bob} = (0.5 \ \ 8 \ \ 0.3 \ \ 7.1)^T$.

By comparing these vectors, we can classify individuals. Since the dimension of the vector does not affect our discussion, let us consider the simplest case, that is, the case where μ_{bob} consists of two elements; i.e., $\mu_{bob} = (\mu_1 \ \ \mu_2)^T$. When the μ of each individual is known, we can assign a location to each person in the 2-dimensional space, as illustrated in Fig. 3.

Seen this way, our proposal is understood as a natural extension of Conceptual Spaces framework for lexical semantics [10,11], or the studies working on Persona-based semantics/pragmatics [6,17]. Putting aside the theoretical choice of partitioning the space in Fig. 3, we can easily see that Alice and Bob are different from the other individuals in the way they choose honorific forms. For instance, if μ_1 is the age difference, and μ_2 is the formality, Alice and Bob do not strongly prioritize age difference but are sensitive to the difference in formality. In other words, we can identify a behavioral pattern for the group of Alice and Bob, a type of personal characteristics. On the other hand, we can also find a

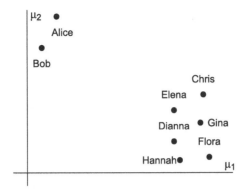

Fig. 3. Distribution of personae

cluster for the other individuals. In terms of the size of the group, this could be seen as a 'mainstream' persona (cf., [6]).

Upon this view, mainstream and anti-mainstream personae are not fixed single locations, but seen as emergent regions that become apparent only after we have estimated many people's locations. We thus predict that a mainstream persona can change, which is borne out by a well-known fact that that an existing politeness-oriented expression gradually becomes analyzed less 'polite' and a new respect-expressing strategy gets utilized to encode a high-level politeness. To create a superpolite publicized self-image people try to deviate from the mainstream location. The synchronic deviation in Fig. 3 is seen as a symptom of an emergent, diachronic language change.

5   Conclusion and Theoretical Implications

In this paper, we have described how Japanese and Spanish 'politeness'-oriented expressions are associated with sociolinguistic and pragmatic factors. , We then developed a pragmatic model explaining the inter-/intra-speaker variation and their prior/posterior relation with the context. In the presented model, the audience is invited to infer the persona of each speaker by observing how they take the contextual factors into consideration when they make a decision regarding the use of a 'politeness'-oriented expression.

Although we have chiefly examined the data from Japanese and Spanish, we believe our proposal can be extended to account for data in other languages. The following anecdote from a native German speaker serves as an example. The speaker, a man in his mid-thirties, went to the barbershop to have his hair cut. His barber was male and appeared to be the same age. The two men spent the duration of the haircut speaking in the third-person (equivalent to English 'one') because neither of them was confident to commit to a formal (*Sie* 'you') or familiar (*du* 'you') address form and corresponding relationship. The speaker relayed this story still with ambivalence about how he should have acted. Anecdotes from other German speakers reveal similar hesitation about committing to certain personal identities, instead opting to be publicly agnostic about their own personalities. Most speakers defer to the formal *Sie*, given that respect is a good default but also, notably, because this form allows the speaker more 'distance' from the addressee in the conversation. In German and other T/V languages (Spanish included), speakers may also use a back-off strategy to avoid committing to a specific singular address form by using a plural address form. Under our analysis, the fear of revealing one's personality is understood as an avoidance of locating oneself in the persona space as shown in Fig. 3.

We predict that languages place differing weights on social hierarchy from Japanese and Spanish. With appropriate data sets, future studies can identify the mainstream use in each language, making us easily detect the variation among language communities.

It is also important to examine how each language encodes politeness. Politeness can be encoded in the verbal domain as honorificity (Japanese), and in the nominal domain (Spanish). Is the pragmatic effect we have discussed read off from the same feature in the syntax? If so, where does the feature exist? Is this a feature provided in the NP-periphery, or is it a clause-level feature [26]? Detailed examinations of the logical forms will surely allow us to promote our understanding of politeness-oriented phenomena across languages.

References

1. Bishop, K., Michnowicz, J.: Forms of address in Chilean Spanish. Hispania **93**(3), 413–429 (2010)
2. Borrás-Comes, J., Sichel-Bazin, R., Prieto, P.: Vocative intonation preferences are sensitive to politeness factors. Lang. Speech **58**(1), 68–83 (2015)
3. Brown, P., Levinson, S.: Politeness: some universals in language usage (1987 [1978])
4. Brown, R., Gilman, A.: The pronouns of power and solidarity. In: Sebeok, T.A. (ed.) Style in Language, pp. 253–276. MIT Press, Cambridge (1960)
5. Brown, L., Prieto, P.: (Im)politeness: prosody and gesture. In: Culpeper, J., Haugh, M., Kádár, D. (eds.) The Palgrave handbook of linguistic (im) politeness, pp. 357–379. Palgrave Macmillan, London (2017)
6. Burnett, H.: A persona-based semantics for slurs. Grazer Philosophische Studien **97**, 31–62 (2020)
7. Carricaburo, N.: Las fórmulas de tratamiento en el español actual [second ed]. Arco Libros, Madrid (2015)
8. Donatelli, L.: The morphosemantics of Spanish gender: evidence from small nominals. Ph.D. thesis, Georgetown University (2019)
9. Fernández-Mallat, V.: Forms of address in interaction: evidence from Chilean Spanish. J. Pragmat. **161**, 95–106 (2020)
10. Gärdenfors, P.: Conceptual spaces: the geometry of thought. MIT Press, Cambridge (2000)
11. Gärdenfors, P.: The Geometry of Meaning: Semantics Based on Conceptual Spaces. MIT Press, Cambridge (2014)
12. Helincks, K.: Negotiation of terms of address in a Chilean television talk show. Bull. Hispanic Stud. **92**(7), 731–753 (2015)

13. Henderson, R., McCready, E.: Dogwhistles, trust and ideology. In: Proceedings of the Sixteenth International Workshop of Logic and Engineering of Natural Language Semantics, (LENLS16), vol. 16, pp. 1–2 (2019)
14. Kikuchi, Y.: Honorifics. Kadokawa Shoten, Tokyo [reprinted in 1997, Kodansha, Tokyo] (1997 [1994])
15. Landone, E.: Discourse markers and politeness in a digital forum in Spanish. J. Pragmat. **44**(13), 1799–1820 (2012)
16. McCready, E.: A semantics for honorifics with reference to Thai. In: Proceedings of Pacific Asia Conference on Language, Information and Computing (PACLIC) 28, pp. 503–512 (2014)
17. McCready, E.: Honorification and Social Meaning. Oxford University Press, New York (2019)
18. Portner, P.: Commitment to priorities. In: Fogel, D., Harris, D., Moss, M. (eds.) New Work on Speech Acts, pp. 296–316. Oxford University Press, Oxford (2018)
19. Portner, P., Pak, M., Zanuttini, R.: The speaker-addressee relation at the syntax-semantics interface. Language **95**, 1–36 (2019)
20. Potts, C.: The Logic of Conventional Implicatures. Oxford University Press, Oxford (2005)
21. Prieto, P., Borrás-Comes, J., Crespo-Sendra, V., Thorson, J., Vanrell, M.M.: Entonación y pragmática en los enunciados interrogativos absolutos del espa nol en un corpus de habla dirigida a niños. Oralia **14**, 227–255 (2011)
22. Real Academia Española (RAE): Nueva gramática de la lengua espa nola manual. Espasa (2010)
23. Rivadeneira Valenzuela, M.: Sociolinguistic variation and change in Chilean voseo. In: Moyna, M.I., Rivera-Mills, S. (eds.) Forms of Address in the Spanish of the Americas, pp. 87–117. John Benjamins, Amsterdam (2016)
24. Shibatani, M.: Honorifics. In: Jacob, M. (ed.) Concise encyclopedia of pragmatics, pp. 341–350. Elsevier, Amsterdam (1998)
25. Watts, R.J.: Politeness. Cambridge University Press, Cambridge (2003)
26. Yamada, A.: The syntax, semantics and pragmatics of Japanese addressee-honorific markers. PhD. Thesis, Georgetown University, Washington D.C. (2019)

JURISIN2020

Fourteenth International Workshop on Juris-Informatics (JURISIN 2020)

Juris-informatics is a new research area that studies legal issues from the perspective of informatics. The purpose of the International Workshop on Juris-informatics (JURISIN) is to discuss both the fundamental and practical issues among people from various backgrounds such as law, social science, information, intelligent technology, logic, and philosophy, including the conventional "AI and law" area. JURISIN 2020 was held in the International Symposia on AI by the Japanese Society of Artificial Intelligence (JSAI-isAI).

JURISIN 2020 is a two-day workshop consisting of the ordinal JURISIN session and COLIEE session. COLIEE stands for the Competition on Legal Information Extraction/Entailment, which consists of the following tasks, and it has been held since 2015.

1. The legal case retrieval task
2. The legal case entailment task
3. The statute law retrieval task
4. The legal question answering data corpus

We called for papers for both sessions, and three program committee members reviewed each submitted paper; thus, twenty-four papers are selected for oral presentations. Furthermore, we invited two lectures. Takehiko Kasahara of Toin Yokohama University gave a lecture titled "AI and Judicial Policy," and Akira Shimazu of JAIST gave a lecture titled "Semantic Parsing for Legal Engineering - Studies So Far and in the Future -."

After JURISIN 2020, according to comments of reviewers and discussion during the workshop, authors revised their papers and submitted them for the post-proceedings. Each paper was reviewed again, and we selected ten excellent papers, among which three papers were selected from the ordinal JURISIN session, and seven papers were from the COLIEE session. This volume includes these selected papers.

We thank all the Steering Committee, Advisory Committee, and Program Committee of JURISIN 2020, all authors who submitted papers, and all the members of the Organizing Committee of JSAI-isAI.

April 2021

Yasuhiro Ogawa
Nguyen Le Minh
Ken Satoh

AI and Judicial Policy

Takehiko Kasahara[✉]

Toin University of Yokohama, Yokohama, Japan
kasahara@toin.ac.jp

Abstract. The use of AI in the judiciary is limited to the use of IT and later ICT, and the use of AI for judging functions has just begun to sprout. In this paper, judicial ICT use in Japan, then the trends around the world are summarized: those of the United States, Germany and Spain. Then apart from court issues, the impact and potential of AI technology beyond actual use are discussed; especially block chain technology and legal-XML. Finally, the current state of AI trials, the problems of AI judges, and the possibility of ADR will be discussed.

1 Preface

The JURISIN of this year is held online caused by the Corona epidemic. Even as I write this manuscript, the number of victims is still increasing. It goes without saying that this corona pandemic is a disaster, but for Japan it revealed the delay in digitization. The pandemic compelled us to engage in remote work and digitization of our society. The "paper and stamp" culture in Japan has historically played a major role, but at the same time it was a factor that hindered digitization. I hope that it will not end as a preliminary and emergency measure, but will lead to the acceleration in ICT use.

In this paper I will figure out the situation of Japanese judiciary and furthermore the possibility of AI in the field of judicial policy.

2 Application of IT to Court

2.1 Video Link System, Triophone

It was often described as "the introduction of IT in Japanese judiciary is twenty years behind", but in fact, the introduction of one form of technology was early: "Video Link System" and the "Triophone".

2.1.1 Remote Witness Cross-Examination by Video Link System

For civil trials, in 1998 the ISDN video conferencing system was introduced nationwide in 50 District Courts and their major branches (video link). As a result, with respect to witness cross-examination, if you live far from the court where the case is heard, you can go to the nearby district court to participate in the witness cross-examination procedure (Civil Procedure Act, hereinafter referred to as CPA, Article 204). The objective was

N. Okazaki et al. (Eds.): JSAI-isAI 2020 Workshops, LNAI 12758, pp. 147–161, 2021.
https://doi.org/10.1007/978-3-030-79942-7_10

for witnesses involved in trials to save time and expense and, as a result, to make trials more "convenient and speedy".

In 2001, technology was also introduced in criminal trials. It was adopted to eliminate the feeling of strong mental pressure in order to separate the accused and the victim, especially in sex crimes, due to the presence of the accused in the same courtroom as the victim. It replaced the conventional wooden screen.

2.1.2 Preparatory Procedure by Triophone

At the same time, "Triophone", a conference call system that uses a three-way calling system, was also introduced. It was used for proceedings; as expressed in the statute, it was "a method which enables court and both parties to communicate simultaneously by transmitting and receiving voice (CPA §170 (3)".

Initially it was of limited use only by the preparatory proceedings, but it was expanded to include the withdrawing an action, waiving a claim by the plaintiff and acknowledging a claim by the defendant, and also the entering into a settlement.

2.2 Judicial System Reform – "The Supreme Court to Judge the Memories of the Case."

Due to administrative reforms in the 1990s in Japan, administrative restrictions on the pre-dispute adjustment function were relaxed, and as the result, judicial trials as a post-dispute resolution function became the focus of attention.

"The Supreme Court judges the recollection of the case" said former Prime Minister Koizumi who was skilled in catchphrases. He made fun of trials which cost time and money. The Act on Court Acceleration (Law No. 107 on July 16, 2003) came into force in 2003 with the goal of making it possible to end all cases of first instance in the shortest possible period of time within a maximum of two years [1].

In the judicial system reform of June 12, 2001, the Judicial Reform Council issued the Judicial Reform Promotion Plan; then, the government Judicial Reform Promotion Headquarters was created, and on March 19th, 2002, the headquarters and the Japan Federation of Bar Associations issued the judicial system reform plan. The next day the Supreme Court issued the "Outline of the Judicial Reform Promotion Plan". With respect to the introduction of IT, the Supreme Court said, "By promoting networking using homepages, etc., necessary measures should be taken to draw up and publish a plan to strengthen the provision of information including ADR, legal counseling, and legal assistance systems, In cooperation with related organizations, necessary measures will be taken, and promote the active introduction of information and communication technology (IT) in various aspects such as court proceedings, paperwork, and information provision."

Various reforms such as the lay judge trial system were introduced and the legal consulting center, "law terrace", was created. The court websites have been enhanced. (case law disclosure, statistics disclosure, online demand procedure system, etc.), with respect to the use of IT, but the praxis of the trial procedure itself has been only slightly digitized.

2.2.1 Lay Judge Trial

Although few Japanese know it, a jury trial had been held in Japan since 1928, however, in 1943 the jury system was suspended during World War II. After the war, the jury law remained suspended, and even under the present day judicial reform, a lay judge system was adopted instead of the jury. As in EU countries, lay judges do not judge independently like Jurors, but together with professional judges.

2.2.2 Demand Procedure

"Demand procedure" is a simplified civil procedure for a claim the object of which is the payment of a certain amount of money or other fungible or securities. If the plaintiff had to lodge a lawsuit even when there was no dispute, for example only to prevent the statute of limitations, it would be a waste of time and money for all parties.

The following demand procedures have been established for such cases:

Article 382 Civil Prodedure Act (CPA)

Upon the application of the creditor, the court clerk may issue a demand for the payment of a claim whose object is the payment of a certain amount of money or other fungible or securities; provided, however, that this applies only if it is possible to serve the demand in Japan, by a means other than service by publication.

If the debtor does not challenge it and after specified period of time, it has the same effect as a judgment. Since it is applied in a simple case about a fixed amount of payment, it is easy to use a computer to carry it out, so this procedure has been digitized and handled online since 2004, based on revised Article 397 of the CPA.

2.2.3 Experimental Implementation of e-filing

Although the provision for e-filing in court was subscribed (CPA §132–10), the corresponding order was not enacted. In addition, only few petitions are allowed online and the most important documents, the complaint, written answer and a brief detailing an allegation, have not been recognized for this purpose. One experiment was attempted at the Sapporo District Court in Hokkaido, but terminated on the March 20th, 2008. The lack of users was the reason of the termination.

The introduction of IT in courts has not progressed at all in almost 20 years since this attempted reform [2].

2.3 Headquarters for Japan's Economic Revitalization

The current civil trial reform for use of ICT is based on the efforts of the government and not of the courts. The "Japan revival strategy - Japan is Back - (2013)" was aimed at developed countries within 3 places among the 35 OECD members countries in the World Bank's business environment ranking in 2020. Japan's ranking has been declining year by year. Among many problems "conflict resolution" was cited as one of the areas with low evaluation [3]. In order to reform this situation two Cabinet decisions have been made led by "the Headquarters for Japan's Economic Revitalization" and the digitization of courts has started again.

On June 9, 2017, the "Report on Priority Measures and Others for Innovative Business Activity Action Plan 2017" [4] was issued, and "the IT implementation study group for court procedures" [5] was appointed. The result of the study group, "Summary for IT implementation of court procedures -Toward the realization of three "e"s, was summarized on March 30, 2018 and was released on June 15th, 2018, in the "Report on Priority Measures and Others for Innovative Business Activity Action Plan 2018 [6]" in a second decision. The "three "e"s are "e-filing", "e-Court" and "e-Case Management". They will be realized by dividing them into three stages: what can be done under existing laws, which provisions need to be revised, and future development [7].

In addition, on September 27 2019 under the Headquarters for Japan's Economic Revitalization has instituted "the ODR activation Study Group" [8], and online alternative dispute resolution was examined. The Legislative Council for Civil Procedure Law (IT-related) was established to address the revision of the law. The first meeting was held on the June 10, 2020 [9].

In the following discussion, trends in the field of ICT and the possibility of application of AI in court are described.

3 Cyber Court Research in Japan

Contrary to the court's inertia, research activities listed below were actively conducted and a large amount of grants were provided. I will summarize some experiments and what we had proposed.

2002–2005: "Cyber Campus & Cyber Court Project": Research commissioned by the Ministry of Education Culture, Sports, Science and Technology (Toin Univ. of Yokohama)

2003–2005: Workshop for Cyber Court of the academic society "Information Network Law"

2003–2010: Workshop for "e-supported Court" of the "Workshop for Advanced Technology" (Kyushu Univ.)

2009–2010: "Survey research for promoting the utilization of ICT in legal service" Research commissioned by the Ministry of Internal Affairs and Communications (Kyushu Univ.)

In these projects, a video conferencing system on the IP network, a voice recognition system and automatic creation of digital video records were tested, and some of them are now adopted. Court records are automatically created in the form of digital video records. Especially when it comes to recording witness cross-examinations, videos are better. This is because facial expressions, gaze, hesitation etc. can be observed. The problem was the burdensomeness of cueing videotape, but it can be solved by using thumbnail software.

3.1 Thumbnail Software

Thumbnail software adds a table of contents to videos. It can be used to add a table at regular intervals, or to add a table when the speaker changes. Furthermore, if you combine it with voice recognition software, you can play the video from the relevant part while reading the contents and click the sentence.

3.2 Annotation Software

Annotation software is available to help reuse digital video. This picture shows an annotation software called Diver.

Diver is software made by a professor at Stanford University at the time, who had made Apple's software "Quicktime". The bottom part was actually designed for a video which photograph 360-degrees camera. Judges and attorneys can add comments as meta-information such as "This point contradicts the previous statement" while watching the video. If this system is situated in the centre of the courtroom, all trial records are kept. This system can also be used via the Internet and it can handle remote trials and remote interpretation.

The above joint research was interrupted because the budget was exhausted and the Stanford's professor moved to the private sector. The plan of the project was to save the video in MPeg7 format, a tag set was created and information other than video could has been saved together using XML.

4   3 Types of Digitizing of Court [10]

The author has observed three types of judicial IT initiatives: American type, German type and Spanish type. Representing each is a slogan: the United States type, "total disclosure of trial information", German type, "replacement of documents", Spain type, "paradigm shift".

4.1 American Type

The feature of the American type is total disclosure of court information. At the federal level, the "Case Management/Electronic Case Filing" (CM/ECF) system, and "Public Access to Court Electronic Records" (PACER) for public disclosure of court records have been created.

Furthermore, at the state level, there are various unique initiatives such as the introduction of IT in the bankruptcy court that started in Minnesota Bankruptcy Court [11], and the Michigan Cyber court Act [12]. The State of Michigan's Cyber Court was ambitious effort to perform all the procedures online, but was rejected by the state legislature because of its large budget [13].

4.1.1 CM/ECF Case Management/Electronic Case Filing (Case Management and Electronic Application System)

The objective is to manage cases of the court's cases and to enable electronic filings to each court. It is possible to file a case and send documents to the court 24 h a day, 365 days a year via the Internet. When a case is filed, the other party is automatically notified by e-mail. It is free of charge but, the application fee to be paid to the court separately with a credit card.

Each court issues a login ID and a password, and it is accessible for lawyers and petitioners in bankruptcy. The court often requires them to have training in advance to use the system.

4.1.2 PACER Public Access to Court Electronic Records (General Use System for Digitized Court Records)

The purpose is to provide electronic access to trial records. Access to case information of each Federal court is available online via Internet. Logging in to the Party US/Case Index and federal district courts and bankruptcy courts, you can find a case by the party name, court name, case number, and the filing date. There is a charge, but it is very inexpensive [14]. Materials that can be viewed with this system include court dockets and documents.

A major issue is full disclosure of information online, including case record, and so its security is not strictly considered. Personal authentication requires only ID and password; there are no plans to use digital signatures in the future [15]. In addition, trials may be open to the public by cable TV and online videos on the network [16].

4.2 German Type

Germany is conventional; it reforms its practice step by step, and carefully. Compared to Spain, which will be described later, the computerization retains the concept of written legal documents. Since the Civil Procedure Act of Japan was modeled after German law and is very similar, the German reform became a model. In the EU, however, Germany is viewed as a country where IT applications in courts have been delayed [17]. Nonetheless the Landshut District Court, close to Munich, has an IT center [18], and IBM and the court are jointly building a system.

4.2.1 June 2001: "Law for Revising Service Procedures in Court Procedures (Service Law Amendment Law)", July 2001: "Law for Adapting New Information Exchange to Provisions on Private Law Styles and Other Provisions (Private Law Compliance Law)"

These two laws digitize the filing of cases and the service of judgements, and also stipulate that "qualified electronic signatures" are presumed to be authentic provenance. They make possible service of documents, including the judgement by electronic documents available for lawyer use without limitations and for other persons with explicit consent. IC card and ID are used [19] with a PIN (Personal authentication number) code and an electronic signature, [20] however, it was pointed out that in the future, it would be necessary to introduce biometrics authentication such as fingerprints or voiceprints because "80% of lawyers work by teaching secretaries his PIN code which should not be given out to others [21]". A video conferencing system has also been introduced. The parties are also able to hold a remote trial (referred to in the German Code of Civil Procedure (hereinafter referred to as "ZPO") §128. It is noteworthy that the introduction of IT use in the judiciary has been taken almost 20 years from this point to the present.

4.2.2   March 2005: "Act on the Use of Electronic Information Forms for Judiciary (Judiciary Informatization Act)"

In the year 2005 the Judicial Informatization Law, commonly known as the Electronic Civil Procedure Law, made it possible to digitize civil procedure in general, including case records. The electronic document with the above-mentioned qualified electronic signature was recognized as a document in courts (§130a ZPO, §298a). On April 21 of the same year, the "Basic technical guidelines for the exchange of electronic information between the court and the public prosecutor's office" [22] were issued, and Legal-XML was adopted to maintain sharing information and the compatibility between federal states.

Data sharing and compatibility has become a major issue, especially in Japan today. (The need for Legal-XML will be described later.) This basic guideline stipulates the establishment of a communication office (Kommunikationsstellen), which is a specialized department in the court and the public prosecutor's office [23].

4.2.3   October 2013: "Court Electronic Information Exchange Promotion Law (Electronic Judiciary Law)", July 2017: "Law for the Introduction of Electronic Documents and Further Promotion of Information Exchange in the Judiciary"

In October 2013 Court Electronic Information Exchange Promotion Law (Electronic Judiciary Law) [24] was enacted, and digitization of case records became mandatory (former §130a of ZPO). However, according to this law, states were mandatory to issue ordinance (Rechtsverordnung) in which to cut the time limit to introduce digitized procedure. According to the law of 2017 it was prescribed all courts by January 1, 2018; and for law firms and government agencies by the January 1, 2022 digitization will be required (Article ZPO 130d). [25].

It should be noted that just before the enactment of the "Electronic Judiciary Law", the "Law on the Electronic Administration Promotion" [26] was passed, and the introduction of IT in the judiciary and the administration is being promoted simultaneously. In Japan, courts independently consider networks and their security, but in Germany, "the government and courts adopt the same standards for cyber security." "Because it addresses the personal information in court and also in administration, the need for and the degree of security is the same. Data management and storage of the government and the court are in the same place. However, access rights are clearly managed separately" [27].

Even with the separation of powers, it is obvious it is not always necessary to create and manage network equipment separately. Currently, a preparation department has been set up for the establishment of the Digital Agency in Japan. Still unknown is the relationship between the Cabinet Cyber Security Center and the Digital Agency. Although regardless of the administrative and judicial role, with respect to the security of network, the security should be left to a specialized agency and not to courts, so that courts can focus on trials. In the words of the Munich Magistrates' Judge, "Security is not a court issue, but a court/administrative network (Elektronisches Gerichts- und Verwaltungspostfach) issue. We, as judges, have not touched it" [28].

Regarding the security of communication, it is resolved by adopting a separately created secure communication method according to Article ZPO 130a, instead of the security unique to the court. In Paragraph 4 of this Article, "A secure communication method is 1. De-Mail (see below), 2. Electronic PO Box (beA Postfach) according to Article 31a of the Lawyer Law 3. Communication between the PO Box of a government office or public corporation (Postfach) and the electronic PO Box of a court (Poststelle)." In addition, "4. Other methods of transmission common within the federal government, approved by federal legislation and order with the consent of the Federal Trade Commission," is also accepted, but the authenticity, integrity, and ease of use of the data (Barrierefreiheit) is required [29].

De-Mail is electronic registered mail distribution with identity verification and authentication signal service. The functioning of a document of registered mail is also implemented online [30]. The beA is a "bar association network". "By exchanging of e-mails with an authorized electronic signature, it is necessary to put an electronic signature on all documents. It is cumbersome and difficult to prevail. By using the beA, it is necessary to authenticate only at the time of login and in the network no more digital signature is necessary." [31] For example, the Federal Patent Court have allowed to use the beA with EGVP encryption from January 1, 2018 in addition to the De-Mail.

The Federal Department of Justice has planned to create a portal site for the viewing of case records online. A bill for online browsing has been submitted on July 14, 2017 [32]. It was Introduced on a trial basis from 2018 to 2020. It differs from U.S.A in that only the parties have access authority. Also, after downloading, secondary use of the record is prohibited with punishment.

4.3 Spanish Type - ARCONTE

The introduction of IT in Spanish courts was promoted by a system called "Arconte". It is used in 2,600 courts (81%) and about 1,500,000 trials are recorded (500,000 h or more/about 50TB) per year. It issues an annual 2,880,000 copies using self-service print terminal and Kiosk touch panel terminals for lawyers. Like the system in Germany, this Spanish system has been built with Barcelona Fujitsu over a period 19 years since the first introduction to the Court of Valencia in 2001.

The unique feature of "Arconte" is that it does not create a document but makes a proceeding record only by video using two cameras. The author, who received an explanation of the system at the District Court Barcelona in 2018, was surprised, and asked about whether the original judgment was enforceable title for a debt for the compulsory execution and also about the original judgment rendered by the court of appeals, as well as various other questions. The answer was very simple: "You can get it if you look at the video." I thought about the possibility for the Japanese practice all day long and realized that the appeal rate was low [33], and the practice of summary court is very simplified also in Japan. [34] I considered for whom the judgment is. I came to think that it is one solution, whether it is acceptable in Japan or not. For example, this method would be acceptable if the parties would not appeal nor ask for a written judgment.

5 AI and Trial

5.1 Definition of AI

So far, the term "AI" has been deliberately avoided, but the concept of AI has been used in many other ways. Most broadly, it can be defined as "a technology that allows a computer to perform intellectual actions such as language understanding, reasoning, and problem solving on behalf of humans." In relation to law, it has been dealt with in legal informatics.

The initial artificial intelligence boom was in the late 1950s and 1960s. It was possible to "infer" and "search" by the computer, and to present a solution to a particular problem.[35] Machine translation by natural language processing was particularly focused. The second artificial intelligence boom was symbolized by "machine learning". Deployments such as expert systems, case-based reasoning (CBR), and Bayesian networks could be seen. The third artificial intelligence boom was symbolized by "deep learning". Computers began to learn automatically to discover the characteristics of specific data from big data without human intervention.

5.2 Possibility of AI and Judicial Policy

In light of such developments in AI, what is and will be the impact to the judicial policy?

5.2.1 Impact of AI Technology Prevailent Society on Law

Even now, AI-based traffic lights have been put into practical use for the mitigation of traffic congestion. It is an AI signal with autonomous decentralized signal control, in which each signal independently judges [36]. Furthermore, in the future, if all vehicles become fully autonomous and the vehicles can recognize each other's positions, such signals could disappear from the intersection. In that case, many Road Traffic Act regulations will be unnecessary.

5.2.2 Major Transformation of Finance by Digital Currencies and Assets and Impact on Financial Legislation

A larger impact from AI is found in the financial legislation. A small number of individuals who use SWIFT via banks for overseas remittances but the "Transfer Wise". It is very easily explained: if a person in country A wants to send $10,000 to an account in country B, and another person want to remit the same amount from country B to A, if both persons are connected on the matching site and send each other's domestic remittances to the other party's remittance destination, they do not have to pay high exchange fee and overseas remittance fee. They can instead remit the amount as a domestic remittance and need not exchange any currency. Similarly, if you use digital currency, it is also unnecessary to change it into foreign currency.

Digital currency (virtual currency) became a hot topic due to the bankruptcy of the Japanese Bitcoin exchange, Mt.Gox; it was often reported negatively. Initial use of Bit Coin was primarily by individuals who want to avoid expensive international remittance charges by financial institutions. It was used for international settlement but later attracted other attention, when adopted as a vehicle for market speculation. In other words it was characterized as "assets" rather than as an "currency" by some people. (encryption Asset [37]) Because there is no function of national assurance and it is unlike currencies issued by public institutions, there were some countries which adopted the position that it was not recognized as a currency. On the other hand, currencies issued by current public institutions, especially banknotes, have evolved from promissory notes and have a history of only about 200 years. In addition, In the past, currencies were linked to gold or silver, and it was only possible to issue currencies commensurate with such precious metal holdings, so that eventually they could be exchanged for gold (convertible banknotes). Since the Nixon shock of 1971 such exchange is no longer possible. Nowadays based on the national credit, and everyone believes that it is worthwhile; if the nation's credit is lost and the currency cannot be backed by credit, hyperinflation will occur and paper banknotes will run out, as has been observed in countries in Latin America, for example.

Things are actually the same, in the sense that gold and silver are also valuable because people believe that they are valuable. It is not meaningful to deny that a virtual currency is not a legal currency, insofar as there are people who believe that it has value, thus it will continue to be used as currency. There are already multiple virtual currencies proposed to be linked to governmental currencies, such as Facebook's Libra, which would make use as the payment method the main use, rather than using it as a speculative target. EU and China are even eyeing the digitization of their own governmental currencies.

When such electronic data exchange between individuals (Peer to Peer) is made possible by networks, the function of monetary policy will be weakened that has been monopolized by the state, such as in state control and the management of money supply. Due to cryptocurrency(s anonymity, criminal investigations such as tax evasion and money laundering crackdowns have become difficult. Negative responses to crypto assets of some developed countries seem to be caused by the anxiety about these problems. In any case, it has a great influence on not only financial laws but also criminal laws.

5.2.3 Possibility of Blockchain Technology

In the sense that individuals are directly connected without authority, the Blockchain technology is attracting attention in all aspects of society. It became famous through virtual currency but is an open, distributed ledger that can record transactions between two parties efficiently, in a verifiable and permanent way. Once recorded it is not possible to change the data in the block retrospectively. Falsification can be prevented by making the books public and connecting all the records. Using a hash value, it prevents having the contents of the individual records seen, and a tampering changes the hash value.

By utilizing this technology, for example, a huge server of bank transactions protected by strict security becomes unnecessary, and remittance can be safely performed between individuals. In addition, contracts and settlements that require the creation and storage of evidence can be easily made. It is used already for the collection of copyright fees for music distribution [38] and remittances using virtual currency, and is attracting attention of industries that require reliable document preparation such as banks and the real estate industry [39]. Furthermore, it has the potential to change the conventional legal functions, which require official certifications such as the registration and notarization systems. Even if a public institution does not guarantee the reliability of information, it is possible through the Blockchain to store reliable information that has not been tampered.

This Blockchain technique is applicable to various records to store safely, e.g. for Information, which has been handled by public institutions or similar institutions because it requires a high degree of reliability and safety, like medical records, or even for the archiving of official documents.

Presumably the changes will progress through actions by financial and public institutions themselves. They will adopt Blockchain technology. Since it is originally a P2P technology, there is a possibility that even financial institutions and public institutions would be partially unnecessary, and it will surely affect the laws related to registration and financial institutions.

It is necessary for courts to create a system that is compatible with the use of data in a society. It should be made compatible with real estate registrations and EDI contracts and should be used in trials. If they have compatibility with each other, it is technically possible to end the compulsory execution of electronically recorded claims by operating from the keyboard of the judge's seat at the moment of judgment.

As for compatibility, Legal-XML is also important in this sense.

5.2.4 Legal-XML

The COVID-19 Pandemic forced our workshop to be held as a Zoom meeting. In Japanese companies remote work is now widespread, and universities are now engaged in distance learning. At the same time, it has made many people aware of the delay of digitization in Japan.

The number of people who were found to be infected with the coronavirus, the number of people who underwent PCR tests, etc., could not be accurately calculated even three months after the problem occurred. This is due to the fact that the network of medical information has not progressed as much as expected, and that the method of aggregation is different due to the difference in the report format between the health center and the medical associations. Similar problems occur not only in many government agencies but also in educational institutions that are forced to give distance lectures. The problem is that big data that cannot be linked sufficiently with each organization and even across organizations, and there are various types of commercial software that ignores data compatibility, and thus even within the organization they cannot cooperate with each other. The COVID-19 problem has highlighted the fact that information cannot be networked in Japan when needed. The courts also suffered from the same problem until a few years ago, that spent a lot of cost and time in order to organize the data that was not take compatible with more than 150 systems.

In the United States, XML (eXtensible Markup Language) is adopted as the description language for official document data. Previously, in 1986 the defined ISO SGML (Standard Genralized Markup Language) was adopted. XML is defined as the successor in 1998 W3C [40] which has been recommended to assure data integrity and compatibility. This XML has been adopted not only in the United States but also in German judiciary [41]. Also in private sector of e-commerce, it has become popular in the form of XML-EDI [42].

Using MPeg7 or other video protocol with tagging to legal XML all records, documents, still images, video storage, are treatable in one record collectively [43].

5.2.5 AI Judge

The ultimate form of using AI for judiciary would be that AI, not humans, would judge. They are called a "robot judge" or an "AI judge". The technological singularity of 2045 has been talked about, but will the replacement of a human being by an AI judge be realized?

In Estonia, the "Robot Judge" project was underway, but it is currently suspended. In China, an AI-based sentencing standardization system called "AI Judge" is used in Hainan Province. It is reported that it comprehensively uses AI technologies such as big data processing, natural language processing, graph structure data, with deep learning. In addition, an online court dealing with online-related disputes has been established to provide an AI-based litigation risk assessment tool and a function to create automatically litigation-related documents using machine translation and voice recognition technology [44]. In the United States, ROSS Intelligence developed AI. "ROSS" provides a service that presents highly relevant information and judicial precedents related to bankruptcy [45]. These AI Judges nevertheless seem a combination of so-called big data and AI search, and AI Judge may not reach to make a legal decision by himself.

A similar and talked-about thing is IBM's application "Watson". Tokyo University Hospital and IBM did joint research in which Watson input 20 million research papers, information on the drug that exceeds 15 million reviews and genetic information with cancer. It aimed to improve the diagnosis capability. A patient had been diagnosed "acute myeloid leukemia" and administered an anticancer drug in vain. Entering the patient's genetic information into the Watson, a different diagnosis was made in about 10 min, and being treated on this information, the patient recovered and was discharged safely. It became a hot topic in the media that the AI surpassed specialists.

As an application of the Watson to the legal field is "the Legal Consultation for Everyone" by "the Bengoshi.com", which is used by law firms [46]. A contract creation AI combined with the cloud "the Ri-ga-ru check" [47] is also available. It is a "cloud legal support AI" that can create contracts without expertise.

5.2.6 Online ADR (ODR) Site

A successful ODR site is "Rechtwijzer (guidepost of the justice)" in Netherland [48]. It is the Online ADR (ODR) site for divorce using AI. Entering age, income, education, custody of the child, residence etc. of a couple, AI presents a compromise. It also has child support calculations and consent drafting functions, as well as an optional professional brokerage service. It is reported that only about 5% of all such cases go to trial without being resolved.

In particular, the ODR field is an area that is familiar to IT use, and more progress is expected.

6 Conclusion

In Japanese society, many people were satisfied with the current state of things, and during the period of the long deflationary economy, defensive company management that does not spend money was widely carried out, leading to an extraordinary accumulation of reserves. (Coincidentally, this reserve has helped companies during COVID-19.) Universities and the judiciary had made little progress, even though more digitization had been proposed since over twenty years ago.

The degitization of the judiciary of the earlier time was led by administrative leadership, but now need for digitalization of society as a whole is widely recognized. It is expected that the judiciary will take this opportunity and actively approach it.

Since the judiciary and society are now twenty years behind, a considerable speedup is required just for catching up. The other countries mentioned in this paper have engaged in reform over a long span, looking ahead ten to twenty years. It is expected that the system will be designed in anticipation of not only the technical problems at hand but also the judiciary aspires to be like twenty years from now.

The pandemic of Coronavirus that has spread all over the world will have a great impact on people's lives. It will change their way of life and will probably continue to affect our lives. In Japan, for example, the problem of overconcentration in Tokyo would be released, which was not improved but accelerated. The relocation of people from the city center is about to proceed. By being forced to work remotely, its availability and usefulness have become widely recognized.

Corona pressed forcibly the society for the DX (Digital Transformation). Of course, the pandemic of corona itself is an unfortunate event for human being as a whole. The only positive impact of this seems to me this transformation. It is not, or it should not be an emergency evacuation, but it is necessary to thoroughly examine the current changes and think about what the next generation should be. It is now expected that we could collaborate and discuss about the future of post corona.

References

1. In fact, as far as the judicial statistics are concerned, Japanese courts are fast and cheap. In particular criminal cases are very short due to the confession-oriented practice and "precision judiciary" which means higher than 99% are convicted, which based on principle of discretionary prosecution. See "Court Data Book 2019". https://www.courts.go.jp/vc-files/courts/file4/db2019_P75-P88.pdf
2. More info. Takehiko Kasahara "Civil trial and IT", 70 Jubilee of Takeshi Kojima (continuation) - the legal system and judicial policy for the rights enforceable, Commercial Law (2009)
3. http://www.kantei.go.jp/jp/singi/keizaisaisei/saiban/index.html
4. https://www.kantei.go.jp/jp/singi/keizaisaisei/pdf/miraitousi2017_t.pdf

5. https://www.kantei.go.jp/jp/singi/keizaisaisei/saiban/index.html
6. https://www.kantei.go.jp/jp/singi/keizaisaisei/pdf/miraitousi2018_zentai.pdf
7. Refer to "Report of the Study Group on IT in Civil Court Procedures Toward the Realization of IT in Civil Court Procedures" https://www.shojihomu.or.jp/documents/10448/6839369/%E6%B0%91%E4%BA%8B%E8%A3%81%E5%88%A4%E6%89%8B%E7%B6%9A%E7%AD%89%EF%BC%A9%EF%BC%B4%E5%8C%96%E7%A0%94%E7%A9%B6%E4%BC%9A%20%E5%A0%B1%E5%91%8A%E6%9B%B8.pdf/f0c69150-e413-4e26-9562-4d9a7620031b
8. https://www.kantei.go.jp/jp/singi/keizaisaisei/odrkasseika/
9. See below for materials and minutes. http://www.moj.go.jp/shingi1/shingi04900001_00016.html
10. "Survey and research work report on IT implementation of civil court procedures in major developed countries". http://www.moj.go.jp/content/001322234.pdf
11. http://www.mnb.uscourts.gov/Calendar/CalSelect2.html
12. For various IT movements, see the CD attached to the report of the Japan Federation of Bar Associations, "Judiciary Reform and Lawyer Business - In the Age of Significant Increase in the Number of Lawyers-" and "3. 2005 American Report"
13. https://www.americanbar.org/groups/business_law/publications/blt/2013/01/03_toering/
14. 1 page, 10 cents (54 lines per page in principle. However, the maximum is $ 3 per document, and charged if exceed $ 15 every quarter. With one login ID and password PACER can be used at any states (mostly federal courts)
15. According to an interview at the Bankruptcy Court in New York District in 2005. Note 12), US Report 3rd Subcommittee "02 US Survey Report" "Chapter 3 Chapter 2–5_US Report_G2.PDF"
16. Article 2716 (B) of the Michigan Cyber Court Oder
17. Prior to Germany, Austria promoted IT. However, Austria did not step into the digitization of case record and prioritized the introduction of IT only in the so-called e-filing. http://www.univie.ac.at/frisch/isegov/aushaengUniWien/IT-JustizSchneider210003.pdf
18. https://www.justiz.bayern.de/gerichte-und-behoerden/landgericht/landshut/
19. All citizens have an ID card also as passport, alike to my number care in Japan
20. Digital signatures are unpopular, and as of three years ago, most practitioners avoided using them. The bar association created the beA (Electronic Post Box. §31a Lawyer Act) to eliminate the need for electronic signatures on documents
21. Helmut, R.: Saarland University, Germany (at that time), invited lecture "Cybercourt" in November, Toin University of Yokohama (2003)
22. Organisatorisch-technische Leitlinien für den elektronischen Rechtsverkehr mit den Gerichten und Staatsanwaltschaften (OT-Leit-ERV)
23. The Basic Guidelines subscribed Equipment may be installed by the state judiciary and public prosecutor's office (e.g., computer center)
24. Gesetz zur Förderung des elektronischen Rechtsverkehrs mit den Gerichten vom 10. Okt. 2013 (eJustice -Gesetz), BGBl: https://www.bgbl.de/xaver/bgbl/start.xav?startbk=Bundesanzeiger_BGBl&start=//*[@attr_id=%27bgbl113s3786.pdf%27]#_bgbl_%2F%2F*%5B%40attr_id%3D%27bgbl113s3786.pdf%27%5D_1508663584138
25. Introduction page of the Ministry of Justice. https://www.justiz.nrw.de/JM/schwerpunkte/erv/index.php
26. Gesetzes zur Förderung der elektronischen Verwaltung sowie zur Änderung weiterer Vorschriften vom 25, Juli 2013
27. According to an interview with the Federal Ministry of Justice in September 2017. For the criminal case, because the court records was a huge, case record was stored in to electronic form without statue text. Papers are scanned and stored for six months

28. Same as above note (27), according to an interview with the Munich District Court. The Landshut District Court take as the court's own security that the access is not possible except for certified and registered PCs and access control is performed twice, the computer center and the IT center

29. Paragraphs 5 and 6 of the same Article stipulate the arrival time of electronic documents and incomplete transmission as follows. (5) The electronic document shall be deemed to have received when it was recorded in the (electronic information) system of the court designated for receipt. (6) If the transmitted electronic document is not suitable for the processing of the court, the court must notify without delay to the sender, that transmitting (Eingang) is invalid, send the available technical manual. Sender retransmits in a form suitable for processing of the court without delay and the document contents is prima facie showing to be identical, the document is deemed to have been sent at the precedent transmission

30. Tsuneharu, Y.: "Current Status of Electronic Signatures in Germany and the Electronic Administrative Procedure Act," Quarterly Published Political Management Research No. 101, p. 23 et seq., "Outline of the German De-Mail Service Bill --Secure and Reliable Communication on the Internet" As an attempt to improve the basic legal system", Information Network Law Review, Vol. 10, p. 149, Shoji Homu (2011). As available online, the same "Examination of the German Trust Service Law". https://core.ac.uk/download/pdf/286608155.pdf

31. According to an interview with the Munich Bar Association in September 2017

32. §147 StPO, Gesetz zur Einführung der elektronischen Akte in der Justiz und zur weiteren Förderung des elektronischen Rechtsverkehrs vom 5. Juli 2017, BGBl Teil 1 Nr.45

33. The appeal rate for district court decisions is in civil case 10.0% (report on verification of speeding up trials (2nd)) and in criminal 9.5% (judicial statistics 2016)

34. Takehiko, K.: ITization of trials of summary courts -from the perspective of citizens, Citizens and Law, No. 124, p . 3 et seq.

35. "History of Artificial Intelligence (AI) Research", Ministry of Internal Affairs and Communications. White Paper on Information and Communications (2016)

36. https://miraicolabo.willsmart.co.jp/giojsdal

37. With respect to the concept of "encryption assets". https://Gendai.Ismedia.Jp/articles/-/55035 reference

38. https://ujomusic.com/

39. https://www.coindeskjapan.com/16565/

40. Abbreviation for "World Wide Web Consortium", non-profit organization that sets standards for Web technology

41. See XJustiz (Judiciary IT Project) in Germany. https://xjustiz.justiz.de/

42. e.g. Japanese logistics, see "Commentary" Easy-to-understand XML/ED, Japan Logistics Association. https://www.butsuryu.or.jp/edi/xml/desc

43. Atsushi, I., Takeshi, U., Takehiko, K., Katsuhiko, T.: Lecture/Symposium "Regal XML" Information Network Law Review, vol. 9, no. 2

44. BarandBench. http://www.barandbench.com/columns/is-artificialintelligence-replacing-jud ging

45. https://zuuonline.com/archives/125364

46. https://www.bengo4.com/bbs/

47. https://lisse-law.com/service/?utm_source=yahoo&utm_medium=cpc&utm_campaign= 1utm_content=1utm_term=%E6%B3%95%E5%8B%99%20%E3%82%B7%E3%82% B9%E3%83%86%E3%83%A0

48. https://www.hiil.org/news/rechtwijzer-why-online-supported-dispute-resolution-is-hard-to-implement/

Differential Translation for Japanese Partially Amended Statutory Sentences

Takahiro Yamakoshi[(✉)], Takahiro Komamizu, Yasuhiro Ogawa,
and Katsuhiko Toyama

Nagoya University, Nagoya, Japan
yamakoshi@kl.i.is.nagoya-u.ac.jp

Abstract. We propose a *differential* translation method that targets statutory sentences partially modified by amendments. After a statute is amended, we need to promptly update its translations for international readers. We must focus on the *focality* of translation. In other words, we should modify only the amended expressions in the translation and retain the others to avoid causing misunderstanding of the amendment's contents. To generate focal, fluent, and adequate translations, our method incorporates neural machine translation (NMT) and template-aware statistical machine translation (SMT). In particular, our method generates *n*-best translations by an NMT model with Monte Carlo dropout and chooses the best one by comparing them with the SMT translation. This complements the weaknesses of each method: NMT translations are usually fluent but they often lack focality and adequacy, while template-aware SMT translations are rather focal and adequate but not fluent. In our experiments, we showed that our method outperformed both the NMT-only and SMT-only methods.

Keywords: Japanese statutory sentences · Differential translation · Amendment

1 Introduction

In the world's globalized society, governments must quickly publicize their statutes worldwide to facilitate international trade, investments in their economy, legislation support, and so on. The Japanese government, to cope with this issue, launched the Japanese Law Translation Database System (JLT) [15] in April 2009 where it publicizes English translations of Japanese statutes. However, as of January 2020, only 23.4% (163/697) of the translated statutes in JLT correspond to their latest versions. After amending a statute, we need to promptly update its translation, or international readers may be confused about whether it remains in effect. However, statutes are much tougher to be translated than ordinary documents because the former are highly technical, complex, and long.

Machine translation is a promising solution because such methods can produce translations fast and conveniently. Such neural machine translation (NMT) methods as Transformer [16] output very fluent sentences. The typical input to a machine translation model is one source language sentence, and the output is one target language

© Springer Nature Switzerland AG 2021
N. Okazaki et al. (Eds.): JSAI-isAI 2020 Workshops, LNAI 12758, pp. 162–178, 2021.
https://doi.org/10.1007/978-3-030-79942-7_11

sentence. However, this setting has a problem in producing translations of amended statutory sentences that are partially modified.

From the perspective of a statute distributor who intends to precisely publicize statutes, making *focal* translations is more optimal for such sentences; that is, we should only modify expressions that are changed by the amendment without modifying the others. For example, assume that the following statutory sentence must be revised: "The Minister of Defense shall designate one Self-Defense Forces personnel who is a physician." The revision needs to indicate that three physicians should be designated. The following revision satisfies the focality requirement: "The Minister of Defense shall designate <u>three</u> Self-Defense Forces personnel who <u>are physicians</u>," which contains the minimum modifications. On the other hand, although "Three Self-Defense Forces personnel who are physicians shall be designated by the Minister of Defense" is fluent and adequate, it is unsuitable for the revised sentence from the focality perspective because its sentence structure is drastically changed. Typical machine translation methods do not assure to output focal translations, since it takes only a source language sentence to be translated as the input data.

For such problems, it is preferable to use a machine translation method that incorporates a translation template: a pair comprised of a source sentence and its corresponding target sentence. In this methodology, we can make a translation of the post-amendment sentence by modifying the translation of the pre-amendment sentence in accordance with the difference between the input sentence (i.e., the post-amendment sentence) and the pre-amendment sentence. Koehn's statistical machine translation (SMT) method [7] incorporates a translation template, which identifies a satisfactory template from a translation memory (TM), and determines expressions to be translated based on edit distance and only translates those expressions. Kozakai's SMT method [8] adapted Koehn's method to partially modified Japanese statutory sentences. To identify expressions to be translated, it utilizes a comparative two-column table that indicates the differences between pre- and post-amendment statutes. Although these methods can generate focal translations, the translation quality is inadequate for three reasons. First, an SMT model's performance is typically worse than NMT's. Second, their methods completely lock unchanged expressions, which is a too strong restriction. Third, they use word alignment to find target language expressions that correspond to source language expressions, whose errors lead to incorrect translations.

From this background, we propose a new machine translation method for partially modified Japanese statutory sentences that aims to ease strain on human translators. Our method incorporates NMT and template-aware SMT to satisfy focality, fluency, and adequacy. We obtain n-best translations from an NMT model as candidates and choose the best one based on similarity with the template-aware SMT translation. Since a template-aware SMT retains the unchanged expressions, we expect that the best candidate will be the most focal among all candidates and more fluent than the template-aware SMT translation. Here we apply Monte Carlo (MC) dropout [2] to the NMT model. NMT with MC dropout generates more diverse translations by making some neurons inactive during translation generation, increasing the chance to find a better candidate.

	第百六十四条①第四項を削り、②第三項後段を削り、③同項第一号中「の父母」を「（十五歳以上のものに限る。）」に改め、④同項第二号中「前号に掲げる」を「…に対し親権を行う」に改め、⑤同項第三号を削り、⑥同項を同条第六項とし、⑦同項の次に次の一項を加える。 7　特別養子適格の…（省略）
Amendment sentence in a reform act (Act No. 34 of 2019)	
Translation	In Article 164, ①delete paragraph 4, ②delete the latter part of paragraph 3, ③replace "the parents of" with "(limited to a child of 15 years of age or older)" in item (i) of the same paragraph, ④replace "set forth in the preceding item" with "who exercises parental authority over …" in item (ii) of the same paragraph, ⑤delete item (iii) of the same paragraph, ⑥regard the same paragraph as paragraph 6 of the same Article, ⑦add the following paragraph next to the same paragraph: 7 ··· of special adoption eligibility ··· (omitted)

Fig. 1. Amendment sentence

This paper contributes to amended statutory sentence translation tasks by reviewing the task requirements, proposing a method that meets the requirements, and describing its performance. Also, we expect that our method makes the whole statutory sentence translation process efficient because amendment acts occupy most of enacted statutes.

This paper is organized as follows. In Sect. 2, we position our task by introducing the amendment procedure in Japanese legislation. In Sect. 3, we explain related work. In Sect. 4, we describe our method. Section 5 presents our evaluation experiments and discussions. Finally, we summarize and conclude in Sect. 6.

2   Task Definition

In this section, we clarify the background and the objective of our task. First, we introduce the amendment process in Japanese legislation from the viewpoint of document modification. Next we position the objective of our task in the amendment process.

2.1   Partial Amendment in Japanese Legislation

In Japanese legislation, partial amendment is done by "patching" modifications to the target statute, which are prescribed as amendment sentences in a reform statute. Such modifications can be categorized as follows [12]:

1. Modification on part of a sentence: (a) Replacement, (b) Addition, and (c) Deletion.
2. Modification on statute structure elements such as sections, articles, items, sentences, etc.: (a) Replacement, (b) Addition, and (c) Deletion.
3. Modification on element numbers: (a) Renumbering, (b) Attachment, and (c) Shift.
4. Combined modification of element renumbering and replacement of its title string.

In modifying part of a sentence, Japanese legislation rules [5] dictate that the expressions to be modified must be uniquely specified by chunks of meaning.

Figure 1 shows an example of an actual amendment sentence prescribed by a reform act. Any of the seven modifications in the amendment sentence can be assigned one

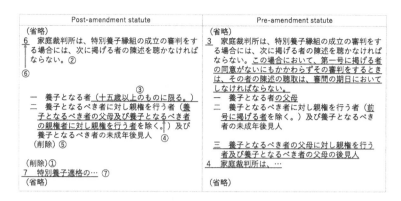

Fig. 2. Comparative table (circled numbers correspond to modifications described in Fig. 1)

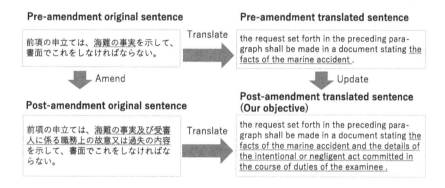

Fig. 3. Differential translation in an amended statutory sentence

of the categories described above: Modifications ①, ②, and ⑤ belong to 2. (c) of a paragraph, a sentence, an item, respectively; Modifications ③ and ④ belong to 1. (a); Modification ⑥ belongs to 3. (c); Modification ⑦ belongs to 2. (b).

Usually, a comparative table that corresponds to a reform statute is publicized, which shows the amendment contents by aligning pre-amendment and post-amendment statutes and underlining the expressions modified in the amendment. Figure 2 is a sample of a comparative table for the amendment sentence in Fig. 1.

2.2 Objective

Our task addresses post-amendment statutory sentences. Among the categories described in the previous section, we focus on category 1. (i.e., replacement, addition, and deletion of part of a sentence), and thus this task resembles a *differential translation task*. In the case of Fig. 1, modifications ③ and ④ are our targets. Here, we also target those that insert an additional sentence (e.g., a proviso) to an existing element or delete a sentence from the element, since additions or deletions affect the main sentence. For example, modification ② in Fig. 1, removing the latter part, is such a case.

Our task takes a triplet of sentences (*a pre-amendment original sentence*, *a post-amendment original sentence*, and *a pre-amendment translated sentence*) as input and generates a translation for the post-amendment original sentence called *a post-amendment translated sentence*. A pre- and post- amendment original sentence is a statutory sentence in a statute before and after an amendment, respectively. A pre-amendment translated sentence is a translation of the pre-amendment original sentence. Figure 3 illustrates this task.

In generating post-amendment translated sentences, it is better to only modify expressions that are changed by the amendment without modifying the others. There are two reasons from the viewpoint of precise publicization. First, such sentences clearly represent the amendment contents, which helps international readers to understand the contents. Second, the expressions in pre-amendment translated sentences are reliable so that reusing them ensures the translation quality. In the case of Fig. 3, we should replace "the facts of the marine accident" with "the facts of ... of the examinee" and keep other expressions which correspond to the following instruction: "Replace「海難の事実」 (*kainan no jijitsu*) with「海難の事実及び…過失の内容」(*kainan no jijitsu oyobi ... kashitsu no naiyo*)." We call this requirement *focality*, which is the third requirement along with fluency and adequacy that are the primary metrics of general machine translation.

We define our task as follows:

Input:
    Pre-amendment original sentence $W_{\text{pre-org}}$;
    Post-amendment original sentence $W_{\text{post-org}}$;
    Pre-amendment translated sentence $W_{\text{pre-tr}}$.
Output: Generated post-amendment translated sentence $\hat{W}_{\text{post-tr}}$.
Requirements:
    focality: $\hat{W}_{\text{post-tr}}$ should be generated based on expressions of $W_{\text{pre-tr}}$, and $\hat{W}_{\text{post-tr}}$ should exactly reflect amendment from $W_{\text{pre-org}}$ to $W_{\text{post-org}}$;
    fluency: $\hat{W}_{\text{post-tr}}$ should be natural in terms of phrasing and syntax;
    adequacy: $\hat{W}_{\text{post-tr}}$ should have $\hat{W}_{\text{post-org}}$'s contents without excesses or inadequacies.

3   Related Work

In this section, we review related work. We introduce template-aware SMT methods in Sect. 3.1 and NMT methods in Sect. 3.2.

3.1   Template-Aware Statistical Machine Translation

Koehn et al. [7] proposed an SMT-based translation method incorporated with translation memory (TM). Figure 4 outlines this method, which generates translations by the following procedure:

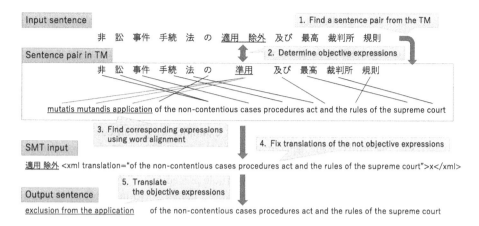

Fig. 4. Procedure of Koehn's method

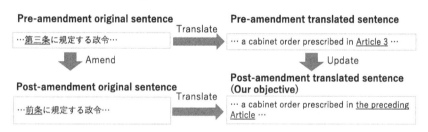

Fig. 5. Example that shows how Kozakai's method copes better

1. Extract a source language sentence and its corresponding target language sentence from the translation memory. Hereinafter, we call the former sentence the TM source sentence and the latter the TM target sentence. We extract a pair whose TM source sentence resembles the input sentence.
2. Determine the objective expressions that must be retranslated. This process is based on the edit distance calculation, where we determine the minimal edits that transform a TM source sentence into an input sentence. Then we mark the edited words as objective expressions.
3. Find expressions in the TM target sentence that correspond to the objective expressions by word alignment.
4. Lock the expressions in the TM target sentence that do not correspond to the objective expressions.
5. Finally, translate the objective expressions by an SMT model and concatenate them with the locked expressions in the previous procedure.

This method utilized Moses [6] for the SMT model. Moses can lock translations by annotating them with XML tags (Fig. 4).

Kozakai et al. [8] adapted this method to our task by applying the following two modifications. First, they used a pre-amendment original sentence and its translation instead of a relevant pair from the translation memory. Second, to determine the objective expressions, they used underlined information in the comparative table instead of the edit distance. The underlined information is more reasonable as a translation unit than the edit distance since sentence modification is done by a chunk of meaning in Japanese legislation. A critical example is shown in Fig. 5. We have underlined information between "第三条 (*dai san jo*)" and "前条 (*zen jo*)." Both objective expressions denote specific articles. By applying this underlined information, we get the following adequate translation: "... a cabinet order prescribed in <u>the preceding article</u> ..." On the other hand, if we use edit distance for this example, we get an edit that replaces "第三 (*dai san*; the third)" with "前 (*zen*; preceding)," since "条 (*jo*; article)" is common in these sentences. Applying Koehn's method, we finally get the following inadequate translation: "... a cabinet order prescribed in Article <u>preceding</u> ..." According to Kozakai et al.'s experiments, Kozakai's method achieved higher performance than Koehn's method in both BLEU [13] and RIBES [4].

Both methods can meet our focality requirement by locking the unchanged expressions in the pre-amendment translated sentences. However, the translation quality, especially fluency, suffers for the following three reasons. First, they use SMT for the translation model, whose performance is typically worse than that of NMT. Second, their methods completely lock the unchanged expressions, which may strongly restrict translations. Third, they use word alignment to find English expressions that correspond to Japanese expressions, which may weaken their performance due to alignment error.

3.2 Neural Machine Translation

Neural machine translation (NMT) is the most common machine translation scheme because of its fluent output. A typical NMT model embeds an input sentence into a vector or multiple vectors and outputs a translated sentence by referencing the vector(s). One of the most powerful and influential NMT architectures is Transformer [16], which is comprised of two attention mechanisms: self-attention and cross-attention. These attentions capture such contexts as dependency and adjacent word information [17].

Some studies have focused on the incorporation of NMT and TM. For example, Cao et al. [1] proposed an NMT architecture that encodes an input sentence and its relevant TM target sentence into each vector and utilizes them for predicting target words by balancing two vectors based on context. Xia et al. [18] proposed a Transformer-based architecture that accepts TM target sentences by encoding them with a graph network.

However, a naive NMT model does not guarantee that unchanged expressions will be retained. The TM-incorporated NMT methods described above also fail to provide such guarantees because the expressions in the TM sentences are embedded and outputting them is influenced by probability.

4   Proposed Method

In this section, we propose our method. Sections 4.1 and 4.2 explain the translation procedure and the criterion for focality evaluation, respectively.

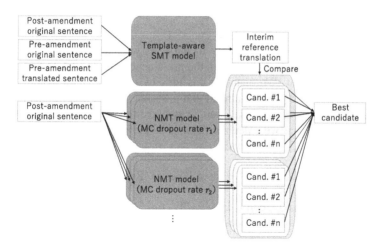

Fig. 6. Procedure of our method

4.1 Translation Procedure

Figure 6 shows our translation procedure. Our method uses an NMT model and a template-aware SMT model. We let the NMT model output *n*-best translations, which is done by applying a beam search. We then choose the most similar translation to the *interim* reference translation that is generated from the template-aware SMT model. With this methodology, we expect that these two methods compensate for the disadvantage of each method:

- An NMT model can output natural sentences, but it may modify or drop expressions that should not be tampered with.
- Although a template-aware SMT model can retain unchanged expressions during the translation process, its output may not be fluent.

We assume that the best candidate from the NMT model should cover more unchanged expressions than the other candidates, and that the best candidate is more fluent than the template-aware SMT translation.

We hope the NMT model to output more diversified sentences to identify a better candidate. Therefore, we apply Monte Carlo (MC) dropout [3] to the model for generating NMT translations. By removing neurons from the NMT model, it can output more diversified translations based on its uncertainty about the input [2]. Therefore, we can gather more various kinds of translations and perhaps locate a better candidate nearer the reference translation. We merge translations from different dropout rates, including dropout rate $r = 0.0$, which means that no MC dropout was applied.

In sentence comparisons, we can substantially utilize any criterion that assesses the similarity between two sentences. However, we believe that BLEU is a good criterion because its calculation is based on an *n*-gram concordance rate, which does not heavily penalize drastic word order changes compared to word matching-based metrics like RIBES. We should not penalize the NMT translations according to translations of template-aware SMT models that contain word order errors.

4.2 Focality Criterion

We design an n-gram base criterion for focality. As we discussed in Sect. 2.2, focal translations should contain expressions in the pre-amendment translation that are unaffected by the amendment. We quantize this idea by calculating the recall of the n-grams shared by both the pre-amendment and post-amendment translations. With pre-amendment translated sentence $W_{\text{pre-tr}}$ and actual post-amendment translated sentence $W_{\text{post-tr}}$ written by human, we calculate focality score $\text{Foc}(\hat{W}_{\text{post-tr}}; W_{\text{pre-tr}}, W_{\text{post-tr}})$ of generated sentence $\hat{W}_{\text{post-tr}}$ as follows:

$$\text{Foc}(\hat{W}_{\text{post-tr}}; W_{\text{pre-tr}}, W_{\text{post-tr}}) = \text{RP}(W_{\text{post-tr}}, \hat{W}_{\text{post-tr}}) \cdot \text{Rec}(\hat{W}_{\text{post-tr}}; W_{\text{pre-tr}}, W_{\text{post-tr}}), \quad (1)$$

where $\text{RP}(W_{\text{post-tr}}, \hat{W}_{\text{post-tr}}) = \min(1, \exp(1 - |\hat{W}_{\text{post-tr}}| / |W_{\text{post-tr}}|))$ avoids overestimating the scores of the redundant sentences. $|W|$ is the word count of W. The recall Rec is calculated as follows:

$$\text{Rec}(\hat{W}_{\text{post-tr}}; W_{\text{pre-tr}}, W_{\text{post-tr}}) \quad (2)$$
$$= \frac{\sum_{s \in \text{CN}(\{\hat{W}_{\text{post-tr}}, W_{\text{pre-tr}}, W_{\text{post-tr}}\})} \min(c_{\hat{W}_{\text{post-tr}}}(s), c_{W_{\text{pre-tr}}}(s), c_{W_{\text{post-tr}}}(s))}{\sum_{s \in \text{CN}(\{W_{\text{pre-tr}}, W_{\text{post-tr}}\})} \min(c_{W_{\text{pre-tr}}}(s), c_{W_{\text{post-tr}}}(s))},$$

where $c_W(s)$ is the number of occurrences of the n-gram s in W, and $\text{CN}(\mathcal{W})$, where $\mathcal{W} = \{W_1, W_2, \cdots, W_m\}$, returns common n-grams of $W_1, W_2, \cdots, W_m$:

$$\text{CN}(\mathcal{W}) = \left\{ s \mid s \in \bigcap_{W_i \in \mathcal{W}} \text{ngrams}(W_i) \right\}, \quad (3)$$

where $\text{ngrams}(W)$ returns n-grams in W. We consider the multiple lengths of n-gram:

$$\text{ngrams}(W) = \bigcup_{i=1}^{N} i\text{-gram}(W), \quad (4)$$

where $i\text{-gram}(W)$ returns the i-grams of W.

5 Experiment

Next we experimentally evaluated the effectiveness of our method.

5.1 Outline

For training data, we used a bilingual-statutory-sentence corpus compiled by Kozakai et al. [8] from JLT[1]. This corpus consists of 158,928 sentence pairs from 407 statutes. As test data, we used 158 sets of sentence amendment examples that consist of pre-amendment original sentences, post-amendment original sentences, pre-amendment

---

[1] http://www.japaneselawtranslation.go.jp/.

Table 1. Experimental results

Model	BLEU	RIBES	Focality
Transformer + Kozakai model + MC Dropout (Proposed 1)	**62.43**	**88.19**	84.27
Transformer + Koehn model + MC Dropout (Proposed 2)	62.08	87.74	84.59
Transformer + Kozakai model	60.52	87.50	82.35
Transformer + Koehn model	60.68	87.58	82.42
Naive Transformer	58.72	86.86	80.11
Naive Kozakai model	59.86	83.04	**85.60**
Naive Koehn model	59.22	82.52	85.21
Naive Moses	40.67	64.31	54.95
Transformer + $W_{\text{post-tr}}$ + MC Dropout	69.13	89.95	87.24

Table 2. Successful case

Model	Output
$(W_{\text{pre-org}})$	（講習の業務の休廃止）
$(W_{\text{pre-tr}})$	(suspension or abolition of <u>training</u> services)
$(W_{\text{post-org}})$	（エネルギー管理講習の業務の休廃止）
$(W_{\text{post-tr}})$	(suspension or abolition of <u>energy management training</u> services)
Proposed 1	(suspension or abolition of energy management training services)
Proposed 2	(suspension or abolition of training services for energy management)
Transformer	(suspension or abolition of energy management training)
Kozakai	(suspension or abolition of energy management of training services)
Koehn	(suspension or abolition of training services) energy management
Moses	(suspension or abolition of training services energy management)

translated sentences, and post-amendment translated sentences, where the pre- and post-amendment original sentences have underlined information. We acquired these sentence amendment examples from 17 amendments.

We used Transformer [16] for the NMT model. Here are the settings of the NMT model: six encoder/decoder hidden layers, eight self-attention heads, 512 hidden vectors, a batch size of eight, and an input sequence length of 256. We implemented the training and prediciton codes based on the TensorFlow official model [2]. We used SentencePiece [9] as a tokenizer and set the vocabulary size to 32,768. We chose a dropout rate of 0.1 for training, which is the default setting of the official Transformer implementation. In the prediction phase, we executed the model with two dropout rates, 0.0 and 0.1, where a 0.0 dropout means that no dropout was applied. We set the number of beam search candidates to four and the number of MC dropout trials to 20 and acquired $20 \times 4 = 80$ candidates for each dropout rate.

---

[2] https://github.com/tensorflow/models.

For the template-aware SMT model, we compared Kozakai's SMT model [8] (hereinafter the Kozakai model) and Koehn's SMT model [7] (Koehn model). The following are the settings of these template-aware SMTs: GIZA++ [11] for the word alignment, SRILM [14] for the language model generation, and Moses [6] for the decoder. We used MeCab [10] for the Japanese tokenizer.

We used BLEU and RIBES to evaluate the fluency and adequacy. For focality, we use Eq. 1 with maximum n-gram length $N = 4$, which is the same as the standard BLEU score calculation. To cope with edge words, we padded the sentences when we acquired n-grams of them. We tested the following translation models as comparison methods: naive Transformer, naive Moses [6], naive Kozakai model, naive Koehn model, a combination of Transformer and Kozakai model without MC dropout, and a combination of Transformer and Koehn model without MC dropout.

5.2 Results

Table 1 shows the experimental results. Among the proposed methods, Proposed 1 achieved higher BLEU and RIBES, while Proposed 2 achieved a higher focality score. Comparing these methods with the naive methods, we observe that the combination of NMT and template-aware SMT raises both BLEU and RIBES. Although these proposed methods output one of the Transformer candidates that are generated only from the post-amendment original sentence, their focality scores were not degraded much from the naive template-aware SMT methods. We also confirm the effectiveness of MC dropout by comparing the proposed methods with ones without MC dropout. However, there is room for improvement in interim reference translations. When we used actual post-amendment translated sentence $W_{post-tr}$ as the interim reference translation instead of the output of Kozakai model, we get 6.70, 1.76, and 2.97 points higher performance in BLEU, RIBES, and focality, respectively.

Hereinafter, we conduct qualitative analysis. Table 2 shows a successful case. The naive Transformer model output "suspension or abolition of energy management training," where "services" was missing. On the other hand, Proposed 1 chose the correct candidate by referencing the output of the template-aware SMT model: the naive Kozakai model. The choice of Proposed 2 is also focal; however, its sentence structure is different from $W_{post-tr}$. Table 3 shows an unsatisfactory case. Since the original sentence dropped the subject, "the permitted manufacturer," the Transformer model needed to estimate it. The proposed methods theoretically can exploit their advantage of candidate selection in this case. However, both Proposed 1 and Proposed 2 failed to output an adequate choice because the dropped subject did not appear among the candidates.

Table 4 shows a case of a long sentence. We need to add an expression "業種別のエネルギーの使用の合理化の状況" (, the status of the rational use of energy by each type of business) in this amendment [3]. Proposed 1 translated the expression in an almost correct manner, while the naive Transformer model could not. The naive Kozakai model wrongly inserted the expression to the beginning of the sentence possibly because of alignment errors. The Moses output seems not to be very fluent.

---

[3] This example is not perfectly focal because the replacement of "taking into consideration" with "considering" is not affected by the Japanese sentences.

Table 3. Failure example

Model	Output
($W_{\text{pre-org}}$)	第十八条第一項の規定による命令に違反したとき。
($W_{\text{pre-tr}}$)	where the permitted manufacturer has violated an order under the provisions of Paragraph (1) of Article 18.
($W_{\text{post-org}}$)	第十八条の規定による命令に違反したとき。
($W_{\text{post-tr}}$)	where the permitted manufacturer has violated an order under the provisions of Article 18.
Proposed 1	the person has violated an order under the provisions of Article 18.
Proposed 2	the person has violated an order under the provisions of Article 18.
Transformer	the designated calibration organization has violated an order under the provision of Article 18.
Kozakai	where the permitted manufacturer has violated an order under the provisions of Article 18 of
Koehn	where the permitted manufacturer has violated an order under the provisions of Article 18
Moses	when he/she violated an order pursuant to the provisions of Article 18.

5.3 Discussion

First, we look at the generation ability of MC dropout. Figure 7 shows the outputs of the Transformer model with three MC dropout trials. In this case, the sentence structures of the outputs in dropout #3 were different from dropouts #1 and #2. On the other hand, the outputs in each dropout are rather similar. For example, they have minor word or phrase usage differences: "trial vs. hearing" and "conducted vs. carried out" in dropout #1 and "chief trial examiners vs. presiding judge" in dropout #2. One exception is expression "in case of. . .," which was omitted in two outputs of dropout #3. This implies that MC dropout contributed to the generation of diversified translations and avoided bad translations.

Next, we assessed the quantitive performance of the MC dropout sentences. First, we focus on the relationship between the number of MC dropout trials and the BLEU performance (Fig. 8). As we increased the MC dropout trials, the BLEU performance also generally rose. However, the growth rate was higher when we used actual post-amendment translated sentences as the interim reference translations. This result may reflect the limitation of the Kozakai model's performance.

Second, we focused on the relationship between the number of MC dropout trials and the number of selections of non-MC dropout sentences. This investigation addresses whether doing more MC dropouts raises the chances of identifying a better translation. Figure 9 shows such relationship in Proposed 1. As we increased the MC dropout trials, the number of selections of non-MC dropout sentences decreased. However, the number eventually became saturated. This result suggests that more MC dropout trials generally lead to better translations, although this claim has limitations.

Table 4. Example of long sentence (We omit the output of Proposed 2 and Koehn model because of space limitations)

Model	Output
($W_{\text{pre-org}}$)	前項に規定する判断の基準となるべき事項は、エネルギー需給の長期見通し、エネルギーの使用の合理化に関する技術水準その他の事情を勘案して定めるものとし、これらの事情の変動に応じて必要な改定をするものとする。
($W_{\text{pre-tr}}$)	the standards of judgment prescribed in the preceding paragraph shall be established by taking into consideration long-term energy supply-demand forecasts, the technical level related to the rational use of energy, and other circumstances, and shall be revised if necessary depending on any changes in these circumstances.
($W_{\text{post-org}}$)	前項に規定する判断の基準となるべき事項は、エネルギー需給の長期見通し、エネルギーの使用の合理化に関する技術水準、業種別のエネルギーの使用の合理化の状況その他の事情を勘案して定めるものとし、これらの事情の変動に応じて必要な改定をするものとする。
($W_{\text{post-tr}}$)	the standards of judgment prescribed in the preceding paragraph shall be established by considering long-term energy supply-demand forecasts, the technical level related to the rational use of energy, the status of the rational use of energy by each type of business and other circumstances, and shall be revised if necessary depending on any changes in these circumstances.
Proposed 1	the standards of judgment prescribed in the preceding paragraph shall be established by taking into consideration long-term energy supply-demand forecasts, the technical level related to the rational use of energy, the status of the rational use of energy by type, and other circumstances, and shall be revised if necessary due to any changes in these circumstances.
Transformer	the standards of judgment prescribed in the preceding paragraph shall be established by taking into consideration long-term energy supply-demand forecasts, the technical level related to the rational use of energy, and other circumstances, as well as necessary revisions shall be made to the standards depending on the changes in these circumstances.
Kozakai	the type of the rational use of energy and the status of the standards of judgment prescribed in the preceding paragraph shall be established by taking into consideration long-term energy supply-demand forecasts, the technical level related to the rational use of energy, and other circumstances, and shall be revised if necessary depending on any changes in these circumstances.
Moses	the standards of judgment prescribed in the preceding paragraph, the long-term outlook for energy supply and demand, the technical level related to the rational use of energy, for each type of the status of the rational use of energy and other circumstances shall be established by taking into consideration the change in these circumstances necessary depending on.

Next, we discuss the effectiveness of the dropout rates. Figure 10 shows the sentence-level correlation coefficients between the metric scores and the sentence features. The metric scores include the BLEU, RIBES, and the focality scores of each sentence at different MC Dropout rates: 0.0, 0.1, 0.2, 0.3, 0.4, and 0.5. As for dropout

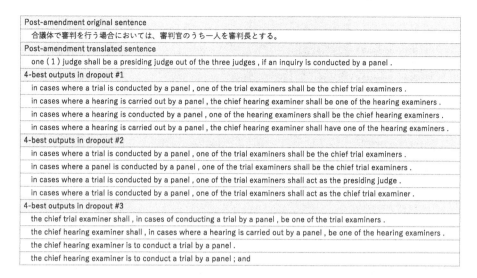

Post-amendment original sentence
合議体で審判を行う場合においては、審判官のうち一人を審判長とする。
Post-amendment translated sentence
one (1) judge shall be a presiding judge out of the three judges , if an inquiry is conducted by a panel .
4-best outputs in dropout #1
in cases where a trial is conducted by a panel , one of the trial examiners shall be the chief trial examiners .
in cases where a hearing is carried out by a panel , the chief hearing examiner shall be one of the hearing examiners .
in cases where a hearing is conducted by a panel , one of the hearing examiners shall be the chief hearing examiners .
in cases where a hearing is carried out by a panel , the chief hearing examiner shall have one of the hearing examiners .
4-best outputs in dropout #2
in cases where a trial is conducted by a panel , one of the trial examiners shall be the chief trial examiners .
in cases where a panel is conducted by a panel , one of the trial examiners shall be the chief trial examiners .
in cases where a trial is conducted by a panel , one of the trial examiners shall act as the presiding judge .
in cases where a trial is conducted by a panel , one of the trial examiners shall act as the chief trial examiner .
4-best outputs in dropout #3
the chief trial examiner shall , in cases of conducting a trial by a panel , be one of the trial examiners .
the chief hearing examiner shall , in cases where a hearing is carried out by a panel , be one of the hearing examiners .
the chief hearing examiner is to conduct a trial by a panel .
the chief hearing examiner is to conduct a trial by a panel ; and

Fig. 7. Example of MC dropout sentences

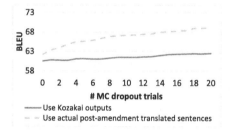

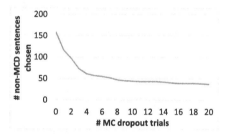

Fig. 8. BLEU transition on number of MC dropout trials

Fig. 9. Relationship between numbers of MC dropout trials and selections of non-MC dropout sentences

rates of 0.2 and larger, we trained a model at the new dropout rate. Sentence features include the total word count of $W_{\text{post-tr}}$, the unique word count of $W_{\text{post-tr}}$, the 4-gram language model probability of $W_{\text{post-tr}}$, the unedited word ratio between $W_{\text{pre-org}}$ and $W_{\text{post-org}}$, and the unlined word ratio between $W_{\text{pre-org}}$ and $W_{\text{post-org}}$ of each translation instance. We found some interesting results. First, adjacent dropout rates have relatively high correlations in metric scores, especially in focality. This suggests that we can get translations with similar scores using similar dropout rates. Second, weak negative correlations exist between metric scores in strong dropout rates and some sentence features, including total word count, unique word count, unedited word ratio, and unlined word ratio. The result of the total and unique word counts suggests that Transformer models with a higher dropout rate tend to work more poorly against longer sentences. Concerning the result of the unedited or unlined word ratio, our hypothesis models with a higher

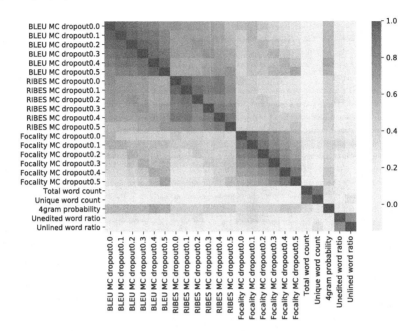

Fig. 10. Correlation between metric scores and sentence features

dropout rate produced more diverse translations, and thus we needed more trials to get better sentences that more closely match the unchanged expressions.

Finally, we discuss the recall of common n-grams in each method to investigate our method's focality capabilities. The bar graph in Fig. 11 shows the total number of occurrences of the same n-grams in $CN(\{W_{\text{pre-tr}}, W_{\text{post-tr}}\})$, that is, the number of common n-grams $W_{\text{pre-tr}}$ and $W_{\text{post-tr}}$ through the amendment. The line graphs in the figure show the n-gram match rate between $CN(\{\hat{W}_{\text{post-tr}}, W_{\text{pre-tr}}, W_{\text{post-tr}}\})$ and $CN(\{W_{\text{pre-tr}}, W_{\text{post-tr}}\})$, that is, the recall of the common n-grams. Proposed 1, Kozakai model, and naive Transformer retain high match rates in long n-grams. Compared with naive Transformer, Proposed 1 achieves around 3 to 6 points better recall. Compared with Kozakai model, Proposed 1 achieves higher recall in longer n-grams: Proposed 1 has 77.70% recall in 10-grams while Kozakai model has 75.68% recall. This result might come from alignment errors in Kozakai model: as we saw in Table 4, they can cause wrong word insertions, which divide continuous common n-grams. On the other hand, Kozakai model is good at shorter n-grams possibly because of its stronger fixation of unchanged expressions.

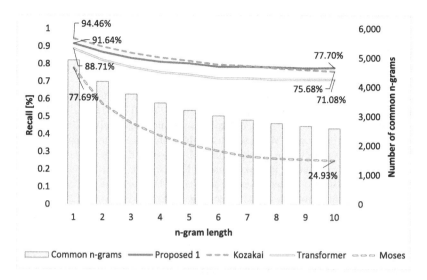

Fig. 11. Recall of common *n*-grams in different lengths

6 Summary

We proposed a differential translation method for amended statutory sentences. Our method incorporates an NMT model and a template-aware SMT model, where the former outputs natural translation candidates and the latter outputs an interim reference translation that retains the contents of the pre-amendment statutory sentences. We augmented candidates with high diversity by applying Monte Carlo dropout to generate NMT translations. Our method outperformed NMT or template-aware SMT alone.

Our future work will address the following two tasks. First, we need to investigate the validity of the focality metric. Second, we must find a better solution to generate interim reference translations, since our NMT model has the potential to output better translations.

Acknowledgments. This work was partly supported by JSPS KAKENHI Grant Number 18H03492.

References

1. Cao, Q., Xiong, D.: Encoding gated translation memory into neural machine translation. In: Proceedings of the 2018 Conference on Empirical Methods in Natural Language Processing, pp. 3042–3047 (2018)
2. Fomincheva, M., Specia, L., Guzm'an, F.: Multi-hypothesis machine translation evaluation. In: Proceedings of the 58th Annual Meeting of the Association for Computational Linguistics, pp. 1218–1232 (2020)
3. Gal, Y., Ghahramani, Z.: Dropout as a Bayesian approximation: representing model uncertainty in deep learning. In: Proceedings of the 33rd International Conference on Machine Learning, p. 10 (2016)

4. Hirao, T., Isozaki, H., Sudoh, K., Duh, K., Tsukada, H., Nagata, M.: Evaluating translation quality with word order correlations. J. Nat. Lang. Process. **21**(3), 421–444 (2014). (In Japanese)
5. Hoseishitumu-Kenkyukai: Workbook Hoseishitumu (newly revised second edition). Gyosei (2018). (In Japanese)
6. Koehn, P., et al.: Moses: Open source toolkit for statistical machine translation. In: Proceedings of the ACL 2007 Demo and Poster Sessions, pp. 177–180 (2007)
7. Koehn, P., Senellart, J.: Convergence of translation memory and statistical machine translation. In: AMTA Workshop on MT Research and the Translation Industry, pp. 21–31 (2010)
8. Kozakai, T., Ogawa, Y., Ohno, T., Nakamura, M., Toyama, K.: Shinkyutaishohyo no riyo niyoru horei no eiyaku shusei. In: Proceedings of NLP2017, p. 4 (2017). (In Japanese)
9. Kudo, T., Richardson, J.: Sentencepiece: a simple and language independent subword tokenizer and detokenizer for neural text processing. In: Proceedings of the 2018 Conference on Empirical Methods in Natural Language Processing (System Demonstrations), pp. 66–71 (2018)
10. Kudo, T., Yamamoto, K., Matsumoto, Y.: Applying conditional random fields to Japanese morphological analysis. In: Proceedings of the 2004 Conference on Empirical Methods in Natural Language Processing, pp. 230–237 (2004)
11. Och, F.J., Ney, H.: A systematic comparison of various statistical alignment models. Comput. Linguist. **29**(1), 19–51 (2005)
12. Ogawa, Y., Inagaki, S., Toyama, K.: Automatic consolidation of Japanese statutes based on formalization of amendment sentences. In: New Frontiers in Artificial Intelligence: JSAI 2007 Conference and Workshops, Revised Selected Papers, Lecture Notes in Computer Science 4914, Springer, pp. 363–376 (2008)
13. Papineni, K., Roukos, S., Ward, T., Jing Zhu, W.: BLEU: a method for automatic evaluation of machine translation. In: Proceedings of the 40th Annual Meeting of the Association for Computational Linguistics, pp. 311–318 (2002)
14. Stolcke, A.: SRILM – an extensible language modeling toolkit. Proc. ICSLP **2002**, 901–904 (2002)
15. Toyama, K., et al.: Design and development of Japanese law translation system. In: Law via the Internet 2011, p. 12 (2011)
16. Vaswani, A., Shazeer, N., Parmar, N., Uszkoreit, J., Jones, L., Gomez, A.N., Kaiser, L., Polosukhin, I.: Attention is all you need. Proc. Adv. Neural Inf. Process. Syst. **30**, 6000–6010 (2017)
17. Voita, E., Talbot, D., Moiseev, F., Sennrich, R., Titov, I.: Analyzing multi-head self-attention: specialized heads do the heavy lifting, the rest can be pruned. In: Proceedings of the 57th Annual Meeting of the Association for Computational Linguistics, pp. 5797–5808 (2019)
18. Xia, M., Huang, G., Liu, L., Shi, S.: Graph based translation memory for neural machine translation. In: Proceedings of the Thirty-Third AAAI Conference on Artificial Intelligence, pp. 7297–7304 (2019)

Aspect Classification for Legal Depositions

Saurabh Chakravarty[✉] ⓘ, Satvik Chekuri ⓘ, Maanav Mehrotra, and Edward A. Fox ⓘ

Department of Computer Science, Virginia Tech, Blacksburg, VA 24061, USA
{saurabc,satvikchekuri,maanav,fox}@vt.edu

Abstract. Attorneys have interest in having a digital library with suitable services (e.g., summarizing, searching, and browsing) to help them work with large legal deposition corpora. Their needs often involve understanding the semantics of such documents. In the case of tort litigation associated with property and casualty insurance claims, such as relating to an injury, it is important to know not only about liability, but also about events, accidents, physical conditions, and treatments.

We hypothesize that a legal deposition consists of various aspects that are discussed as part of the deponent testimony. Accordingly, we developed an ontology of aspects in a legal deposition for accident and injury cases. Using that, we have developed a classifier that can identify portions of text for each of the aspects of interest. Doing so was complicated by the peculiarities of this genre, e.g., that deposition transcripts generally consist of data in the form of question-answer (QA) pairs. Accordingly, our automated system starts with pre-processing, and then transforms the QA pairs into a canonical form made up of declarative sentences. Classifying the declarative sentences that are generated, according to the aspect, can then help with downstream tasks such as summarization, segmentation, question-answering, and information retrieval.

Our methods have achieved a classification F1 score of 0.83. Having the aspects classified with good accuracy will help in choosing QA pairs that can be used as candidate summary sentences, and to generate an informative summary for legal professionals or insurance claim agents. Our methodology could be extended to legal depositions of other kinds, and to aid services like searching.

Keywords: NLP · Aspects · Classification · Legal depositions

1 Introduction

Processing and comprehension of legal deposition documents by humans are difficult, time-consuming, and lead to considerable expense since the work typically is carried out by attorneys and paralegals. This process often adds to the

N. Okazaki et al. (Eds.): JSAI-isAI 2020 Workshops, LNAI 12758, pp. 179–195, 2021.
https://doi.org/10.1007/978-3-030-79942-7_12

elapsed time when handling a case or preparing for trial, and may cause real-time staffing problems. Automatic processing and comprehension of the content present in legal depositions would be immensely useful for law professionals, helping them to identify and disseminate salient information in key documents, as well as reducing time and cost.

These documents are comprised of dialogue exchanges between attorneys and deponents, mainly focused on identifying observations and the facts of a case. These conversations are in the form of (possibly quickfire) question-answer (QA) sets. Processing such deposition documents using traditional text analysis techniques is a challenge because of the syntactic, semantic, and discourse characteristics of the QA conversations.

In [8] we proposed methods to transform QA pairs into a canonical form made up of declarative sentences. That allows the text to be processed by workflows for downstream tasks, e.g., summarization. However, preliminary experiments starting with the declarative sentences resulting from the transformation, and feeding them into a summarization method pre-trained on news article corpora, led to poor results. This happens because of a lack of domain understanding on the part of these methods, which have been trained on news articles that are markedly different in content and structure from legal depositions. Many important parts of depositions are present in the middle or end segments in the document, unlike news stories where significant concepts are mentioned in the beginning. There may be very little repetition of some key concepts, such as when a key admission is made, and an attorney deliberately avoids allowing such a statement to be elaborated upon. Such non-repetition diminishes the utility of simple frequency-based scores, that work so well in the news domain.

Consumers of legal deposition summaries are more interested in important parts that relate to the case pleadings or claim complaints as opposed to uniform coverage of the whole deposition document. Coverage of the details of a key event (e.g., accident), and the events before and after it, often is important for legal professionals. Events, entity mentions, and facts are present throughout the length of the deposition. Identifying the aspects covered in a deposition would allow a deposition to be broken up into its constituent topical parts. Summaries can be generated based on a predefined distribution and layout of different aspect sentences present in the deposition. Such a layout and distribution can be learned from existing legal depositions and summaries, and could be further refined based on case pleadings and deponent types.

This work focuses on classifying the various aspects of depositions into a predefined ontology that pertains to property and casualty insurance claims, e.g., relating to an injury. As part of our initial work, we analyzed legal depositions and their summaries generated by legal professionals. These were legal depositions for different cases and varying deponent roles. We started with an ontology of 20 aspects that were later trimmed down to a set of 12 by merging aspects that were similar in nature. The ontology is described in detail in Sect. 3.1.

The core contributions of our work are as follows:

1. An ontology of aspects for accident and injury cases that can be expanded/modified for other kinds of cases.
2. Classification methods to identify the various aspects of QA pairs in the deposition, that fit well in a pipeline for summarization.
3. A dataset that can be used by the community to support and expand their research in legal and other domains.
4. An overall framework to identify the aspects of legal depositions that can be re-purposed for other kinds of cases in the legal domain. This framework also can be used for scientific and medical literature summarization.

2   Related Work

As part of our literature search, we studied works that relate to the comprehension of conversations. Work in [18] introduced the concept of dialog acts (DA) in spoken conversations. A DA represents the communicative intent of a speaker in a two or multi-party conversation. Work in [2,6,13,17,20,21,23,33,34] used different techniques to classify the dialog acts in different settings such as text chats, meetings, etc. Identifying the DAs of conversation sentences provides a way to understand the discourse structure of the conversation.

A challenge with spoken conversation sentences is that the context of the conversation is spread across the question and the answer. This is especially pronounced in the area of legal depositions. One method to process the QA sentences in an efficient way is to fuse the question and answer together into one or a series of sentences. Our work in [8] used the DAs of the questions and answers to transform a QA pair to a declarative sentence. The QA pairs were from a corpus of legal depositions [31]. Transformation rules were developed to break the question and answer sentences into chunks, and words were permuted, deleted, and added from the question and answer sentences, followed by a fusion of the modified question and answer sentences. Different transformation rules were developed based on the combination of the question and answer DA classes. We used the DA ontology for legal depositions from our work in [6] to frame the rules for transformation. Transforming the QA pairs to a text representation that is conducive to other downstream tasks would be useful; here we explore further whether a transformation to a canonical form will help achieve better results.

Classical classification methods such as Naïve Bayes [28], decision tree [29], k-nearest neighbor [11], association rules [1], etc. have been used for classifying text. These methods have been combined with various feature selection techniques such as Gini index [26], conditional entropy [27], χ^2-statistic [5], and mutual information [15]. They have also been augmented with various feature engineering techniques to improve the classification further.

Another class of classification methods uses rich word embeddings like GloVe [25] and word2vec [24]. With them, good results have been reported in various text classification tasks. Using the embeddings helps create a feature representation of the text without the need to perform complicated feature selection or engineering. However, a challenge with both the classical feature selection and the word embedding based methods is that the created representation is a bag-of-words representation and does not factor in the ordering of the words.

Methods based on Deep Learning have further improved upon the established state-of-the-art results in text classification. Sophisticated architectures like encoder-decoder models [9] along with attention [3] were equally effective in text classification. These architectures are very deep and sometimes have multiple layers and a large number of parameters. However, achieving improved performance requires training of these models on a large dataset.

Another recent addition in the text representation space is the introduction of systems that can generate embeddings for sentences. The premise of these systems is to learn a language model (LM) using a large corpus. These models are trained using the principle of self-supervision on targeted natural language processing (NLP) tasks like missing word prediction and next sentence classification. As the model is trained on the targeted task, a side benefit of such training is the intermediate representation that is learned by the system to represent sentences. These sentence embeddings are semantically very rich.

Work on BERT [12] trained a language model using a large corpus of English text. A core contribution of this work was the generation of pre-trained sentence embeddings that have been learned using the left and right context of each token in the sentence. The system was trained in a bi-directional way to learn the semantic and syntactic dependencies between words in both directions. After adding a fully connected neural network layer to the pre-trained embeddings, the authors proposed that these embeddings can be utilized to model any custom NLP task. BERT internally uses the "Transformer" or the multi-layer network architecture presented in [32] to model the input text and the output embedding. The trained system was able to outperform the established state-of-the-art in 11 benchmark NLP tasks. Accordingly, we explore the use of deep learning based methods and BERT sentence embeddings for classification.

3   Methods

As part of our methods, we defined an ontology of aspects for the legal domain. We also developed methods to classify the aspects for the QA pairs in the dataset, according to the defined ontology. The following sections describe the ontology and the classification methods in more detail.

The preprint archive version of this paper [7] contains additional supporting material such as architecture figures of classifiers, experimental setup details, and parameters used for tuning the classifiers for best performance.

3.1   Aspects Ontology

To identify the aspects, we analyzed the legal depositions and their summaries in our dataset. The summaries in the dataset were arranged in paragraphs, where each aspect in the summary was present in a different paragraph. However, there were multiple paragraphs that covered the same aspect. Two authors of our paper created their own taxonomy of aspects initially. They collated all of the aspects together based on their mutual agreement. These aspects were then reviewed by a legal professional and further refined to a final taxonomy of 12 aspects. Note that we use "ontology" rather than "taxonomy" in this paper since in future work we may consider relationships among aspects for more in-depth analysis.

Table 1 lists all of the aspects, with their descriptions.

3.2   Aspect Classification

For our work, we used 3 different methods for classification. Two of the methods used deep neural networks to model the sentence embeddings for the input sentences. The third method used the BERT [12] model to generate sentence embeddings. We wanted to measure whether simple architectures based on a rich sentence embedding would perform competitively compared to a deep neural network. The following sections describe the architecture of these methods.

CNN Based Classifier. Though word embedding based deep averaging methods [16] were able to achieve competitive performance in text classification, one of the challenges with such methods is that they do not account for the word order in the sentence. The final averaged representation of the sentence is the same, as long as it has the same words. This follows a simple analogy with a bag-of-words model. Work in [19] used a convolutional neural network (CNN) to create a classifier that would be able to account for the word order in the sentence that has to be classified. The network used a spanning window of a variable size, which was generally 2–4, to represent the n-gram (e.g., 2–4 word sequence) based representation in a sentence. The convolution filter size of the network was parameterized and was used to control how many n-grams will be run through the convolution process.

We used an architecture similar to [19] for our experiments. The input sentence was tokenized into words. The words were transformed into their embeddings using word2vec. The convolution and max-pooling operations convert the word embeddings of the input words into a fixed-sized representation. This fixed-size representation is the sentence embedding that is generated by the network. Such an embedding, learned after the training process, is semantically rich since it captures the semantic and syntactic relationships between the words. This sentence representation was used next by a fully connected layer, followed by a softmax output layer for classification.

LSTM with Attention Classifier. Even though a CNN based network can capture the semantic and syntactic relationships between the words using the window based convolution operation, it struggles to learn the long term dependencies occurring in longer sentences. Recurrent networks like LSTM [14] have the ability to learn such long term dependencies in long sentences (which are

Table 1. List of aspects for accident/claim cases

Topic ID	Topic	Definition
1	B (Biographical)	This topic covers the background of the witness, family and work history, along with educational background, training, etc.
2	EB (Event Background)	This topic covers events that happened or conditions that existed just before the actual event (e.g., accident) that resulted in the legal claim
3	ED (Event Details)	This topic covers all details about the accident event that resulted in the legal claim
4	EC (Event Consequences)	It covers the results or effects of the event that led to the legal claim, including injuries, pain, medical treatment, or lost income
5	PPC (Prior Physical Condition)	This topic covers what the injured person could do before the injury occurred
6	TR (Treatments Received)	This topic covers all medical treatment received by the plaintiff for the injury. It includes EMT services, diagnostic testing, hospitalization, medications, surgeries, therapy, and counseling
7	EE (Expert Elaboration)	This topic covers any detailed explanation by an expert witness. It usually involves the use of precise medical, engineering, vocational or economic terminology, and may include detailed elaboration on the definition of the terms
8	IP (Impact on Plaintiff)	It covers any description of the physical, mental, emotional, or financial impact of the injury on the plaintiff, including physical limitations, recovery progress, and any planned or potential future treatment
9	DP (Deposition Procedures)	This topic covers the instructions that are often provided to deponents
10	OPS (Operational procedures/ inspections / maintenance / repairs)	Most injury claims involve movable (cars, boats, etc.) or immovable property (buildings, equipment, etc.). This topic covers the condition, operational procedures, inspection, maintenance, or repairs of the property involved in the accident/event
11	PRD (Plaintiff-related Details)	For fact witnesses other than the plaintiff, this topic covers information gathered from them about the plaintiff
12	O (Other)	This is to be used for any topic that the annotator believes is not covered in the list above

often found in depositions). Work in [35] used a bi-directional LSTM with an attention mechanism for neural machine translation (NMT). The context of the input words makes their way back into the beginning of the recurrent network during the back-propagation step in the training phase. This enables the system to learn long-term dependencies. Also, since the network was bi-directional, it also learned the relationship of a word with the words that preceded it, in addition to the words that follow. The hidden states of the network were joined to an attention layer that assigns a weight, known as attention weight, to each term. These attention weights capture the relative importance of the words based on the task. Though the work was used for NMT, we used the same network for classification by joining the attention layer to a dense layer followed by a softmax classification layer. The system was trained end-to-end on the data, and the word embeddings were also learned as part of the training. We added dropout [30] to the embedding, LSTM, and penultimate layers. Additionally, the L2-norm based penalty was applied as part of the regularization.

BERT Embeddings Based Classifier. Work in [32] introduced a new approach to sequence to sequence architectures. In the recent past, RNNs and LSTMs have been used to model text and capture their long term dependencies. The challenge with the encoder-decoder model is that the output of the encoder is still a vector. A sentence loses some of its meaning when it is converted into a single vector via recurrent connections. This loss is even greater when the sentence is long. The architecture proposed in the work did not have any recurrent connections to model the input. The approach used multiple stacked layers of attention in the encoder. The decoder also used the same architecture, but employed a masked multi-head attention layer. This was done to ensure that only the past and present words are available to the decoder, and the future words are masked. The architecture allowed the decoder to have complete access to the input, instead of just considering a single vector. The system was trained using the standard WMT 2014 English-German dataset containing about 4.5 million sentence pairs, and attained state-of-the-art results as measured by BLEU score.

Pre-training of Deep Bidirectional Transformers for Language Understanding (BERT) [12] is a framework to generate pre-trained embeddings for sentences. It also can be used to perform various NLP classification tasks using parameter fine-tuning after adding a single fully-connected layer. The authors make a strong assertion that the embeddings generated by Deep Learning based language models involve a training process that is uni-directional. Such kind of training does not learn the dependencies in both directions. In the self-attention stage, the architecture is required to attend to tokens preceding and succeeding the present token specifically for attention-based question answering tasks.

The system was trained based on two NLP tasks. One of these was to predict a missing word, given a sentence. To create such a training set, large English language corpora were used. A word was selected at random and removed subsequently. The training objective was to predict the word that was missing from the sentence. The other task was to identify the next suitable sentence for a

Table 2. A QA pair with its canonical form.

Type	Text
Question	Were you able to do physical exercises before the accident?
Answer	Yes. I used to play tennis before. Now I cannot stand for more than 5 min
Canonical Form	I was able to do physical exercises before the accident. I used to play tennis before. Now I cannot stand for more than 5 min

Table 3. Dataset class distribution

Class	Counts	% of Total
B	1455	15.73
EB	1468	15.87
ED	522	5.64
EC	220	2.38
PPC	39	0.42
TR	245	2.65
EE	62	0.67
IP	51	0.55
DP	80	0.86
OPS	1011	10.93
PRD	1617	17.48
O	2477	26.78
Total	9247	100

given sentence, from a custom-developed set that consisted of 4 sentences. The corpora used for training were the Books Corpus (800M words) [22] and English Wikipedia (2,500M words) [10]. We used BERT embeddings to model the sentences followed by a single layer neural network for our experiments.

The classification methods will be referred to as CNN, Bi-LSTM, and BERT, respectively, in the experiments section.

3.3   Canonical Representation

A QA pair in a legal deposition has its context spread across the question and answer. We wanted to use a form of the text that can combine the whole QA context into a canonical form of declarative sentences. We hypothesize that a canonical form would be able to assist the classifier better than the question or the answer text. We used the techniques from our work in [8] to transform the QA pair into its canonical form. We used the canonical form of a QA pair in our experiments in addition to the question and answer text. Table 2 shows an example declarative sentence for a QA pair.

4   Dataset

Our classification experiments were performed using a proprietary dataset. This dataset contained about 350 depositions. We randomly selected 11 depositions that pertained to 2 different litigation matters, each with multiple deponent types. We processed the dataset for any noise and removed all of the content from the depositions other than the QA pairs. We ended up with a total of 9247 QA pairs. We divided them into training, validation, and test sets with percentages of

70, 20, and 10, respectively. The dataset was manually annotated by the authors. Table 3 shows the (aspect/topic) class distribution for the dataset.

5 Experiment Setup and Results

5.1 Experimental Setup

We wanted to understand what content from the QA pairs would enable a classification system to capture effectively the semantics of a conversation QA pair. Is it the question, the answer, or the declarative sentence that works best? Or would a combination of these lead to the highest achievable classification results?

The declarative sentences were generated automatically by the transformation method, as described in Sect. 3.3. For the testing phase involving the declarative sentences input, the inference was performed using the declarative sentences as generated by the automated methods.

5.2 Results and Discussion

Table 4 shows the results for each of the 3 systems. We attained the best F1 score of 0.83 for the BERT embeddings based classifier. The classifiers based on CNN and bidirectional LSTM with attention had poor performance with all of the input types. The BERT classifier consistently outperformed all of the other systems for all input types. For the BERT classifier, the best score was attained for the declarative sentences input. It was (pleasantly) surprising to us that concatenation of question and answer text had an inferior performance when used for classification, as compared to the declarative sentences. Equally surprising was the fact that concatenating the question and answer text with the declarative sentences had a slightly lower (non-significant) classification performance, as compared to using just the declarative sentences. We believe that transforming a QA pair into a declarative sentence and using that in downstream tasks would be useful because of its form and content. The results also highlight the superior classification efficacy of the BERT based system. The sentence embeddings generated by it were semantically rich. Using them with a single layer neural network resulted in the best classification results, as compared to other systems.

To further explore the effectiveness of the declarative sentences, we performed another experiment. In our analysis of the declarative sentences (DS-M) generated by our method in [8], we observed that a few of the generated sentences had some noise. This was due to the less than ideal fusion of the question and answer text, which was also highlighted by the authors of the work for some QA pairs. We wanted to explore whether using declarative sentences that are devoid of any noise would provide any improvement in the classification accuracy. To perform this experiment, we used the same dataset and had human annotators write the declarative sentences for the QA pairs. These annotators had learned English as their first language and were proficient in their writing ability.

We trained the BERT classifier as it was the one with the best performance. We wanted to evaluate whether training using declarative sentences written

Table 4. F1-scores for the different methods. Best score in bold.

	CNN	Bi-LSTM	BERT
Question (Q)	0.44	0.43	0.64
Answer (A)	0.35	0.36	0.71
Question+Answer(Q+A)	0.47	0.49	0.75
Declarative Sentences - Machine (DS-M)	0.46	0.46	**0.83**
Question + Answer + Declarative Sentences - Machine (Q+A+DS-M)	0.50	0.49	0.81

Table 5. Experiment results with additional training data using the BERT classifier.

Text used	F1-score
DS-M	0.83
DS-C	0.82
DS-CM	0.83

by human annotators will improve the classification on the machine-generated declarative sentences. We performed the classification on the test set that contained machine-generated declarative sentences. The training was performed using the following different texts: (1) Machine-generated declarative sentences (DS-M); (2) Human-written declarative sentences (DS-C); (3) Concatenated[1] human-written and machine-generated declarative sentences (DS-CM).

Table 5 shows the results of the experiment. We observed that training using the additional declarative sentences written by human annotators did not make any difference, as the F1 score remained constant at 0.83. This highlights that the classifier is resilient to noise, and can perform as well with noisy text as with the human-annotated sentences. Table 6 lists the Precision, Recall, and F1-score for the respective classes in each of the three scenarios. The classification model DS-CM performs well on classes with low amounts of training data, that can be identified in Table 3. When compared with the two other models, DS-CM was relatively better, but a test of significance yielded a p-value of .14, so the difference was not significant. On the other hand, both the DS-M and DS-C models perform well in classes with large amounts of training data, and the DS-CM model is not far behind.

To understand the limitations of the classifier further, we performed another experiment using training and testing on human written declarative sentences. We wanted to explore whether the classifier performs well when it has to perform inference on declarative sentences that are devoid of noise. We trained the BERT embeddings based classifier on the dataset with human-written declarative sentences and achieved an F1-score of 0.94 on the test set. This result shows that the presence of noise in the machine-generated declarative sentences hurts the classification efficacy. We find this result very encouraging and believe that a detailed analysis of the classification results between the human-written and machine-generated declarative sentences would provide some insights in tuning the classifiers further. We plan to address this in our future work.

---

[1] The texts of the DS-M and DS-C declarative sentences are concatenated.

Table 6. Classification scores for BERT

Cls	DS-M			DS-C			DS-CM		
	P	R	F1	P	R	F1	P	R	F1
B	0.92	0.91	**0.91**	0.89	0.89	0.89	0.89	0.90	0.90
EB	0.86	0.86	0.86	0.89	0.84	**0.87**	0.79	0.87	0.83
ED	0.84	0.75	0.79	0.88	0.86	**0.87**	0.89	0.81	0.85
EC	0.74	0.81	0.77	0.55	0.69	0.61	0.80	0.89	**0.84**
PPC	1.00	1.00	**1.00**	1.00	1.00	**1.00**	1.00	1.00	**1.00**
TR	0.59	0.76	0.67	0.71	0.73	0.72	0.75	0.92	**0.83**
EE	0.83	1.00	0.91	0.71	1.00	0.83	1.00	1.00	**1.00**
IP	0.80	0.80	0.80	0.43	0.60	0.50	0.78	1.00	**0.88**
DP	0.57	0.57	0.57	0.50	0.71	0.59	0.86	0.80	**0.83**
OPS	0.77	0.79	0.78	0.75	0.84	**0.79**	0.71	0.75	0.73
PRD	0.81	0.89	**0.85**	0.83	0.88	**0.85**	0.82	0.85	0.84
O	0.84	0.76	**0.80**	0.82	0.71	0.76	0.87	0.73	0.79
Avg	0.83	0.83	**0.83**	0.83	0.82	0.82	0.83	0.83	**0.83**

Table 7. Experiment results with training to test set ratio 60:40

Class	Precision	Recall	F1-score
B	0.88	0.88	0.88
EB	0.85	0.82	0.84
ED	0.90	0.93	0.91
EC	0.86	0.79	0.83
PPC	0.83	0.91	0.87
TR	0.92	0.87	0.89
EE	0.87	0.85	0.86
IP	0.89	0.72	0.80
DP	0.84	0.64	0.73
OPS	0.82	0.82	0.82
PRD	0.79	0.78	0.79
O	0.82	0.87	0.85
Avg.	0.86	0.82	0.84

To check for overfitting, we re-trained and tested the system with a training to test set ratio of 60:40. There were 3444 sentences in the test set, which was selected randomly from the full set of 9247 QA pairs. Table 7 shows the result for the BERT classifier with machine-generated declarative sentences as input.

Table 8. Example of predicted aspects by BERT classifier and the canonical transformation of QA pairs to Declarative Sentences. These sentences correspond to the Expert Witness deponent role.

	QA Pairs	Declarative Sentence	Aspect	Predicted Aspect
Q	Right. So your calculation is basically if he jumped off a 20-foot building?	Right. So my calculation is basically if he jumped off a 20-foot building	EE	EE
A	Essentially, yes			
Q	Is that the product safety signs and labels standard?	That is the product safety signs and labels standard	EE	EE
A	It is			
Q	Okay	Okay	O	O
A	(nodding)			
Q	Are you qualified to perform maintenance on ORG2 telescopic boom lifts?	I am qualified to evaluate the safety of maintenance on ORG2 telescopic boom lifts, not to perform it	B	B
A	My specialty is safety engineering. I'm qualified to evaluate the safety of maintenance, not to perform it			
Q	With regard to your education that's listed on your CV, which parts of your education did you apply to this case?	I did apply to this case my mechanical engineering education, and my education of just working on heavy equipment as I grew up, and light equipment, for that matter, but –	B	OPS
A	My mechanical engineering education, and my education of just working on heavy equipment as I grew up, and light equipment, for that matter, but –			
Q	And so the five percent figure would refer to income?	The five percent figure would refer to income	B	B
A	Correct			

An example of the output of our system is shown in Table 8. The Declarative Sentences are machine-generated through our prior work in [8] that transform QA pairs. The table also displays the aspects assigned to each sentence by human annotators and the predicted aspect by the BERT classifier.

Table 9. Error analysis

Class	Analysis
B (Biographical)	Most of the misclassifications attributed to the incorrect class assignment to "OPS," and "O" classes. Sentences assigned to the "OPS" class have similar words often found in the listing of skills of a person, which are used in the "B" class This inclusion of these words without proper context results in misclassification. The declarative sentences generated by the automated methods sometimes remove the context. For example, a human-written declarative sentence such as "i left ORG165 due to difference of opinion" includes the background with not so much reliance on other sentences in the block. But in a machine-generated declarative sentence, "i did leave there due to difference of opinion" does not convey the context unless the previous and preceding declarative sentences are also included. Such sentences are often assigned to the "O" class
EB (Event Background)	The misclassification in this class concerns the sharing of certain words in the training example with the "ED" and "EC" classes
ED (Event Details)	The few misclassifications for this class are assigned to the "O" class. Mostly these sentences do not include the essential terms/context but are just repeated sentences by a deponent during the deposition
EC (Event Consequences)	Training data for this class is less, making it hard for the classifier to learn words associated with this class as compared to "ED," "EB," "IP"
TR (Treatments Received)	The sharing of terms in the training data with the "PPC" class confuses the classifier re learning the correct word associations
IP (Impact on Plaintiff)	The medical impact of the injury on the plaintiff as against the other kind of impacts is often misclassified in this class. The inclusion of terminology in these classes is the primary reason for this misclassification
DP (Deposition Procedures)	Possible misclassifications in this class are due to a limited amount of training data and frequent use of the word "deposition," which is also found in the "B" class
OPS (Operational procedures/ inspections/ maintenance/ repairs)	The majority of the misclassifications are assigned to the "EB" and "PRD" classes. The "OPS" and "PRD" classes are only covered as part of the witness deponent roles such as Related Organization Witness, leading to the terminology cross over in the training data
PRD (Plaintiff-related Details)	Conversations about acquaintance with the plaintiff and other related people are mostly considered part of the "B" class which leads to most misclassifications
O (Other)	Sentences not assigned to any of the previous classes are assigned to "O", making it a mix of many variants of terminology and context. Resulting sentence assignment errors lead to low recall

5.3   Error Analysis

We chose the best performing classification system results, as shown in Table 4, and performed a detailed error analysis on the misclassifications. For the analysis, we only included classes that had either an F1-score < 0.9, or a number of misclassifications greater than a threshold of 10. Table 9 discusses the errors associated with each aspect. In future work we may reduce the number of errors.

6   Conclusion and Future Work

It is difficult to apply traditional and state-of-the-art NLP and summarization techniques to corpora that consist of question-answer pairs. Applying summarization methods as-is on QA pairs leads to less than ideal results because of their form. Consequently we designed a multi-step approach to summarization, that started with classifying QA pairs as to dialog act [6], and then used the DA classification to guide the transformation of QA pairs into a declarative canonical form [8]. However, even then, our initial use of the canonical form did not improve the summarization results by much. Hence we sought a summarization method that is customized for the legal domain, but can be extended to other domains. Having a way to break a legal deposition into its constituent aspects topically would help segment the various parts of the depositions in a manner that would be useful for summarization. To achieve this, we developed an ontology of aspects that pertains to the legal domain, especially for property and casualty insurance claims. This ontology can be expanded or modified for other kinds of cases or for different domains. So we could automatically classify the canonical forms according to the aspects in that ontology, we annotated a dataset of 9247 QA pairs as to aspect. This dataset helped us in training and evaluating our classifiers.

We developed three methods for classifying according to the aspects present in legal depositions: CNN with word2vec embeddings, Bi-directional LSTM with attention mechanism, and BERT sentence embeddings based classifier. We plan to improve and extend this work in the following ways.

1. Add more training examples to the dataset for the aspects that had classification errors due to a smaller number of training examples.
2. Provide more context to the classifier using the preceding classes from the previous 2 QA pairs [4] to classify the current QA pair, to improve the classification accuracy.
3. Create a framework as part of our summarization pipeline to group certain aspects into specific ones based on deponent type (e.g., Plaintiff:{B, EB, ED, EC, PPC, TR, IP}) that could allow us to structure a summary better in terms of aspect distribution and layout.
4. Analyze the classifications on the test set involving human written declarative sentences. Identify the classification differences vis-a-vis with the machine-generated declarative sentences to improve the classifiers further.

5. Use additional data we have collected for training our classifiers, so as to increase the classification score further. Attorneys and paralegals have annotated this data. Accordingly, we plan to evaluate these results with the legal experts who helped us in annotating this data.
6. Develop NLP and deep learning techniques to identify segments within the legal deposition that are centered around the same topic. Using the aspects would help create these segments that can be used to generate summaries.
7. Develop explainable AI methods to correlate summary sentences back to the parts in the deposition that provide their support.

Acknowledgments. This work was made possible by Virginia Tech's Digital Library Research Laboratory (DLRL). In accordance with Virginia Tech policies and procedures and our ethical obligation as researchers, we are reporting that Dr. Edward Fox has an equity interest in Mayfair Group LLC, which provided data used in this research. Dr. Fox has disclosed those interests fully to Virginia Tech, and has in place an approved plan for managing any potential conflicts arising from this relationship.

References

1. Agrawal, R., Srikant, R., et al.: Fast algorithms for mining association rules. In: Proceedings of the 20th International Conference on Very Large Data Bases, VLDB, vol. 1215, pp. 487–499 (1994)
2. Ang, J., Liu, Y., Shriberg, E.: Automatic dialog act segmentation and classification in multiparty meetings. In: Proceedings of the IEEE International Conference on Acoustics, Speech, and Signal Processing, vol. 1, pp. I-1061 (2005)
3. Bahdanau, D., Cho, K., Bengio, Y.: Neural machine translation by jointly learning to align and translate. In: Proceedings of the International Conference on Learning Representations (ICLR) (2014)
4. Bothe, C., Weber, C., Magg, S., Wermter, S.: A context-based approach for dialogue act recognition using simple recurrent neural networks. In: Proceedings of the 11th International Conference on Language Resources and Evaluation (2018)
5. Brank, J., Grobelnik, M., Milic-Frayling, N., Mladenic, D.: Interaction of feature selection methods and linear classification models. In: Workshop on Text Learning held at ICML (2002)
6. Chakravarty, S., Chava, R.V.S.P., Fox, E.A.: Dialog acts classification for question-answer corpora. In: Proceedings of the 3rd Workshop on Automated Semantic Analysis of Information in Legal Text (ASAIL) (2019)
7. Chakravarty, S., Chekuri, S., Mehrotra, M., Fox, E.A.: Aspect Classification for Legal Depositions. arXiv e-prints arXiv:2009.04485 (September 2020)
8. Chakravarty, S., Mehrotra, M., Chava, R.V.S.P., Liu, H., Krivansky, M., Fox, E.A.: Improving the processing of question answer based legal documents. In: Proceedings of the JURIX Conference: Legal Knowledge and Information Systems (2019)
9. Cho, K., van Merrienboer, B., Bahdanau, D., Bengio, Y.: On the properties of neural machine translation: Encoder-decoder approaches. In: Proceedings of the 8th Workshop on Syntax, Semantics and Structure in Statistical Translation, pp. 103–111 (2014)
10. Coster, W., Kauchak, D.: Simple English Wikipedia: a new text simplification task. In: Proceedings of the 49th Annual Meeting of the Association for Computational Linguistics: Human Language Technologies, vol. 2, pp. 665–669 (2011)

11. Cover, T., Hart, P.: Nearest neighbor pattern classification. IEEE Trans. Inf. Theory **13**(1), 21–27 (1967)
12. Devlin, J., Chang, M., Lee, K., Toutanova, K.: BERT: pre-training of deep bidirectional transformers for language understanding. In: Proceedings of the Conference of the North American Chapter of the Association for Computational Linguistics: Human Language Technologies, vol. 1, pp. 4171–4186 (2019)
13. Fernandez, R., Picard, R.W.: Dialog act classification from prosodic features using support vector machines. In: Speech Prosody 2002, International Conference (2002)
14. Hochreiter, S., Schmidhuber, J.: Long short-term memory. Neural Comput. **9**(8), 1735–1780 (1997)
15. Ikonomakis, M., Kotsiantis, S., Tampakas, V.: Text classification using machine learning techniques. WSEAS Trans. Comput. **4**(8), 966–974 (2005)
16. Iyyer, M., Manjunatha, V., Boyd-Graber, J., Daumé III, H.: Deep unordered composition rivals syntactic methods for text classification. In: Proceedings of the 53rd Annual Meeting of the Association for Computational Linguistics and the 7th International Joint Conference on Natural Language Processing. vol. 1, pp. 1681–1691 (2015)
17. Ji, G., Bilmes, J.: Dialog act tagging using graphical models. In: Proceedings of IEEE International Conference on Acoustics, Speech, and Signal Processing, vol. 1, pp. I-33 (2005)
18. Jurafsky, D., Shriberg, E., Fox, B., Curl, T.: Lexical, prosodic, and syntactic cues for dialog acts. J. Discourse Relat. Discourse Mark. **4**, 1–7 (1998)
19. Kim, Y.: Convolutional neural networks for sentence classification. In: Proceedings of the Empirical Methods in Natural Language Processing (EMNLP), pp. 1746–1751 (2014)
20. Král, P., Cerisara, C.: Automatic dialogue act recognition with syntactic features. Lang. Resour. Eval. **48**(3), 419–441 (2014)
21. Liu, Y.: Using SVM and error-correcting codes for multiclass dialog act classification in meeting corpus. In: 9th International Conference on Spoken Language Processing (2006)
22. Davies, M.: Google Books corpora (2011). http://googlebooks.byu.edu/. Accessed 28 April 2019
23. Mast, M., et al.: Dialog act classification with the help of prosody. In: Proceedings of the of 4th International Conference on Spoken Language Processing, vol. 3, pp. 1732–1735. IEEE (1996)
24. Mikolov, T., Sutskever, I., Chen, K., Corrado, G.S., Dean, J.: Distributed representations of words and phrases and their compositionality. In: Advances in neural information processing systems, pp. 3111–3119 (2013)
25. Pennington, J., Socher, R., Manning, C.: GloVe: global vectors for word representation. In: Proceedings of the conference on empirical methods in natural language processing (EMNLP), pp. 1532–1543 (2014)
26. Porath, E.B., Gilboa, I.: Linear measures, the Gini index, and the income-equality trade-off. J. Econ. Theory **64**(2), 443–467 (1994)
27. Porta, A., et al.: Entropy, entropy rate, and pattern classification as tools to typify complexity in short heart period variability series. Trans. Biomed. Eng. **48**(11), 1282–1291 (2001)
28. Rish, I., et al.: An empirical study of the naive Bayes classifier. In: Proceedings of the IJCAI workshop on empirical methods in artificial intelligence, vol. 3, pp. 41–46 (2001)
29. Safavian, S.R., Landgrebe, D.: A survey of decision tree classifier methodology. IEEE Trans. Syst. Man Cybern. **21**(3), 660–674 (1991)

30. Srivastava, N., Hinton, G., Krizhevsky, A., Sutskever, I., Salakhutdinov, R.: Dropout: a simple way to prevent neural networks from overfitting. J. Mach. Learn. Res. **15**(1), 1929–1958 (2014)
31. UCSF Library: Truth Tobacco Industry Documents (2002). https://www.industrydocuments.ucsf.edu/tobacco
32. Vaswani, A., et al.: Attention is All you Need. In: Advances in Neural Information Processing Systems 30, pp. 5998–6008. Curran Associates, Inc. (2017)
33. Venkataraman, A., Ferrer, L., Stolcke, A., Shriberg, E.: Training a prosody-based dialog act tagger from unlabeled data. In: Proceedings of the IEEE International Conference on Acoustics, Speech, and Signal Processing, vol. 1, pp. I-I (2003)
34. Webb, N., Hepple, M., Wilks, Y.: Dialog act classification based on intra-utterance features. cs-05-01. Department of Computer Science, University of Sheffield, UK (2005)
35. Zhou, P., et al.: Attention-based bidirectional long short-term memory networks for relation classification. In: Proceedings of the 54th Annual Meeting of the Association for Computational Linguistics, vol. 2, pp. 207–212 (2016)

COLIEE 2020: Methods for Legal Document Retrieval and Entailment

Juliano Rabelo[1,2], Mi-Young Kim[1,3], Randy Goebel[1,2],
Masaharu Yoshioka[4,5(✉)], Yoshinobu Kano[6], and Ken Satoh[7]

[1] Alberta Machine Intelligence Institute, Edmonton, AB, Canada
{rabelo,miyoung2,rgoebel}@ualberta.ca
[2] University of Alberta, Edmonton, AB, Canada
[3] Department of Science, Augustana Faculty, Camrose, AB, Canada
[4] Graduate School of Information Science and Technology, Hokkaido University,
Kita-ku, Sapporo-shi, Hokkaido, Japan
yoshioka@ist.hokudai.ac.jp
[5] Global Station for Big Date and Cybersecurity, Global Institution for Collaborative
Research and Education, Kita-ku, Sapporo-shi, Hokkaido, Japan
[6] Faculty of Informatics, Shizuoka University, Naka-ku, Hamamatsu-shi,
Shizuoka, Japan
kano@inf.shizuoka.ac.jp
[7] National Institute of Informatics, Hitotsubashi, Chiyoda-ku, Tokyo, Japan
ksatoh@nii.ac.jp

Abstract. We present a summary of the 7th Competition on Legal
Information Extraction and Entailment. The competition consists of four
tasks on case law and statute law. The case law component includes an
information retrieval task (Task 1), and the confirmation of an entailment relation between an existing case and an unseen case (Task 2). The
statute law component includes an information retrieval task (Task 3)
and an entailment/question answering task (Task 4). Participation was
open to any group based on any approach. Ten different teams participated in the case law competition tasks, most of them in more than one
task. We received results from 9 teams for Task 1 (22 runs) and 8 teams
for Task 2 (22 runs). On the statute law task, there were 14 different
teams participating, most in more than one task. Eleven teams submitted a total of 28 runs for Task 3, and 13 teams submitted a total of 30
runs for Task 4. We summarize the approaches, our official evaluation,
and analysis on our data and submission results.

Keywords: Legal documents processing · Textual entailment ·
Information retrieval · Classification · Question answering

1 Introduction

The Competition on Legal Information Extraction/Entailment (COLIEE) was
initiated to help develop the state of the art for information retrieval and

© Springer Nature Switzerland AG 2021
N. Okazaki et al. (Eds.): JSAI-isAI 2020 Workshops, LNAI 12758, pp. 196–210, 2021.
https://doi.org/10.1007/978-3-030-79942-7_13

entailment using legal texts. It is usually co-located with JURISIN, the Juris-Informatics workshop series, which was created to promote community discussion on both fundamental and practical issues on legal information processing, with the intention to embrace various disciplines, including law, social sciences, information processing, logic and philosophy, including the existing conventional "AI and law" area. In alternate years, COLIEE is organized as a workshop the International Conference on AI and Law (ICAIL), which was the case in 2017 and 2019. Until 2017, COLIEE consisted of two tasks: information retrieval (IR) and entailment using Japanese Statute Law (civil law). Since COLIEE 2018, IR and entailment tasks using Canadian case law were introduced.

Task 1 is a legal case retrieval task, and it involves reading a new case Q, and extracting supporting cases S_1, S_2, ..., S_n from the provided case law corpus, hypothesized to support the decision for Q. Task 2 is the legal case entailment task, which involves the identification of a paragraph or paragraphs from existing cases, which entail a given fragment of a new case. For the information retrieval task (Task 3), based on the discussion about the analysis of previous COLIEE IR tasks, we modify the evaluation measure of the final results and ask participants to submit ranked relevant articles results to discuss the detailed difficulty of the questions. For the entailment task (Task 4), we performed categorized analyses to show different issues of the problems and characteristics of the submissions, in addition to the evaluation accuracy as in previous COLIEE tasks.

The rest of this paper is organized as follows: Sects. 2, 3, 4, 5 describe each task, presenting their definitions, datasets, list of approaches submitted by the participants, and results attained. Section 6 presents final some final remarks.

2   Task 1 - Case Law Information Retrieval

2.1   Task Definition

This task consists in finding which cases, in the set of candidate cases, should be "noticed" with respect to a given query case. "Notice" is a legal technical term that denotes a legal case description that is considered to be relevant to a query case. More formally, given a query case q and a set of candidate cases $C = \{c_1, c_2, ..., c_n\}$, the task is to find the supporting cases $S = \{s_1, s_2, ..., s_n \mid s_i \in C \wedge noticed(s_i, q)\}$ where $noticed(s_i, q)$ denotes a relationship which is true when $s_i \in S$ is a noticed case with respect to q.

2.2   Dataset

The training dataset consists of 520 base cases, each with 200 candidate cases from which the participants must identify those that should be noticed with respect to the base case. The training dataset contains a total of 104,000 candidates cases with 2,680 (2.57%) being true noticed cases. The official COLIEE test dataset has 130 cases. For those cases, the golden labels are only disclosed after the competition results were published. The test dataset has a total of 26,000 candidates cases with 636 (2.44%) being true noticed cases.

2.3 Approaches

Eight teams submitted a total of 22 runs for this task. IR techniques and machine learning based classifiers were commonly used. More details are described below:

- **cyber (three runs)** [18] created a method based on a selection of the top 30 candidate cases using a paragraph similarity score based on a universal sentence encoder, and then applied a Support Vector Machine (SVM) model based on the vector representation between base case and candidate case in Term Frequency-Inverse Document Frequency (TF-IDF) space. The base method is augmented by applying additional auto-weighting of classes in SVM training and by using a TF-IDF vectorizer trained on all available texts, including test samples.
- **UB (two runs)** [6] uses a Learning to Rank approach with features generated from Terrier weighting models such as BM25 and TF-IDF. All documents from the training and test datasets were used to build the ranking model. A Learning to Rank approach with a combination of text similarity and distance metrics' generated features was also used.
- **iiest (three runs)** [9] applied filtered-bag-of-ngrams (FiBONG), BM25 and other techniques in three runs. FiBONG is an extended version of BOW and uses several pre-processing filters (stopword removal, POS filtering, lemmatization, etc.) over unigrams, bigrams and trigrams. The first run used BM25 upon a FiBONG representation of the case documents. In the second run, the FiBONG representation was used with a different scoring function. A modified version of BM25 where the new IDF term is multiplied with a standardized and normalized value of the collection frequency. The third run used the FiBONG representation with a different scoring function called "PSlegal" [8].
- **TLIR (three runs)** [14] applied the word-entity duet (weduet) framework which uses 11 interaction features to generate the ranking scores. The authors also submitted a run based on the usage of the BERT-PLI framework, with one-layer forward GRU as the RNN component. The uncased-base BERT model is used and fine-tuned on the data of COLIEE 2019 Task 2. LMIR (Language model for Information Retrieval) is used to select top-30 candidate cases in the first stage. Last, they use the 11-dimensional features in "weduet" and extract the output vector (2-dimensional) of the softmax function in "bertgru". The authors also apply the seed-driven Document Ranking algorithm and obtain 2-dimensional features (similarity scores calculated based on words and entities, respectively). Then the first paragraph of the query and a candidate case are used as input of BERT to fine-tune a sentence pair classification task and extract the vector (2-dimensional) given by the softmax function as additional features. In total, 17-dimensional features are obtained and applied to a RankSVM model.
- **TR (three runs)** [5] used a ranking approach followed by a classification task. First the the candidate cases for a given case are ranked based on their similarity. Next the dataset is split into subdatasets based on their ranks to classify if a candidate case is a supporting case. The ranking task

is straightforward and does not require specific parameters. XGBoost is used for the classification task.

– **AUT99 (three runs)**, which applied a model based on CEDR [7] with different parameters. The authors haven't submitted a paper with a detailed description of their method.
– **DACCO (one run)**: We were not able to obtain its technical details.
– **TAXI (one run)** [1] uses Catboost with the following features as input: 400 word limit summarized documents input to Count Vectorizer with n-gram ranged 1–2 and 60,000 maximum features and TF-IDF with IDF smoothing.
– **JNLP (three runs)** [10] applies a system which is based on the BERT base model, fine-tuned for a text-pair classification task. The text-pairs are extracted from candidate cases using designed heuristics. The text-pair supporting scores and lexical matching scores (BM25) are computed from comparing paragraph-paragraph to measure query case-candidate case relevance. Machine learning model and setting: BERT [3] with 768 hidden nodes, 12 layers, 12 attention heads, 110M parameters, 512 max input length.

2.4   Results

The F1-measure is used to assess performance in this task. We use a simple baseline model that uses the Universal Sentence Encoder to encode each candidate case and base case into a fixed size vector, and then applies the cosine distance between both vectors. The baseline result was 0.3560. The actual results of the submitted runs by all participants are shown on Table 1, with the cyber team attaining the best F1 score. TLIR and cyber also achieved good results.

Table 1. Results attained by all teams on the test dataset of task 1.

Team	File	F1	Team	File	F1
Cyber	Task1 cyber02.txt	0.6774	TLIR	T1_run1_thuir.txt	0.5148
Cyber	Task1 cyber03.txt	0.6768	Iiest	Iiest_ps_t1_1.txt	0.4821
TLIR	T1_run3_thuir.txt	0.6682	TR	Submission2	0.3800
Cyber	Task1 cyber01.txt	0.6503	TR	Submission3	0.3792
JNLP	JNLP.task1.BMW25.txt	0.6397	TR	Submission1	0.3388
TLIR	T1_run2_thuir.txt	0.6379	AUT99	AUTIRT1R1.txt	0.2658
JNLP	JNLP.task1.W25.txt	0.6358	DACCO	T1 DACCO.txt	0.2077
JNLP	JNLP.task1.W30.txt	0.6278	AUT99	AUTIRT1R2.txt	0.1617
UB	UB_RUN1.res	0.5866	AUT99	AUTIRT1R3.txt	0.0898
Iiest	Iiest_bm26_t1_3.txt	0.5288	UB	UB_RUN2.res	0.0592
Iiest	Iiest_bm25_t1_2.txt	0.5272	Taxi	Task1_TAXICATTFCV.txt	0.0457

3 Task 2 - Case Law Entailment

3.1 Task Definition

Given a base case and a specific fragment from it, and a second case relevant to the base case, this task consists in determining which paragraphs of the second case entail that fragment of the base case. More formally, given a base case b and its entailed fragment f, and another case r represented by its paragraphs $P = \{p_1, p_2, ..., p_n\}$ such that $noticed(b, r)$ as defined in Sect. 2 is true, the task consists in finding the set $E = \{p_1, p2, ..., p_m \mid p_i \in P\}$ where $entails(p_i, f)$ denotes a relationship which is true when $p_i \in P$ entails the fragment f.

3.2 Dataset

The training dataset has 325 base cases, each with its respective entailed fragment in a separate file. For each base case, a related case represented by a list of paragraphs is given, from which the paragraph(s) that entail the base-case-entailed fragment must be identified. The training dataset contains 11,494 paragraphs in the related cases, 374 (3.25%) of which are true entailing paragraphs. The test dataset has 100 cases and was initially released without the golden labels, which were only disclosed after the competition results were published. It contains 3,672 paragraphs, with 125 (3.40%) being true entailing paragraphs.

3.3 Approaches

Eight teams submitted a total of 22 runs to this task. The most used techniques were those based on transformer methods, such as BERT [3] or ELMo [11]. More details on the approaches are show below.

- **cyber (three runs)** [18], whose method is based on the selection of top 10 candidate paragraphs, using a sentence similarity score based on a universal sentence encoder, and then applying an SVM model based on the vector formed between the base case and candidate case representations in TF-IDF. The authors also submitted runs augmenting the base approach and training a TF-IDF vectorizer on all available texts, including test samples and excluding certain anomalous samples excluded from training.
- **DACCO (one run)** We were not able to obtain its technical details.
- **iiest (three runs)** [9] based their submissions in techniques such as filtered-bag-of-ngrams (FiBONG) and BM25 as in task 1. The first run used BM25 upon a FiBONG representation of the case documents. In the second run, the FiBONG representation was used with a different scoring function. A modified version of BM25 where the new IDF term is multiplied with a standardized and normalized value of the collection frequency. The third run used centroids of word embeddings to represent the candidate paragraphs and the base judgements. Cosine distance was used to measure similarity. The word embeddings are taken from Law2Vec[1].

---

[1] https://archive.org/details/Law2Vec.

- **JNLP (three runs)** [10] applied an approach similar to the one used in Task 1. The system has a model capturing the supporting relation of a text pair, based on the BERT base model, then fine-tuned for a supporting text-pair classification task. The set of supporting text-pairs includes the text-pairs from Task 1 candidate cases using designed heuristics, and the gold data of Task 2 (decision-paragraph). The system also has a BERT model fine-tuned on SigmaLaw (a law dataset) for the masked language modeling task. Together with scoring by the BERT models, lexical matching (BM25) is also considered for predicting decision-paragraph entailment.
- **tax-i (three runs)** [1] applied an Xgboost classifier with the following features as input: NLI probability (BERT-NLI), similarity between entailed fragment and paragraphs based on fine-tuned BERT (bert-base-uncased), and BM25 similarity between entailed fragment and paragraphs. The authors also submitted runs using other features as input: n-grams, BM25, NLI, and EUR-LEX (81,000 sentences from EU legal documents) fine-tuned ROBERTA and BERT (bert-base-uncased) derived similarity features.
- **TLIR (three runs)** [14] fine-tune BERT (uncased-base) in a sentence pair classification task. If the total input tokens exceed the length limitation (512), the texts are truncated symmetrically. The model is trained for no more than 5 epochs with $lr = 1e - 5$ and selected according to the F1 measure on the validation set. The difference in the second run is the truncation of text asymmetrically. They limit the tokens of decision fragment to 128 and only truncate the tokens in the candidate paragraph if the total length of the text pair exceeds 512 tokens. In their last run, the authors extract the output vector of the fully-connected layer of the two previous models (4-dimensional in total) as features. Besides, they calculate the BM25 scores (1-dimensional). The position ID and the length of the paragraph are used as 2 additional features. In total, 7-dimensional features are generated and then a RankSVM model is applied.
- **TR (three runs)** [5], whose approach consists of two stages: (1) similarity features-based ranking and (2) Random Forest binary classification. Paragraphs are ranked according to a criterion that combines the individual ranks given by the cosine similarity coefficients obtained using different sentence vectorizers (n-grams, universal sentence encoder, averaged glove embeddings, topic modelling probability scores). The likelihood of the relevant paragraph falling into the top K paragraphs is estimated for different values of K using the training data. Then for a specific value of likelihood, similarity features are computed on the top K paragraphs and fed to a random forest classifier.
- **UA (three runs)** [12], which applied transformer-based techniques to generate features which were then fed to a Random Forest classifier. The features were generated by fine-tuning a pre-trained BERT model text entailment on the provided training dataset and using the score produced in this task, two transformer-based models fine-tuned on a generic entailment data set, and another one applying zero-shot techniques by using BERT fine tuned for paraphrase detection. They also used data augmentation techniques based on back translation to increase the size of the training data.

3.4 Results

The F1-measure is used to assess performance in this task. The score attained by a simple baseline model which uses the Universal Sentence Encoder to encode each candidate paragraph and the entailed fragment into a fixed size vector and applies the cosine distance measure between both vectors was 0.1760. The actual results of the submitted runs by all participants are shown in Table 2, from which it can be seen that the JNLP team attained the best results. The TAXI and TLIR teams also achieved good results for the F1-score.

Table 2. Results attained by all teams on the test dataset of task 2.

Team	Submission file	F1-score	Team	Submission file	F1-score
JNLP	JNLP.task2.BMWT.txt	0.6753	Cyber	Task2 cyber01.txt	0.5600
JNLP	JNLP.task2.BMW.txt	0.6222	TLIR	T2_run3_thuir.txt	0.5495
Taxi	T2-taxiXGBaft.txt	0.6180	TLIR	T2_run1_thuir.txt	0.5428
TLIR	T2_run2_thuir.txt	0.6154	UA	UA1.txt	0.5425
JNLP	JNLP.task2.WT+L.txt	0.6094	UA	UA2.txt	0.5179
Taxi	T2-taxiXGBaf.txt	0.5992	Iiest	Iiest_l2v_t2_3.txt	0.5067
Taxi	T2-taxiXGB3f.txt	0.5917	UA	UA_translate.txt	0.4647
Cyber	Task2 cyber03.txt	0.5897	TR	Submission1.txt	0.4107
Iiest	Iiest_bm25_t2_1.txt	0.5867	TR	Submission3.txt	0.4107
Iiest	Iiest_bm26_t2_2.txt	0.5867	TR	Submission2.txt	0.4018
Cyber	Task2 cyber02.txt	0.5837	DACCO	T2 DACCOr.txt	0.0622

4 Task 3 - Statute Law Retrieval

4.1 Task Definition

This task involves reading a legal bar exam question Q, and retrieve a subset of Japanese Civil Code Articles S_1, S_2,..., S_n to judge whether the question is entailed or not ($Entails(S_1, S_2, ..., S_n, Q)$ or $Entails(S_1, S_2, ..., S_n, notQ)$).

4.2 Dataset

For task 3, questions related to Japanese civil law were selected from the Japanese bar exam. Since there was update of Japanese Civil Code at April 2020, we revised text for reflecting this revision for Civil Code and its translation into English. However, since English translated version is not provided for a part of this code, we exclude these parts from the civil code text and questions related to these parts. As a results number of the articles used in the dataset is 768. Training data (the questions and relevant article pairs) was constructed by using previous COLIEE data (696 questions). In this data, questions related to revised articles are reexamined and ones for excluded articles are removed from the training data. For the test data, new questions selected from the 2019 bar exam are used (112 questions). The number of questions classified by the number of relevant articles is as follows (1 answer: 87, 2 answers 22, 3 answers 3) [2].

4.3 Approaches

The following 11 teams submitted their results (28 runs in total). Three teams (HUKB, JNLP, and UA) had participated in previous COLIEE editions, and eight teams (CU, Cyber, GK_NLP, HONto, LLNTU, OvGU, TAXI, TRC3) were new competitors. Compared to previous years, many teams use BERT [3] for analyzing text. From the results, BERT-based approach is good for improve the retrieval quality. In addition, this approach also allows the team to select two or more articles for one question. Other common techniques used were well known IR engines such as elasticsearch Indri [15], Hierachical Optimal Topic Tranport (HOTT) [20] based on topic model, gensim, scikit-learn with various scoring function such as TF-IDF, BM25. For the indexing of ordinal IR system, the most common method was ordinal word base indexing with stemming. Several teams use N-gram, word sequence, word embedding using legal texts.

- **CU (three runs)** [2] uses TF-IDF and BERT model with different settings.
- **cyber (three runs)** [18] calculate similarity between the sentence in the articles using TF-IDF and BM25 and aggregate the results.
- **GK_NLP (one run)** GK_NLP uses elastic search using TF-IDF model.
- **HONto (three runs)** [17] uses HOTT for calculating the similarity between question and article using different word embedding methods.
- **HUKB (three runs)** [19] uses BERT-based IR system and Indri for the IR module and compare the result of each system output to make final results.
- **JNLP (three runs)** [10] uses BERT model with different settings to classify the articles are relevant or not.
- **LLNTU (one run)** [13] uses BERT to classify articles as relevant or not.
- **OvGU (three runs)** [17] uses TF-IDF and BM25 with different indexing methods.
- **TAXI (three runs)** [1] uses TF-IDF model and IR model that uses word embeddings based on the legal texts.
- **TRC3 (three runs)** [5] uses TF-IDF for the basic IR system and Wikibooks on Japanese civil law to calculate similarity between the query and articles.
- **UA (two runs)** uses TF-IDF and language model as an IR module.

---

[2] There is one question (R1-23-1: relevant articles are 554 and 1002) that have a relevant article excluded by this competition (1002). We also calculated the results by excluding this question, but there is no significant difference with official evaluation results. So we use the official evaluation results for this paper.

4.4   Results

Table 3 shows the evaluation results of submitted runs (due to page limit constraints, only the best run in terms of F2 is selected from each team). The official evaluation measures used in this task were macro average of precision, recall and F2 measure. We also calculate the mean average precision (MAP), recall at k (R_k: recall calculated by using the top k ranked documents as returned documents) by using the long ranking list (100 articles).

This year, LLNTU is the best among all runs. JNLP achieves good performance when they submit an answer. However, since there are several questions that returns no relevant article, overall performance of JNLP is lower than LLNTU. We confirmed recent development of deep learning technology based on BERT is also effective to retrieve relevant articles for the questions.

Table 3. Evaluation results (Task 3)

Sid	Lang	Return	Retrieved	F2	Precision	Recall	MAP
LLNTU	J	122	**84**	**0.659**	**0.688**	**0.662**	**0.760**
JNLP.tfidf-bert-ensemble	E	104	76	0.553	0.577	0.567	0.662
Cyber1	E	204	70	0.529	0.506	0.554	0.554
HUKB-1	J	250	75	0.516	0.420	0.591	0.569
CUBERT1	E	126	68	0.514	0.540	0.519	0.585
TRC3_1	J	159	65	0.501	0.456	0.536	0.598
OvGU_bm25	E	248	69	0.477	0.400	0.534	0.510
TAXI_R3	E	230	64	0.455	0.439	0.509	0.506
GK_NLP	E	224	64	0.427	0.286	0.499	0.498
UA.tfidf	E	112	48	0.391	0.429	0.387	0.478
HONto_hybrid	E	162	36	0.282	0.254	0.299	0.014

Figure 1.2 shows average of evaluation measure for all submission runs. As we can see from left part of Fig. 1, there are many easy questions that almost all system can retrieve the relevant article. Easiest question is R01-12-U whose relevant article is almost same as a question. However, there are also many queries for which none of the systems can retrieve the relevant articles (Fig. 1 right). R1-14-U[3] is an example of such a question. The relevant article is Article 87 [4]. It is necessary to interpret the relationship between the "building and leased land" in the question as "first thing attaches a second thing" in the article. Even though BERT is good at ranking articles that take into account the context, it is

---

[3] "In cases where a mortgage is created with respect to a building on leased land, the mortgage may not be exercised against the right of lease.".

[4] "(1) If the owner of a first thing attaches a second thing that the owner owns to the first thing to serve the ordinary use of the first thing, the thing that the owner attaches is an appurtenance. (2) An appurtenance is disposed of together with the principal thing if the principal thing is disposed of.".

difficult because this example shows an instance which requires legal knowledge to interpret the context.

One characteristic difference from the previous COLIEE is improvement of the retrieval quality for questions with multiple answers. In the previous COLIEE, most teams returned only one article for each question to keep a good precision. This year, many teams returned two or more answers to such questions. As a result, there are 4 questions whose recall is higher than 0.5. For COLIEE 2019, but there were no questions with multiple answers with recall higher than 0.5.

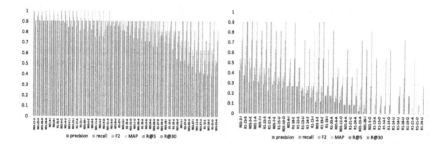

Fig. 1. Avg. of prec., rec., F2, MAP, R_5 and R_30 (questions with 1 relevant article)

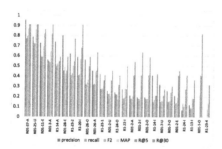

Fig. 2. Avg. of prec., rec., F2, MAP, R_5 and R_30 (questions with 1+ relevant article)

5   Task 4 - Statute Law Entailment

5.1   Task Definition

Task 4 is a task to determine entailment relationships between a given problem sentence and article sentences. Competitor systems should answer "yes" or "no" regarding the given problem sentences and given article sentences. Until COLIEE 2016, the competition had pure entailment tasks, where t1 (relevant article sentences) and t2 (problem sentence) were given. Due to the limited number of available problems, COLIEE 2017, 2018 did not retain this style of task. In the Task 4 of COLIEE 2019 and 2020, we returned to the pure textual entailment task to attract more participants, allowing more focused analyses.

5.2 Dataset

Our training dataset and test dataset are the same as Task 3. Questions related to Japanese civil law were selected from the Japanese bar exam. The organizers provided a data set used for previous campaigns as training data (768 questions) and new questions selected from the 2019 bar exam as test data (112 questions).

5.3 Approaches

The following 12 teams submitted their results (30 runs in total). 3 teams (JNLP, KIS, and UA) had experience in submitting results in the previous campaign. We describe each system's overview below.

- **CU (two runs)** [2] uses multilingual cased BERT model for sequence classification trained and evaluated only with given relevant articles (CUGIVEN), plus additional articles returned using TFIDF (CUPLUS).
- **cyber (one runs)** [18] uses RoBERTa based method which is fine-tuned on sentence pair classification with the SNLI corpus. The resulting model fine-tuned on text pair classification with COLIEE training data.
- **GK_NLP (one run)** uses similarity measure on BERT embeddings and GloVe word embeddings with lightgbm classification model.
- **HONto (three runs)** [17] uses linear kernel SVM with TF-IDF and n-grams.
- **JNLP (three runs)** [10] uses BERT; JNLP.BERT and JNLP.TfidfBERT with the Google's original BERT_Base, JNLP.BERTLaw pretrained by American cases of 8.2M sentences/182M words in English. JNLP.BERTLaw and JNLP.BERT were fine-tuned by lawfulness classification on Augmented JAPAN Civil Code + COLIEE training data; JNLP.TfidfBERT was fine-tuned by COLIEE training data, no cross-fold validation.
- **KIS (three runs)** [4] built a range of Japanese legal dictionaries for predicate argument structures and paraphrases, which can integrate PROLEG, an legal logic language. KIS is their rule-based ensemble NLP system; KIS_2 uses SVM instead of rules in KIS; KIS_3 uses PROLEG to answer some of the questions in KIS_2.
- **LLNTU (one run)** [13] combines each query from COLIEE training dataset with all civil law articles, trains BERT-based ensemble models.
- **OvGU (three runs)** [17] uses Bidirectional LSTM and a modified Bahdanau's attention with inputing Law2Vec embeddings (baseline_attention.task4.OvGU), with the similarity measure and negations (sim_neg.task4.OvGU), adding POS of each token (POS_simneg.task4.OvGU).
- **tax-i (two runs)** [1] uses legal embeddings (FastText trained on US Caselaw) as input to a Bi-directional GRU with 128 Hidden Layers and 1 GRU layer (LEBIGRU), last hidden state of BERT base-cased was used as input to an XGBoost classifier (BERTXGB).
- **TRC3 (three runs)** [5] uses GloVe word embedding. Multee (TRC3mt) was trained phase one against single sentence NLI datasets (SNLI, MutliNLI) and then trained phase two on multiple sentence NLI datasets (OpenbookQA,

COLIEE). The Text-To-Text Transfer Transformer (T5) run (TRC3t5) was fine-tuned on three denoising tasks (Civil Code Article, Civil Code Titles, Translated Wikibook Articles) and one entailment task (COLIEE).

- **UA (three runs)** [12] uses a decomposable attention model, which is a simple neural architecture for natural language inference, decomposing a problem into sub-problems (UA_attention_final), a RoBERTa trained model (UA_roberta_final), their previous model that showed the best performance in COLIEE 2019 (UA_structure).
- **UEC (three runs)** [16] translates t1 texts into an easier one (t1p) with a paraphrase dictionary, extracts subject/predicate/object tuples from the main and conditional clauses, then constructs tuple-based similarity features for <t1p, t2> pair (UEC1 and UEC2), for both the <t1, t2> and <t1p, t2> pairs (UECplus). LightGBM is used for binary classification.

5.4   Results

Table 4 shows evaluation results of Task 4 (accuracy was used as the metric). Because an entailment task is a complex composition of different subtasks, we manually categorized our test data into categories, depending on what sort of technical issues are required to be resolved. Table 5 shows our categorization results. As this is a composition task, overlap is allowed between categories. Our categorization is based on the original Japanese version of the legal bar exam.

Table 4. Evaluation results of submitted runs (Task 4). L: Dataset Language (J: Japanese, E: English), #: number of correct answers (112 problems in total)

Team	L	#	Accuracy	Team	L	#	Accuracy
JNLP.BERTLaw	E	81	0.7232	KIS_3	J	61	0.5446
TRC3mt	E	70	0.6250	sim_neg.OvGU	E	61	0.5446
TRC3t5	E	70	0.6250	UEC1	J	61	0.5446
UA_attention_final	?	70	0.6250	taxi_BERTXGB	E	60	0.5357
UA_roberta_final	?	70	0.6250	UECplus	J	60	0.5357
KIS_2	J	69	0.6161	CUGIVEN	E	58	0.5179
llntu	J	69	0.6161	CUPLUS	E	58	0.5179
cyber	E	69	0.6161	linearsvm_no_ngram.HONto	E	57	0.5089
UA_structure	?	68	0.6071	POS_simneg.OvGU	E	57	0.5089
GK_NLP	?	63	0.5625	taxi_le_bigru	E	57	0.5089
linearsvm.HONto	E	63	0.5625	TRC3A	E	56	0.5000
JNLP.BERT	E	63	0.5625	UEC2	J	55	0.4911
KIS	J	63	0.5625	baseline_attention.OvGU	E	54	0.4821
linearsvm_no_ngram.HONto	E	62	0.5536	AUT99-BERT-MatchPyramid	E	52	0.4643
JNLP.TfidfBERT	E	62	0.5536	AUT99-LSTM-CNN-Attention	E	50	0.4464

Table 5. Technical category statistics of questions, correct answer ratios of submitted runs for each category in percentages sorted in the order of ranks for each run.

Team rank	Conditions	Predicate argument	Negation	Legal fact	Person role	Person Relationship	Verb paraphrase	Morpheme	Dependency	Anaphora	Entailment	Normal terms	Case role	Article search	Itemized	Normal terms	Ambiguity	Calculation
Total #	74	73	69	55	48	48	41	33	24	23	20	16	14	12	11	3	1	1
1	**.42**	**.44**	.43	**.42**	**.40**	**.42**	.44	.58	.46	.52	.55	.38	.50	.50	.64	.00	1.00	1.00
2	.49	.48	.46	.47	.46	.46	.44	.45	.58	**.35**	.50	.44	.50	.42	**.18**	.33	1.00	.00
3	.53	.51	.59	.58	.56	.56	.59	.36	.42	.48	.40	.50	.57	.58	.27	.67	.00	.00
4	.53	.51	.59	.58	.56	.56	.59	.36	.42	.48	.40	.50	.57	.58	.27	.67	.00	.00
5	.62	.64	**.70**	.60	.60	.60	.61	.64	.67	.52	.45	.69	.64	.50	.45	.67	1.00	1.00
6	.61	.52	.51	.53	.46	.48	.49	.70	.63	.57	.60	.56	.43	.67	.36	.00	1.00	.00
7	.57	.53	.58	.55	.52	.52	.49	.64	.46	.48	.60	.44	**.36**	**.25**	.45	.67	1.00	.00
8	.54	.53	.54	.53	.50	.50	.46	.67	.54	.52	.60	.50	**.36**	**.25**	.45	.67	1.00	.00
9	.50	.48	.55	**.42**	.44	.44	.49	.64	.54	.39	.55	.38	**.36**	**.25**	.36	.67	1.00	1.00
10	.53	.56	.49	.53	.52	.54	.59	.79	.63	.61	.35	.69	.57	.75	.64	.33	.00	.00
11	**.64**	**.78**	.68	**.67**	**.73**	**.73**	**.78**	**.91**	**.75**	**.74**	**.80**	**.75**	.64	.58	.55	**1.00**	1.00	.00
12	.59	.51	.54	.58	.54	.58	.51	.58	.50	.43	.55	.56	.64	**.83**	.64	.67	.00	.00
13	.59	.55	.61	.51	.50	.48	.51	.67	.58	.57	.60	.56	.57	**.25**	.45	.67	1.00	1.00
14	.59	.62	.58	.62	.60	.63	.63	.82	.71	.65	.55	.56	.64	.75	.64	.33	.00	.00
15	.57	.52	.58	.47	.50	.48	.49	.67	.50	.61	.60	.56	.50	.33	.45	.67	1.00	.00
16	.61	.63	.59	.60	.60	.60	.66	.64	.67	.61	.60	.56	.71	.75	.64	.67	1.00	.00
17	.54	.48	.57	.55	.48	.48	.46	**.33**	**.33**	.57	.55	**.31**	.50	.42	.55	.67	1.00	.00
18	.57	.53	.52	.49	.48	.50	.56	.52	.58	.52	.55	.63	.64	.58	.55	.67	1.00	.00
19	.53	.59	.59	.58	.58	.58	.61	.52	.58	.57	.55	.56	.71	.67	.55	.33	1.00	1.00
20	.55	.55	.51	.45	.44	.44	.49	.58	.54	.57	.65	.50	.57	.42	.64	.67	.00	.00
21	.57	.52	.58	.53	.48	.48	.54	.39	.46	.57	.50	.44	.71	.58	**.73**	.67	1.00	.00
22	.49	.49	.49	.55	.52	.54	.46	.58	.58	.43	**.30**	.63	.43	.67	.55	.67	.00	.00
23	.62	.62	.67	.55	.60	.60	.61	.61	.71	.65	.55	.44	.64	.50	.55	**1.00**	.00	1.00
24	.58	.64	.58	.62	.52	.54	.63	.67	.67	.65	.55	.56	**.79**	.75	.64	.67	.00	.00
25	.58	.62	.65	.62	.63	.63	.56	.67	.58	.61	.60	.63	.64	.58	.45	.67	.00	1.00
26	.53	.66	.59	.62	.63	.60	.49	.70	.63	.70	.55	.63	.64	.50	.36	.33	1.00	1.00
27	.58	.60	.61	.58	.54	.52	.54	.73	.67	.57	.55	**.75**	.57	.42	.64	**1.00**	1.00	1.00
28	.57	.56	.51	.55	.60	.63	.49	.48	.67	.61	.55	.56	.50	.58	.55	.33	.00	1.00
29	.46	.49	**.42**	.49	.52	.56	**.41**	.45	.54	.52	.50	.50	.43	.67	.45	.33	.00	.00
30	.54	.49	.54	.62	.58	.60	.46	.52	.54	.48	.35	.63	.50	.75	.64	.67	.00	.00

6   Final Remarks

We have summarized the results of COLIEE 2020, and attempted to capture the diversity of methods used by the competitive teams. Task 1 deals with the retrieval of noticed cases, and Task 2 poses the problem of identifying which paragraphs of a relevant case entail a given fragment of a new case. Task 3 is about retrieving articles to decide the appropriateness of the legal question, and Task 4 is a task to entail whether the legal question is correct or not. Ten (10) different teams participated in the case law competition (most of them in both tasks). We received results from 9 teams for Task 1 (a total of 22 runs), and

8 teams for Task 2 (a total of 22 runs). Regarding the statute law tasks, there were 14 different teams participating, most in both tasks. Eleven (11) teams submitted 28 runs for Task 3, and 13 teams submitted 30 runs for Task 4.

A variety of methods were used for Task 1: exploitation of the case structure information, deep learning based techniques (such as transformer methods and tools such as the Universal Sentence Encoder), lexical and latent features, different text embedding techniques, information retrieval techniques and different classifiers (such as tree based and SVM) were the main ones. For Task 2, transformer-based tools were used (among which BERT was prevalent), but IR techniques and textual similarity features have also been applied. Some teams leveraged techniques similar to the ones they developed for task 1, which shows the tasks are somewhat connected. The results attained were satisfactory, but there is much room for improvement, especially if one considers the related issue of explaining the predictions made; deep learning methods, which attained the best results this year, would not be so appropriate in a scenario where explainability is necessary. For future editions of COLIEE, we plan on continuing expanding the data sets in order to improve the robustness of results, as well as evaluating ways of introducing explainability-aware tasks into the competition.

For Task 3, we confirmed that BERT-based approach improves overall retrieval performance. However, there are still numbers of questions that are difficult to retrieve by any systems. It is better to discuss the type of information necessary to find out the relationship between question and articles for the next step. For Task 4, overall performance of the submissions is still not sufficient to use their systems in real applications, mainly due to lack of coverage for some classes of problems, such as anaphora resolution. We found this task is still a challenging one to discuss and develop deep semantic analysis issues in the real application and natural language processing in general.

Acknowledgements. This research was supported by JSPS KAKENHI Grant Numbers, JP17H06103 and JP19H05470, the National Institute of Informatics, Shizuoka University, Hokkaido University, and the University of Alberta's Alberta Machine Intelligence Institute (Amii). Special thanks to Colin Lachance from vLex for his unwavering support in the development of the case law data set, and to continued support from Ross Intelligence and Intellicon.

References

1. Alberts, H., Ipek, A., Lucas, R., Wozny, P.: COLIEE 2020: Legal information retrieval and entailment with legal embeddings and boosting. In: COLIEE (2020)
2. Aydemir, A., de Castro Souza, P., Gelfman, A.: Using BERT and TF-IDF to predict entailment in law-based queries. In: COLIEE (2020)
3. Devlin, J., Chang, M., Lee, K., Toutanova, K.: BERT: pre-training of deep bidirectional transformers for language understanding. CoRR abs/1810.04805 (2018)
4. Hayashi, R., Kiyota, N., Fujita, M., Kano, Y.: Legal bar exam solver integrating legal logic language proleg and argument structure analysis with legal linguistic dictionary. In: COLIEE (2020)

5. Hudzina, J., et al.: Information extraction and entailment of common law and civil code. In: COLIEE (2020)
6. Leburu-Dingalo, T., Thuma, E., Motlogelwa, N., Mudongo, M.: Ub_Botswana at COLIEE 2020 case law retrieval. In: COLIEE (2020)
7. MacAvaney, S., Yates, A., Cohan, A., Goharian, N.: Cedr: contextualized embeddings for document ranking. In: SIGIR (2019)
8. Mandal, A., Ghosh, K., Pal, A., Ghosh, S.: Automatic catchphrase identification from legal court case documents. In: Proceedings of the Conference on Information and Knowledge Management, pp. 2187–2190. ACM, New York, NY, USA (2017)
9. Mandal, A., Ghosh, S., Ghosh, K., Mandal, S.: Significance of textual representation in legal case retrieval and entailment. In: COLIEE (2020)
10. Nguyen, H.T., et al.: JNLP team: deep learning for legal processing in COLIEE 2020. In: COLIEE (2020)
11. Peters, M.E., et al.: Deep contextualized word representations. In: Proceedings of NAACL (2018)
12. Rabelo, J., Kim, M.Y., Goebel, R.: Application of text entailment techniques in COLIEE 2020. In: COLIEE (2020)
13. Shao, H.L., Chen, Y.C., Huang, S.: BERT-based ensemble model for the statute law retrieval and legal information entailment. In: COLIEE (2020)
14. Shao, Y., Liu, B., Mao, J., Liu, Y., Zhang, M., Ma, S.: THUIR@COLIEE-2020: leveraging semantic understanding and exact matching for legal case retrieval and entailment. In: COLIEE (2020)
15. Strohman, T., Metzler, D., Turtle, H., Croft, W.B.: Indri: a language model-based search engine for complex queries. In: Proceedings of the International Conference on Intelligent Analysis, pp. 2–6 (2005)
16. Suematsu, Y., Matsuyoshi, S., Utsumi, A.: Recognizing textual entailment for Japanese legal text using lexical simplification and tuple-based matching and similarity features. In: COLIEE (2020)
17. Wehnert, S., et al.: Legal information retrieval and entailment detection: hybrid approaches of traditional machine learning and deep learning. In: COLIEE (2020)
18. Westermann, H., Šavelka, J., Benyekhlef, K.: Paragraph similarity scoring and fine-tuned BERT for legal information retrieval and entailment. In: COLIEE (2020)
19. Yoshioka, M., Suzuki, Y.: HUKB at COLIEE 2020 information retrieval task. In: COLIEE (2020)
20. Yurochkin, M., Claici, S., Chien, E., Mirzazadeh, F., Solomon, J.: Hierarchical optimal transport for document representation (2019)

COLIEE 2020: Legal Information Retrieval and Entailment with Legal Embeddings and Boosting

Houda Alberts⬤, Akin Ipek⬤, Roderick Lucas^(✉)⬤, and Phillip Wozny⬤

Deloitte NL, tax-i team, Amsterdam, The Netherlands
{hdevries-alberts,aipek,rlucas,pwozny}@deloitte.nl

Abstract. In this paper we investigate three different methods for several legal document retrieval and entailment tasks; namely, new low complexity pre-trained embeddings, specifically trained on documents in the legal domain, transformer models and boosting algorithms. Task 1, a case law retrieval task, utilized a pairwise CatBoost resulting in an F1 score of .04. Task 2, a case law entailment task, utilized a combination of BM25+, embeddings and natural language inference (NLI) features winning third place with an F1 of 0.6180. Task 3, a statutory information retrieval task, utilized the aforementioned pre-trained embeddings in combination with TF-IDF features resulting in an F2 score of 0.4546. Lastly, task 4, a statutory entailment task, utilized BERT embeddings with XGBoost and achieved an accuracy of 0.5357. Notably, our Task 2 submission was the third best in the competition. Our findings illustrate that using legal embeddings and auxiliary linguistic features, such as NLI, show the most promise for future improvements.

Keywords: Legal information retrieval · Textual entailment · Classification · Natural language inference · Ranking · Legal embeddings · BERT · Boosting

1 Introduction

Search engines have become the gateway to the internet for both the layman and the scholar alike [28]. Google, the largest search engine by market share [6], has become an indispensable tool for academic researchers [37]. However, legal researchers have unique needs that require unique search tools [1]. As the methods that search engines use to rank results shape how the user interacts with web content [12], it is critical that legal researchers have access to tools designed with them in mind. Given the size of corpora that legal researchers must search through, any methods to increase the efficiency of legal research have disruptive potential for the industry [7]. The use of machine learning in the legal

Supported by the tax-i team within Deloitte. Each author contributed equally and is responsible for one specific task; In order of the authors, responsible for task 3, 1, 2 and 4.

© Springer Nature Switzerland AG 2021
N. Okazaki et al. (Eds.): JSAI-isAI 2020 Workshops, LNAI 12758, pp. 211–225, 2021.
https://doi.org/10.1007/978-3-030-79942-7_14

domain has the potential to reduce the amount of time required for legal research and reasoning [7]. Within tax-i[1], we develop machine learning tools built with legal researchers in mind, offering specialized search functionalities such as cross-lingual search.

Two main machine learning applications in the legal domain are entailment and information retrieval [7,36]. Entailment aims to address the question of whether a given proposition is true or false based on a piece of evidence [29]. Machine learning systems can then reason over entailed claims [25]. Information retrieval involves searching through a corpus of documents and ranking them according to their relevance to a query [20]. These are only two examples of how machine learning can disrupt the legal industry through the automation of costly, yet repetitive tasks [13].

As a means of cultivating research in these domains University of Alberta, along with a host of co-sponsors, hosts the Competition on Legal Information Extraction/Entailment (COLIEE). In its current iteration, COLIEE comprises four tasks. Task one requires identifying the set of cases from a case law corpus which support the decision of a query case. Given the decision fragment of a case that is supported by another case, task two aims to discern which paragraph of the supporting case entail the fragment. Tasks three and four use statutory data and bar exam questions. Task three involves retrieving statutory articles relevant to a bar exam question. Task four aims to determine the entailment of a bar exam question by a set of relevant articles.

1.1 Contributions

Our aims in COLIEE are the following:

- We intend to employ the state of the art natural language processing (NLP) methods to address the four tasks.
- Second, we address the fact that many state of the art language models do not transfer well to the legal domain. We do this by training our own embeddings on legal text.

The rest of the paper is as follows: Sect. 2 continues with the related work and Sect. 3 explains our novel approach with our legal embeddings. Next, in Sect. 4, 5, 6, and 7 we will focus on the methodology, experimental set-up and results for task 1, 2, 3 and 4 respectively. Finally, Sect. 8 concludes our paper with possible extensions for our research.

2   Related Work

In this section, we will focus on related research on both legal information retrieval and legal entailment. Although both serve different purposes, they can be addressed using common methods.

---

[1] https://tax-i.deloitte.nl/.

Classic information retrieval techniques include BM-25 [24] and TF-IDF [19], which obtain normalized bag of word representations of a corpus of documents and a query. The aforementioned are then compared to rank the queried documents by relevancy. Such practices are common in the legal domain [10,14,33].

Richer document representation methods introduced in legal information retrieval include, Doc2Vec [16] and more advanced transformer methods [32], such as BERT [8]. One shortcoming of BERT is that it takes a fixed sequence length of 512 tokens, which is problematic given the length of legal documents[2]. Previous attempts to address this shortcoming have involved using summarization tools such as Gensim [26] or trimming sequences to the maximum length [10]. Another downside of out-of-the-box BERT is its inability to generalize to specific domains due to the fact that it was trained on Wikipedia-like data [11].

BERT can also be used only as means of generating features from text without invoking the entire transformer architecture [8]. Common methods of using BERT derived features include taking the mean of the last four hidden layers, taking a weighted sum of the last four hidden layers, or just using the last hidden layer [8]. BERT derived features can then be used as input to a separate model [10].

Both information retrieval and entailment tasks can be configured as classification problems through pairwise relevance prediction and binary classification, respectively. Legal classification problems can be addressed through deep learning methods. For instance, Chalkidis, Androutsopoulos & Aletras (2019) employed a Bi-Directional Gated Recurrent Unit with Attention (Bi-GRU-ATT) model [4] to predict the outcome of European Court of Human Rights (ECHR) cases. Bi-GRU-ATT models are useful in the legal domain because they are sensitive to context [3]. Previous COLIEE submissions have illustrated the effectiveness of encoding entailment inputs into separate Long Term Short Term Memory (LSTM) models whose combined output is used for binary classification [33].

Non deep learning methods can also be used for classification, such as K-Nearest Neighbor, Random Forest, and boosting algorithms [26]. The downside of this latter problem framing is that class imbalanced become more common due to more non-relevant documents; however, tree-based approaches such as XGBoost [5] or CatBoost [9] tend to handle such imbalances better. XGBoost is therefore often the model of choice in competitive machine learning environment [21]. Furthermore, tree based methods can make use of meta information, such as the date or header, alongside textual features [35].

3   Legal Embeddings

As explained in Sect. 2, most competitive embedding based models are trained on a general corpus, such as Wikipedia or (short) stories. However, when applied to legal data, the results fall short. Legal English is different than regular English with respect to syntax, semantics, vocabulary and morphology, which explains

---

[2] https://eur-lex.europa.eu/legal-content/NL/ALL/?uri=CELEX%3A61996CJ0349.

this shortage in performance [34]. Based on these findings, we trained a legal FastText model[3] at the start of this year for our own applications within our intelligent information retrieval system[4], tax-i. The need for legal embeddings is verified by recent research that has found that training a legal BERT does aid in legal-based entailment and question answering [11].

To train our FastText [2] model, we make use of a partition of legal data that we have available in our tax-i platform. We only use US-related content and take roughly 1/3rd of this which translates to 1M US cases. We pre-process the data by lowercasing the text, removing punctuation, and converting numbers to text and use this during training.

We then use the unsupervised FastText[5] to train embeddings with the legal data via a skipgram model, training for 4 epochs, 6 threads, no wordngrams, a 300-dimensionality for the word embeddings and all remaining parameters remain default. This yields a final loss of around ~ 0.05. The legal embeddings resulted in sub-par performance on tasks one and two during initial experimentation; therefore, alternative methods were employed.

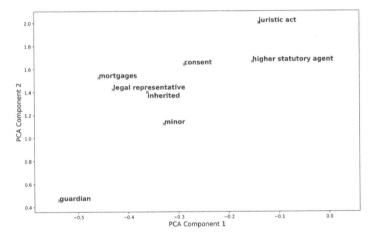

Fig. 1. Our legal embeddings visualized for several legal terms in a 2D space with the use of PCA.

When we visualize different legal terms with our legal embeddings, we can distinguish related and non-related legal concepts. Though, the usefulness of a PCA visualization of an embedding space depends on the between group and within group variance of the words being compared, it is standard practice for visualizing word relationships [17]. However, that is not an issue here as our intuition of these words corresponds with the visualization; we know that legal

---

[3] We opted for FastText rather than BERT due to limited computational resources.

[4] We are currently in the process of making parts of our AI functionalities open source.

[5] https://github.com/facebookresearch/fastText.

representatives are important when dealing with inheritance and mortgages. We can also observe that a legal representative and higher statutory agent are more similar than a guardian, which have different roles to a person, showing that these legal embeddings show an understanding of the legal corpus. Furthermore, the utility of these legal embeddings has been validated by subject matter experts within the context of retrieving suggested documents on the tax-i platform. Documents retrieved by embedding similarity were found to be more relevant to a query than those retrieved by standard TF-IDF similarity methods.

While these short concepts contain rich information in their embeddings, we have observed that they do not contribute to improved performance in task 1 and 2 compared to task 3 and 4. This is likely due to the fact that, while these embeddings can be (mathematically) combined, the longer the sequence the less informative these embeddings become. Since the first two tasks involve large pieces of text, they struggle to obtain a balanced combination of the separate word embeddings. Therefore, legal embeddings were not used for task 1 and 2.

4   Task 1: Case Law Information Retrieval

The first task focuses on case law information retrieval where given a case law document, Q, we want to retrieve relevant case law to this document from a finite set of candidates $S_1, S_2, ...S_n$.

4.1   Methodology

We formulate this retrieval task into a pairwise classification problem meaning, where each candidate is labeled as relevant or not. We use English case law and have a fixed amount of candidates per case, namely 200, where the candidates differ for each base case.

To classify each candidate, we conjoin the query document and a summary of the candidate case, extracted using either Gensim or regex, to generate TF-IDF with IDF weight smoothing and absolute word count features using uni- and bi-grams. These features are then put into a boosting algorithm, either XGBoost [5] or CatBoost [23], where the latter has shown promising results in text-related tasks [27,30]. Afterwards, we use precision, recall and the F1 measure to assess how this model performs by only taking the ones classified as relevant into account for these measures. That is, we do not take the non-relevant cases into account to get a proper estimation of the classification in this retrieval task.

4.2   Experimental Setup

We use a 90-10% split on the training data to obtain a training and validation set. Using absolute counts and TF-IDF features with XGBoost and CatBoost resulted in F1 scores of 0.37 and 0.54, respectively. As such, we determined the superior method to be CatBoost with 1500 iterations, a learning rate of 0.1, l2 leaf regularization of 3.5, and depth of 4.

4.3   Results

Among the COLIEE 2020 submissions this year the used method, absolute counts and TF-IDF into CatBoost, we obtain a test F1 score of 0.0457, where the top-3 submissions obtain 0.6774 (team cyber), 0.6768 (team cyber) and 0.6682 (team TLIR) in descending order. The difference between the final test results and the training data test results was due to human error in the method of document summarization employed. That is, the model was trained on Gensim summarized documents and the model was evaluated on extracted summary documents via regular expressions. Applying Gensim summarization to the 2020 test data resulted in an actual F1 score of .18. The drop in performance is indicative of overfitting. This can be caused by the use of a pairwise TF-IDF approach which depends on a shared vocabulary between train and test data. This can be overcome by using the cosine distance between TF-IDF vectors as a feature. Furthermore, repeated evaluation on the training data showed high variance model performance with values between 0.43 and 0.54.

5   Task 2: Case Law Entailment

The case law entailment task requires finding an entailing paragraph from a case, given a base case with a specified fragment. Or put formally: Given a base case, Q, its entailed fragment, f, and another related case, R, composed of the paragraph set $P = \{p_1, p_2, \ldots, p_n\}$, find the paragraph set $E = \{p_1, p_2, \ldots, p_m \mid p_i \in P\}$, such that p_i entails f.

5.1   Methodology

The three feature groups are ensembled in a XGBoost classifier in order to predict the probability of p_i entailing f. XGBoost was chosen for the same reason that it is often the model of choice in competitive machine learning environments: it is robust to the curse of dimensionality, is performs feature selection automatically, and is capable of generating rich feature representations [21].

The feature groups are classical features, embedding similarity and Natural Language Inference (NLI).

Feature Group 1 - Classical Features. These consist of classical word features, such as length of the paragraph p_i, place of paragraph within the article, count of overlapping words between f and p_i and a BM-25 ranking.

Feature Group 2 - Embedding Similarity. This consists of the similarity of the means of three different word-embeddings: RoBERTa [18], BERT [8] and a fine-tuned version of the latter all uncased on the COLIEE 2020 training data. As a similarity measure between the embedded p_i and the embedded f, we use the cosine similarity.

Feature Group 3 - Natural Language Inference. NLI is the task of determining whether two statements entail or contradict each other. Ideally this would be done utilizing a fine-tuned model for the legal domain. However, due to the training and validation time constraints, we use the pre-trained BERT NLI model.

Ensemble Model. The previous mentioned feature groups are all min-max normalized over all paragraphs in each related case R. Predictions are the probabilistic output of a XGBoost classifier. For every base case Q, we check how many paragraphs p_i of related case R are predicted to be entailing fragment f. If no paragraphs are found for a base case, the algorithm picks the one with the highest probabilistic outcome (albeit it with a low probability). If more than two are predicted, only the two with the highest scores are allowed in the submitted results.

5.2   Experimental Setup

After experimentation it was found that fine-tuned BERT embeddings provided the best performing similarity measure for feature group 2. As such, all approaches used fine-tuned BERT embeddings for feature group 2 and fed features into an XGBoost classifier. The three different approaches based on the aforementioned feature groups were the following. The Feature Importance approach used only features deemed important by analysing xgboost feature weights. The XGBoost approach used all features with a grid search hyperparameter tuning. Finally, the XGBoost Bayesian used all features with bayesian optimization hyperparameter tuning. We cross validate the training set with five folds, and our results can be found in Table 1. It is evident that we try to optimize precision over recall for more precise results.

Table 1. Validation results of the models for task 2 using 5-fold cross validation.

Approach	Precision	Recall	F1
Feature importance	0.5990	0.5800	0.5855
XGBoost	0.6168	0.5855	0.5984
XGBoost Bayesian	0.7054	0.4785	0.5674

5.3   Results

Applying the previous mentioned models on the official COLIEE 2020 test set, we get the results as described in Table 2. All of the models achieve F1 scores high enough for the top seven submissions this year. Using Bayesian tuning, we obtain the best results from our own submissions and obtain third place, showing the importance of proper tuning.

Table 2. The top seven F1 scores of COLIEE 2020 task 2.

Team	F1
JNLP BMWT	0.6753
JNLP BMW	0.6222
TAXI XGBoost Bayesian	0.6180
TLIR	0.6154
JNLP WT	0.6094
TAXI XGBoost	0.5992
TAXI feature importance	0.5917

Analysis. Upon further analysis of the features, we can see that using the most important features is necessary, but not sufficient for state-of-the-art results. Furthermore, grid search hyperparameter tuning improves performance, but not as much as Bayesian optimization methods.

Upon inspecting the test result data and XGBoost Bayesian predictions, we found the following to be true. The model performs better on longer candidate paragraphs. The average paragraph lengths for correctly and incorrectly predicted examples were 108 and 91 tokens, respectively. This suggests that the longer the paragraph the more BERT is capable of comparing contextual information. With respect to shared vocabulary, the model seems to perform better when shared vocabulary is slightly higher. The count of number of shared tokens in correctly and incorrectly predicted examples were 122 and 111, respectively. It appears that word level similarity increases the similarity between paragraphs in embeddings as well.

6   Task 3: Statute Law Information Retrieval

The statue law information retrieval task focuses on finding relevant articles $S_1, S_2, ..S_N$ from the complete Japanese Civil Code to a legal bar exam question Q, such that the use of these articles in combination with the exam question would yield entailment or not. We use the English version of this data, which is the translated version of the original Japanese dataset.

6.1   Methodology

We will use three different approaches to generate a feature embedding for each bar exam question and all articles. These are then compared and ranked using cosine similarity. We then always return the most similar article, and any additional ones based on the difference δ between the previously retrieved article and the next most similar article. If that difference is below a certain threshold H, we continue to return more articles until either the threshold is exceeded or a maximum amount of retrieved articles R is found. To evaluate our models, we use the macro-average of precision, recall and the F-2 measure, where the latter is chosen due to the higher importance of recall.

Approach 1 - TF-IDF Vectors. This feature approach, which is based on last year's winner [15], is TF-IDF with IDF weight smoothing. We generate TF-IDF vectors for each article and bar exam question, containing the relative frequency of each word in a given vocabulary.

Approach 2 - Legal Embeddings. The other approach is based on our legal embeddings, discussed in Sect. 3. Embeddings have been proven to capture context, whereas a simple word approach as TF-IDF does not, hence the choice of using embeddings as well. For all the articles and bar exam questions, we generate a legal question/article embedding by finding the legal embeddings for its words and take the average for the final representation.

Approach 3 - Combination. Given that the earlier mentioned approaches have their own shortcomings as well as strengths, we propose another approach to combine the best of both. We use both approaches separately and combine their top 100 retrieved articles and re-evaluate the order with the same ranking mechanism as explained before.

6.2   Experimental Setup

Since each of these approaches has parameters to tune, we use a grid search method to find the best parameters via the hold out validation set. This yields for the TF-IDF implementation a maximum amount of 3 retrieved articles and a $\delta = 0.007$ which results in a larger recall over precision. For the legal embedding approach we set a maximum amount of 4 retrieved articles and $\delta = 0.007$. Lastly, for the combined model, the maximum amount of retrieved articles is 4 and $\delta = 0.015$. Moreover, the embeddings use lowercasing, punctuation removal, stopword removal and number to text conversion. For the TF-IDF, we keep casing, do not remove punctuation, use number to text conversion, keep stopwords and use both uni- and bigrams.

We split our training data into a train and validation set to obtain intermediate results as well as having interpretable numbers during hyper-tuning and use 600 examples for training and 96 for validation. These results are shown in Table 3, where we can observe that recall is indeed larger. Critically, the combination of the two features show a more balanced precision and a larger recall.

Table 3. Validation results of the models for task 3, where LE stands for the legal embedding approach.

Approach	Precision	Recall	F2
TF-IDF	0.5130	0.5217	0.5117
LE	0.3823	0.5382	0.4490
Combination	0.4790	0.5660	0.5161

6.3 Results

When evaluating our models against other COLIEE 2020 participants on the test set, we get the results mentioned in Table 4. Our legal embeddings on their own do not cover enough semantics and context to obtain sufficient performance; however, in combination with TF-IDF they do boost the recall considerably, showing that they have promising prospects.

Table 4. Quantitative results on task 3 by the top-3 participants on COLIEE 2020 and our three submissions. R1, R2 and R3 stand for the TF-IDF, legal embedding and combination approach respectively.

Team	Precision	Recall	F2	MAP	R@5	R@10	R@30
LLNTU	0.6875	0.6622	0.6587	0.7604	0.8071	0.8571	0.9214
JNLP.tfidf-bert-ensemble	0.5766	0.5670	0.5532	0.6618	0.6857	0.7143	0.7786
Cyber1	0.5058	0.5536	0.5290	0.5540	0.5500	0.6929	0.8000
TAXI_R3	0.4393	0.5089	0.4546	0.5057	0.5714	0.6143	0.6786
TAXI_R1	0.4435	0.4152	0.4112	0.4883	0.5857	0.6214	0.7214
TAXI_R2	0.2872	0.4182	0.3400	0.3741	0.3786	0.4214	0.5643

Analysis

Training Statistics. When we evaluate the cosine similarities values between the bar exam questions and all possible articles, we can see a clear difference in their similarity values, which is shown in Table 5. The TF-IDF similarity values indicate a large difference between relevant and non-relevant articles compared to a bar exam question. However, there is a large standard deviation among relevant articles, indicating that some relevant articles to bar exam questions are not found by TF-IDF which are found by our legal embeddings.

Table 5. Mean cosine similarity value ± their standard deviation for relevant and non-relevant articles to the bar exam questions on the training data with both feature methods.

Approach	Relevant	Non-relevant
TF-IDF	0.1651 ± 0.1629	0.0092 ± 0.0184
LE	0.9264 ± 0.0436	0.8754 ± 0.0437

Strengths and Shortcomings. When we manually evaluate the performance of both the TF-IDF and legal embeddings on a few test examples, we can see a clear difference in their strengths and shortcomings. TF-IDF tends to work quite well on finding relevant articles to bar exam questions when the vocabulary used is the same. However, our legal embeddings also find the correct relevant articles to a bar exam question even without shared vocabulary between them. For example, it has learned that a *higher statutory agent* can also be a *legal representative*, which gives us a good indication that these embeddings are essential for improved text comparison.

7   Task 4: Statute Law Entailment

The statue law entailment task requires determining whether a legal bar exam question, Q, is entailed in the text of a set of articles, $S_1, S_2, ... S_N$ relevant to Q. Entailment is taken to mean whether Q is true or false given the content of $S_1, S_2, ... S_N$. This was done in two ways: using a BERT-XGBoost combination and using the legal embeddings with a Bi-GRU. The former is inspired by the previous 2019 COLIEE submission of Gain and colleagues (2019) for the purposes of bench-marking the latter.

7.1   Methodology

BERT-XGBoost Combination. For each example, the set of articles S were concatenated to each other, then to the question, Q, with a separator token, and summarized with Gensim if necessary. The last hidden layers of the BERT base cased model were then input to XGBoost.

Legal Embeddings Bi-GRU. For each example, the set of articles S were concatenated to each other and then to the question, Q, with a separator token. Stop words were not removed as they contain important information regarding negation and affirmation. The tokenized and padded data was then fed to the Bi-GRU.

7.2   Experimental Setup

XGBoost, was then hyperparameter tuned using five-fold cross validation and Bayesian optimisation methods. The hyperparameters tuned were the following: subsample; the amount of training data to be used per sample, max depth; the maximum tree depth, eta; the learning rate, colsample by level; the subsample ratio per tree used when making a level, and colsample by tree; the subsample ratio per column used when making a tree. Resulting values are .60, 4, .50, .34, .98, respectively. The tuned model was evaluated on a hold out validation set of 20% of the data yielding an average precision, recall and F1 of .63.

Initial experiments found that the Bi-GRU-ATT used in previous legal prediction tasks [3] has too many parameters for such a small dataset. Therefore, we used only one GRU layer and removed the attention. Due to time constraints the model was not fully hyperparameter tuned. The resulting precision, recall, accuracy and F1 on the test set were .59, .58, .58, .56, respectively.

7.3   Results

The results of our two submissions, taxi_BERTXGB and taxi_le_brigru, can be found in Table 6 alongside the top three wining submissions. The former answered 60 questions correct with an accuracy of 0.5357 and the latter answered 57 questions correct with an accuracy of 0.5089.

Table 6. The top three performing models of COLIEE 2020 task 4 along with our two submissions.

Model	Number correct	Accuracy
JNLP.BERTLaw	81	0.7232
TRC3mt	70	0.6250
TRC3t5	70	0.6250
Taxi_BERTXGB	60	0.5357
taxi_le_bigru	57	0.5089

Analysis. By using TF-IDF cosine similarity as a measure of shared vocabulary we can elucidate both models' strengths and shortcomings.

The necessity of shared vocabulary for the BERTXGB implementation is evident in the similarity difference between correctly and incorrectly predicted labels, 0.4252 and 0.3429, respectively. However, BERTXGB was not competitive with the top performing submissions. This is likely due to the fact that BERT cased has not been trained on legal text.

The shortcomings of the Bi-GRU model are less explicit, as the TF-IDF cosine similarity is actually higher in the incorrectly predicted labels than in the correctly predicted labels. Indeed, the Bi-GRU implementation was not much better than random chance.

8   Conclusion

In this paper, we propose several approaches to both legal information retrieval and entailment. For task 1, the case law retrieval task, we use CatBoost with both absolute word counts and TF-IDF features obtaining a F1 score of 0.04. The second task, the case law entailment task, makes use of Information Retrieval features such as BM-25, NLI probabilities and fine-tuned embeddings. This model achieves a F1 score of 0.6180, while also achieving third place in the competition. The third task, the statutory information retrieval task, utilizes pre-trained legal embeddings in combination with TF-IDF obtaining a F2 of 0.4546. Lastly, task 4, the statutory entailment task, achieves an accuracy of 0.5357 with BERT embeddings into XGBoost.

The use of extra linguistic features, such as NLI, have been shown to be important and useful to obtain better and state-of-the-art performance. Moreover, we showed that even though the current legal embeddings are not state-of-the-art, they do indicate an understanding of legal terms that is necessary for obtaining better performance.

Both this and earlier years do show that on average scores on the Japanese data is higher than the English one. Since both languages differ much in semantic and structural properties, it would be worth checking whether the Japanese text contains richer token information to expand to multilingual models.

Operationally, we could have better shared methodologies across similar tasks. Sharing of best practices could have no only prevented the human error, but also lead to improved performance across the board.

Future research will involve re-training the legal embeddings using a contextually sensitive model such as BERT for a deeper understanding of legal nuance, and focusing on a more precise low complexity model to transform the rich word legal embeddings to rich legal document representations. Furthermore, we see future opportunities in the addition of new tasks to the competition given our perspective as one of the few participants from the private sector. First, there is industry demand for argumentation mining systems capable of performing the following sub-tasks: extraction from unstructured text, type classification, and relation identification. There is currently only one dataset containing annotated legal argumentation structures [31]. Second, there is industry demand for functionality to score the complexity of legal documents to estimate the difficulty of taking on a case. The European Court of Human Rights ascribes an importance level to each case in the meta data which can be used as a proxy for a complexity label [22].

References

1. Benjamins, V.R., Casanovas, P., Breuker, J., Gangemi, A. (eds.): Law and the Semantic Web. LNCS (LNAI), vol. 3369. Springer, Heidelberg (2005). https://doi.org/10.1007/b106624
2. Bojanowski, P., Grave, E., Joulin, A., Mikolov, T.: Enriching word vectors with subword information. Trans. Assoc. Comput. Linguist. **5**, 135–146 (2017)
3. Chalkidis, I., Androutsopoulos, I., Aletras, N.: Neural legal judgment prediction in english. arXiv preprint arXiv:1906.02059 (2019)
4. Chalkidis, I., Fergadiotis, M., Malakasiotis, P., Aletras, N., Androutsopoulos, I.: Extreme multi-label legal text classification: a case study in eu legislation. arXiv preprint arXiv:1905.10892 (2019)
5. Chen, T., He, T., Benesty, M., Khotilovich, V., Tang, Y.: Xgboost: extreme gradient boosting. R Package Version (4-2), 1–4 (2015)
6. Clement, J.: Worldwide desktop market share of leading search engines from january 2010 to April 2019. Accessed 12 March 2019 (2019)
7. Dale, R.: Law and word order: Nlp in legal tech. Nat. Lang. Eng. **25**(1), 211–217 (2019)
8. Devlin, J., Chang, M.W., Lee, K., Toutanova, K.: Bert: pre-training of deep bidirectional transformers for language understanding. arXiv preprint arXiv:1810.04805 (2018)

9. Dorogush, A.V., Ershov, V., Gulin, A.: Catboost: gradient boosting with categorical features support. arXiv preprint arXiv:1810.11363 (2018)
10. Gain, B., Bandyopadhyay, D., Saikh, T., Ekbal, A.: Iitp in coliee@ icail 2019: legal information retrieval using bm25 and bert (2019)
11. Holzenberger, N., Blair-Stanek, A., Van Durme, B.: A dataset for statutory reasoning in tax law entailment and question answering. arXiv preprint arXiv:2005.05257 (2020)
12. Introna, L.D., Nissenbaum, H.: Shaping the web: why the politics of search engines matters. Inf. Soc. **16**(3), 169–185 (2000)
13. Kerikmäe, T., Hoffmann, T., Chochia, A.: Legal technology for law firms: determining roadmaps for innovation. Croatian Int. Relat. Rev. **24**(81), 91–112 (2018)
14. Kim, M.Y., Rabelo, J., Goebel, R.: Statute law information retrieval and entailment. In: Proceedings of the Seventeenth International Conference on Artificial Intelligence and Law, pp. 283–289 (2019)
15. Kim, M.Y., Rabelo, J., Goebel, R.: Statute law information retrieval and entailment. In: Proceedings of the Seventeenth International Conference on Artificial Intelligence and Law, pp. 283–289. ICAIL 19, Association for Computing Machinery, New York, NY, USA (2019). https://doi.org/10.1145/3322640.3326742
16. Le, Q., Mikolov, T.: Distributed representations of sentences and documents. In: International Conference on Machine Learning, pp. 1188–1196 (2014)
17. Liu, S., Bremer, P.T., Thiagarajan, J.J., Srikumar, V., Wang, B., Livnat, Y., Pascucci, V.: Visual exploration of semantic relationships in neural word embeddings. IEEE Trans. Vis. Comput. Graph. **24**(1), 553–562 (2017)
18. Liu, Y., et al.: Roberta: a robustly optimized bert pretraining approach (2019)
19. Manning, C.D., Schütze, H., Raghavan, P.: Introduction to Information Retrieval. Cambridge University Press, Cambridge (2008)
20. Mitra, B., Craswell, N.: Neural models for information retrieval. arXiv preprint arXiv:1705.01509 (2017)
21. Nielsen, D.: Tree boosting with xgboost-why does xgboost win every machine learning competition? Master's Thesis, NTNU (2016)
22. Opijnen, M.V.: Towards a global importance indicator for court decisions. In: Legal Knowledge and Information Systems: JURIX 2016: The Twenty-Ninth Annual Conference, vol. 294, p. 155. IOS Press, Amsterdam (2016)
23. Prokhorenkova, L., Gusev, G., Vorobev, A., Dorogush, A.V., Gulin, A.: Catboost: unbiased boosting with categorical features (2017)
24. Robertson, S.E., Walker, S., Jones, S., Hancock-Beaulieu, M.M., Gatford, M., et al.: Okapi at trec-3. Nist Spec. Publ. Sp **109**, 109 (1995)
25. Rocktäschel, T., Grefenstette, E., Hermann, K.M., Kočiskỳ, T., Blunsom, P.: Reasoning about entailment with neural attention. arXiv preprint arXiv:1509.06664 (2015)
26. Rossi, J., Kanoulas, E.: Legal information retrieval with generalized language models. In: Proceedings of the 6th Competition on Legal Information Extraction/Entailment. COLIEE (2019)
27. Saha, P., Mathew, B., Goyal, P., Mukherjee, A.: Hateminers: detecting hate speech against women. arXiv preprint arXiv:1812.06700 (2018)
28. Salehi, S., Du, J.T., Ashman, H.: Use of web search engines and personalisation in information searching for educational purposes. Inf. Res. Int. Electr. J. **23**(2) (2018)
29. Sammons, M., Vydiswaran, V.V., Roth, D.: Ask not what textual entailment can do for you... In: Proceedings of the 48th Annual Meeting of the Association for Computational Linguistics, pp. 1199–1208 (2010)

30. Shelmanov, A., Pisarevskaya, D., Chistova, E., Toldova, S., Kobozeva, M., Smirnov, I.: Towards the data-driven system for rhetorical parsing of russian texts. Proc. Workshop Discourse Relat. Parsing Treebanking **2019**, 82–87 (2019)

31. Teruel, M., Cardellino, C., Cardellino, F., Alemany, L.A., Villata, S.: Increasing argument annotation reproducibility by using inter-annotator agreement to improve guidelines. In: Proceedings of the Eleventh International Conference on Language Resources and Evaluation (LREC 2018) (2018)

32. Vaswani, A., et al.: Attention is all you need. In: Advances in neural information processing systems, pp. 5998–6008 (2017)

33. Wehnert, S., Hoque, S.A., Fenske, W., Saake, G.: Threshold-based retrieval and textual entailment detection on legal bar exam questions. arXiv preprint arXiv:1905.13350 (2019)

34. Wydick, R.: Plain english for lawyers: Teacher's manual (2005)

35. Yoshioka, M., Song, Z.: Hukb at coliee 2019 information retrieval task - utilization of metadata for relevant case retrieval. In: Proceedings of the 6th Competition on Legal Information Extraction/Entailment (2019)

36. Zhong, H., Xiao, C., Tu, C., Zhang, T., Liu, Z., Sun, M.: How does nlp benefit legal system: A summary of legal artificial intelligence. arXiv preprint arXiv:2004.12158 (2020)

37. Zientek, L.R., Werner, J.M., Campuzano, M.V., Nimon, K.: The use of google scholar for research and research dissemination. New Horiz. Adult Educ. Hum. Res. Dev. **30**(1), 39–46 (2018)

BERT-Based Ensemble Model for Statute Law Retrieval and Legal Information Entailment

Hsuan-Lei Shao[1] (ORCID), Yi-Chia Chen[2], and Sieh-Chuen Huang[3,4](✉) (ORCID)

[1] Department of East Asian Studies, National Taiwan Normal University, Taipei, Taiwan
hlshao@ntnu.edu.tw
[2] Department of Computer Science and Information Engineering, National Taiwan Normal University, Taipei, Taiwan
40647045s@ntnu.edu.tw
[3] College of Law, National Taiwan University, Taipei, Taiwan
schhuang@ntu.edu.tw
[4] Center for Research in Econometric Theory and Applications, National Taiwan University, Taipei, Taiwan

Abstract. The Competition on legal information extraction/entailment (COLIEE) is an international information processing and retrieval competition. As an aid to future participants as well as question designers, this article describes how to connect legal questions taken from past Japanese bar exams to relevant statutes (articles of the Japanese Civil Code, Task 3) and how to construct a Yes/No question answering system for legal queries (Task 4) incorporating background materials on Japanese law. We restructured the given data to a dataset which contains all possible combinations of queries and articles as continuous strings as our samples. In this way, the difficult pairing task has been turned into a simpler classification task and samples for training became sufficient in number. Next, we used three BERT-based models to solve binary questions in order to achieve stable performance. As a result, the model achieved an F2-score of 0.6587 in Task 3 (ranked 1st) and an accuracy of 0.6161 in Task 4.

Keywords: Textual entailment · Information retrieval · Legal AI · BERT-based ensemble model · Legal analytics · COLIEE 2020

1 Introduction

The Competition on Legal Information Extraction/Entailment (COLIEE), a famous international information retrieval competition, had its seventh run in 2020 [1–3]. Four tasks were included in the 2020 competition: Tasks 1 and 2 were the case law competition, and tasks 3 and 4 were the statute law competition. Task 1 was a legal case retrieval task, requiring the participants to develop an approach capable of reading a new case Q, and extracting supporting cases S1, S2, …, Sn from the provided case law corpus, to support the decision for Q. Task 2 was a legal case entailment task, which involved the

All authors contributed equally to this work.

© Springer Nature Switzerland AG 2021
N. Okazaki et al. (Eds.): JSAI-isAI 2020 Workshops, LNAI 12758, pp. 226–239, 2021.
https://doi.org/10.1007/978-3-030-79942-7_15

identification of a paragraph from existing cases that entailed the decision of a new case. Similar to the tasks featured in previous COLIEE competitions, Task 3 was to consider a yes/no legal question Q and retrieve relevant statutes from a database of the Japanese Civil Code; Task 4 was to confirm entailment of a yes/no answer from the retrieved Civil Code statutes [4].

Our team, the *Legal Analytics Laboratory of National Taiwan University (LLNTU)*, participated in Task 3 (the Statute Law Retrieval Task) and Task 4 (the Legal Question Answering Task). Although this is the first time we participated in this competition, we are no strangers to Civil Codes and bar exams. Perhaps this is why we do not feel unfamiliar with the data. We provided a solution to Task 3 using classification of pair sequences and an ensemble of three BERT models. Fortunately, the BERT-based structure built a fine model for retrieving information: the F2-score was 0.6587 on Task 3 (the best score among all participants). Then we applied the same model to Task 4, as to which the accuracy was 0.6161 (rank 6).

2 Competition Data and Task Description

The COLIEE organizer provided the "*Statute Law Competition Data Corpus*," in which legal questions were drawn from Japanese bar exams, and all Japanese civil law statues were also provided in both Japanese and English. The format of the COLIEE competition corpora has been derived from an NTCIR work [4], offering confirmed relationships between questions and the articles and cases relevant to answering the questions, as in the following example:

"H18-1-2"

<pair label="Y" id="H18-1-2">

 <t1>

  (Seller's Warranty in cases of Superficies or Other Rights)Article 566 (1)In cases where the subject matter of the sale is encumbered with for the purpose of a superficies, an emphyteusis, an easement, a right of retention or a pledge, if the buyer does not know the same and cannot achieve the purpose of the contract on account thereof, the buyer may cancel the contract. In such cases, if the contract cannot be cancelled, the buyer may only demand compensation for damages…

 </t1>

 <t2>

  There is a limitation period on pursuance of warranty if there is restriction due to superficies on the subject matter, but there is no restriction on pursuance of warranty if the seller's rights were revoked due to execution of the mortgage.

 </t2>

</pair>

The <t2> part is the bar exam question Q, and the <t1> part is the article of Japan Civil Code related to Q. The above is an example where the query id "H18-1-2" is confirmed to be answerable within the preview of Article 566 (relevant to Task 3). The pair labeled "Y" in this example means the answer for this query is "Yes", which is entailed from the relevant articles (relevant to Task 4) [4]. For Tasks 3 and 4, the training data will be the same. We used them for the following two sub-tasks:

1) Task 3: Legal Information Retrieval Task. The input is a bar exam 'Yes/No' question and the output should be the relevant civil law articles.
2) Task 4: Recognizing Entailment between legal Articles and Queries. The input is a bar exam 'Yes/No' question. After retrieving the relevant articles using our method, we determined 'Yes' or 'No' as the output [4].

For Task 3, the evaluation measures involved precision, recall and the F2-measurement (instead of the ordinary F1-measure). The COLIEE organizer placed more emphasis on recall because the goal of information retrieval is to select articles to be used in the next entailment process [4], which is:

$$F2 - measure = \frac{(5 \times Precision \times Recall)}{(4 \times Precision + Recall)}$$

$$Precision = \frac{average\ of\ (the\ number\ of\ correctly\ retrieved\ articles\ for\ each\ query}{(the\ number\ of\ retrieved\ articles\ for\ each\ query)}$$

$$Recall = \frac{average\ of\ (the\ number\ of\ correctly\ retrieved\ articles\ for\ each\ query)}{(the\ number\ of\ relevant\ articles\ for\ each\ query)}$$

The goal of Task 4 is to construct Yes/No question answering systems for legal queries, by entailment from the relevant articles. The task investigates the performance of systems that answer 'Yes' or 'No' to previously unseen queries by comparing the meanings between queries and retrieved Civil Code articles. For Task 4, the evaluation measure is accuracy. Training data consist of a set containing a query, relevant article(s), a correct answer "Y" or "N". Test data offered by the COLIEE organizer includes only queries, but no 'Y/N' label, no relevant articles [4].

3 Data Preprocessing

Our research processed only the Japanese-language data corpus provided by the COLIEE organizer, not the English-language data corpus. At the beginning, we had 696 bar exam questions as <t2> from H18–H30, and 767 Civil Code Articles as <t1>. Our design was to input the combinations of "bar exam questions Q" and "articles from the Japanese Civil Code" as continuous strings. That is to say, for the <t2> component for each pair, <t2> was combined with every article of the Civil Code, producing 767 samples (the number of articles in the Part I–III of the Civil Code). Among these, only the sample containing the relevant article was labeled as "1" and other samples containing non-relevant articles were labeled as "0". For example, as Table 1 shows, as specified by <pair label = "Y" id = "H18-1-2"> in the training data, the query id "H18-1-2" was deemed relevant to Article 566, so we labeled it as 1. On the other hand, regarding the non-relevant articles such as Article 1 and 2, the label was "0".

Table 1. Reconstruction of the training dataset

Index	Bar exam questions "H18-1-2" (<t2>)	Japan Civil Code Articles (<t1>)	Label
1	Bar exam questions "H18-1-2" 目的物に地上権による制限があった場合の担保責任追及には期間制限があるが，抵当権の行使によって買主が権利を失った場合の担保責任追及には期間制限がない。 (There is a limitation period on pursuance of warranty if there is restriction due to superficies on the subject matter, but there is no restriction on pursuance of warranty if the seller's rights were revoked due to execution of the mortgage.)	Japan Civil Code Article 566 （目的物の種類又は品質に関する担保責任の期間の制限）第五百六十六条　売主が種類又は品質に関して契約の内容に適合しない目的物を買主に引き渡した場合において、買主がその不適合を知った時から一年以内にその旨を売主に通知しないときは、買主は、その不適合を理由として、履行の追完の請求、代金の減額の請求、損害賠償の請求及び契約の解除をすることができない。ただし、売主が引渡しの時にその不適合を知り、又は重大な過失によって知らなかったたときは、この限りでない。 ((Limitation on Period of Warranty with Respect to Kind or Quality of Subject Matter) Article 566 If the subject matter delivered by the seller to the buyer does not conform to the terms of the contract with respect to the kind or quality, and the buyer fails to notify the seller of the non-conformity within one year from the time when the buyer becomes aware of it, the buyer may not demand cure of the non-conformity of performance, demand a reduction of the price, claim compensation for loss or damage, or cancel the contract, on the grounds of the non-conformity; provided, however, that this does not apply if the seller knew or did not know due to gross	1 (given correct pair)

(continued)

Table 1. *(continued)*

		negligence the non-conformity at the time of the delivery.	
2	Bar exam questions "H18-1-2" 目的物に地上権による制限があった場合の担保責任追及には期間制限があるが，抵当権の行使によって買主が権利を失った場合の担保責任追及には期間制限がない。 (There is a limitation period on pursuance of warranty if there is restriction due to superficies on the subject matter, but there is no restriction on pursuance of warranty if the seller's rights were revoked due to execution of the mortgage.)	Japan Civil Code Article 1 （基本原則）第一条　私権は、公共の福祉に適合しなければならない。2　権利の行使及び義務の履行は、信義に従い誠実に行わなければならない。3　権利の濫用は、これを許さない。 ((Fundamental Principles) Article 1　(1)　Private rights must conform to the public welfare. (2) The exercise of rights and performance of duties must be done in good faith. (3)　No abuse of rights is permitted.)	0 (fictitious wrong pair)
3	Bar exam questions "H18-1-2" 目的物に地上権による制限があった場合の担保責任追及には期間制限があるが，抵当権の行使によって買主が権利を失った場合の担保責任追及には期間制限がない。 (There is a limitation period on pursuance of warranty if there is restriction due to superficies on the subject matter, but there is no restriction on pursuance of warranty if the seller's rights were revoked due to execution of the mortgage.)	Japan Civil Code Article 2 （解釈の基準）第二条　この法律は、個人の尊厳と両性の本質的平等を旨として、解釈しなければならない。 ((Standard for Construction) Article 2　This Code must be construed in accordance with honoring the dignity of individuals and the essential equality of both sexes.)	0 (fictitious wrong pair)
...	...	...	...
533,831	Bar exam questions "H28-35-3" 地上権者は，土地所有者の承諾を得ることなく地上権を第三者に譲渡することができるが，賃借人は，賃貸人の承諾又はそれに代わる裁判所の許可を得なければ，土地賃借権を譲渡することができない。 (A superficiary may assign the superficies without obtaining the approval of the owner of the land	Japan Civil Code Article 724 （不法行為による損害賠償請求権の消滅時効）第七百二十四条　不法行為による損害賠償の請求権は、次に掲げる場合には、時効によって消滅する。一　被害者又はその法定代理人が損害及び加害者を知った時から三年間行使しないとき。二　不法行為の時から二十年間行使しないとき。	0 (fictitious wrong pair)

(continued)

Table 1. (*continued*)

	but a lessee may not assign the lessee's rights without obtaining the approval of the lessor or the court's permission in lieu of it.)	((Extinctive Prescription of Claim for Compensation for Loss or Damage Caused by Tort) Article 724 In the following cases, the claim for compensation for loss or damage caused by tort is extinguished by prescription: (i) the right is not exercised within three years from the time when the victim or legal representative thereof comes to know the damage and the identity of the perpetrator; or (ii) the right is not exercised within 20 years from the time of the tortious act.)		
533,832	Bar exam questions "H28-35-3" 地上権者は，土地所有者の承諾を得ることなく地上権を第三者に譲渡することができるが，賃借人は，賃貸人の承諾又はそれに代わる裁判所の許可を得なければ，土地賃借権を譲渡することができない。 (A superficiary may assign the superficies without obtaining the approval of the owner of the land but a lessee may not assign the lessee's rights without obtaining the approval of the lessor or the court's permission in lieu of it.)	Japan Civil Code Article 724-2 （人の生命又は身体を害する不法行為による損害賠償請求権の消滅時効）第七百二十四条の二 人の生命又は身体を害する不法行為による損害賠償請求権の消滅時効についての前条第一号の規定の適用については、同号中「三年間」とあるのは、「五年間」とする。 ((Extinctive Prescription of Claim for Compensation for Loss or Damage Arising from Death to Person or Injury to Person Caused by Tort) Article 724-2 For the purpose of the application of the provisions of item (i) of the preceding Article with regard to the extinctive prescription of the claim for compensation for loss or damage for death or injury to person caused by tort, the term "three years" in the same item is deemed to be replaced with "five years".)	0 (fictitious wrong pair)

After combining each query with all articles, we constructed a dataset composed of 533,832 samples (the 696 questions times 767 articles). Next, we allocated the samples from going back 11 years (H18–H28) to the training set which had 435,656 samples (the 568 questions times 767 articles), samples in the year before the latest year (H29) as a validation set which contained 44,486 samples (the 58 questions times 767 articles), and samples in the latest year (H30) as a test set, containing 53,690 samples (70 questions time 767 articles). Because the positive samples (samples labeled "1") are very few (about 1/700) and hence the dataset is unbalanced, we simply upsampled positive ones in the training set to be 100 times. The aforementioned process can be seen as a kind of data augmentation. After data preprocessing, we transformed the pairing task into a binary classification task.

4   Model Training and the Result

We used above-mentioned samples as inputs, then adopted three BERT-based models to train them. The first one was *BERT-base_mecab-ipadic-char-4k_whole-word-mask* [5], which abbreviated is *BERTjpcwwm*. We preserved only the first 384 words (maximum length, *maxlen* 384) which was sufficient to perform well (Fig. 1). The second BERT model is *BERTjpcwwm* with maxlen 512 and the third one is *ALBERTjp* with maxlen 512 (v2) [6]. Afterwards, we also attempted other models such as the XLM-RoBERTa. But compared to the initial *BERTjpcwwm384*, other models did not improve. Finally, we concluded that the best combination is: *BERTjpcwwm*(maxlen384), *BERTjpcwwm*(maxlen512), and *ALBERTjp*(maxlen512).

We used Adam [7] as optimizer with a learning rate of 4e-5, batch size: 48, loss function: binary cross entropy, epoch: 1. The valid loss of our model is approximately 0.64.

A sigmoid layer was put finally in the model. This model indicated how much <t1> and <t2> were relevant. We trained each model (*BERTjpcwwm* 384, *BERTjpcwwm* 512, *ALBERTjp* 512) independently as usual. Next, each validation sample or test sample was fed into these three models, yielding values between 0 and 1. Finally, in the ensemble layer, these three values were averaged to provide the final prediction value (as shown in the following Fig. 2).

Adopting three BERT-based models rather than a single BERT model is due to its performance. For example, we compared F2-score performance of a single model (ALBERT model) with the ensemble model in each threshold (as shown in the following Fig. 3). The ensemble model always works much better than the single model. At our final selected threshold 0.8 (details described in the next paragraph), the gap of their F2-score is approximately 0.13. It is assumed that ensemble model can reduce bias weight of specific words or their combination at least. The ensemble layer can also reduce the bias of a single one. Performances of the other two models (*BERTjpcwwm 384, BERTjpcwwm 512*) are similar to the ALBERT.

The threshold to decide whether a pair is "relevant or irrelevant" is 0.8. We tested different numbers for the threshold, ranging from 0.2 to 0.99, and recorded the F2-score performance of the validation set and the test set of each threshold to confirm model sensitivity (as shown in the following Fig. 4). The validation set curve (blue) reached

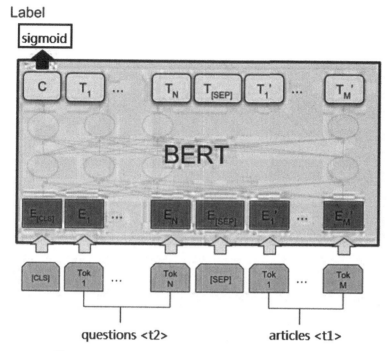

Fig. 1. Continious squence BERT model, modified from [8]

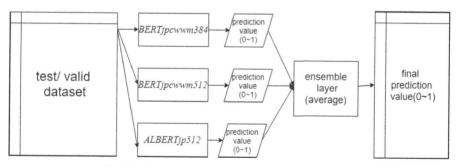

Fig. 2. The structure of BERT-based ensemble model

a peak at the threshold of 0.7. Meanwhile, the test set curve (orange) plateaued at a threshold ranging from 0.75 to 0.82. In order to acquire stable results, an average curve (green) of the validation set and the test set was drawn, displaying that 0.8 is a relatively reliable and rational decision of the threshold.

With the threshold of 0.8, it may be possible that more than one article is recognized as relevant at the same time. On the other hand, it also happens that no article has a F2-score value greater than 0.8. In this case, we obtained the maximum index as the most likely relevant article using the arguments of the maxima (argmax) function. The COLIEE organizer also encouraged participants to submit a rank list with 100 candidates for each

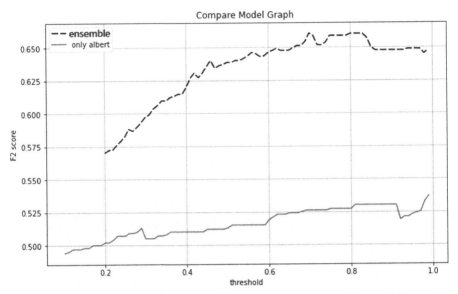

Fig. 3. The comparison of F2-score performance of a single model and the ensemble model

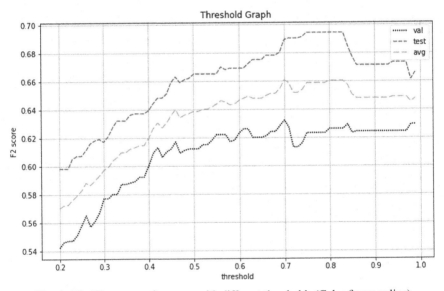

Fig. 4. The F2-score performance with different thresholds (Color figure online)

query as the "long answer", which gave us more opportunities to hit the target. The "R_5" value means recall by using the top 5 ranked documents as returned documents [1], "R_10" for our top 10, and "R_30" means our top 30, which are listed in the following Table 2.

Table 2. The result of BERT-based ensemble model on Task 3

Team	F2-score	Precision	Recall	MAP	R_5	R_10	R_30
LLNTU	0.6587	0.6875	0.6622	0.7604	0.8071	0.8571	0.9214

In terms of performance, as the Table 2 indicates, the F2-score of our model is 0.6587, the precision is 0.6875, and the recall is 0.6622. It is a stable model. In addition, with a wider rank list, we can provide 80% of the correct answers in the top five trial, and over 90% in the top 30 hits.

5 TASK 4: Yes/No Question Answering

The goal of Task 4 was to construct Yes/No question answering systems for legal queries, by entailment from the relevant articles provided by the COLIEE 2020 organizer. That is to say, a 'Yes/No' legal bar exam question was provided as <t2>, and relevant Civil Code articles were given as <t1>. Task 4 was to answer 'Yes' or 'No' to queries <t2> based on these articles <t1> [4]. Training data consisted of a set of a query, relevant article(s), a correct answer "Y" or "N". Test data included only queries and relevant articles, but no 'Y/N' label.

The core of Task 4 is to train the model to recognize the relationship between queries <t2> and answer "Y" or "N". Even if we added irrelevant articles by ourselves like what we did in Task 3, it would not change the answer label ("Y" or "N"), meaning that we had no ways to use the same approach to enhance our samples. Compared to sufficient samples in Task 3, in Task 4 we had only 568 samples to learn from. Specifically speaking, the questions from going back 11 years (H18–H28) constitute the training set which had 568 samples, questions in the year before the latest year (H29) became the validation set which contained 58 samples, and questions in the latest year (H30) made the test set, containing 70 samples. We appointed the answer label Yes as "1" and No as "0" and used the same BERT ensemble model to decide the answer.

Our model's Task 4 accuracy is 0.6161, which has 69 correct answers for all 112 questions. It was ranked the 6th.

6 Failure Analysis: Problems of Extraction-Based Question Answering

Our model shares the same limitations as extraction-based question answering, meaning that answer strings (often noun phrases or named entities) would be found in the query texts [10]. The model's failing answers can be categorized into two types:

First, when there is no common word for the correct <t1> and the respective query <t2>, our model has difficulty recognizing their relevancy and hence points to the wrong <t1>. For example, in <pair id = 'R01-1-O'>, the query is: 成年被後見人の行為であることを理由とする取消権の消滅時効の起算点は、成年被後見人が行為能力者となった時である (*The period of the extinctive prescription of the right to rescind about the act performed by an adult ward commences* **from the time** *of* **becoming a person with capacity to act***).* The golden answer is that the query shall be related to Article 124: *(1) The ratification of a voidable act does not become effective unless it is made after* **the circumstances that made the act voidable cease to exist** *and the person ratifying the act becomes aware of the right to rescind it. (2) In the following cases, the ratification referred to in the preceding paragraph is not required to be made after the circumstances that made the act voidable cease to exist: (i) if a legal representative or a curator or assistant of a person with the legal capacity ratifies the act; or (ii) if a person with qualified legal capacity (excluding an adult ward) makes the ratification with the consent of a legal representative, curator or assistant.* and Article 126: *The right to rescind an act is extinguished by the operation of prescription if it is not exercised within five years* **from the time when it becomes possible to ratify the act***. The same applies if 20 years have passed from the time of the act*, which are the rules governing prescription. However, our model incorrectly identified Article 9, *the juristic acts of a ward is voidable,* as the most relevant article, with a low prediction value of 0.45. To answer this query correctly, as a human, it is necessary to understand that the word "起算点(from the time)" in the query has the same meaning as "時から *(from the time)*" in Article 126. The connection between these two Japanese phrases might have not been established in the BERT model. Furthermore, the query states "行為能力者となった*(becoming a person with capacity to act)*," which is a situation in which a ward recovers capacity so that his/her act is not voidable anymore but completely valid, which equals "取消しの原因となっていた状況が消滅し *(the circumstances that made the act voidable cease to exist)*" as stipulated in Article 124. In other words, it is necessary to pair the idea of *"becoming a person with capacity to act"* in the query with the idea of *"the circumstances that made the act voidable cease to exist"* in Article 124. However, our model does not succeed in doing this concept retrieval perhaps due to the lack of common words in the query and Article 124. This kind of mistake happens because the model cannot find sufficient hints to make a good decision. It needs additional information to derive the associations required to identify words belonging to similar concepts, such as legal domain knowledge.

Another incorrect answer pattern occurs when there are several common words for the <t2> and <t1> pair so that it easily catches the model's attention. For example, in <pair id = 'R01-2-E'>, the query is: Aがその財産の管理人を置かないで行方不明となったことから、家庭裁判所は、Bを不在者Aの財産の管理人として選任した。Aが被相続人Fの共同相続人の一人である場合、BがAを代理してFの他の共同相続人との間でFの遺産について協議による遺産分割をす るためには、家庭裁判所の許可を得る必要はない *(The family court appointed B as the administrator of the property of absentee A, as A went missing without appointing anyone. In cases where A is one of the joint heirs of decedent F, B doesn't need to obtain the permission of a family court when dividing inherited F's property by agreement between the other joint heirs as an agent of A).* Human would understand that this query is about the authority of an administrator. The golden answer is Article 28, which is the specific provision governing the authority of an administrator. However, the word "権限(authority)" does not exist in the query so our model ignores Article 28 and the second answer, Article 103, which is cited by Article 28, also providing rules for the authority of an agent. In spite of the lack of the word "権限(authority)" in the query, Article 28 contains the same phrase "家庭裁判所の許可を得(obtain the permission of a family court)" as the query. But our model fails to recognize this information in the query to connect to Article 28. Instead, it gives Article 27 (stipulating that the administrator has an obligation to compile a property inventory): *(1) An administrator who is appointed by the Family Court pursuant to the provisions of the preceding two Articles must prepare a list of the property he/she is to administer. In such a case, the expenses incurred shall be disbursed from the property of the absentee. (2) In case it is not clear whether an absentee is alive or dead, if so requested by any interested person or a public prosecutor, the family court may also order the administrator appointed by the absentee to prepare list set forth in the preceding paragraph. (3) In addition to provisions of the preceding two paragraphs, the family court may issue an order to the administrator to effect any action which the court may find to be necessary for the preservation of the property of the absentee.* as the wrong answer. Probably because the word "property (遺産・財産)" appears once in the query and three times in Article 27, our model made the wrong decision. Similar errors occur repeatedly in <pair id = 'R01-2-O'>, <pair id = 'R01-2-I'>, <pair id = 'R01-2-U'>, and <pair id = 'R01-2-A'>, where the queries are all related to the powers or authority of the administrator. In these cases, the golden answers are Article 28 and Article 103, but our model incorrectly linked them to Article 27. It seems our model was not thorough enough when making the decision, then fell into the trap like a careless student.

After the competition, the COLIEE organizer provided a report on the level of difficulty of every query based on the performance of all teams. There are "easy questions" which most participants answered correctly, while there are also "hard questions" that none of systems retrieved relevant statutes [12]. This analysis helps us to reexamine our failure. By comparing our answers in Task 3 to the report offered by the organizer, it is found that overall the mistakes made by our system are similar to other teams. A typical failure is the one such as R1-14-U indicated by the organizer. The relevant article is Article 87, but our model pointed to Article 370 with very low confidence (0.16), revealing that our model was not sure about the answer at all. Another example of this kind of error is R1-21-O, which was also identified as a "hard question" by the organizer [12]. The correct answer is Article 520, while our model decided Article 179 wrongly with a relatively low prediction value of 0.56. In fact, both Article 179 and Article 520 are rules of merger (meaning that a claim and an obligation became vested in the same person), where the former is governing ownership and rights in rem, and the latter relates to claims from a contract. The query R1-21-O was asking a claim based on a lease contract, not a claim based on a right in rem. Hence, the answer should be Article 520. In fact, our system chose Article 179 wrongly perhaps because this article and the query share the same word "ownership." But since they share only this one word, the model's prediction value is not high (0.56). This situation can be recognized as the first failure pattern, i.e., the scarcity of common word and low confidence in prediction, that we raised.

On the other hand, there are also "hard questions" to which our model answered incorrectly with a high confidence level. For example, query R1-19-O was identified one of the hard questions [12] about whether a person B can perform his/her debts to C not by monetary payments but by transferring B's claim towards A to C. The golden answer was Article 482 (substitute performance). But the model answered Article 474 (performance by third party) with a high prediction value (0.85). As a human, we understand that in the context of the query, the third party, A, did not pay debts for the benefit of B at A's will, so it cannot be categorized as a "performance by a third party" in any sense. But there are several common words both in the query and Article 474 such as "a third party (第三者)", "against the will of (の意思に反して)", "obligor (債務者)", "obligee (債権者)", "perform the obligation (弁済)." This can be seen as the second failure pattern which we described as a rash person. That is, too many common words misled the model.

In general, our model shows similar weakness facing "hard questions" as other teams. But failure may be derived from different reasons. The two above-mentioned patterns of errors in our model indicate that approaches using BERT may solve a certain kind of extraction-based question answering problem [11], but perform weaker when abstract legal concepts and reasoning are necessary. We are considering integrating some legal domain knowledge with our approach as a mean to improve the performance of the model next year.

7   Conclusion

What we contributed to a knowledge base was to combine <t2> s with both articles listed in <t1> s and articles not listed in <t1> s as continuous strings as our samples. In this way, the difficult pairing task has been transformed into a simpler classification task, while producing a sufficient number of samples for training. Next, we used three BERT-based models to solve binary questions in order to achieve more stable performance.

Our BERT-based ensemble model received the best score in Task 3, but it did not perform as well in Task 4. A direct and short answer was that BERT was not good enough at the yes/no questions [9], not to mention legal-related complex ones. Adding some rule-based models can perhaps improve the performance.

Acknowledgments. This work was financially supported by: Hsuan-Lei Shao, "From Knowledge Genealogy to Knowledge Map-China Studies in Big Data and Machine Learning" (MOST 107-2410-H-003 -058 -MY3), Sieh-Chuen Huang, Center for Research in Econometric Theory and Applications (Grant no. NTU-110L900203) from The Featured Areas Research Center Program within the framework of the Higher Education Sprout Project by the Ministry of Education (MOE) and Ministry of Science and Technology (MOST 109-2634-F-002-045) in Taiwan.

References

1. Rabelo, J., Kim, M.-Y., Goebel, R., Yoshioka, M., Kano, Y., Satoh, K.: A summary of the COLIEE 2019 competition. In: Sakamoto, M., Okazaki, N., Mineshima, K., Satoh, K. (eds.) JSAI-isAI 2019. LNCS (LNAI), vol. 12331, pp. 34–49. Springer, Cham (2020). https://doi.org/10.1007/978-3-030-58790-1_3
2. Yoshioka, M., Kano, Y., Kiyota, N., Satoh, K.: Overview of Japanese statute law retrieval and entailment task at COLIEE-2018. In: The Proceedings of the 12th International Workshop on Juris-Informatics (JURISIN 2018), pp. 117–128. The Japanese Society of Artificial Intelligence (2018)

3. Kano, Y., et al.: COLIEE-2018: evaluation of the competition on legal information extraction and entailment. In: Kojima, K., Sakamoto, M., Mineshima, K., Satoh, K. (eds.) JSAI-isAI 2018. LNCS (LNAI), vol. 11717, pp. 177–192. Springer, Cham (2019). https://doi.org/10.1007/978-3-030-31605-1_14

4. COLIEE organizer. COLIEE-2020. https://sites.ualberta.ca/~rabelo/COLIEE2020/

5. Cl-tohoku, BERT-base_mecab-ipadic-char-4k_whole-word-mask. https://github.com/cl-tohoku/bert-japanese

6. Alinear-corp, albert-japanese. https://github.com/alinear-corp/albert-japanese

7. Kingma, D.P., Ba, J.: Adam: a method for stochastic optimization. arXiv preprint arXiv:1412.6980 (2014)

8. Devlin, J., Chang, M.W., Lee, K., Toutanova, K.: BERT: pre-training of deep bidirectional transformers for language understanding. arXiv preprint arXiv:1810.04805 (2018)

9. Clark, C., Lee, K., Chang, M.W., Kwiatkowski, T., Collins, M., Toutanova, K.: BoolQ: exploring the surprising difficulty of natural yes/no questions. arXiv preprint arXiv:1905.10044 (2019)

10. Barskar, R., Ahmed, G., Barskar, N.: An approach for extracting exact answers to question answering (QA) system for English sentences. Procedia Eng. **30**, 1187–1194 (2012). https://doi.org/10.1016/j.proeng.2012.01.979

11. Li, X., et al.: Entity-relation extraction as multi-turn question answering. arXiv preprint arXiv:1905.05529 (2019)

12. Rabelo, J., Kim, M.Y., Goebel, R., Yoshioka, M., Kano, Y., Satoh, K.: COLIEE 2020: methods for legal document retrieval and entailment. In: Proceedings of the International Workshop on Juris-Informatics 2020 (JURISIN 2020), pp. 114–127 (2020)

The Application of Text Entailment Techniques in COLIEE 2020

Juliano Rabelo[1,3], Mi-Young Kim[1,2]([✉]), and Randy Goebel[1,3]

[1] Alberta Machine Intelligence Institute, University of Alberta, Edmonton, Canada
{rabelo,miyoung2,rgoebel}@ualberta.ca
[2] Department of Science, Augustana Faculty, University of Alberta, Edmonton, Canada
[3] Department of Computing Science, University of Alberta, Edmonton, Canada

Abstract. We develop a method to identify entailment relationships in the texts of case law documents, in the context of two tasks of the Competition on Legal Information Extraction and Entailment (COLIEE 2020). The first task consists in, given a 1) base case, 2) a text fragment from that base case, and 3) the list of paragraphs from a noticed case, identify which of those paragraphs entail the given text fragment. For that problem, we apply a combination of transformer-based and textual similarity techniques. The second task consists in identifying entailment relationships between yes/no questions extracted from the Japanese law bar exam and paragraphs extracted from the Japanese statute legislation. Our approach is to first define a set of classes of textual entailment that cover our analysis of the statute law data, and then implement a pre-processing step to construct the statute law-specific entailment types before exploiting them with deep learning.

Keywords: Legal textual entailment · Binary classification · Imbalanced datasets

1 Introduction

Tools to help legal professionals handling the large volume of legal documents are becoming more and more necessary. The volume of information produced in the legal sector by its many actors (such as law firms, law courts, independent attorneys, legislators, and many other sources) is overwhelming. To help build a legal research community, COLIEE was created, and focuses on four specific problems in the legal domain: case law retrieval, case law entailment, statute law retrieval and statute law entailment. In this paper, we provide details of our approaches for the two entailment tasks.

Initial techniques for open-domain textual entailment focused on shallow text features, and has currently evolved to the usage of word embeddings, logical models and machine learning in general. The current state of the art, especially

© Springer Nature Switzerland AG 2021
N. Okazaki et al. (Eds.): JSAI-isAI 2020 Workshops, LNAI 12758, pp. 240–253, 2021.
https://doi.org/10.1007/978-3-030-79942-7_16

for problems which have access to enough labelled data, rely on deep learning based approaches (more notably those based on transformer methods), which have shown very good results in a wide range of textual processing benchmarks, including benchmarks specific to entailment tasks.

Our method for the task of case law entailment presented builds on our methods of the past two editions [26, 27]: it combines similarity based features, transformer methods and a simple post processing technique based on *a priori* probabilities. For similarity calculations, we now used two methods: a sentence distributed vector representation and a simple bag of words representation using noun phrases as tokens. The cosine measure was used to calculate a similarity between documents, represented as described above.

The transformer methods relied on the BERT framework [10]: one by fine tuning, and another one leveraging two BERT models fine tuned on a generic entailment data set, then another that applied zero-shot techniques by using BERT, but fine tuned for paraphrase detection. We also used data augmentation techniques based on back translation to increase the size of the training data.

The rest of this paper is organized as follows: in Sect. 2 we briefly review open the literature background on domain textual entailment and the special cases of case law entailment and statute law entailment. Section 3 describes our approaches to both case law and statute law entailment tasks in COLIEE 2020. Section 4 describes our experiments with an analysis of the results. Section 5 concludes the paper and comments on future work.

2   Related Work

Textual entailment is a logic task in which the goal is to determine whether one sentence can be inferred from another. In COLIEE, teams are challenged with the task of classifying two case law textual fragments possessing a "positive entailment" relationship or not (i.e., either they have "positive entailment" or "neutral entailment"). The statute law entailment task (Task 4) in COLIEE is the same: the participants are required to decide if a query is entailed from the relevant civil law articles or not.

In the following subsections, we will discuss related research on textual entailment in general and techniques developed specifically for case law entailment.

2.1   Open-Domain Textual Entailment

Textual entailment is useful as a task per se or as a component in larger applications. For example, question-answering systems may apply textual entailment techniques to identify an answer from previously stored databases [3]. Textual entailment may also be used to enhance document summarization (e.g., to measure sentence connectivity or as additional features to summary generation [21]). Recently increased interest on textual entailment has motivated the creation of public benchmarks to evaluate such systems (e.g., [4, 31]).

Early approaches for open-domain textual entailment relied heavily on exploiting surface syntax or lexical relationships, and then a wide range of tools, including word embeddings, logical models, graphical models, rule systems and machine learning [1]. A modern research trend for open-domain textual entailment is an application of general deep learning models, such as ELMo [25], BERT [10] and ULMFit [14].

These methods build on the approach introduced in [9], which showed how to improve document classification performance by using unsupervised pre-training of an LSTM [13] followed by supervised fine-tuning for specific downstream tasks. The pre-training is done on very large datasets, which do not need to be labeled and are intended to capture general language knowledge (usually, the pre-training is considered as a language modeling task). Subsequently, supervised learning is used as a fine-tuning step, thus using a significantly smaller labeled dataset, aiming at adjusting the weights of the final layers of the model and making it suitable for the specific task. These models have achieved impressive results in a wide range of publicly available benchmarks of different common natural language tasks, such as RACE (reading comprehension) [17], COPA (common sense reasoning) [30] and RTE (textual entailment) [8].

2.2   Case Law Textual Entailment

The specific task of assessing textual entailment for case law documents is quite new. The first COLIEE edition which included this task was in 2018 [15]. Chen et al. [7] proposed the application of association rules for the problem. They applied a machine learning-based model using Word2Vec embeddings [22] and Doc2Vec [18] as features. This approach has two main problems: the lack of sufficient training data to make the models converge and generalize, and the computational cost of training, which increases exponentially on the size of the dataset. To overcome that issue, they proposed two association rule models: (1) the basic association rule model, which considers only the similarity between the source document and the target document, and (2) the co-occurrence association rule model, which uses a relevance dictionary in addition to the basic model. Another approach [26] worth mentioning approached the task as a binary classification problem, and built feature vectors comprised of the measures of similarity between the candidate paragraph and (1) the entailed fragment of the base case, (2) the base case summary and (3) the base case paragraphs (actually a histogram of the similarities between each candidate paragraph and all paragraphs from the base case). Those feature vectors are used as input to a Random Forest [5] classifier. To overcome the problem of severe data imbalance in the dataset, the dominant class was under-sampled and the rarer class was over-sampled by SMOTE sample synthesis [6]. In [27], the method for case law entailment combines similarity based features which rely on multi-word tokens instead of single words, and exploits the BERT framework [10], fine-tuned to the task of case law entailment on the provided training dataset.

2.3   Statute Law Textual Entailment

In addition to the case law entailment task, past editions of COLIEE included a task on statute law entailment, whose goal is to identify entailment relationships between Japanese bar exam questions and relevant legal statute articles. The best performance on that task for all past COLIEE editions has been achieved by a combination of legal information retrieval and textual entailment approach, which exploits semantic information using a logic-based representation [16]. In that approach, a meaning extraction process uses a selection of features based on a kind of paraphrase, coupled with a condition/conclusion/exception analysis of articles and queries, while additionally exploiting negation patterns extracted from the articles. The logic-based representation is constructed by a semantic analysis, which is used to classify questions according to their difficulty level, by analyzing the logic representation. If a question is in the "easy" category, the entailment answer is obtained in a straightforward manner from the logic representation; otherwise, an unsupervised learning method is applied.

3   Text Entailment in COLIEE 2020

3.1   Case Law Entailment

The task of case law entailment in COLIEE may be defined as follows: given a base case b and one fragment of text f contained within b, and a second case r which is relevant in respect to b, the task consists in determining which paragraph(s) of r entail f. More formally, given b, f and r as above (r represented by its paragraphs $P = \{p_1, p_2, ..., p_n\}$), we need to find the set $E = \{p_1, p_2, ..., p_m \mid p_i \in P\}$ where $entails(p_i, f)$ denotes a relationship which is true when $p_i \in P$ entails the fragment f.

We frame that problem as a binary classification problem, by considering each paragraph p_i in r an entailment candidate, which must then be classified as entailing f or not. To do so, we created a classifier which processes each pair (p_i, f) with the following features:

- Score from a BERT model fine-tuned with the COLIEE training data;
- Scores from BART and Roberta (also transformer-based models) fine-tuned to a different text entailment dataset;
- Score from a transformer-based model fine-tuned for paraphrase detection;
- Distance-based features between embedding representations of p_i and f;
- Distance-based features between bag of words representations of p_i and f which only take into consideration noun phrases.

We applied different transformer based models[1] in an attempt to cover different challenges posed by the samples in the dataset. The main model is of course the BERT model fine tuned on the competition data, but we also figured

---

[1] The transformer models used in our experiments were implemented by Hugging-Face.co.

that similar models (such as BART and Roberta) fine tuned on more general text entailment dataset could provide reasonable results in a legal text entailment competition. By using their scores as features for a separate classifier, we hoped to be able to correctly classify cases that would be missed by one specific classifier used in isolation.

These features are then fed to a Random Forest classifier, which provides the final classification score for each (p_i, f). Those scores are post processed before the final output is produced[2]. Details on each one of these components will be provided in the next subsections. To give an idea of each component importance, we calculated the individual scores on the validation dataset for each one, assuming simple heuristics. The results are shown on Table 1:

Table 1. Results for each task 2 component in the validation dataset

Component	Heuristic	Precision	Recall	F1
BERT	Model output	0.5789	0.3666	0.4489
BART	Entail score > Contradiction score	0.0545	0.7272	0.1015
Roberta	Entail score > Contradiction score	0.0661	0.6711	0.1203
Paraphrase	Score > 0.5	0.5882	0.1069	0.1809
Distance based	Distance > 0.5	0.6153	0.1283	0.2123

BERT Model Fine-Tuned on the COLIEE Training Data. The main component of our method applies BERT [10] by fine tuning it on the provided traning dataset. BERT is a framework designed to pre-train deep bidirectional representations by jointly conditioning on both left and right context in all layers. This leads to pre-trained representations which can be fine-tuned with only one additional output layer on downstream tasks, such as question answering, language inference and textual entailment, but without requiring task-specific modifications. BERT has achieved impressive results on well-known benchmarks such as GLUE [31], MultiNLI [32] and MRPC [11].

We used a BERT model pre-trained on a large (general purpose) dataset (the goal being make it acquire general language "knowledge"[3]) which can be fine-tuned on smaller, specific datasets (the goal being to make it learn how to combine the previously acquired knowledge in a specific scenario). This makes BERT a good fit for this task, since we do not have a large dataset available

---

[2] We also tried data augmentation to generate more training samples, but due to computing and time constraints we could not generate all features for the augmented dataset and had to combine the output of the BERT model fine-tuned on that augmented dataset with the original model through simple heuristic rules.

[3] Calling the kind of representations learned by BERT (or any other transformer based model) "knowledge" is a stretch and even some sort of anthropomorphization but, well, it seems to be appropriate in the context of machine "learning".

for training the model[4]. Our BERT model is then fine-tuned on the COLIEE training dataset, receiving as inputs pairs of entailment fragment f and candidate paragraph p_i, and outputting whether there is an entailment relationship or not.

Transformer Models Fine-Tuned for Text Entailment on Different Datasets. Even if one cannot immediately apply a general text entailment classifier in COLIEE (recall the difference between COLIEE's case law entailment task and the usual text entailment tasks, as explained in Sect. 2), it is possible to easily adapt a system able to identify the 3 usual entailment classes to the COLIEE task. One immediate approach would be to consider contradiction and neutral to represent the "not entailment" class and combine those scores somehow (e.g., averaging or summing them up). In our approach, we used the 3 scores output by the entailment model (actually, since the models we used apply a softmax layer on its outputs, the scores sum up to 1 for each sample, so we discard the neutral score and keep the entailment and contradict scores, since for machine learning purposes the neutral score would be redundant). We used two transformer based models which were fine tuned on the MultiNLI dataset:

- one based on BART [19], which uses a standard seq2seq architecture with a bidirectional encoder (like BERT [10]) and a left-to-right decoder (like GPT [28]). BART is commonly used for text generation text but also presents good results for text "comprehension" tasks.
- another one based on RoBERTa [20], which builds on BERT and modifies key hyperparameters, removing the next-sentence pretraining objective and training with much larger mini-batches and learning rates.

BERT Model for Paraphrase Detection. A BERT model fine tuned on the MRPC paraphrase detection dataset [11], under the assumption that sometimes an entailment relationship consists of paraphrasing.

Distance-Based Features Between Sentence Embedding Representations. Distributed vector representations [22] are a great tool to represent semantics of isolated words. In [26], we applied those word embeddings to larger text fragments by using the Word Mover's Distance, but that is quite expensive and does not capture the full semantics of those larger text fragments. In an attempt to generate a more accurate representation for our inputs f and p_i, we applied a sentence embedding technique, which creates distributed vector representations for sentences, thus theoretically capturing their semantics more appropriately. To apply the sentence embedding model, we first segmented the input text fragments into sentences and calculated the cosine distances [2] between each sentence from f and p_i. Out of that set of measurements, we

---

[4] As it is explained before, we tried to enlarge the training dataset through data augmentation techniques, since even though BERT is capable of grasping part of the correlations from the training dataset, it can certainly benefit from larger datasets.

extracted some distance based statistics (average, standard deviation, minimum and maximum distances), which were then used as features in the final classifier.

Distance-Based Features Considering only Noun Phrases. A classic technique for measuring similarity between documents is the representation of the text as a bag of words, and then calculating the cosine distance between those document representations in the vector space [2]. Often the text tokenization considers each word as a token (i.e., punctuation marks and spaces are seen as token delimiters), thus completely neglecting the possibility that sentences formed by the same words in different order may have different meanings. n-grams is one of the usual techniques which can be used to tackle that problem, but here we experimented with a different option: we detect the noun phrases[5] and use those as tokens. Then we created a bag of words representation of the entailed fragment f and each paragraph p_i then calculated the distance between the text fragments using the cosine distance. The similarity score generated by this process is used as a feature in the end Random Forest classifier.

Data Augmentation. Being aware that the provided training data in COLIEE is not large enough to satisfactorily inform transformer-based models, we performed data augmentation by applying back translation on the training dataset using two separate pipelines with different intermediate languages. The first pipeline used a convolutional based model [12] for English $\rightarrow$ German $\rightarrow$ English translation. The second one applied a transformer based model [23] for back translating with Russian as the intermediate language. However, due to time constraints, we could not generate all features for the augmented dataset. Thus, the produced BERT model fine-tuned on the augmented training dataset and the model which combined all the features trained on the original training dataset were applied separately to the test dataset. We changed the response of the original model by applying simple heuristic rules, which consists of changing the score produced by the full featured model if it was not too high (<0.8) and the corresponding score produced by the augmented BERT model was very high (>0.9). Our hypothesis was that we could take advantage of the scores produced by a separate model when that model presented a high confidence and the original model was not too sure.

Final Classifier and Post-processing. At the end of the pipeline, all the calculated scores are used as features and fed to a Random Forest [5] classifier. The confidence score output by this classifier is then post processed as such: by analyzing the *a priori* probabilities of the dataset, we see that the majority of the cases have exactly one entailing paragraph among all candidates. So we

---

[5] The actual implementation detects noun chunks, a good enough approximation. See https://spacy.io/ for more details.

establish that, for each case, we will return at least one candidate, even if its confidence score is lower than the threshold. Moreover, we also establish that at most 2 answers should be returned for each case, no matter how many candidates have confidence scores higher than the threshold.

3.2   Statute Law Entailment

Textual entailment, which is sometimes called Natural Language Inference (NLI), is an important problem in language understanding, and we need a system that can learn various semantic fragments, e.g., Boolean coordination, quantification, conditionals, and monotonicity reasoning. [29] indicated that the state-of-the-art models, including BERT, that are pre-trained on existing NLI benchmark datasets perform poorly on these semantic fragments, even though these phenomena are central to the general problem of natural language inference.

Table 2. NLI types in the statute law entailment

Type	Civil law article	Query	
Example case	If a manager engages in benevolent intervention in another's business in order to allow a principal to escape imminent danger to the principal's person, reputation, or property, the manager is not liable to compensate...(omitted)	In cases where an individual rescues another person from getting hit by a car by pushing that person out of the way, causing the person's luxury kimono to get dirty, the rescuer does not have to compensate damages for the kimono	Y
Background knowledge required	A juridical act performed by an adult ward is voidable; provided, however, that this does not apply to the purchase of daily necessities or to any other act involved in day-to-day life	In cases where an adult ward receives the gift of a building, the adult ward cannot rescind the relevant gift contract	N
New legal term	If the land and a building on that land belong to the same owner, a mortgage is created with respect to that land or building, and the enforcement of that mortgage causes them to belong to different owners, it is deemed that a superficies has been created with respect to that building. In this case, the rent is fixed by the court at the request of the parties	Statutory real rights granted by way of security exist, but statutory usufructuary rights do not exist	N
'only if' condition	The principal secured by a revolving mortgage is crystallized in the following cases:...(omitted)... provided, however, that this provision applies only if the commencement of either auction procedures or execution procedures against earnings from immovable collateral, or an attachment has been effected	Even if procedures for auctions petitioned by a lower rank security interest holder have begun, since the first rank -revolving mortgagee has priority over the lower rank security interest holder regarding selection of the timing of the auction, the first rank revolving mortgagee can stop the auction procedures without fixing the principal	N

(*continued*)

Table 2. (*continued*)

Type	Civil law article	Query	
Connection to the previous paragraph	In order to effect an assignment under the provisions of the preceding paragraph, the approval of the person that holds the rights for which that revolving mortgage is the subject matter must be obtained	Since a revolving mortgage before the fixing of principal can be described as a right which dominates the value of the maximum amount detached from the secured claim, it can be transferred in whole or in part, but since the obligor and the secured claim may change, approval must be obtained from the revolving mortgagor	Y
Exceptional case	...(omitted) provided, however, that this does not apply if the third party knew or did not know due to negligence that the other person has not been granted the authority to represent	a person who has manifested to a third party that he/she has granted certain authority of agency to other person(s) shall be relieved of his/her liability of apparent authority, if there is any proof that the third party knew or was negligent that the other person had not been granted authority of agency	Y
Addition of conditional	A juridical act performed by an adult ward is voidable; provided, however, that this does not apply to the purchase of daily necessities or to any other act involved in day-to-day life	In cases when the adult ward performs juristic acts other than acts related to everyday life, even if the adult ward obtains approval from the guardian of the adult in advance for the relevant juristic act, the adult ward can rescindthe juristic act	Y
Relations between new entities	Except in cases prescribed in Article 438, Article 439, paragraph (1), and the preceding Article, any circumstances which have arisen with respect to one of the joint and several obligors is not effective in relation to other joint and several obligors	When jointly and severally liable guarantor person C acknowledges a claim from person A to person B before the prescription period has elapsed, the effect of interruption of prescription also affects main obligor person B	N
Reference to other articles	Except in cases prescribed in Articles 438, Article 439, paragraph (1), and the preceding Article, any circumstances which have arisen with respect to one of the joint and several obligors is not effective in relation to other joint and several obligors	When jointly and severally liable guarantor person C acknowledges a claim from person A to person B before the prescription period has elapsed, the effect of interruption of prescription also affects main obligor person B	N
Different condition, same conclusion	A person that commences the possession of movables peacefully and openly by a transactional act acquires the rights that are exercised with respect to the movables immediately if the person possesses it in good faith and without negligence	A seller that cancelled a movable sale contract on the basis of duress can demand return of the movable based on its ownership from the person who bought the movable from the buyer prior to the cancellation without knowledge or any negligence	N

In addition to these phenomena, we have found more NLI types in the statute law textual entailment dataset. Some of the semantic phenomena came from the characteristics of the law field. Table 2 shows the category of the found semantic fragments in statute law NLI.

According to the types of the NLI for statute law textual entailment, as shown in Table 2, we need to recognize condition, conclusion, and exceptional cases. Additionally, we need to re-generate the conclusion of the exceptional case by taking the negation of the conclusion of the general case. References to other articles or previous paragraphs also need to be resolved.

To solve the problem of the small training data size, we use the SNLI[6] dataset, a standard benchmark data in NLI. Here, we see another challenge: while the SNLI dataset has one sentence for each premise and hypothesis, our COLIEE dataset has different lengths between the two input texts: premise (statute law, here relevant civil law article) and hypothesis (query). While a query usually consists of one sentence, a civil law article consists of many paragraphs. Even some queries have multiple civil law articles as input. This unbalanced length can be an issue when we use an attention model to align between the two inputs. To make the alignment easier, we choose the most relevant sentence with the query amongst many sentences and paragraphs in the relevant civil law articles.

To help with the detection of various NLI types in statute law textual entailment, we use the following pre-processing step:

(1) Split a civil law piece into condition, conclusion and exceptional case by [16].
(2) Referring to preceding paragraphs or cases of other articles is replaced by the corresponding paragraphs or case descriptions in other articles.
(3) Re-generate a sentence for the exceptional case by adding the negated conclusion of the general case.
(4) Extract only one sentence relevant to a query that shares the most terms with the query.

We submitted the results of following three models in COLIEE 2020:

(1) a decomposable attention model [24], which is a simple neural architecture for natural language inference. This model is decomposing a problem into sub-problems that can be solved separately. The approach consists of the 'Attend', 'Compare', and 'Aggregate', and outperformed considerably more complex neural methods aiming for text understanding.
(2) RoBERTa, a robustly optimized BERT pretraining approach [20]. This model modified the original BERT to measure the impact of many key hyperparameters and training data size. Their modifications are (a) training the model longer, with bigger batches, over more data, (b) removing the next sentence prediction objective, (c) training on loner sequences, and (d) dynamically changing the masking pattern applied to the training data. This model established a new state-of-the-art on NLI over the original BERT.
(3) the use of [16]'s approach, which showed the best performance in COLIEE 2019.

---

[6] https://nlp.stanford.edu/projects/snli/.

4 Results

4.1 Case Law Entailment

The official COLIEE 2020 results for this task are shown in Table 3. Our two best submissions (0.45 and 0.51 f1 scores) were based on our fine tuned BERT model and use the full set of additional features. The only difference between them is the hyperparameters used while training the BERT model: the first one was trained for 5 epochs and the second one for 3 epochs. Our worst submission (f1 score of 0.46) consists of the BERT model trained for 5 epochs combined with a separated BERT model fine tuned for 1 epoch on the augmented training dataset, as explained in Sect. 3.1. As it can be seen from Table 3, the applied heuristics actually compromised model performance.

Table 3. Official COLIEE 2020 results on the test dataset.

Team	F1	Team	F1	Team	F1	Team	F1	Team	F1	Team	F1
JNLP	0.6753	JNLP	0.6094	iiest	0.5867	TLIR	0.5495	iiest	0.5067	TR	0.4018
JNLP	0.6222	taxi	0.5992	iiest	0.5867	TLIR	0.5428	**UA**	**0.4647**	DACCO	0.0622
taxi	0.6180	taxi	0.5917	cyber	0.5837	**UA**	**0.5425**	TR	0.4107		
TLIR	0.6154	cyber	0.5897	cyber	0.5600	**UA**	**0.5179**	TR	0.4107		

4.2 Statute Law Entailment

Table 4 shows the comparison of the accuracy between applying the pre-processing step and without the pre-processing step. For this experiment, we used 70 pairs out of the training dataset as the validation data. Through this result, we can conclude that applying the pre-processing step is helpful improving the NLI performance in the statute law entailment.

Table 4. Comparison of accuracy according to the usage of a pre-processing step

	Model	Validation accuracy
Without using our pre-processing step	Attention	0.486
	RoBERTa	0.457
Using our pre-processing step	Attention	0.657
	RoBERTa	0.629

In Task 4 of COLIEE 2020, the training data consists of 13 xml files with 696 pairs of <query, relevant civil law article(s)>, and the test data consists of 112 pairs. Table 5 shows the results of the statute law entailment competition. Our two models (attention and RoBERTa) were ranked No. 2, and the third model was ranked No. 9 amongst the 30 submissions.

Table 5. Official COLIEE 2020 results on Task4

Team	Acc.	Team	Acc.	Team	Acc.
JNLP.BERTLaw	0.7232	linearsvm.HONto	0.5625	CUGIVEN	0.5179
TRC3mt	0.6250	JNLP.BERT	0.5625	CUPLUS	0.5179
TRC3t5	0.6250	KIS	0.5625	linearsvm-no-ngram-nofuzz.HONto	0.5089
UA-attention-final	0.6250	linearsvm-no-ngram.HONto	0.5536	POS-simneg.OvGU	0.5089
UA-roberta-final	0.6250	JNLP.TfidfBERT	0.5536	taxi-le-bigru	0.5089
KIS_2	0.6161	KIS_3	0.5446	TRC3A	0.5000
llntu	0.6161	sim_neg.OvGU	0.5446	UEC2	0.4911
cyber	0.6161	UEC1	0.5446	baseline-attention.OvGU	0.4821
UA_structure	0.6071	taxi_BERTXGB	0.5357	AUT99-BERT-MatchPyramid	0.4643
GK_NLP	0.5625	UECplus	0.5357	AUT99-LSTM-CNN-Attention	0.4464

5   Conclusions

We have described our approach for two complex textual entailment tasks on the domain of legal documents: case law and statute law entailment. For case law entailment, our method relied on the usage of transformer models. The most relevant component was the one fine tuned on the training dataset provided in the competition. The other components in isolation presented lower scores, but the final f1 score from the combined components was lower than expected, probably because the components where not complementary. For statute law entailment, our pre-processing step considering the NLI types in the statute law improved the performance and our submission results were ranked No. 2.

We plan to extend this work by performing the following actions:

- Train BERT using a larger case law dataset and check whether it is capable of grasping law-related knowledge. There are publicly available case law corpus (e.g., Canadian Supreme Court Reports) which can be used as input;
- Fine tuning the framework with a larger dataset of case law entailment would be probably more effective, but there are not other case law entailment datasets known to the authors. We will generate such a dataset by applying simple heuristics or semiautomatic approaches on case law documents;
- Given the golden labels of the official COLIEE test dataset, perform an error analysis to identify the characteristics of the errors and if the different components are complementary or redundant;
- Use back translation fully integrated into the final model.

Acknowledgements. This research was supported by Alberta Machine Intelligence Institute (AMII), and would not be possible without the significant support of Colin Lachance from vLex and Compass Law, and the guidance of Jimoh Ovbiagele of Ross Intelligence and Young-Yik Rhim of Intellicon.

References

1. Androutsopoulos, I., Malakasiotis, P.: A survey of paraphrasing and textual entailment methods. CoRR abs/0912.3747 (2009). http://arxiv.org/abs/0912.3747
2. Baeza-Yates, R.A., Ribeiro-Neto, B.: Modern Information Retrieval. Addison-Wesley Longman Publishing Co. Inc., Boston (1999)
3. Ben Abacha, A., Demner-Fushman, D.: A question-entailment approach to question answering. CoRR abs/1901.08079 (2019). http://arxiv.org/abs/1901.08079
4. Bowman, S.R., Angeli, G., Potts, C., Manning, C.D.: A large annotated corpus for learning natural language inference. In: Proceedings of the Conference on Empirical Methods in Natural Language Processing. ACL (2015)
5. Breiman, L.: Random forests. Mach. Learn. **45**(1), 5–32 (2001)
6. Chawla, N.V., Bowyer, K.W., Hall, L.O., Kegelmeyer, W.P.: SMOTE: synthetic minority over-sampling technique. J. Artif. Int. Res. **16**(1), 321–357 (2002)
7. Chen, Y., Zhou, Y., Lu, Z., Sun, H., Yang, W.: Legal information retrieval by association rules. In: Twelfth International Workshop on Juris-Informatics (2018)
8. Dagan, I., Glickman, O., Magnini, B.: The PASCAL recognising textual entailment challenge. In: Quiñonero-Candela, J., Dagan, I., Magnini, B., d'Alché-Buc, F. (eds.) MLCW 2005. LNCS (LNAI), vol. 3944, pp. 177–190. Springer, Heidelberg (2006). https://doi.org/10.1007/11736790_9
9. Dai, A.M., Le, Q.V.: Semi-supervised sequence learning. CoRR (2015)
10. Devlin, J., Chang, M., Lee, K., Toutanova, K.: BERT: pre-training of deep bidirectional transformers for language understanding. CoRR abs/1810.04805 (2018)
11. Dolan, W.B., Brockett, C.: Automatically constructing a corpus of sentential paraphrases. In: Proceedings of the 3rd International Workshop on Paraphrasing (2005)
12. Gehring, J., Auli, M., Grangier, D., Yarats, D., Dauphin, Y.N.: Convolutional sequence to sequence learning. CoRR abs/1705.03122 (2017)
13. Hochreiter, S., Schmidhuber, J.: Long short-term memory. Neural Comput. **9**(8), 1735–1780 (1997). https://doi.org/10.1162/neco.1997.9.8.1735
14. Howard, J., Ruder, S.: Fine-tuned language models for text classification. CoRR abs/1801.06146 (2018). http://arxiv.org/abs/1801.06146
15. Kano, Y., et al.: COLIEE-2018: evaluation of the competition on legal information extraction and entailment. In: 12th International Workshop on Juris-Informatics (2018)
16. Kim, M.Y., Goebel, R.: Two-step cascaded textual entailment for legal bar exam question answering. In: Proceedings of the 16th Edition of the International Conference on Artificial Intelligence and Law, pp. 283–290. ACM, New York (2017)
17. Lai, G., Xie, Q., Liu, H., Yang, Y., Hovy, E.H.: RACE: large-scale reading comprehension dataset from examinations. CoRR abs/1704.04683 (2017)
18. Le, Q.V., Mikolov, T.: Distributed representations of sentences and documents. CoRR abs/1405.4053 (2014)
19. Lewis, M., et al.: BART: denoising sequence-to-sequence pre-training for natural language generation, translation, and comprehension (2019)
20. Liu, Y., et al.: Roberta: a robustly optimized BERT pretraining approach (2019)
21. Lloret, E., Ferrández, Ó., Muñoz, R., Palomar, M.: A text summarization approach under the influence of textual entailment. In: NLPCS - 5th International Workshop on Natural Language Processing and Cognitive Science, pp. 22–31, January 2008
22. Mikolov, T., Sutskever, I., Chen, K., Corrado, G., Dean, J.: Distributed representations of words and phrases and their compositionality. CoRR (2013)

23. Ng, N., Yee, K., Baevski, A., Ott, M., Auli, M., Edunov, S.: Facebook fair's WMT19 news translation task submission. CoRR abs/1907.06616 (2019)
24. Parikh, A.P., Töckström, O., Das, D., Uszkoreit, J.: A decomposable attention model for natural language inference. In: Proceedings of EMNLP, pp. 2249–2255 (2016)
25. Peters, M.E., et al.: Deep contextualized word representations. In: Proceedings of NAACL (2018)
26. Rabelo, J., Kim, M.Y., Babiker, H., Goebel, R., Farruque, N.: Legal information extraction and entailment for statute law and case law. In: Twelfth International Workshop on Juris-Informatics (JURISIN) (2018)
27. Rabelo, J., Kim, M.Y., Goebel, R.: Combining similarity and transformer methods for case law entailment. In: Proceedings of the Seventeenth International Conference on Artificial Intelligence and Law, ICAIL 2019, pp. 290–296. Association for Computing Machinery, New York (2019)
28. Radford, A., Wu, J., Child, R., Luan, D., Amodei, D., Sutskever, I.: Language models are unsupervised multitask learners (2018)
29. Richardson, K., Hu, H., Moss, L., Sabharwal, A.: Probing natural language inference models through semantic fragments. In: Proceedings of AAAI, pp. 8713–8721 (2020)
30. Roemmele, M., Bejan, C., Gordon, A.: Choice of plausible alternatives: an evaluation of commonsense causal reasoning. In: AAAI Spring Symposium Series (2011)
31. Wang, A., Singh, A., Michael, J., Hill, F., Levy, O., Bowman, S.R.: GLUE: a multi-task benchmark and analysis platform for natural language understanding. CoRR abs/1804.07461 (2018). http://arxiv.org/abs/1804.07461
32. Williams, A., Nangia, N., Bowman, S.R.: A broad-coverage challenge corpus for sentence understanding through inference. CoRR abs/1704.05426 (2017)

Information Extraction/Entailment of Common Law and Civil Code

John Hudzina(✉) ⒾD, Kanika Madan ⒾD, Dhivya Chinnappa ⒾD,
Jinane Harmouche ⒾD, Hiroko Bretz ⒾD, Andrew Vold ⒾD, and Frank Schilder ⒾD

Center for AI and Cognitive Computing, Thomson Reuters, Eagan, USA
`john.hudzina@thomsonreuters.com`
`https://www.thomsonreuters.com/en/artificial-intelligence.html`

Abstract. With the recent advancements in machine learning models, we have seen improvements in Natural Language Inference (NLI) tasks, but legal entailment has been challenging, particularly for supervised approaches. In this paper, we evaluate different approaches on handling entailment tasks for small domain-specific data sets provided in the Competition on Legal Information Extraction/Entailment (COLIEE). This year COLIEE had four tasks, which focused on legal information processing and finding textual entailment on legal data. We participated in all the four tasks this year, and evaluated different kinds of approaches, including classification, ranking, and transfer learning approaches against the entailment tasks. In some of the tasks, we achieved competitive results when compared to simpler rule-based approaches, which so far have dominated the competition for the last six years.

Keywords: Legal AI · Information retrieval · Textual entailment · Natural language processing · Multi-task learning · Transfer learning

1 Introduction

The Competition on Legal Information Extraction/Entailment (COLIEE) has run a challenge for extraction and entailment since 2014 that examines the decision process for both case-based and statute-based legal systems. We explored several approaches for information extraction and text entailment related to both common law and civil code. In general, both legal systems provide a rationale for a decision. For common law, judges base legal decisions on past precedents via a process known as *stare decisis*. For civil code, judges base legal decisions on applying one or more statutes to a given situation without altering the central legal issue, i.e., *mutatis mutandis*.

For each legal system, COLIEE lays out a two-step process. The first step *retrieves* the relevant cases or statutes to apply to a decision. Once the system discovers the relevant text, the second step determine if the relevant text supports or *entails* the decision. Our approach for each step is further described in the following sections:

© Springer Nature Switzerland AG 2021
N. Okazaki et al. (Eds.): JSAI-isAI 2020 Workshops, LNAI 12758, pp. 254–268, 2021.
https://doi.org/10.1007/978-3-030-79942-7_17

- **Section** 2 - **Task 1:** Common Law Retrieval
- **Section** 3 - **Task 2:** Common Law Entailment
- **Section** 4 - **Task 3:** Civil Code Retrieval
- **Section** 5 - **Task 4:** Civil Code Entailment.

2   Task 1: The Legal Case Retrieval Task

The goal of Task 1 is to explore and evaluate legal document retrieval technologies that are both effective and reliable. The task investigates the performance of systems that search a set of case laws that support an unseen case law. In response to a query case, the task aims to return *supporting* cases in the given collection. A case is *supporting* to a query case if it supports the decision of the query case. In this task, the query case does not include the decision, because the goal is to determine how accurately a machine can capture decision-supporting cases for a new case (with no decision yet).

The corpus used for training is composed of case laws from the Federal Court of Canada. The training data contains query cases alongside a pool of case laws, and the gold *supporting cases*. Thus for a given case, the goal is to identify *supporting cases* from a pool of candidate cases. To first find out cases which are similar to the query case and to train our machine learning models, we start with a ranking approach, followed by a classification task. To identify *supporting cases* of a given query case, we first rank all the candidate cases based on their similarity to the base case. Then, depending on the rank a candidate case receives, we build classification models to identify the *supporting cases* from this ranked pool of candidate cases.

The training dataset consists of 520 query cases with 200 candidate cases per query case. The frequency of *supporting cases* against the number of base cases is depicted in Fig. 1. As we can see from the figure, there are 97 base cases with 1 *supporting case* and there is 1 base case with 31 *supporting cases*. We conduct experiments to choose the *supporting cases* by pairing each base case with the 200 associated candidate cases. Thus we work with 104,000 instances containing *supporting* and *unsupporting* cases. We observe that there are 2,680 (2.57%) *supporting* pairs and 101,320 *unsupporting* pairs in the dataset.

2.1   Experiments

To identify *supporting* pairs, we begin by ranking the candidate cases based on similarity scores and then conduct classification experiments based on the ranking. Thus our experiments include two tasks.

1. The ranking task
2. The classification task

We pre-processed each case document by removing stop words and punctuation. Each word in the case document is lowercased before undergoing any similarity calculation.

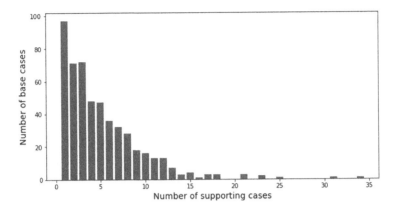

Fig. 1. Frequency of supporting cases vs. number of base cases

The Ranking Task: We calculated four similarity scores to rank the candidate cases. We used one or more of these ranking methods to identify the *supporting* cases.

1. **Jaccard similarity**: Jaccard similarity between the set of tokens in the base case and the set of tokens in each candidate case. Jaccard similarity is defined as the size of the intersection divided by the size of the union of the sample sets.
2. **BOW similarity**: Cosine similarity between the bag-of-words vector between the base case and each candidate case.
3. **GloVe embedding similarity**: Cosine similarity between the *average GloVe* [7] *embedding* between the base text and each candidate case. The *average GloVe embedding* is obtained by averaging the GloVe pretrained embedding of the most frequent 2,000 words from a case text.
4. **Word2Vec embedding similarity** is the cosine similarity between the *average word2vec* [3] *embedding* between the base text and each candidate case. The *average word2vec embedding* is obtained by averaging the google news pretrained word2vec embedding of the most frequent 2,000 words from a case text.

Table 1. Percentages of supporting cases distributed across ranks based on different methods for Task 1. The total number of supporting cases are 2,680.

Rank range	Method										
	GloVe	w2v	BOW	Jacc.	GloVe+ w2v	GloVe+ BOW	GloVe+ Jacc.	w2v+ BOW	w2v+ Jacc.	BOW+ Jacc.	All
≤50	66	72	10	84	70	7	77	10	78	19	64
>50 & <150	21	18	17	15	18	31	14	43	15	64	26
≥150	13	10	73	1	12	62	9	47	7	17	10

We ranked the candidate cases based on each of these scores and also by combining them. When combining two methods, we calculated the scores for ranking by adding the two similarity scores. Table 1 shows the range of ranks of *supporting* pairs based on one or more of the similarity scores. Our goal is to identify the methods that rank the *supporting* cases in the top. Clearly, despite being a simple method, Jaccard similarity ranks *supporting* cases on the top. Additionally, a combination of Jaccard similarity and Word2Vec embedding similarity, and Jaccard similarity and GloVe embedding similarity also ranks the *supporting* pairs at the top.

The Classification Task: We use this ranking approach to divide our dataset into subdatasets. We do so to group similar instances together. We believe that dividing the dataset based on the ranks would help the classifiers learn better in identifying the *supporting* cases.

We use the best performing similarity methods—methods with more *supporting* cases in the top 50—to split the dataset. Thus we conduct and present results by splitting the dataset into subdatsets using (i) Jaccard similarity, (ii) Jaccard similarity + Word2Vec embedding similarity, and (iii) Jaccard similarity + Glove embedding similarity.

Table 2. Results obtained in the development set over the subdatasets for Task 1 on the *supporting* cases.

Rank range	Method	Precision	Recall	F1-score
≤50	Jaccard	0.67	0.43	0.52
	Jaccard+w2v	0.68	0.41	0.51
	Jaccard+glove	0.68	0.42	0.52
>50 & <150	Jaccard	0.37	0.23	0.28
	Jaccard+wv2	0.72	0.18	0.29
	Jaccard+glove	0.72	0.12	0.20
≥150	Jaccard	0.33	0.06	0.10
	Jaccard+wv2	0.50	0.09	0.19
	Jaccard+glove	0.63	0.27	0.38

2.2   Results

First, we divide the dataset into three subdatasets based on the ranks (≤50, >50 & < 150, and ≥150) using each of the aforementioned chosen methods. Then we build classification models for each of the subdataset. We used all individual similarity scores, their combinational scores, and all ranks as features for the classifiers. We experimented with support vector machines(SVM), logistic regression and xgboost classifiers. We found that the Logistic regression models always performed worse than SVMs and xgboost classifiers, and hence based on our pilot experiments, we decided to work with xgboost classifiers as they were comparable to SVMs in performance but have a faster execution time. We created a 80/20 stratified split for training and development over each of the subdataset. The stratification ensures that the training set and the development set have the same distribution of labels (*supporting/unsupporting* cases). The results on the development set for each subdataset is presented in Table 2. The test predictions were obtained by ranking the cases first and then building models for each subdatasets. We used the Jaccard+glove model over each of the subdatasets to obtain the predictions. The final results on the test set, with F1 score of 0.38, was lower than our cross validation numbers reported here, which we believe happened due to overfitting of our models to the small dataset. In this task, imbalance in the data distribution played a big factor, and we intend to focus on improving it in the next year.

3   Task 2: Legal Case Entailment

Task 2 consists of recognizing entailment between a new case and a relevant case. Input is a decision fragment from an unseen case and a relevant case. Output is one or more specific paragraphs from the relevant case, which entail the given fragment of the unseen case. The approach we took consists of two stages: (1) similarity features-based ranking and (2) binary classification.

The first stage tries to rank the paragraphs of the relevant case based on their similarity with the given decision fragment. We evaluate this ranking process on the training dataset with respect to the total number of paragraphs of each relevant case. This evaluation allows us to set a variable threshold for the top K paragraphs selected in the subsequent classification stage. The approach shows promising results on the training set, yet less on the test set, due to the multiple parameters that the approach involves and which require fine-tuning to get the best performance for a specific dataset.

3.1   Experiments and Results

In the ranking phase, the paragraphs of the relevant case are ranked according to their similarity with the decision paragraphs. The similarity score is decided by combining different ranking given by multiple sentence vectorizers.

The vectorizers used include n-gram vectors, topic distribution vectors obtained through latent semantic analysis, universal sentence encoder vectors and averaged GloVe embeddings. The vectorizers are used with different levels of pre-processing (removing numbers, with and without stopwords, with and without lemmatization, etc.). With every sentence vectorizer, pairwise cosine coefficients are computed between the sentences of a paragraph from the relevant case and the decision paragraph. Then, paragraphs of the relevant case are ranked according to the maximum cosine coefficient. In order to get the final ranking, two parameters, K_1 and K_2 are set. The first parameter, K_1, is function of the total number of paragraphs within the relevant case. Let us denote the number of paragraphs N. Then, $K_1 = \alpha N$, where $\alpha < 1$. Each paragraph p is given a rank R_i^p by the vectorizer v_i. Let F_p be the rate of the paragraph p falling into the top K_1, in other words, the proportion of times $R_i^p < K_1$. The paragraphs are then ranked according to the factor F_p.

We evaluate this ranking process on the training dataset by locating the golden paragraph in the obtained order. Table 3 summarizes the ranking results, where the rank at 80 percentile means the rank obtained for 80% of data-points/cases.

Table 3. Ranking results on the dataset for Task 2

Number of paragraphs	Frequency	Rank at 80 percentile
$N \leq 30$	57%	3
$30 < N \leq 50$	26%	5
$N > 50$	17%	8

In the classification stage, a variable number of paragraphs, denoted K_2, are selected according to the table above (third column). 100 percentiles of the pairwise cosine coefficients of the top K_2 paragraphs are considered as features and fed to a classifier. Three random forest classifiers are trained, one for each interval of the number of paragraphs. Results of cross validation are presented in the Table 4.

Table 4. Cross validation results from Random Forest classifier for Task 2

Number of paragraphs	Frequency	Precision	Recall	F1-score
$N \leq 30$	57%	0.71	0.66	0.68
$30 < N \leq 50$	26%	0.66	0.68	0.67
$N > 50$	17%	0.37	0.39	0.38

Although results on the training dataset are promising, the experiments have shown sensitivity of the results to the parameters K_1 and K_2, potentially explaining the relatively low global accuracy obtained on the unseen dataset. Our final test unseen F1 score was 0.41, indicating the models did not generalize very well on the test set. Detailed results are shown in Table 5.

Given the size of the datasets, adding more regularization and trying out simpler methods might result in better performance on the test set, which we intend to focus more on the next year's tasks.

Table 5. Test results for Task 2

Number of paragraphs	$N \leq 30$	$30 < N \leq 50$	$N > 50$
F1-score	38%	32%	50%

4   Task 3: Civil Code Article Retrieval

Task 3 involves selecting the most relevant Japanese Civil Code articles needed to answer given legal questions. The questions are from Japanese legal bar exams and given in the form of true/false questions. More than 70% of the questions can be answered by a single article, but some questions need multiple articles to infer the answer, while some questions have multiple associated articles each of which can answer them independently. Selecting the right number of articles for each question is important.

The text for Japanese Civil Code is provided by the competition organizers both in Japanese and English. Questions from past exams were used for training, and the test set for this year's COLIEE competition were also provided in Japanese and English. For task 3, we chose to use Japanese text to leverage Japanese domain knowledge from the team. We attempted multiple approaches but the ones that yielded most promising results were based on TF-IDF, which was motivated by the approach of last year's winning team [5]. After retrieving candidates, we ranked them based on the cosine similarity and applied a threshold to select only the relevant articles. For some types of questions, TF-IDF performed poorly. To accommodate those questions we used additional training data which we will explain in the next section.

4.1   Experiments

TF-IDF on Civil Code. For task 3, we used TF-IDF and for each question, we computed cosine similarity between the question and articles from the civil code, and choose the closest article. Dealing with Japanese text has additional challenges because there are no spaces to indicates word segmentation. We decided to develop our own tokenizer instead of relying on third-party libraries to have control over how we segment the text. Japanese writing system has 3 components, kanji, hiranaga, and katakana. Kanjis are characters imported from Chinese and each character carries meanings. Hiragana and katanaka characters both originated in Japan, and each character do not carry meanings much like English alphabet. Hiragana is mainly used for conjunctions, post positional particles, and kanji suffixes. Katakana is typically used to phonetically represent words imported from foreign languages (e.g. computer, Internet, etc.). Since the legal terminologies and idioms are almost exclusively written in kanji, we extracted consecutive kanji characters and used hiragana and other punctuation characters as delimiters which we did not include as tokens. We did not explicitly exclude katakana words, but they are rare in the data set. We excluded some conjunctions that contain kanji characters such as 及び (and), 又は (or), and 若しくは

(or), since they can appear adjacent to kanji terminologies, causing improper segmentation. This approach has an advantage of preserving idioms and terminologies. With traditional tokenizer such as Macab, idioms and terminologies are divided into smaller segments. For example, 家庭裁判所 (family court) is further divided into 家庭 (family) and 裁判所 (court). However, since a legal term carries specific meanings only when the words in it are put together, it is much more meaningful to consider it as a single token.

TF-IDF on Wikibook. TFIDF approach is effective for definition questions where the definition of the article is directly asked. In such questions, there are many overlapping words between them and their corresponding articles. However, many questions are more indirect and complex. For example, consider the following question-article pair in Table 6.

Table 6. Question article pair examples: Task 3

Question	An unborn child may not be given a gift on the donor's death
Article	(1) The enjoyment of private rights commences at birth
	(2) Unless otherwise prohibited by applicable laws, regulations, or treaties, foreign nationals enjoy private rights

In such cases, since there is no overlapping words, the TF-IDF approach did poorly. In the attempt to alleviate this problem, we searched for additional data to close the gap. We chose ja.wikibooks.org which has an entry for each civil code article. For each entry, there are additional explanation of the article as well as the original definition. It also has a section for cases, each of which is linked to the public court documents. We extracted the court documents as well. We appended the text from each article to the corresponding article from the provided COLIEE civil code article data, and used that as training data. However, this had mixed results. Even though it helped some specific cases, overall the training data without the additional data performed slightly better. Our highest scoring run (TRC3_1) was trained without those additional data.

4.2 Results

Table 7 displays the evaluation results from the competition. Of the 3 runs submitted, TRC3_1 was the best run. In the competition, the results were evaluated based on the F2 Score. Our team ranked the 6th with the F2 score of 0.5011. As you see in the R_5, R_{10}, and R_{30} recall metrics, we ranked 2nd in those criteria. This means our approach effectively selected the right articles in the pool, but we were not successful in rank them, which resulted in lower f2 score.

Table 7. Evaluation results compared to other runs (Task 3).

Run	lang	F2	Prec.	Recall	MAP	R_5	R_{10}	R_{30}
LLNTU	E/J	**0.6587**	0.6875	0.6622	**0.7604**	**0.8071**	**0.8571**	**0.9214**
JNLP.tbe	E/J	0.5532	0.5766	0.5670	**0.6618**	0.6857	0.7143	0.7786
cyber1	E/J	0.5290	0.5058	0.5536	0.5540	0.5500	0.6929	0.8000
HUKB-1	J	0.5160	0.4196	0.5908	0.5687	0.6714	0.7214	0.8143
CUBERT1	E/J	0.5139	0.5402	0.5193	0.5848	0.6429	0.6857	0.7071
TRC3_1	J	0.5011	0.4561	0.5357	**0.5978**	**0.6929**	**0.7714**	**0.8429**
OVGU_bm25	E/J	0.4768	0.4003	0.5342	0.5095	0.5929	0.6143	0.7214
TAXI_R3	E/J	0.4546	0.4393	0.5089	0.5057	0.5714	0.6143	0.6786
GK_NLP	E/J	0.4273	0.2857	0.4985	0.4982	0.5571	0.6357	0.7214
UA.tfidf	E/J	0.3913	0.4286	0.3869	0.4777	0.5429	0.6071	0.6714
HONto_hybrid	E/J	0.2822	0.2545	0.2991	0.0142	0.0071	0.0071	0.0500

5 Task 4: Civil Code Entailment

COLIEE has run an entailment challenge over Japanese bar exam questions since 2014. Before this year, the entailment task has resisted deep learning approaches because of the large premise sizes and the relatively small training set size. We implemented recent work on transfer-learning [8] and multi-sentence entailment [10] to set a foundation for moving beyond rule-based heuristics.

Although teams have attempted machine learning entailment models in past years [9], civil code entailment remains challenging because the system must evaluate several inter-dependent articles $[P_1, P_2, \ldots P_n]$ against a statement H to determine if H is true or false. Each civil code article represents a set of conditions, exceptions, and conclusions. H represents a set of facts and a conclusion. The system must apply the facts to the articles' conditions and determine if H came to the correct conclusion [5]. Table 8 shows a single sentence example matching the conditions with facts. In contrast, standard entailment datasets, like MultiNLI, remain comparatively simple because they focus on single sentence entailment [12].

Table 8. An example with conclusions , conditions , and facts : Task 4

Sentence	Sentence text
P_1	A mandate shall terminate when the mandator or mandatary dies
H	The mandate terminated upon the mandator's death

In addition to the multiple sentence entailment, deep learning approaches have performed especially poorly on the Japanese Civil Code entailment tasks because the training set size is comparatively small to similar entailment tasks. Table 9 compares COLIEE 2020 civil code entailment data set to other single and multiple sentence data sets. The COLIEE data is 2 to 5 times smaller than the multiple sentence data set and 1000x smaller than the single sentence data sets. The COLIEE data set alone is too small for supervised machine learning [14].

Table 9. Entailment data set sizes.

Dataset	MultiNLI	SNLI	MultiRC	OpenBookQA	**COLIEE**
Train	392,702	550,152	5,131	4,957	**626**
Dev	20,000	10,000	4,848	500	**70**
Test	20,000	10,000	4,583	500	**112**

We investigated one supervised approach and two transfer learning approaches to address the premise length and data set size issues. The naive supervised approach demonstrates the issue with supervised learning on small datasets. We then implemented a multi-sentence Natural Language Inference (NLI) model, Multee [10], which applies transfer learning from a single-sentence NLI dataset. Finally, we evaluated a multi-task model, Text-To-Text Transfer Transformer (T5) [8], which applies transfer learning across related NLP tasks.

5.1 Experiments

Naive Feature-Based Approach. In order to determine the performance gain of our transformer classifiers on our validation data set, it was decided that a simple TF-IDF based classifier would be used as a benchmark. This TF-IDF approach utilized our team's customized tokenizer over all of the unigrams and bigrams in the data. The TF-IDF vectorizer was fit on all of the articles, wikibook data, and the public court documents.

With this TF-IDF vectorizer, features for both the questions and articles were created and then concatenated to form a unique feature vector for each question/article pair. Due to the high dimensionality of TF-IDF vectors, training and inference of machine learning models is expensive in both computation and memory. In order to mediate this, the dimensionality of the feature space was reduced to maintain 99% of its cummulative explained variance ratio. This resulted in a dimensionality reduction from 60969 to 585 features. After reducing the feature space dimensionality, the next task was to identify and train a machine learning model with said features. A linear SVM classifier, a random forest classifier, and a gradient boosting classifier were all studied with various hyperparameter configurations. By studying the accuracy of the models' performance on the validation data set, it was determined that the gradient boosting classifier with 2 estimators and a .5 sampling fraction was the best model, achieving a validation accuracy of 64%.

Multiple Sentence NLI. Based on the observations from past decomposable attention approaches [4,9], we experimented with Multee because it both increases the training set size and deals with multiple sentence entailment. Multee trains the model in two phases: single sentence pre-training and multiple sentences entailment. The first phase remained utterly unchanged compared to Multee's original experiments [10]. This phase pre-trained against the relatively massive SNLI and MultiNLI data sets and produced weight uses in the second training phase.

The second phase required some modifications to the Multee original experiments because the COLIEE data set is not multiple choice. The COLIEE model implemented a binary cross-entropy loss function for a single hypothesis. The second phase's training set includes both COLIEE and OpenBookQA examples because the OpenBookAQ provided a useful generalized multi-sentence entailment data set with complete sentences in the hypothesis. To make both data sets consistent with each other, we made two changes. First, we labeled the COLIEE example as entailment and neutral for the Y and N, respectively. Second, we converted the OpenbookQA pairs in a single hypothesis format.

Unlike our next approach, both phases leveraged GloVe word embedding (680 Billion Words, 300 dimensions) instead of contextual embedding (i.e., BERT-style embeddings). A contextual embedding was not possible with this specific model because the premise sequence length create an attention matrix too large to fit on a 16GB GPU. Although the Multee weights each sentence, the model still performs cross-attention over the entire premise passage. The GloVe embeddings were chosen to avoid a truncated premise.

Once the second phase completed, we evaluated the COLIEE 2020 task 4 test set.

T5 Multi-task. For the second transfer-learning approach, we leverage T5 [8], which is a sequence to sequence model implemented with PyTorch transformers [13]. Like most BERT-style transformers, T5 includes both pre-training and fine-tuning stages. We decided to leverage the "t5-base" embedding for the pre-training because the domain-specific training sets tend to over-fit [8]. The t5-base embedding was pre-trained on an unsupervised denoising task. The pre-training task denoised text from the Colossal Clean Crawled Corpus (C4) [8].

While we leveraged generalized embedding, the fine-tuning stage updated the model with tasks against legal data. Each task followed the same format with an identifying prefix, input text and target text. The input and target text varied based on the task type and the format is noted in Table 10.

Table 10. Fine tuning tasks: Task 4

Task type	Input text	Target text
Entailment	hypothesis: An unborn ... premise: Article 3 (1) ...	Y or N
Denoise	The enjoyment of private rights commences <id_1>	<id_1> at birth

For the entailment task, the input text includes both the hypothesis (i.e., the exam question) and premise (i.e., the articles) with a prefix denoting the start of each respective sequence. The target text contains either "Y" for entailment or "N" representing does not entail.

For the denoising task, we followed the replacement span procedure documented in the T5 study [8]. The denoise task uses an unsupervised object where the data prep corrupts random text spans. The corrupted spanned is then replaced with a single identifier token, for example "<id_1>" in Table 10. The target text contains each span identifier, followed by the missing text span.

The submitted T5 run (TRC3t5) used the following hyper-parameters, development set, and training sets. The model was fine-tuned with the transformer library T5-base's default settings except a learning rate of 1e-4, max target sequence of 100, and batch size of 16. The model trained on four separate tasks:

1. **Entailment:** COLIEE task 4 pairs (years from H18 to H29)
2. **Denoise:** Japanese Civil Code Article text
3. **Denoise:** Japanese Civil Code Article titles
4. **Denoise:** Wikibook articles on the Japanese Civil Code[12].

The TRC3t5 run configured early stopping. The early stopping process saves the model's parameters every training epoch and selects the best epoch based on an evaluation metric. Instead of using the run-time loss, the training run selected the epoch with the highest entailment accuracy on a validation set (year H30).

5.2 Results

Our Civil Code Entailment results are noted in Table 11. Given a bar exam question as a hypothesis H and a set of relevant articles as the premise $P = [P_1, P_2, \cdots P_n]$, determine if P entails H or not (i.e. Y or N). The baseline in the chart below assumes all 122 questions are entailed by the relevant statues. Of the 122 questions only 59 questions are support by the statute, thus the baseline has an accuracy of 0.5268. Our worst run (TRC3A) score below the baseline. Our two best runs (in bold) tie for second with UA at 0.625 accuracy.

Run TRC3mt. The Multee approach preformed surprisingly well compared to this year's approaches with 70 out of 122 questions correct and tied for the second place. It's ranking is surprising for two reasons: lack of a legal training set and the passé non-contextual embeddings. Although Multee leverages a slightly more complicated 2-stage attention architecture, training data was mostly comprised of general NLI datasets. The result may indicate that at least some questions are answerable with generalize reasoning instead of domain-specific legal reasoning.

---

[1] Extracted pages 民法第1条 to 民法第726条 from https://ja.wikibooks.org/wiki/ コ ンメンタール民法

[2] The articles where translated from Japanese to English using the Google translation API.

Table 11. Evaluation results for Task 4 runs.

Run	Correct	Accuracy	Run	Correct	Accuracy
Baseline	59/122	0.5268	Baseline	59/122	0.5268
JNLP.BERTLaw	81	0.7232	**TRC3mt**	**70**	**0.6250**
UA_attention_final	70	0.6250	**TRC3t5**	**70**	**0.6250**
UA_roberta_final	70	0.6250	TRC3A	56	0.5000

Additionally, Multee's ranking is surprising because the model used a simplistic non-contextual embedding, GloVe. If tuned properly, NLI models leveraging contextual should have outperformed Multee on multiple sentence entailment. In the SuperGlue leaderboard [11], both RoBERTa and T5 outperformed Multee's MultiRC F1a score of 69.9, with 84.4 and 88.1, respectively [6,8,10]. While contextual embedding have outperformed in a standard multi-sentence NLI benchmarks, both our T5 and UA's RoBERTa submission tied with the Multee on COLIEE specific task.

Run TRC3t5. Despite our best efforts to diversify the training set with multiple domain specific tasks, the T5 run appears to have over-fit on the training set. The T5 run's accuracy on the validation set (H30) was 0.6714 compare to 0.6250 on the test set. The domain specific training performed equally well compared to the more generalized training set used in the TRC3mt run (Table 11).

However, the two models similar performance isn't necessarily a negative result. If we compare the T5 runs to the Multee predictions, the models differed on 36 different questions. This opens up the potential for an ensemble model in the future.

Although the multi-task approach didn't perform as expected, the winning approach provides a potential explanation. The BERTLaw approach pre-trained on legal text where as the T5 run only fine-tuned on legal text. As a consequence, the BERTLaw model contained a legal specific vocabulary and updated the entire model based on legal text. Comparatively, fine-tuning doesn't change the vocabulary and only updates the adaptor layer's parameters. We expect the multi-task approach to improve if we include the domain specific task during pre-training because the vocabulary will include legal-specific tokens and will be encoded in all the parameters. During the T5 study, multi-task pre-training performed well compared to unsupervised pre-training on GLUE, SuperGLUE, and SQuAD benchmarks [8].

5.3   Discussion

Given BERT-style transformers topped the leader board this year, we need to discuss the statutory entailment tasks potential evolution. Although the transformer mechanisms demonstrate the ability to handle statutory entailment this year, they aren't actually demonstrating legal reasoning because they're mainly learning the legal's text linguistic form instead of learn the article's communicative intent [1]. Given the task binary nature, it's difficult to even assess what the models learned because attention-based models aren't transparent to legal experts [2]. Instead of a yes or no answer, the task should explain the conditions under a scenario matches the statutes and the resulting consequence [5].

6   Summary

In this paper, we demonstrated a variety of approach to all four COLIEE information extraction and entailment tasks. In the information extraction tasks (tasks 1 & 3) we examined TF-IDF and semantic similarity matching with mixed results. When dealing with small data sets, sometimes more simplistic approaches work best. While TRC3_1 leverage TF-IDF cosine-similarity and rudimentary word segmentation, it performed well with the MAP, R_5, R_{10}, and R_{30} metrics compared to other approaches.

In the entailment tasks (tasks 2 & 4), we explore similarity features and transfer learning. With the entailment tasks, the transfer learning approaches perform comparably well to the other participants. For task 4, we submitted two transfer learning approaches which fined-tuning on a generalize NLI dataset and domain specific task. Both approach tied for second with 0.6250 accuracy, yet yielded different answers on 36 questions.

References

1. Bender, E.M., Koller, A.: Climbing towards NLU: on meaning, form, and understanding in the age of data. In: Proceedings of ACL 2020 (2020). https://doi.org/10.18653/v1/2020.acl-main.463
2. Branting, K., et al.: Semi-supervised methods for explainable legal prediction. In: Proceedings of ICAIL 2019 (2019). https://doi.org/10.1145/3322640.3326723
3. Goldberg, Y., Levy, O.: word2vec explained: deriving Mikolov et al'.s negative-sampling word-embedding method (2014). http://arxiv.org/abs/1402.3722
4. Hudzina, J., Vacek, T., Madan, K., Custis, T., Schilder, F.: Statutory entailment using similarity features and decomposable attention models. In: Proceedings of COLIEE 2019 (2019)
5. Kim, M., Rabelo, J., Goebel, R.: Statute law information retrieval and entailment. In: Proceedings of ICAIL 2019 (2019). https://doi.org/10.1145/3322640.3326742
6. Liu, Y., et al.: Roberta: a robustly optimized BERT pretraining approach (2019). https://arxiv.org/abs/1907.11692
7. Pennington, J., Socher, R., Manning, C.D.: Glove: global vectors for word representation. In: Proceedings of EMNLP (2014)
8. Raffel, C., et al.: Exploring the limits of transfer learning with a unified text-to-text transformer. J. Mach. Learn. Res. **21**(140), 1–67 (2020). http://jmlr.org/papers/v21/20-074.html
9. Son, N.T., Phan, V.A., Minh, N.L.: Recognizing entailments in legal texts using sentence encoding-based and decomposable attention models. In: Proceedings of COLIEE 2017 (2017). http://www.easychair.org/publications/paper/347231

10. Trivedi, H., Kwon, H., Khot, T., Sabharwal, A., Balasubramanian, N.: Repurposing entailment for multi-hop question answering tasks. In: Proceedings of NAACL 2019 (2019). https://doi.org/10.18653/v1/N19-1302
11. Wang, A., et al.: SuperGLUE: a stickier benchmark for general-purpose language understanding systems. arXiv preprint arXiv:1905.00537 (2019)
12. Williams, A., Nangia, N., Bowman, S.: A broad-coverage challenge corpus for sentence understanding through inference. In: Proceedings of NAACL-HLT 2018 (2018). http://aclweb.org/anthology/N18-1101
13. Wolf, T., et al.: HuggingFace's transformers: state-of-the-art natural language processing. ArXiv abs/1910.03771 (2019)
14. Yoshioka, M., Kano, Y., Kiyota, N., Satoh, K.: Overview of Japanese statute law retrieval and entailment task at COLIEE-2018 (2018). https://sites.ualberta.ca/~rabelo/COLIEE2019/COLIEE2018_SL_summary.pdf

Paragraph Similarity Scoring and Fine-Tuned BERT for Legal Information Retrieval and Entailment

Hannes Westermann[1]([✉]), Jaromir Savelka[2], and Karim Benyekhlef[1]

[1] Cyberjustice Laboratory, Faculté de droit, Université de Montréal,
Montréal, QC H3T 1J7, Canada
`hannes.westermann@umontreal.ca`
[2] School of Computer Science, Carnegie Mellon University,
Pittsburgh, PA 15213, USA

Abstract. The assessment of the relevance of legal documents and the application of legal rules embodied in legal documents are some of the key processes in the field of law. In this paper, we present our approach to the 2020 Competition on Legal Information Extraction/Entailment (COLIEE-2020), which provides researchers with the opportunity to find ways of accomplishing these complex tasks using computers. Here, we describe the methods used to build the models for the four tasks that are part of the competition and the results of their application. For Task 1, concerning the prediction of whether a base case cites a candidate case, we devise a method for evaluating the similarity between cases based on individual paragraph similarity. This method can be used to reduce the number of candidate cases by 85%, while maintaining over 80% of the cited cases. We then train a Support Vector Machines model to make the final prediction. The model is the best solution submitted for Task 1. We use a similar method for Task 2. For Task 3, we use an approach based on BM25 measure in combination with the identification of similar previously asked questions. For Task 4, we use a transformer model fine-tuned on existing entailment data sets as well as on the provided domain-specific statutory law data set.

Keywords: Legal entailment · Universal sentence encoder · Approximate nearest neighbor · Support vector machine · BM25 · BERT

1 Introduction

Assessing the relevance of, and the relationship between, textual documents is one of the key skills used in the legal profession. Attorneys and judges need to know which previous legal case is relevant to a current case, in order to craft their argument and decide on the merits of a case. Law students need to assess whether a piece of legislation is relevant to a fact pattern in an exam and determine the

N. Okazaki et al. (Eds.): JSAI-isAI 2020 Workshops, LNAI 12758, pp. 269–285, 2021.
https://doi.org/10.1007/978-3-030-79942-7_18

effect of the legislation on which answer they should give. This assessment of relevance can be very difficult, requiring complex analysis and determinations. Automating this task, even partially, could have tremendous implications for the legal profession and support judges, lawyers, researchers, students, and the public in their use and understanding of the law.

The focal point for researchers to develop and compare their efforts in understanding and comparing legal texts is the Competition on Legal Information Extraction/Entailment (COLIEE). The competition consists of 4 tasks. Task 1 is the Legal Case Retrieval Task, concerned with determining which of 200 candidate cases are cited by a base case. Task 2, the Legal Case Entailment task, focuses on which paragraph in a cited case is cited by a specific fragment in a base case. Task 3, The Statute Law Retrieval Task, focuses on the retrieval of relevant legal articles for questions in a bar exam. Task 4 focuses on providing the answer to bar exam questions, using the relevant sections of the law. We work with a number of methods and combinations thereof, including sentence encoding models based on deep neural networks, Support Vector Machines (SVM), nearest neighbor searches, rankings based on BM25 measure, and fine-tuned language models (BERT).

Our placements on the team level in the four challenges are:

- Task 1: **1st Place**
- Task 2: 4th Place
- Task 3: 3rd Place
- Task 4: 4th Place (shared)

This paper describes our approaches to the different tasks. We go through the tasks one by one. For each task, we provide a short description, explain our methodology, and present and briefly discuss our results.

2   Task 1 - The Legal Case Retrieval Task

2.1   Task Description

The goal of Task 1 is to identify cases that are noticed (e.g. cited) by a base case. The data consists of 650 samples, 520 samples with labels for training, and 130 samples for testing. Each sample consists of one base case and 200 candidate cases. The aim of the task is to identify which of the 200 cases was noticed by the judge in the base case.

From a classification perspective, the data set is heavily unbalanced. Only around 2.5% of the provided candidate cases are noticed by the corresponding base case. Imbalanced datasets present a difficult problem for most machine learning methods. There are a number of approaches to tackle this issue, such as under-sampling and cost-sensitive learning [12]. This issue has been discussed in papers submitted for previous COLIEE editions. (see e.g. [6]).

Our solution is based on making the dataset more balanced via preliminary filtering. The filter excludes 85% of the candidate cases while maintaining over 80% of the positive samples. On the remaining 15% of the data, we train a traditional ML classifier to generate the final prediction.

2.2 Methodology

Our approach consists of three steps—data pre-processing, preliminary filtering via our paragraph similarity method that narrows the space of candidate matches from 200 to 30, and a Support Vector Machine (SVM) model that makes the final prediction as to which case is noticed.

The approach relies on several insights about the dataset. These are:

– Noticed cases might only be relevant to a single paragraph in the base case. For example, a judge might summarize an entire noticed case in a single paragraph in the base case. Conversely, only a single paragraph in the noticed case might be relevant to the base case. For example, a judge might refer to a specific issue in a noticed case, which is only discussed in a single paragraph in that case. Therefore, it is advantageous to work on the paragraph level and to compare paragraphs in a many-to-many fashion. (Compare [27] which models interactions between paragraphs using BERT.)
– Paragraphs in a certain section of the base case are more likely to cite other cases. When discussing the facts of a case, the judge is less likely to cite other cases. When describing the application of legal rules to a case, however, the judge is more likely to cite cases. When searching for a noticed case, it is, therefore, advantageous to only consider the latter paragraphs.

Pre-processing. Each case is split into paragraphs. Each paragraph is turned into a vector representation, using a Universal Sentence Encoder. This model relies on deep transformer networks, trained on multiple tasks with the aim of being used for transfer learning [2]. We use the pre-trained implementation provided from Google on tf-hub.[1] For each paragraph in the case, the model produces a 512-dimension vector. The Universal Sentence Encoder has been used in previous COLIEE editions (e.g. [17,20]).

Next, we create a method to quickly identify all paragraphs across the 200 candidate cases that are similar to a given paragraph. For this, we use the Spotify Annoy[2] library, which implements a fast and scaleable Approximate Nearest Neighbors algorithm. For each sample, we create a search tree for all paragraphs contained in the 200 candidate cases.

The combination of Sentence Encoders and the approximate nearest neighbor approach was used in [28] to retrieve text elements that are relevant for annotation. In this work, we instead use the similarity scores to surface entire cases that are relevant to a base case, by accumulating the similarity of paragraphs on a per-case basis.

Paragraph Similarity Score. The next step is to filter out cases that are unlikely to be noticed. The aim is to employ a low-precision filter with high recall. This enables us to create a more balanced dataset suitable for traditional

---

[1] https://tfhub.dev/google/universal-sentence-encoder/4.
[2] https://github.com/spotify/annoy.

prediction. As discussed above, comparing the entire text between the base case and the candidate case at this stage might not give the desired results, as only certain paragraphs in the base case might be relevant for the candidate case, and vice-versa. Therefore, we identify the candidate cases with the most paragraphs that are similar to paragraphs in the base case.

First, we identify the section of the case where the judge is likely to cite other cases, by taking paragraphs with keywords indicating suppressed citations and a few surrounding paragraphs. The paragraphs with suppressed citations are used as a proxy to identify something akin to the "reasoning" section of a case, where the judge applies the law to a factual situation. This is the area where the judge is likely to refer to jurisprudence to explain a decision. While the use of keywords for suppressed citations is specific to the COLIEE dataset, it could be replaced by a method of scanning for standard citations in a real-world dataset.

We step through these paragraphs. For each of them, we identify the 10 most semantically similar paragraphs, across all the paragraphs in the candidate cases, using the nearest neighbor method and sentence encoders described above. Whenever a paragraph of a candidate case appears in the top 10 most similar paragraphs for a paragraph in the base case, we increase the score for that candidate case by an amount corresponding to the euclidean proximity of the two paragraphs. This aims to create a many-to-many comparison of paragraphs in the base case and candidate cases. The 30 candidate cases with the highest similarity score are retrieved for subsequent processing.

Support Vector Machines. As the next step, a traditional ML model is trained to determine whether one of the 30 candidate cases is noticed or not. First, we transform the base cases and candidate cases into a single vector, by taking a Bag of Word representation of words and bigrams and running them through a Term Frequency and Inverse Document Frequency (TF-IDF) transformer. This method aims to determine the relevancy of terms by weighting them depending on how often they appear in a document and across the corpus. We use the implementation from the python library scikit-learn [18]. We cap the maximum amount of features at 6000. Next, we subtract the vector for thecandidate case from that of the base case.

Finally, we train an SVM model on the resulting vector to predict whether the candidate case is noticed by the base case. SVMs map examples with different labels into a high-dimensional space, to find clear divisions between examples of different classes [5]. We use the SVM implementation from scikit-learn [18], using the "rbf" kernel. Further, we balance the predictions by weighting the classes in Run 2 and Run 3. The output of this model is the final prediction, with all cases outside of the top 30 as previously selected being set to negative. The case with the highest similarity score is further always predicted as positive.

2.3   Results

Table 1 shows the results of a hypothetical scenario where only the similarity measure is used for prediction (S1, S7 and S30), and the final three runs we

Table 1. Results for runs using only the similarity score (S1, S7 and S30), and the official runs using the similarity score and support vector machine.

	Train			Eval			Test		
	P	R	F1	P	R	F1	P	R	F1
S@1	.69	.13	.22	.75	.14	.24	.75	.15	.25
S@7	.37	.51	.43	.45	.60	.51	.42	.61	.50
S@30	.14	.81	.24	.16	.91	.27	.15	.93	.26
Run 1				.79	.48	.59	.81	.54	.6503
Run 2				.72	.66	.69	.69	.66	**.6774**
Run 3				.72	.65	.68	.69	.66	.6768

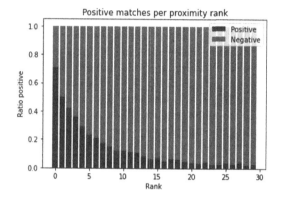

Fig. 1. Positive examples at different ranks as determined by paragraph similarity assessment.

submitted. We split the data into the following partitions: Train (Sample 1–449), Eval (Sample 450–520), Test (Sample 521–650) set. For the evaluation on the Eval split, the model is trained on the Train split. For the evaluation on the Test split, the Train and Eval splits are used for training.

Specifically, the Table presents the following results:

- S@1 - Hypothetical results of predicting the most similar case (based on the paragraph similarity score) only as noticed.
- S@7 - Hypothetical results of predicting the top seven most similar cases as noticed. This is the highest-scoring approach using only the similarity score.
- S@30 - Hypothetical results of predicting the top 30 most similar cases as noticed. These 30 cases are further used by the SVM for the submitted runs.
- Run 1 - Support Vector Machine, without balancing via class-weights.
- Run 2 - The same as run 1, with balancing via class-weights.
- Run 3 - The same as run 2 using TF-IDF transformer trained on all available text, including the text of test samples.

Figure 1 shows the distribution of positive and negative examples along the axis of the cases with the highest similarity score. The x-axis shows the rank of the candidate case, while the y-axis shows the percentage of cases at that rank that are positive (e.g. the candidate case is noticed) vs negative (e.g. the candidate case is not noticed).

2.4   Discussion

The proposed architecture was the best-performing one submitted for COLIEE 2020 Task 1 (the winning model).

The main problem to overcome in this task is the unbalanced dataset (from the classification perspective). As only 2.5% of the examples are positive, classification models trained on the full dataset tend to only predict the negative class. In order to overcome this, we developed the paragraph comparison to identify relevant cases, by comparing paragraphs from the base case to paragraphs from the candidate cases. This method results in picking the 30 most similar cases. This reduces the size of the dataset by 85%, while retaining 80% to 90% of the positive examples, meaning that around 15% of the data now consists of positive cases. As can be seen in Fig. 1, the similarity scoring does a good job of placing cases that are likely to be noticed at the highest positions in the ranking. The candidate case ranked as the closest is around 70% likely to be noticed.

After we have selected the 30 top highest ranked cases using the similarity score, we train an SVM model on the TF-IDF vector between the base case and the noticed case. The balancing of the classes improved the performance of the model, as can be seen by the strong performance of Run 2 and Run 3, which scored first and second of all the submitted runs. Pre-training the TF-IDF vectorizer on the test sample texts gave no performance improvement, which could indicate that the train and test data has a similar distribution in terms of topics.

There are a number of ways this model could be improved. It currently uses entire cases to determine whether one case noticed another case in the final prediction step. This works well, however it is possible that the performance could be improved by focusing on similar sections. Furthermore, the use of neural networks and language models could improve performance. These tend to have trouble with long sequences, such as the cases used in Task 1, however recently models that are able to handle thousands of tokens have emerged (e.g. [11]).

3   Task 2 - The Legal Case Entailment Task

3.1   Task Description

Task 2 is somewhat similar to Task 1, in that it concerns the detection of citations from one case to another. However, while Task 1 focuses on the entire case, Task 2 focuses on paragraphs within a case. As such, the data provided is a base case, an entailed fragment of the base case, and a noticed case, split into its paragraphs. The task is to determine which paragraph from the noticed case is cited by the entailed fragment.

In total, the organizers provided 325 training samples and 100 test samples. Again, the data is sparse. 85% of the entailed fragments cite only a single paragraph, while 13% cite two paragraphs. For each pair of an entailed fragment and a candidate cited paragraph, only 3.3% are positive. Just like for Task 1, overcoming this imbalance was the key step in building a well-performing model. The method we use is similar to the one we used for Task 1, except that we based the model on sentences instead of entire paragraphs.

3.2   Methodology

The methodology is very similar to that we use for Task 1. We create a many-to-many sentence comparison method that narrows the potentially matching paragraphs down to the top ten most likely matches. We then train an SVM model to make the final predictions.

Pre-processing. Paragraphs are read from the files and grouped by sample. Each paragraph is split into sentences, using the SpaCy library.[3] Each sentence is turned into a 512-dimension vector representation, using the Google Universal Sentence Encoder model. Finally, we use the Annoy library to create a nearest-neighbor search method of all sentences contained in the candidate paragraphs for a specific sample (see Sect. 2.2 for pointers to the individual methods).

Sentence Similarity Score. Next, we perform a per-sentence comparison between the entailed fragment and the candidate paragraphs, to determine the semantic similarity between the two. Comparing the paragraphs on a per-sentence level allows us to capture situations where only a few of the sentences in the entailed fragment or the candidate paragraphs are similar. In some entailed fragments, for example, the text discusses the present case and then supports the reasoning with a single sentence referring to the noticed case.

We iterate through the sentences in the entailed fragment and retrieve the ten closest sentences from all sentences in the candidate paragraphs. For each candidate paragraph, we keep track of how often a contained sentence appears in the top ten most similar sentences of the sentences in the entailed fragment. Finally, we select the ten paragraphs with the highest score (see Sect. 2.2).

Support Vector Machines Classifier. We train an SVM model to predict the candidate paragraph that is the most likely to be cited by the entailed fragment. SVM does not return probabilities. However, we use the Platt-scaling implemented in scikit-learn, which trains an additional sigmoid function on top of the SVM model in order to turn the raw scores into probabilities [19]. We train a TF-IDF vectorizer on the case texts and use it to transform all paragraphs into

---

[3] https://spacy.io/.

Table 2. Results for runs using only the similarity score, and the official runs using the similarity score and support vector machines.

	Train			Eval			Test		
	P	R	F1	P	R	F1	P	R	F1
S@1	.44	.39	.41	.60	.49	.54	.48	.38	.43
S@10	.10	.88	.18	.12	.96	.21	.11	.88	.20
Run 1				.75	.61	.67	.63	.50	.5600
Run 2				.70	.61	.65	.63	.54	.5837
Run 3				.74	.65	.70	.63	.55	**.5897**

their TF-IDF representation. We use only unigrams for the vectorization, and cap the number of features at 6,000. Next, for each pair of an entailed fragment and a candidate paragraph, we subtract the TF-IDF vector of the candidate paragraph from that of the entailed fragment.

We also introduce two additional features. First, we calculate the average cosine distance between all the encoded sentences in the entailed fragment and the sentences in the candidate paragraph, to capture semantic relatedness beyond vocabulary overlap. Further, we introduce the length of the candidate paragraph as a feature, based on the experimental observation that cited paragraphs are often long.

For prediction, we obtain the probability for each pair of entailed fragment and candidate paragraph. We then accumulate these based on the entire sample and take the pair with the highest probability as the prediction. Further, for Run 2 and 3, we introduce a system that accumulates prediction probabilities for all paragraphs not initially selected. This list is ordered by probability, and the top 10% of these paragraphs are also predicted to be matching, to capture some of the cases where two paragraphs are cited. (see [20] which used post-processed BERT confidence scores to determine the cited fragments).

3.3 Results

We split the data into Train (Samples 1–284), Eval (Sample 285–325) and Test (Sample 326–425).

Table 2 shows the following model runs:

- S@1 - Hypothetical result of only predicting the most similar paragraph based on the sentence similarity score as entailed.
- S@10 - Hypothetical result of only predicting the top ten paragraphs based on the sentence similarity score as entailed. The resulting data is further used as input data for the SVM models.
- Run 1 - Regular run of the similarity many-to-many matching combined with an SVM model.
- Run 2 - The same as Run 1, but the TF-IDF vectorizer is fitted on both the training and test data.

– Run 3 - The same as Run 2, except that the cases between 182 and 225 (corresponding to the test data of COLIEE 2019) are excluded from the training data. Oddly, this particular partition seems to confuse the model (determined heuristically), and we found that training without this data consistently improved the performance.

3.4   Discussion

Overall, the model performs reasonably well, enough to place us at the fourth place. The sentence similarity comparison works well as a way to make the dataset more balanced. When taking the top ten paragraphs, it is able to retain around 90% of the positive examples, while excluding 72% of the candidates.

The final model based on SVM, however, did not perform as well as it did for Task 1. This could potentially be explained by less data being available overall, and each sample (in the form of paragraphs) being shorter than the whole cases used in Task 1, making it more difficult to find a vocabulary overlap.

There are many ways the model could be improved upon. First of all, the spaCy model used to separate the sentences might not be ideal for case law. Alternatives, e.g. [26], could be used. Further, the SVM model does not seem perfect for detecting entailment between short sequences. Instead, modern language models such as BERT could be used, as in [20]. We tried these, but have not yet been able to use them to outperform SVM. Finally, information from the entire base case could be used additionally to the entailed fragment.

4   Task 3 - Statutory Law Retrieval Task

4.1   Task Description

The task consists of a set of statements that could be either true or false with respect to the provisions of the Japanese civil code translated to English. The civil code is divided into 782 articles. The task is to retrieve one or more relevant articles in response to a statement. An article is considered to be relevant if a query statement can be evaluated as true or false on the basis of the article. If a combination of multiple articles is required to evaluate a statement, then all of them are considered relevant. Finally, if multiple articles enable the assessment of a statement independently, then all of them are relevant as well. As such, the task is an example of an ad hoc document retrieval where a statement is a query and the civil code articles are the documents. The competition organizers provided 696 statements paired with the relevant articles as the training set and 112 statements without the pairing as the test set.[4]

---

[4] https://sites.ualberta.ca/~rabelo/COLIEE2020/.

4.2 Methodology

Pre-processing. As the first step, we segment the statements and civil code articles into sentences using a sentence segmentation model from [26], which is specifically trained to work well on legal texts. This transforms the data set of 696 statements to 751 statement sentences and the data set of 782 civil code articles to 1,415 article sentences. Then, we turned the sentences into the lists of lemmas excluding stopwords. We found that the commonly used SpaCy library had some issues with dealing with the legal texts. Therefore, we used the LemmInflect[5] library for lemmatization instead of SpaCy. Further, we adopted the PubMed list[6] of stopwords, rather than the one included in SpaCy. We manually curated the list to fit the domain of law.

Sentence Retrieval. In the next step, we measure the similarity between each statement sentence and each article sentence. For the three submitted runs we retrieved the $n = \{1, 2, 3\}$ top similar article sentences for each statement sentence. Notably, we also matched each statement sentence to other statement sentences from the training set. Again, for the three runs, we retrieved $n = \{1, 2, 3\}$ top similar statement sentences for each statement sentence. As the training statements are associated with civil code articles we retrieve the respective articles associated with the retrieved sentence. This follows the intuition that statements that are very similar are likely to rely on the same articles from the civil code. Note that models employing smaller n will have better precision while the models employing greater n will improve recall.

Our approach to measuring the similarity of statement sentences to article sentences is based on the Okapi BM25 function, from the well-known TF-IDF family. The function is defined as follows:

$$\text{BM25} = \sum_{t \in q} TF \cdot IDF \cdot QTF$$

$$\text{TF} = \frac{(k_1 + 1) \cdot tf_{td}}{k_1 \cdot \left(1 - b + b \cdot \frac{L_d}{L_{avg}}\right) + tf_{td}}$$

$$\text{IDF} = log\left(\frac{N - df_t + \frac{1}{2}}{df_t + \frac{1}{2}}\right) \qquad \text{QTF} = \frac{(k_3 + 1) \cdot tf_{tq}}{k_3 + tf_{tq}}$$

Here, N is the size of the collection (i.e., the number of article sentences), df_t is the number of sentences in which t occurs, tf_{td} is the frequency of term t in document d (i.e., an evaluated article sentence), tf_{tq} is the frequency of term t in query q (i.e., an evaluated statement sentence), L_d and L_{avg} are the length of d and the average document length for the whole collection. k_1, k_3 and b are tuning parameters. We use the typical values of $k_1, k_3 = 1.2$ and $b = 0.75$. [14,

---

[5] https://github.com/bjascob/LemmInflect.
[6] https://pubmed.ncbi.nlm.nih.gov/help/#help-stopwords.

Table 3. Results of the different variants of the retrieval system on the training set. The top section shows performance of the system that does not employ any filter. The middle sections show the improvements gained by using the individual filters (see Sect. 4.2). The bottom section demonstrates the gain obtained by using both filters in tandem. The numbers after each method (1,2,3) refer to the number of sentences retrieved, see Sect. 4.2.

	F_2	P	R
no_filter1	.5577	.4479	.6293
no_filter2	.5246	.2774	.7306
no_filter3	.4684	.2005	.7717
high_coverage1	.5730	.5056	.6218
high_coverage2	.5684	.4031	.7107
high_coverage3	.5330	.3491	.7432
max_filter1	.5686	.5166	.6094
max_filter2	.5908	.4525	.6970
max_filter3	.5820	.4237	.7264
cyber1	.5735	.5440	.6034
cyber2	.5962	.4949	.6786
cyber3	.5902	.4712	.7027

p. 233] In [15] the authors emphasize that BM25 is an example of a probabilistic approach to IR, [21] where the 2-Poisson model forms the basis for counting term frequency [8, 22]. The idea is that there are two types of documents having term frequencies from different Poisson distributions—documents that are about a term and documents that only mention the term. The goal in IR is to distinguish between the two types. In order to achieve the goal, the common version of BM25 considers query terms only, assuming that non-query terms are less useful for document ranking [15].

Filtering and Prediction. The above-described method results in the initial set of candidate articles that we subject to subsequent filtering. We first examine the word overlap between the matched sentences. If the ratio of the shared words is higher than 0.7 for at least one of the sentences, the match with the highest ratio is picked as the only result. We refer to this filter as *high coverage*. The other retrieved sentences are discarded. If the first filter is not applicable, the maximum similarity match score is detected (*max*). Any sentences that were matched with a score that is lower than $0.7 * max$ are discarded. We refer to this filter as *max filter*. These filters, determined heuristically, improve precision while causing a rather minimal hit to recall. After applying these filters, the remaining articles are predicted as being matching, i.e. supporting the candidate statement.

Table 4. Results of the 3 runs submitted for COLIEE 2020 Task 3 on the test set.

	F_2	P	R	MAP	R_5	R_{10}	R_{30}
cyber1	.5290	.5058	.5536	.5540	.5500	.6929	.8000
cyber2	.5251	.4353	.5967	.5540	.5500	.6929	.8000
cyber3	.5175	.4134	.6235	.5540	.5500	.6929	.8000

4.3 Results

The results of different variants of our system evaluated on the training set are shown in Table 3. Note that since the number of parameters we are setting is small (only $n = 1, 2, 3$ and usage of the two filters) we optimize directly on the training set. It is apparent that the application of the filters improves the performance of the system irrespective of the number n of retrieved sentences. The systems employing both filters in tandem perform the best.

For the competition, we submitted 3 runs the technical details of which are described in the preceding section. The best F_2 score of 0.529 was achieved by the model focused on precision ($n = 1$). However, the differences among the performance of the three models are minimal as the models are quite similar to each other. The most successful cyber1 model ended up as the third out of the total number of 28 submitted runs, while the cyber2 model ended up fourth and cyber3 model 6th. The performance of the submitted models on the test set is shown in Table 4.

It is apparent that the performance of our models is lower on the test set than on the training set. Also, the cyber1 model which was the weakest one (of those employing both filters) on the training set ended up performing the best on the test set. This suggests that there is a difference between the training set and the test set. Our models were not able to adapt to this difference very well.

4.4 Discussion

The articles are relatively short pieces of text that typically consist of one or at most several sentences. It appears to be well-established that the traditional approach to ranking, based on computing similarity between the query and retrieved documents, is less effective for very short documents (see, e.g., [16]). Usually, the main cause of the decreased performance is the lack of a robust overlap between a query and a document. In larger documents, an unusually high occurrence of a term strongly indicates that the document might be "about" the term. This "aboutness" assumption often works surprisingly well for longer documents. In shorter documents, there is typically just one exact occurrence of the term. Even in the case of more than one occurrence, it is questionable if the "aboutness" assumption would still be as solid as for longer documents.

5   Task 4 - Statutory Law Entailment Task

5.1   Task Description

The task uses the same data as Task 3 (Sect. 4). This means that there is a set of statements that could be either true or false with respect to the provisions of the Japanese civil code (782 articles). Here, the task is to predict if a statement is true or false given a set of relevant articles. Hence, a method developed for Task 3 would constitute the first step in a full question answering (QA) system where a statement would be considered a question. A method developed for this task would then be the second step. The QA system would directly provide a 'yes' or 'no' answer to a question (i.e., a statement). The task is an example of entailment detection where a statement and an article constitute a document pair. The 696 training statements paired with the relevant articles were also equipped with the 'Y' or 'N' label encoding the entailment relation. The relevant articles for the 112 statements from the test set were also provided.

5.2   Methodology

We leverage a bidirectional encoder representation from transformers (BERT) model that has been recently shown as an effective solution for a general entailment task. The SemBERT [30] model is currently reported as the state of the art in the task based on the Stanford Natural Language Inference (SNLI) data set.[7] We employ the base model resulting from the Robustly Optimized BERT Pre-training Approach (RoBERTa base) with 25 million parameters [13]. RoBERTa is using the same architecture as BERT. However, the authors of [13] conducted a replication study of BERT pre-training and found that BERT was significantly undertrained. They used the insights thus gained to propose a better pretraining procedure. Their modifications include longer training with bigger batches and more data, removal of the next sentence prediction objective, training on longer sequences on average (still limited to 512 tokens), and dynamic changing of the masking pattern applied to the training data [13].

We fine-tune the pre-trained RoBERTa base model on the task of sentence pair classification. First, we attempted to fine-tune the model directly on the COLIEE Task 4 data. The resulting performance was rather underwhelming. Since one of the causes was likely the small size of the data set we decided to fine-tune the model on the SNLI data set first. Only after that, we proceeded to fine-tune the model on the COLIEE data. This lead to a major improvement in performance. For both of the fine-tuning stages, we trained the model for 10 epochs using a batch size of 12. After the end of each epoch, we recorded the accuracy of the model on the validation set (33% of training data set aside). In both stages, we picked the model with the best accuracy to work with. In the case of the fine-tuning on SNLI the best model was then used for further fine-tuning on the training data of COLIEE Task 4. The best model resulting

---

[7] https://nlp.stanford.edu/projects/snli/.

Table 5. Results of the model evaluated on the validation set.

	Accuracy
cyber (COLIEE data only)	.5144
cyber	.5690

Table 6. Results of the single run submitted for COLIEE 2020 Task 4 on the test set.

	Correct	Accuracy
cyber	69	.6161

from the second stage of fine-tuning was then used to generate the predictions on the test set.

5.3 Results

The results of our system evaluated on the validation set are shown in Table 5. Our model achieved an accuracy of approximately 57%. While this is a very low accuracy it is a considerable improvement over the system that was exclusively trained on COLIEE data, which barely outperformed a random baseline.

We only submitted one run of the model described in the preceding section. While the accuracy of 0.6161 is quite underwhelming for a binary task the run ended up as the sixth best-performing one (shared with the other two runs) out of the total number of 30 submitted runs. This clearly shows that the task is extremely difficult and much more complicated than the general entailment as encoded in the SNLI data set. There the accuracy of various models based on BERT appears to be very close to .90 in most cases. The performance of the submitted model on the test set is shown in Table 6.

5.4 Discussion

The most important takeaway is that one has to be careful about interpreting the results of various methods evaluated on general language data sets. For example, the performance of models based on BERT on general language entailment tasks, such as SNLI [1] or MNLI [29], gives an impression that the models deal with it very effectively (accuracy above 0.90). However, those data sets mostly consist of short sentences, often with considerable word overlap. The COLIEE Task 4 data are much more complex and the application of the same methods on those data does not appear to lead to similar levels of performance. In the previous run of COLIEE several teams based their solutions to Task 4 on BERT [7,10]. Although, theirs were not the winning submission they performed fairly well in relative terms ([7] ended up third). In [7] the accuracy on the test set was 0.5918 and here we achieved an accuracy of 0.6161. These numbers clearly show that the evaluation of statements' entailment with respect to statutory provisions is much more challenging than general language entailment. Our intuition is that legal reasoning often involves an application of abstract legal rules to concrete factual situations. Even tiny variations in the situation or language might completely alter the result. State-of-the-art language models might have difficulties dealing with this kind of reasoning and understanding.

An alternative explanation could be that BERT models are not well-suited for tasks performed on domain-specific legal texts. However, this does not appear likely since there have been numerous examples of successful applications of BERT on legal texts. In [4] BERT is evaluated on the classification of claim acceptance given judges' arguments. A task of retrieving related case-law similar to a case decided a user provides is tackled in [23]. The authors demonstrate the effectiveness of using BERT for this task while focusing on mitigating the constraint on document length imposed by BERT. In [3] BERT is evaluated as one of the approaches to predict court decision outcome given the facts of a case. BERT has been successfully used for the classification of legal areas of Supreme Court judgments [9]. The authors of [20] combine BERT with simple similarity measure to tackle the challenging task of case law entailment. BERT was also used in learning-to-rank settings for retrieval of legal news [24] and case-law sentences interpreting statutory concepts [25].

6   Conclusions

In this paper we presented four systems focused on statutory and case law retrieval and entailment. The models were submitted to the COLIEE 2020 competition. The model that we submitted for Task 1, focused on case law retrieval, was the best model submitted for the task. The key idea behind the system is to evaluate the similarity between cases on the paragraph level. We used a similar model for Task 2 on case law entailment. For Task 3 focusing on statutory retrieval, we created a system based on the BM25 measure. Finally, we tackled the task on statutory entailment (Task 4) via fine-tuning a sentence pair classification model based on BERT.

Acknowledgements. We would like to thank the Cyberjustice Laboratory at Université de Montréal, the LexUM Chair on Legal Information, and the Autonomy through Cyberjustice Technologies (ACT) project for their support.

References

1. Bowman, S.R., Angeli, G., Potts, C., Manning, C.D.: A large annotated corpus for learning natural language inference. arXiv preprint arXiv:1508.05326 (2015)
2. Cer D., et al.: Universal sentence encoder. arXiv preprint arXiv:1803.11175 (2018)
3. Chalkidis, I., Androutsopoulos, I., Aletras, N.: Neural legal judgment prediction in English. arXiv preprint arXiv:1906.02059 (2019)
4. Condevaux, C., Harispe, S., Mussard, S., Zambrano, G.: Weakly supervised one-shot classification using recurrent neural networks with attention: application to claim acceptance detection. In: JURIX, pp. 23–32 (2019)

5. Cortes, C., Vapnik, V.: Support-vector networks. Mach. Learn. **20**(3), 273–297 (1995). https://doi.org/10.1007/BF00994018

6. El Hamdani, R., Troussel, A. Houvenagel, C.: COLIEE case law competition task 1: the legal case retrieval task. In: COLIEE 2019, pp. 10–15 (2019)

7. Gain, B., Bandyopadhyay, D., Saikh, T., Ekbal, A.: Iitp@coliee 2019: legal information retrieval using BM25 and BERT. In: Proceedings of the 6th Competition on Legal Information Extraction/Entailment, COLIEE 2019 (2019)

8. Harter, S.P.: A probabilistic approach to automatic keyword indexing. Part I. On the distribution of specialty words in a technical literature. J. Am. Soc. Inf. Sci. **26**(4), 197–206 (1975)

9. Howe, J.S.T., Khang, L.H., Chai, I.E.: Legal area classification: a comparative study of text classifiers on Singapore supreme court judgments. arXiv preprint arXiv:1904.06470 (2019)

10. Hudzina, J., Vacek, T., Madan, K., Tonya, C., Schilder, F.: Statutory entailment using similarity features and decomposable attention models. In: Proceedings of the 6th Competition on Legal Information Extraction/Entailment, COLIEE 2019 (2019)

11. Kitaev, N., Kaiser, L., Levskaya, A.: Reformer: the efficient transformer. arXiv preprint arXiv:2001.04451 (2020)

12. Kotsiantis, S., Kanellopoulos, D., Pintelas, P.: Handling imbalanced datasets: a review. GESTS Int. Trans. Comput. Sci. Eng. **30**(1), 25–36 (2016)

13. Liu, Y., et al.: Roberta: a robustly optimized BERT pretraining approach. arXiv preprint arXiv:1907.11692 (2019)

14. Manning, C.D., Schütze, H., Raghavan, P.: Introduction to Information Retrieval. Cambridge University Press, Cambridge (2008)

15. Mitra, B., Nalisnick, E., Craswell, N., Caruana, R.: A dual embedding space model for document ranking. arXiv preprint arXiv:1602.01137 (2016)

16. Murdock, V.G.: Aspects of sentence retrieval. Department of Computer Science, Massachusetts University Amherst (2006)

17. Paulino-Passos, G., Toni, F.: Retrieving legal cases with vector representations of text. In: Proceedings of COLIEE 2019, pp. 50–55 (2019)

18. Pedregosa, F., et al.: Scikit-learn: machine learning in Python. J. Mach. Learn. Res. **12**, 2825–2830 (2011)

19. Platt, J.C.: Probabilistic outputs for support vector machines and comparisons to regularized likelihood methods. Adv. Large Margin Classif. **10**, 61–74 (1999)

20. Rabelo, J., Kim, M.Y., Goebel, R.: Combining similarity and transformer methods for case law entailment. In: Proceedings of the Seventeenth International Conference on Artificial Intelligence and Law, pp. 290–296 (2019)

21. Robertson, S., Zaragoza, H.: The Probabilistic Relevance Framework: BM25 and Beyond. Now Publishers Inc., Delft (2009)

22. Robertson, S.E., Walker, S.: Some simple effective approximations to the 2-Poisson model for probabilistic weighted retrieval. In: Croft, B.W., van Rijsbergen, C.J. (eds.) SIGIR'94, pp. 232–241. Springer, London (1994). https://doi.org/10.1007/978-1-4471-2099-5_24

23. Rossi, J., Kanoulas, E.: Legal search in case law and statute law. In: JURIX, pp. 83–92 (2019)

24. Sanchez, L., He, J., Manotumruksa, J., Albakour, D., Martinez, M., Lipani, A.: Easing legal news monitoring with learning to Rank and BERT. In: Jose, J.M., et al. (eds.) ECIR 2020. LNCS, vol. 12036, pp. 336–343. Springer, Cham (2020). https://doi.org/10.1007/978-3-030-45442-5_42

25. Savelka, J.: Discovering sentences for argumentation about the meaning of statutory terms. Doctoral dissertation, University of Pittsburgh (2020)
26. Savelka, J., Walker, V.R., Grabmair, M., Ashley, K.D.: Sentence boundary detection in adjudicatory decisions in the United States. Traitement automatique des langues **58**, 21 (2017)
27. Shao, Y., et al.: BERT-PLI: modeling paragraph-level interactions for legal case retrieval. In: Electronic Proceedings of IJCAI 2020, vol. 4, pp. 3501–3507 (2020)
28. Westermann, H., Savelka, J., Walker, V.R., Ashley, K.D., Benyekhlef, K.: Sentence embeddings and high-speed similarity search for fast computer assisted annotation of legal documents. In: Legal Knowledge and Information Systems: JURIX 2020, Brno, Czech Republic, 9–11 December 2020, vol. 334. IOS Press (2020)
29. Williams, A., Nangia, N., Bowman, S.R.: A broad-coverage challenge corpus for sentence understanding through inference. arXiv preprint arXiv:1704.05426 (2017)
30. Zhang, Z., et al.: Semantics-aware BERT for language understanding. arXiv preprint arXiv:1909.02209 (2019)

Using BERT and TF-IDF to Predict Entailment in Law-Based Queries

Arman Aydemir[1]([⊠]) [ID], Pedro de Castro Souza[2] [ID], and Andrew Gelfman[1] [ID]

[1] University of Colorado, Boulder, CO 80309, USA
arman.aydemir@colorado.edu
[2] Chemin Eugène-Rigot 2A, 1202 Genève, Switzerland

Abstract. The Competition on Legal Information Extraction/Entailment, COL-IEE for short, is an annual 4-task contest to create a machine learning model that can answer law-based questions. Previous applicants have used a variety of methods to solve the issues presented. Among them are term frequency - inverse document frequency, recurrent neural networks, and structural analysis. Our paper will discuss our attempts to solve two of these tasks. Specifically, we address our approach of Task 3 with BERT and Task 4 with a combination of TF-IDF and BERT. We believe that, while not currently the best result, we created multiple worthy contenders in both tasks with a clear path to improvement for next year.

Keywords: Legal documents processing · Textual entailment · Information retrieval · Classification · Question answering · BERT

1 Background

The challenges we address in this paper come from COLIEE 2020. The Competition on Legal Information Extraction/Entailment (COLIEE) is a series of evaluation campaigns to discuss the state-of-the-art information retrieval and entailment of legal texts. It is an annual event run in association with the International Conference on Artificial Intelligence and Law (ICAIL). We believe the legal domain is an excellent opportunity to apply Natural Language Processing and Information Extraction and to advance the state-of-the-art. We also think the solutions to these challenges could have a significant application both in helping professional lawyers and in assisting everyday people in understanding the laws they live by. There are two datasets and four tasks that are part of the competition. The first dataset and the first two tasks are related to the Federal Court of Canada case laws. The second dataset and third and fourth tasks are related to a dataset of the Japanese legal bar exam questions, along with the Japanese Civil Code. We addressed the second of these datasets and created solutions to Task 3 and Task 4.

Task 3 involves reading a legal bar exam question Q and extracting a subset of Japanese Civil Code Articles S1, S2, ..., Sn from the entire Civil Code which are those appropriate for answering the question such that Entails(S1, S2, ..., Sn, Q) or Entails(S1, S2, ..., Sn, not Q). Given a question Q and the entire Civil Code Articles, the solution must retrieve the set of "S1, S2, ..., Sn" as the answer to this task.

© Springer Nature Switzerland AG 2021
N. Okazaki et al. (Eds.): JSAI-isAI 2020 Workshops, LNAI 12758, pp. 286–293, 2021.
https://doi.org/10.1007/978-3-030-79942-7_19

We used two approaches to solve Task 3. Our first and most basic model for Task 3 is based on Term Frequency and Inverse Document Frequency (TF-IDF) [1], using it to rank articles then applying a heuristic to decide how many articles to return. TF-IDF is a score of how important a term is. Its value increases proportionally to the number of times the word appears in the document and then it is offset by the number of documents the term is used in. Our second model used a BERT [2] sequence classifier to classify query and article pairs as either relevant or not relevant categories.

Task 4, on the other hand, consists of the identification of an entailment relationship such that Entails(S1, S2, ..., Sn, Q) or Entails(S1, S2, ..., Sn, not Q). Given a question Q and relevant articles S1, S2, ..., Sn, determine if the related articles entail "Q" or "not Q".

We used only one approach for Task 4, however, trained and evaluated on slightly different data. The singular approach we used for Task 4 is similar to the BERT approach for Task 3, in that it used a sequence classification model to classify a question and relevant article text pair as either Yes or No. For our first approach, our model only considered the given relevant articles, while in the second approach we also added articles deemed relevant by our TF-IDF model.

2 Methods and Implementation

The first step in our implementation was finding a way to split the raw civil code text into the appropriate list of articles. As a first attempt to do this, we used the same code used by the IITP paper [3], which we found on GitHub. This code was our starting point, but quickly realized significant bugs were causing it not to return the articles correctly. We fixed the code and then went through each article by hand to make sure that articles were delineated correctly. We did our best to make sure that the 'titles' of the articles in parenthesis were also included as part of the text. Further, we made our updated code available on GitHub [4]. However, after reviewing the final solutions, we still have a small issue with our parsing method as there was one article returned that was not in our article set. We will look into this and update our code accordingly.

We formed a six-fold cross-validation set for hyperparameter selection from the training data we had before the competition. We mainly tested for learning rates, which pre-trained BERT model to fine-tune (BERT-large, BERT-cased, multilingual BERT), early stopping criteria, sequence limit, etc. These sets were also the main factor in deciding which models we would submit.

2.1 Task 3: Statute Law Information Retrieval

We used two approaches to solve Task 3. Our first and most basic model for Task 3 is CUTFIDF, based on papers from IITP and UA [5]. On our validation data, we found an average F2 score of 0.553, average precision of 0.574, and average recall of 0.63. We received a cosine similarity ranking for each of the articles in our set using TF-IDF. The formula for finding this score for some term t and document d is found here:

$$tf - idf(t, d) = tf(t, d) * idf(t) \tag{1}$$

Using our hyperparameter validation sets we settled on a heuristic on how many articles to return. This model returned every article with a similarity score within 95% of the top score with a hard maximum of a total of five articles returned.

The second approach had not been attempted in previous editions of this task. The approach was to use BERT sequence classifiers to classify query and article pairs as either relevant or not relevant. This means for each query we performed over 700 classification evaluations since one was needed for each article in our set. We, again, used our hyperparameter validation datasets to settle on our exact specifications.

We evaluated three different BERT models:

- the multilingual BERT model, referred to as 'multi',
- the BERT-large cased model, referred to as 'cased', and
- the BERT-large uncased model, referred to as 'uncased'.

The second submission, CUBERT1, used the multilingual BERT model. The third submission, CUBERT2, used the BERT-large cased model. These two were chosen because they yielded the best two average F2 scores from the datasets. The competition defines precision, recall, and F2 measure as macro averages, with exact equations here:

$$precision = \text{average of}\left(\frac{Number\ of\ Correctly\ Retrieved\ Articles\ for\ Each\ Query}{Number\ of\ Retrieved\ Articles\ for\ Each\ Query}\right) \quad (2)$$

$$recall = \text{average of}\left(\frac{Number\ of\ Correctly\ Retrieved\ Articles\ for\ Each\ Query}{Number\ of\ Relevant\ Articles\ for\ Each\ Query}\right) \quad (3)$$

$$F2\text{measure} = \frac{(5\ \times\ precision\ \times\ recall)}{(4\ \times\ precision\ +\ recall)} \quad (4)$$

For each of our three models, Fig. 1 shows the average precision, recall, and F2 scores, respectively. We decided on our two final models because they got the highest two average F2 scores.

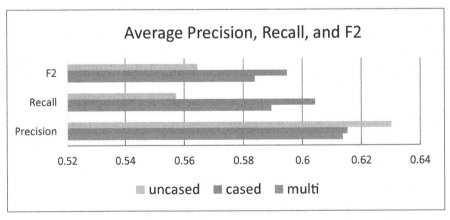

Fig. 1. Averages of precision, recall, and F2 scores for each of our three models over our hyperparameter validation sets.

2.2   Task 4: Statute Law Entailment

For Task 4, we only had one approach. This approach was based on BERT and included two submissions. We used our hyperparameter validation datasets to select which BERT models to use again, but this time we also used it to select what data we would be feeding into the models. We found that for all datasets that we attempted the multilingual BERT model performed best. For the first attempt, we simply fed given related articles, this model is referred to as 'given'. In another, we fed it as much of the whole civil code text that the sequence limit of our BERT models would allow, referred to as 'full'. In the third, we fed it the given related articles plus extra that were returned using our earlier CUTFIDF model for Task 3 and referred to it as 'plus'. We can see from Fig. 2 that our 'given' model yielded the best accuracy on one half of the hyperparameter validation datasets while the 'plus' model achieved the best accuracy on the other half. Because of these scores, these were the two models selected for submission.

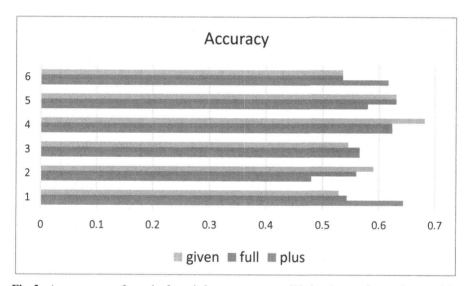

Fig. 2. Accuracy score for each of our six hyperparameter validation datasets for our three models.

3   Results

3.1   Task 3: Statute Law Information Retrieval

Our three submissions for Task 3 were not prize-winning but we still learned a good amount from these results. The submissions were ranked and evaluated based on three main criteria – precision, recall, and F2 – which were all defined earlier. In addition, we submitted our top 100 results to create the MAP, R_5, R_10, and R_30 measures. MAP stands for Mean Average Precision, which is defined as the mean of the average precision for each classification. R_k is defined as recall using the top k rankings of documents. It

Table 1. Task 3 competition results (our methods highlighted in yellow).

Submission Id	F2	Precision	Recall	MAP	R_5	R_10	R_30
LLNTU	0.659	0.688	0.662	0.760	0.807	0.857	0.921
JNLP.tfidf-bert-ensemble	0.553	0.577	0.567	0.662	0.686	0.714	0.779
cyber1	0.529	0.506	0.554	0.554	0.550	0.693	0.800
cyber2	0.525	0.435	0.597	0.554	0.550	0.693	0.800
JNLP.tfidf-lawbert	0.518	0.539	0.527	0.685	0.714	0.771	0.793
cyber3	0.518	0.413	0.624	0.554	0.550	0.693	0.800
HUKB-1	0.516	0.420	0.591	0.569	0.671	0.721	0.814
JNLP.tfidf-bert	0.515	0.541	0.527	0.685	0.714	0.771	0.793
CUBERT1	0.514	0.540	0.519	0.585	0.643	0.686	0.707
HUKB-2	0.514	0.404	0.591	0.574	0.643	0.693	0.793
TRC3_1	0.501	0.456	0.536	0.598	0.693	0.771	0.843
CUBERT2	0.500	0.516	0.510	0.556	0.579	0.650	0.757
TRC3_A	0.491	0.415	0.534	0.554	0.607	0.700	0.843
TRC3_H	0.479	0.431	0.522	0.585	0.707	0.786	0.850
OVGU_bm25	0.477	0.400	0.534	0.510	0.593	0.614	0.721
Ov-GU_combined_bm25	0.470	0.393	0.515	0.548	0.586	0.657	0.700
TAXI_R3	0.455	0.439	0.509	0.506	0.571	0.614	0.679

is noticeable that our TF-IDF method did slightly better than the UA.tfidf method which it was based on. This aligns with our previous work and knowledge. This being true, it still did remarkably worse than both of our BERT models and was second to last in terms of F2 score. This is a good sign that our BERT model has a higher level of understanding than the simple TF-IDF method. Between our two BERT models, CUBERT1 (based on multilingual BERT), did better in every single category compared to CUBERT2 (based on BERT-large cased), except for in the very last category of R_30. While our best model (CUBERT1) was not very close to prize-winning in terms of F2 (9th place), it did fairly well in terms of precision (4th place). We presume our multilingual model performed better because of the many foreign language influenced terms common in legal text. BERT approaches in general did very well this year, earning most of the top spots in the competition. Both LLNTU, the task prize winner, and JNLP, who got second place, had great success with an ensemble of BERT models. In the future, we believe we could make good use of ensemble methods, specifically an ensemble of Transformer models in different languages (Tables 1 and 2).

Table 2. Task 3 competition result (continued) (our methods highlighted in yellow).

Submission Id	F2	Precision	Re-call	MAP	R_5	R_10	R_30
OVGU_tfidf	0.439	0.344	0.491	0.515	0.571	0.621	0.750
GK_NLP	0.427	0.286	0.499	0.498	0.557	0.636	0.721
HUKB-3	0.414	0.438	0.411	0.544	0.629	0.721	0.829
TAXI_R1	0.411	0.444	0.415	0.488	0.586	0.621	0.721
CUTFIDF	0.407	0.445	0.405	0.487	0.550	0.593	0.693
UA.tfidf	0.391	0.429	0.387	0.478	0.543	0.607	0.671

3.2 Task 4: Statute Law Entailment

Our competition results from Task 4 were not nearly as impressive as they were for Task 3 and did not give us much insight into our approaches. Both our CUGIVEN and CUPLUS models got the same accuracy which was worse than the baseline. Here there is opportunity to make some improvements. The most direct improvement could be made by using our BERT results from Task 3 which were clearly superior instead of our TF-IDF results. We also note that the competition winning team, JNLP, found great success in pretraining Transformers with legal text. We believe this method of pretraining models with legal text paired along with the idea of ensemble method with models of two separate languages from the Task 3 results could earn state-of-the-art results (Tables 3 and 4).

Table 3. Task 4 competition results (our methods listed in yellow).

Submission Id	Correct	Accuracy
Base Line	Yes 59/All 112	0.5268
JNLP.BERTLaw	81	0.7232
TRC3mt	70	0.625
TRC3t5	70	0.625
UA_attention_final	70	0.625
UA_roberta_final	70	0.625
KIS_2	69	0.6161
llntu	69	0.6161
cyber	69	0.6161
UA_structure	68	0.6071
GK_NLP	63	0.5625
linearsvm.HONto	63	0.5625
JNLP.BERT	63	0.5625
KIS	63	0.5625

Table 4. Task 4 competition results (continued) (our methods listed in yellow).

Submission Id	Correct	Accuracy
linearsvm_no_ngram.HONto	62	0.5536
JNLP.TfidfBERT	62	0.5536
KIS_3	61	0.5446
sim_neg.OvGU	61	0.5446
UEC1	61	0.5446
taxi_BERTXGB	60	0.5357
UECplus	60	0.5357
CUGIVEN	58	0.5179
CUPLUS	58	0.5179
linearsvm_no_ngram_nofuzz.HONto	57	0.5089
POS_simneg.OvGU	57	0.5089
taxi_le_bigru	57	0.5089
TRC3A	56	0.5
UEC2	55	0.4911
baseline_attention.OvGU	54	0.4821
AUT99-BERT-MatchPyramid	52	0.4643
AUT99-LSTM-CNN-Attention	50	0.4464

References

1. Jones, K.S.: A statistical interpretation of term specificity and its application in retrieval. In: Willett, P. (ed.) Document Retrieval Systems, pp. 132–142. Taylor Graham Publishing, London (1988)
2. Devlin, J., Chang, M., Lee, K., Toutanova, K.: BERT: pre-training of deep bidirectional transformers for language understanding. 2nd version, arXiv.org Abs:1810.04805 (2019). http://arxiv.org/abs/1810.04805
3. Gain, B., Bandyopadhyay, D., Saikh, T., Ekbal, A.: IITP in COLIEE@ICAIL 2019: legal information retrieval using BM25 and BERT (2019)
4. CU_COLIEE_2020. https://github.com/armanaydemir/CU_COLIEE_2020. Accessed 12 Oct 2020
5. Kim, M.-Y., Rabelo, J., Goebel, R.: Statute law information retrieval and entailment. In: Proceedings of the 17th International Conference on Artificial Intelligence and Law. ICAIL 2019 (2019)

Author Index

Printed in the United States
by Baker & Taylor Publisher Services